LIGHT
FANTASTIC

LIGHT
FANTASTIC

ADVENTURES IN THEATRE

JOHN LAHR

THE DIAL PRESS

Published by
The Dial Press
Bantam Doubleday Dell Publishing Group, Inc.
1540 Broadway
New York, New York 10036

Book Design by Julie Duquet

All of the pieces in this collection, with the exception of ''Running
Wilde,'' were originally published in *The New Yorker*.

Library of Congress Cataloging in Publication Data
Lahr, John, 1941–
    Light fantastic : adventures in theatre / by John Lahr.
        p.   cm.
    ISBN 0-385-31546-5
    1. Entertainers—Biography.   2. Dramatists—Biography.
    3. Composers—Biography.   I. Title.
PN1583.L35   1996
791'.0904—dc20   95-21871
                                                                        CIP

Manufactured in the United States of America
Published simultaneously in Canada

March 1996

10   9   8   7   6   5   4   3   2   1

BVG

To
Chip McGrath
&
Connie Booth

CONTENTS

LIGHT
FANTASTIC

INTRODUCTION

A FEW YEARS AGO I BOUGHT a sign in a New York antique shop that read "We Do Not Lease or Rent to Theatricals." It warms my heart to think that there was once a time in the city when theatre folk were a subject of scandal and concern and you could buy greasepaint at any corner drugstore. I count myself "a theatrical," and I'm proud of my raffish pedigree: my father was a clown, my mother a chorus girl. One way or another, most of my life has been spent within shouting distance of a stage: either helping to run theatres, writing plays, or reviewing them. Criticism, of course, is a kind of performance, but with this difference: the artist puts his life on the line, the critic only his words. This is not to minimize the significance of the activity, but to place criticism in its proper context. Criticism is a life without risk; and, therefore, it behooves the critic to honor the craft. To that end, I have tried to redefine theatre criticism to suit my own expressive needs not just as a writer but also as a theatre historian. At the end of an essay, I want the reader to know more about the event than just what I think about it. In my own mind, these essays—whether I've liked a play or not—are collaborations with the makers. They have made a metaphor; and it's my job to interpret it and to make connections to the world we bustle in. I want the makers to be part of the production's story. The essay becomes, to my way of thinking, a more colourful and accurate record of events—a kind of criticism that conjures the life of the theatre as well as the life of the play. We are in danger of losing our theatre culture; and these essays are my little rearguard action to keep the public gaze focussed on the lively language and maverick thought of theatricals—performers, playwrights, directors, designers—who are the "abstracts and brief chronicles of the time."

Most of these essays appeared first in *The New Yorker,* a magazine which since its inception in 1925 has played a considerable part in enlivening America's theatrical scene. *The New Yorker* has had less than a dozen drama critics in its illustrious history; and I'm very aware of both the honor and the responsibility of being in a line of succession which includes Dorothy Parker, Robert Benchley, Wolcott Gibbs, Kenneth Tynan, and Brendan Gill. Their turf and mine differ in one significant detail. Their beat was citywide; mine is national and world-wide. This change has come about because of the changing nature of theatre production and because of the present editor, Tina Brown, who thankfully reached me on holiday in Calistoga, California, in 1992 to offer me the job. While *The New Yorker*'s founder and first editor, Harold Ross, had a couple of plays written about him, including Wol-cott Gibbs's 1952 Broadway hit "Seasons in the Sun," Tina is the only editor who has actually written professional plays. Born and bred in England, she understands the importance of theatre to the community. From the outset, her vision of *The New Yorker* as an international maga-zine and my vision of a more wide-ranging kind of theatre criticism have been happily in synch. These essays, which are written with love and passion, require space and commitment, which has been Tina's editorial gift.

On both sides of the Atlantic these days, the theatre has hit rough weather. In England, where the failure to invest in research and devel-opment is an acute national problem, theatres have been badly con-strained by reduced government subsidy, which has meant a large de-crease in the number of new authors and new plays being produced. In New York, the situation is even more demoralized. A theatre producer who shall remain nameless—Bernie Gersten—informed me recently that Broadway theatre is a nearly billion-dollar-a-year industry. The fact remains that in the 1927–28 season, there were two hundred and sixty-eight shows on Broadway; and this year there will be twenty-eight. The golden egg may still be there; but Broadway's goose is more or less cooked. This does not mean that theatre is either dead or less relevant. "Civilization," Peter Brook told me once, "is what happens between people." And even if it doesn't teach the discipline of com-munity, the theatre calls out of an audience a sense of its necessity.

The shape of theatre may change; but there is an enduring species need to act out our problems together, to show off our personalities, to confide our secrets, to mint new words for the mystery of our singular passage through life.

JL
London,
May 1995

PART 1
COMEDIANS

BILL HICKS

THE GOAT BOY RISES

O N OCTOBER 1, 1993 THE comedian Bill Hicks, after doing his twelfth gig on the David Letterman show, became the first comedy act to be censored at CBS's Ed Sullivan Theatre, where Letterman is now in residence, and where Elvis Presley was famously censored in 1956. Presley was not allowed to be shown from the waist down. Hicks was not allowed to be shown at all. It's not what's in Hicks's pants but what's in his head that scared the CBS panjandrums. Hicks, a tall, thirty-one-year-old Texan with a pudgy face aged beyond its years from hard living on the road, is no motormouth vulgarian but an exhilarating comic thinker in a renegade class all his own. Until the ban, which, according to Hicks, earned him "more attention than my other eleven appearances on Letterman times one hundred," Hicks's caustic observations and mischievous cultural connections had found a wide audience in England, where he is something of a cult figure. I caught up with Hicks backstage on a rainy Sunday last November at the Dominion Theatre, in London, where a record-breaking crowd of two thousand Brits was packed so tightly that they were standing three deep at the back of the dress circle to hear Hicks deliver some acid home truths about the U.S.A., which to him stands for United States of Advertising. Hicks thinks against society and insists on the importance of this intellectual freedom as a way to inspire others to think for themselves. "To me, the comic is the guy who says 'Wait a minute' as the consensus forms," Hicks told me as we climbed the stairs to his dressing room. "He's the antithesis of the mob mentality. The comic is a flame—like Shiva the Destroyer, toppling idols no matter what they are. He keeps cutting everything back to the moment."

Even then, the talk about courting comic danger had Hicks worrying about his prospects in America. "Comedy in the States has been totally gutted," he told me when we'd settled into the dressing room. "It's commercialized. They don't have people on TV who have points of view, because that defies the status quo, and we can't have that in the totalitarian mind-control government that runs the fuckin' airwaves. I can't get a shot there. I get David Letterman a lot. I love Letterman, but every time I go on, we have tiffs over material. They love me, but his people have this fictitious mainstream audience they think they play to. It's untrue. It doesn't exist. I like doing the show, but it's almost like working a puzzle: How can I be me in the context of doing this material? The best thing I do is make connections. I connect *everything*. It's hard to do it in six minutes."

Hicks certainly went for broke and pronounced his real comic self in the banned Letterman performance, which he wrote out for me in a thirty-nine-page letter that also recounts his version of events. Hicks had to write out his set because the tape of it, which the Letterman people said they'd send three weeks ago, had not yet reached him. He doubts it ever will. But the routine, which he had prepared for a Letterman appearance a week earlier (he was bumped because the show ran long), had been, he wrote, "approved and reapproved" by a segment producer of the show. Indicating stage directions and his recollection of significant audience response, Hicks set out some of the "hot points" to which the network took exception.

> You know who's really bugging me these days? These pro-lifers . . . (*Smattering of applause.*)
> You ever look at their faces? . . . "I'm pro-life!" (*Here Bill makes a pinched face of hate and fear; his lips are pursed as though he's just sucked on a lemon.*) "I'm pro-life!" Boy, they look it, don't they? They just exude *joie de vivre*. You just want to hang with them and play Trivial Pursuit all night long. (*Audience chuckles.*)
> You know what bugs me about them? If you're so pro-life, do me a favor—don't lock arms and block medical clinics. If you're so pro-life, lock arms and block cemeteries. (*Audience laughs.*)
> . . . I want to see pro-lifers at funerals opening caskets—"Get

out!'' Then I'd really be impressed by their mission. (*Audience laughs and applauds.*)

I've been travelling a lot lately. I was over in Australia during Easter. It was interesting to note they celebrate Easter the same way we do—commemorating the death and resurrection of Jesus by telling our children a giant bunny rabbit . . . left chocolate eggs in the night. (*Audience laughs.*)

Gee, I wonder why we're so messed up as a race. You know, I've read the Bible. Can't find the words ''bunny'' or ''chocolate'' in the whole book. (*Audience laughs.*)

I think it's interesting how people act on their beliefs. A lot of Christians, for instance, wear crosses around their necks. Nice sentiment, but do you think when Jesus comes back, he's really going to want to look at a cross? (*Audience laughs. Bill makes a face of pain and horror.*)

Ow! *Maybe* that's why he hasn't shown up yet. (*As Jesus looking down from Heaven*) ''I'm not going, Dad. No, they're still wearing crosses—they totally missed the point. When they start wearing fishes, I might go back again. . . . No, I'm not going. . . . O.K., I'll tell you what—I'll go back as a bunny.''

Hicks, who delivered his monologue dressed not in his usual gun-slinger black but in ''bright fall colors—an outfit bought just for the show and reflective of my bright and cheerful mood,'' seemed to have a lot to smile about. Letterman—who Hicks says greeted him as he sat down to talk with ''Good set, Bill! Always nice to have you drop by with an uplifting message!'' and signed off saying, ''Bill, enjoy answering your mail for the next few weeks''—had been seen to laugh. The word in the Green Room was also good. A couple of hours later, Hicks was back in his hotel, wearing nothing but a towel, when the call came from Robert Morton, the executive producer of the Letterman show, telling him he'd been deep-sixed. Hicks sat down on the bed. ''I don't understand, Robert. What's the problem? I thought the show went great.'' The following is a condensed version of what Hicks remembers from the long conversation.

''You killed out there,'' Morton said, and went on to say, according to Hicks, that the CBS office of standards and practices felt that some of the material was unsuitable for broadcast.

"Ah, which material exactly did they find . . ."

"Well, almost all of it."

"Bob, they're so obviously jokes."

Hicks protested that he had run his routine by his sixty-three-year-old mother in Little Rock, Arkansas, and it passed the test. Morton insisted that the situation was out of his hands. He offered to set up another appearance and, according to Hicks, shouldered the blame for not having spent more time beforehand editing out the "hot points."

"Bob, they're just jokes. I don't want to be edited by you or anyone else. Why are people so afraid of jokes?"

"Bill, you've got to understand our audience."

"Your audience! Your audience is comprised of people, right? Well, I understand people, being one myself. People are who I play to every night, Bob. We get along just fine. We taped the show at five-thirty in the afternoon, and your audience had no problem with the material then. Does your audience become overly sensitive between the hours of 11:30 P.M. and 12:30 A.M.? And by the way, Bob, when I'm not performing on your show, *I'm* a member of the audience of your show. Are you saying my material is not suitable for me? This doesn't make any sense. Why do you underestimate the intelligence of your audience?"

"Bill, it's not our decision."

Morton apologized to Hicks, explaining that the show had to answer to the network, and said that he'd reschedule him soon. The conversation ended soon after that exchange, and in the intervening weeks Hicks has had no further word, he says, from Morton or Letterman. He has, however, heard indirectly from the CBS standards-and-practices office. A man who heard an interview with Hicks on the radio and was outraged over the censorship wrote to CBS to upbraid the network for not airing Hicks's set. He faxed the reply from CBS standards-and-practices to the radio station, which faxed it to Hicks's office. "It is true that Bill Hicks was taped that evening and that his performance did not air," the letter said. "What is inaccurate is that the deletion of his routine was required by CBS. In fact, although a CBS Program Practices editor works on that show, the decision was solely that of the producers of the program who decided to substitute his performance with that of another comedian. Therefore, your criticism that CBS censored the program is totally without foundation. Creative judgments must be made in the course of producing and airing any program and, while we regret that you disagreed with this one, the producers felt it necessary and that is not a decision we would override.''

Hicks, who refers to the television set as Lucifer's Dream Box, is now in Lucifer's Limbo. He can't get the Letterman show to send him a tape of his performance. He can't get to the bottom of who censored him. And, as yet, he has no return date on Letterman. I called Robert Morton two weeks ago, and, when pressed, he finally grasped the nettle. He had begun by saying that the decision not to show Hicks's routine was made jointly by the Letterman show and CBS and ended up telling me that the producers of the show were solely responsible. "Ultimately, it was our decision," he said. "We're the packagers and owners of the program. It's our job to deliver a finished product to the network."

"It's been a strange little adventure for Willy," Hicks told me at the Dominion last year, referring to his American comedy career. And so it has proved—stranger, in fact, than Hicks's most maverick imaginings. The farce came full circle in the week following the Letterman debacle. A friend called Hicks to tell him about a commercial she'd seen during the Letterman show—a pro-life commercial. "The networks are delivering an audience to the advertisers," Hicks said later. "They showed their hand. They'll continue to pretend they're a hip talk show. And I'll continue to be me. As Bob Dylan said, the only way to live outside the law is to be totally honest. So I will remain lawless."

Outlaw is how Hicks was styling himself last year for the Dominion performance as he put on his black rifleman's coat and Stetson in the dressing room. When the curtain came up on his performance, Hicks was revealed in his hat, long coat, and cowboy boots, while behind him huge orange flames licked the air. Images of heat and hunting are the perfect backdrop to Hicks's kind of comic attack. He was a hostile sharpshooter taking aim at the culture's received opinions and trying to shoot them down. The British, who have an appetite for this kind of intellectual anarchy, embraced Hicks with a rare and real enthusiasm from the moment he stumbled onto the vivacious English comedy scene in November 1990, as one of eighteen comedians in "Stand Up America!," a six-week limited engagement in the West End. The next year, Hicks was at the Edinburgh Festival, where he outclassed the native talent and won the Critics' Award. This led to his 1992 "Dangerous Tour" of Britain and Ireland, which culminated in appearances in the West End, at the Queen's Theatre, that May. The response was overwhelming, and now Hicks was doing one of the final performances of the "Relentless Tour," his second lap of honor around the British Isles in one year. Hicks was at home with the English, whose sense of irony made them more receptive to his combative humor than the credulous American public had been. "There's a greater respect for the performer," he said. "If you're onstage, people think you've earned it. In America—I'm not kidding—people bark their approval." I looked at him dubiously. "Ask around," Hicks said, and he simulated the sound. "They bark like animals. It's frightening. It's what American society has reduced people to. Ironically, in this show I call myself Goat Boy. They shouldn't be barking, they should be *baaing*."

My first encounter with Hicks was his Gulf War routine, which had been broadcast during the postwar euphoria at the beginning of 1992 on England's Channel 4. My sixteen-year-old son, Chris, was bellowing from the living room for me to come quickly. It was midnight, and he was sprawled, laughing, on the sofa, watching Hicks at the Montreal Comedy Festival calling a massacre a massacre. "So scary, watching the news. How they built it all out of proportion. Like Iraq was ever, or could ever, under any stretch of the imagination, be any threat to us *whatsoever*. But, watching the news, you never would have got that idea. Remember how it started? They kept talking about 'the élite Republican Guard' in these hushed tones, like these guys were the bogeyman or something. 'Yeah, we're doing well now, but we have yet to face . . . the élite Republican Guard.' Like these guys were twelve-feet-tall desert warriors—'NEVER LOST A BATTLE. WE SHIT BULLETS.' Well, after two months of continuous carpet bombing and not *one* reaction at all from them, they became simply 'the Republican Guard'—not nearly as élite as we may have led you to believe. And after another month of bombing they went from 'the élite Republican Guard' to 'the Republican Guard' to 'the Republicans made this shit up about there being guards out there.'

"People said, 'Uh-uh, Bill, Iraq had the fourth-largest army in the world.' Yeah, maybe, but you know what? After the first three largest armies, there's a *real* big fuckin' drop-off. The Hare Krishnas are the fifth-largest army in the world. And they've already got our airports."

Most TV comics trade in brand-name jokes or jokes that play off physical stereotypes. They don't question their culture so much as pander to its insatiable hunger for distraction. But Hicks's mischievous flights of fantasy bring the audience back to reality with a thump. Hicks is a kind of ventriloquist of his contradictory nature, letting voices and sound effects act out both his angst and his appetites. Occasionally, the instinct for Goat Boy comes over him, and Hicks, a man of instincts, goes with it. Goat Boy is Pan, or Hicks's version of him—a randy goat "with a placid look in his eyes, completely at peace with nature"— through which he celebrates his own rampaging libido.

"I am Goat Boy," he would say in the act that night, in a grave baritone. "Come here, my little fruit basket."

"What do you want, Goat Boy?" he answered, in a coy Southern falsetto. "You big old shaggy thing."

"Ha, ha, ha, ha," Hicks growled into the microphone. "I am here to please you."

"How?"

"Tie me to your headboard. Throw your legs over my shoulders, let me roll you like a feed bag." Hicks brought the microphone close to his mouth. He snorted, slurped, and finally screamed, "Hold on to my horns!" Then, as suddenly as the impulse had come upon him, Hicks broke off the fantasy, saying, "I need professional help at this point."

The secret of Hicks's psychic survival has always been comedy. He started writing and performing his jokes as an alienated thirteen-year-old in Houston in 1975, and, by his own count, for the last five years he has been performing about two hundred and sixty-five days a year, sometimes doing as many as three two-hour gigs a night. Few contemporary comics or actors have such an opportunity to get their education in public. Hicks uses the stage time to write his material in front of an audience. "I do it all onstage, *all* of it," he said, and then began to relate how he'd started on his eccentric journey. "When I was about eleven, it dawned on me that I didn't like where I was," he said, speaking of the subdivision where he lived, which was called Nottingham Forest; of Stratford High School, which looked like a prison and where he was bored out of his skull for four years; and of his father, who was a midrange executive with General Motors. The Hicks family lived in "strict Southern Baptist ozone." The memory still rankled. "One time a friend of mine—we were nine—runs over and goes, 'Bill, I just saw some hippies down at the store.' I go, 'No way.' He goes, 'I swear.' My dad goes, 'Get off this property! We don't swear on this property!'

"We were living the American dream. This was the best life had to offer. But there was no life, and no creativity. My dad, for instance, plays the piano. The same song for thirty years—I think it's 'Kitten on the Keys.' I don't play the piano, but all my friends are musicians. My dad goes, 'Do they read music?' I go, 'No.' 'Well, how do they play it?' I go to the piano and I write a song. What's the difference? He can't improvise. That, to me, is the suburbs. You get to a point, and that's it —it's over."

Once he'd seized on the idea of writing jokes, Hicks closeted himself in his bedroom and went to school on comedians. He started watching Johnny Carson. "I thought he was the only comic in the world, because I never stayed up later," he said. Soon Hicks began burning the midnight oil, taping other comic acts on television. "I'd take their jokes and also write my own. I performed them around school, and what I loved was when both got equal laughs. I knew which one was me and which one I'd seen on TV the night before. I learned how to mesh these things. How to get into character. I was very, very popular and known as a comedian at school. I'd always have to have material, constantly, all day. It got to the point where my English teacher gave me five minutes to do before class. My older brother Steve encouraged me. I typed up about two pages of jokes—whimsical stuff in the Woody Allen vein, which really appealed to me—and slipped them under his door. He came in later that night and said, 'What's this?' I said, 'I dunno. I'm writing these things. They're jokes.' He couldn't believe it. 'These are funny, man. Keep doing this.' "

Hicks's first partner in comedy was Dwight Slade, with whom he formed the act Bill and Dwight in the eighth grade. A tape exists of Hicks and Slade giggling through some of their early routines, which involved pretending to be brothers with "many, many problems." "Ladies and gentlemen, the comedy sensation Dwight Slade and Bill Hicks. And here they are!" it begins, and then the two of them collapse into roars of amusement at their own vain attempts to strike adult postures while reading gags about God, sex, abortion, and parents.

The jokes illustrated Hicks's precocity, and suggested how comedy both masked and admitted the hostility that kept him sullen and virtually silent around his family. "I can remember being at dinner when Bill would come down to eat," Steve Hicks told me. "He'd sit there with his face buried in a book. Absolutely no conversation from him or to him. Nothing. Then he would go up to his room and close and lock the door. We had no idea what he was doing." Hicks's room, which had nothing on the walls but a guitar, was a cell of rebellious solitude. He kept a typewriter under his bed and hid his pages of jokes inside its case.

In 1976, there were no comedy clubs in Houston. Except for school, the only outlets for Bill and Dwight's routines were talent shows and nightclubs. They scoured the paper for auditions, and often rode their bikes the seventeen miles into town and back for a tryout. That summer, when they were both fourteen, a talent agent to whom they'd sent a tape liked it enough to get them airtime on Jerry Lewis's Telethon from 2 to 2:45 A.M. Their big break posed three immediate problems: (1) they didn't have forty-five minutes of material, (2) they'd never performed as Bill and Dwight in front of a live audience, and (3) they had to tell their parents. The first two problems were surmountable, but the third proved the sticking point. Hicks's parents said no. Hicks and Slade had to cancel, explaining that they were too young to drive themselves to the job. But in 1978, when the Comedy Workshop opened on San Felipe, in Houston, they talked their way into the lineup. This time, they made the gig. To get to it, Hicks had to climb out his window, shin down the drainpipe to the garage roof, jump from the roof to the ground, and hightail it to the Catholic church behind his house, where Kevin Booth, a friend who had a car, picked him up and then drove both performers to the club. Bill and Dwight did fifteen minutes—a kind of double solo performance, each doing Woody Allen shtick without the actual give-and-take of a comedy team. "What was really funny was when my friends would come and I'd go, 'I . . . uh . . . I have trouble . . . trouble with women,' " Hicks said. "And my friends would go, 'No, you don't!' I'd go, 'My parents are very poor.' 'No, they're not!' They were amazed we were in this adult world. They were seventeen and could drive us there, but when they got us there we were in the adult world."

The comedy team performed five times before Slade moved to Portland, Oregon, where he still lives, working as a standup comic. Hicks put his anarchic energy into a hapless punk-rock group called Stress, in which he sang a song called "I'm Glad I'm Not a Hubcap (Hubcaps Don't Get Laid)." At some point in his seventeenth year, Hicks's parents took him to a psychotherapist. "There was no connection between me and my parents—none," he said. "They had no idea of who I was. They still don't get what I do. How could they have understood it fifteen years ago?" The therapist met with the family, then with Hicks. At the end of the session, the therapist took Hicks aside. " 'Listen, you can continue to come if you feel like it,' " Hicks recalled him saying. " 'But it's them, not you.' " Soon afterward, at the beginning of Hicks's senior year, his father was transferred to Little Rock, Arkansas. He and his wife left Hicks behind in the house and gave him the keys to the car. Hicks began doing comedy every night. His parents thought he was studying. The comedy club put him on first, because he had to get home early. Sometimes the phone would be ringing just as he walked in the door. "The conversations were like this," Hicks said. He fell easily into his father's Southern accent: " 'Where were you?' 'Library.' 'Again?' " Even after his parents left, his material was almost entirely about them.

To this day, Hicks continues to mythologize his parents and his relationship with them, in comic routines that spoof their Southern propriety. But this is only professional acrimony, and doesn't stop Hicks from thanking his parents on his record albums or turning up regularly for ritual family occasions. Hicks, like all comedians, picks at ancient wounds to keep open the soreness that feeds his laughter and to demonstrate his mastery over the past.

In 1982, Hicks's parents finally saw him perform. They had been visiting Steve in Dallas, where the family had assembled for Thanksgiving, and his parents decided to surprise him. The plan was to drive the three hours to Austin, see the show, and drive back to Dallas the same night before setting out the next day for the six-hour ride to Little Rock. Steve and his wife waited up for them but finally fell asleep around 3 A.M. At nine, their phone rang. The Hickses had been so appalled by their son's act that they'd got in their car and driven nonstop to Little Rock. "They were in a state of shock," Steve says. "They didn't say a word to each other for nine hours. They didn't even realize they'd driven through Dallas!"

At one end of Hicks's long, corridorlike dressing room at the Dominion was a window overlooking the stage. Hicks walked over and looked out at the paying customers. "It's about that time," he said. Isolation suddenly fell over him like some fog blown in by his unconscious. Showtime was approaching, and he wanted to be alone. Fifteen minutes later, he brought his aggression roaring onstage. The narrative swung into attack as Hicks, like a man driven to distraction by the media, fought his way free of its overload by momentarily becoming its exaggerated voice: "Go back to bed! America is in control again. . . . Here . . . here is 'American Gladiators.' Watch this! Shut up. Go back to bed. Here's fifty-six channels of it. Watch these pituitary retards bang their fuckin' skulls together and congratulate yourself on living in the land of freedom. Here you go, America! You are free to do as we tell you! You are free!"

Hicks worked at a tremendous rate, pounding away at the absurdities of American culture with short jabs of wit and following up with a flurry of counterpunches. "Ever notice how people who believe in creationism look really unevolved?" he said. "Their eyes real close together. Eyebrow ridges. Big, furry hands and feet. 'I believe God created me in one day.' Looks like he rushed it." Later, near the end of the evening, Hicks drew one final lesson. "The world is like a ride at an amusement park," he said. "And when you choose to go on it, you think that it's real. Because that's how powerful our minds are." A young Englishman three seats away from me shouted "Bollocks!" And, without missing a beat, completely caught up in the dialogue he was having with his audience, Hicks said, "There is a lot of denial in this ride. The ride, in fact, is made up of denial. All things work in Goat Boy's favor!" Thrilled by the improvised insight, the audience burst into applause, and then Hicks guided the rest of the show smoothly to its conclusion, which, for all its combativeness, ended on the word "peace."

Hicks came to my house the next day for tea. He was tired and a little distracted, and was wondering out loud which way to take his quirky talent. "Once this stuff is done, it's over with—I'm not married to any of it," he said. "Goat Boy is the only thing that really intrigues me right now. He's not Satan. He's not Evil. He's Nature." Hicks paused and added, "I'm trying to come up with this thing about 'Conversations with Goat Boy.' " Then, suddenly, the interrogator and Goat Boy started a conversation at my tea table:

"You don't like America?"

"I don't *see* America. To me, there is just a rapidly decreasing wilderness."

Hicks stopped and smiled. "That is Goat Boy. There is no America. It's just a big pavement now to him. That's the whole point. What is America anyway—a landmass including the Philippines? There are so many different Americas. To him, to Nature, it's just land, the earth. Indian spirit—Indians would understand randy Pan, the Goat Boy. They'd probably have a mask and a celebration."

My son wandered into the kitchen and lingered to eavesdrop on the conversation. At one point, he broke in. "I don't know how you have the courage to say those things," he said. "I could never talk like that in front of people."

Hicks smiled but had no response. Saying the unsayable was just his job. He analyzed the previous night's performance, which had been filmed for an HBO special. (It was broadcast in September to good reviews.) "People watch TV *not* to think," he said. "I'd like the opportunity to stir things up once, and see what happens. But I've got a question. Do I even want to be part of it anymore? Show business or art—these are choices. It's hard to get a grip on me. It's also hard for me to have a career, because there's no archetype for what I do. I have to create it, or uncover it." To that end, he said, he and Fallon Woodland, a standup from Kansas City, were writing "The Counts of the Netherworld," a TV comedy commissioned for England's Channel 4 and set in the collective unconscious of mankind. Hicks was doing a column for the English satire magazine *Scallywag*. He was planning a comedy album, called "Arizona Bay," a narrative rant against California with his own guitar accompaniment. Should he stay in England, where he was already a cult figure, or return to America? He recounted a joke on the subject by his friend Barry Crimmins, another American political comedian. " 'Hey, buddy,' this guy says to him after a show. 'America —love it or leave it!' And Crimmins goes, 'What? And be a victim of our foreign policy?' "

As Hicks was about to go, he said, "We are facilitators of our creative evolution. We can ignite our brains with light." The line brought back something his high-school friend Kevin Booth had told me: "Bill was the first person I ever met whose goal was to become enlightened." At various times in his life, Hicks has meditated, studied Hindu texts, gobbled hallucinogens, searched for U.F.O.s—anything to make some larger spiritual and intellectual connection. His comedy takes an audience on a journey to places in the heart where it can't or won't go without him. Through laughter, Hicks makes unacceptable ideas irresistible. He is particularly lethal because he persuades not with reason but with joy. "I believe everyone has this fuckin' poem in his heart," he said on his way out.

Bill Hicks died on February 26, 1994 of pancreatic cancer. He was thirty-two.

JOE ORTON

A REVENGER'S TRAGEDY

ON APRIL 30, 1967, THE comedian Kenneth Williams strolled in Hyde Park with Joe Orton and Kenneth Halliwell, Orton's companion of sixteen years. Williams had starred in the first disastrous production of Orton's "Loot" (1965), which Halliwell had titled and which, revised and remounted, was now the West End comedy hit of the year. In his radio and screen performances in the "Carry On" films, Williams affected outrageousness; but Orton lived it. Williams was always a good audience for the boundless irreverence which distinguished Orton's life and his laughter. On this occasion, Orton was recounting the picking up of a man near a public lavatory. Williams recorded the conversation in his diary:

"We'd been eyeing each other warily—and this fellow asked, 'You got a place we can go?' " Joe said (in front of Halliwell), "I told him that I lived with someone, and it wasn't convenient. The man replied, 'I often get picked up by queers 'round here. Some of them have very nice places. They must be on quite good money. I've had as much as thirty shillings from some of them. They're not all effeminate either, some of them are really manly and you'd never dream they were queer. Not from the look of them. But I can always tell 'cos they've all got LPs of Judy Garland. That's the big give-away.' " I told Joe, "It's marvellous the way you remember dialogue as well as the accents! You really capture the flavor of the personality you're describing." Joe said, "Yes, I've started a diary." I said, "Pepys put all his references to sexual matters in code so that no one would know." Joe said, "I don't care who knows."

"The whole trouble with Western Society today is the lack of anything worth concealing," Orton wrote in his diary, which covered the last eight eventful months of his life. Orton had willed himself into the role of rebel outcast: beyond guilt or shame. At thirty-four, already with a criminal record for comically defacing public library books, Orton had rejected the world of conventional work, conventional sex, and conventional wisdom. He was an iconoclast who believed there was no sense being a rebel without applause.

Orton loved to shock. "Loot" 's success emboldened him. "Well, the sound and fury is over," Orton wrote to a friend on October 4, 1966, sending press clippings which compared him to Ben Jonson, G. B. Shaw and—the sobriquet that stuck—"the Oscar Wilde of Welfare State gentility." " 'Loot' and 'Joe Orton' are a great success. I feel exhausted. 18 months of struggling to vindicate the honor of my play (my own is beyond vindication) has left me weak at the knees." But with acclaim, Orton's literary style and his life acquired a new swagger. Orton's journal, which he began two months later, was called "Diary of a Somebody."

The idea of a diary was first suggested by Orton's agent, Peggy Ramsay, in 1965. "I didn't write the Morocco diary as you wanted," Orton wrote her on August 30, 1965. "I thought there might be difficulties in getting it published." Ramsay continued to press for an account of their Tangier adventures, if not from Orton then from Kenneth Halliwell, whose literary ambitions Orton had inherited and then surpassed. "I urge *one* of you, at least, to start a journal à la Gide. . . . I'm sure it would be a good idea and the publishers would snap at it," she wrote, prematurely, as it turned out. "Why not talk this over with Ken who has real writing talent, but finds stage plots so difficult."

But Halliwell was fast losing what literary confidence he had left. His latest rejection had come the day after "Loot" opened to phenomenal reviews, and was from Orton's agent. "What I've read," Peggy Ramsay wrote, too bored to finish Halliwell's "The Facts of Life," "reads like an adaptation from a novel, because the first speech, for instance, is so damned *literary* and the speeches are nearly always written beyond their 'holding' capacity." Before he finally gave up writing, Halliwell sent the play to a few more agents and to Peter Willes, who produced Orton's television plays. "I'd had several plays sent to me by Ken," Peter Willes recalled. "They were not like Joe's whatsoever. They were like very pseudo–Ronald Firbank."

Halliwell, who never found himself, had also never found his literary voice. Orton had. Orton's unrelenting display of verbal prowess was a terrific offense that masked his own defensiveness; but Halliwell's literary archness only made his insecurity more transparent. Between October and December, when the diary began, Halliwell abdicated the literary obsession that had dominated their adult lives and turned to his collages. "Does my real talent if any lie in this direction?" he wrote to Peggy Ramsay on October 30, 1966. Orton was now the writer; and Halliwell, who had nurtured Orton's skills and ambitions, was increasingly a factotum. Inevitably, the idea of a journal became Orton's project.

"I'm keeping a journal," Orton wrote to Peggy Ramsay from Tangier on May 26, 1967, five months after he'd begun it, "to be published long after my death." To Orton, the value of a diary was its frankness. Reality, as his play insisted, was the ultimate outrage. Orton despised the bogus propriety—the "verbal asterisks"—with which public figures doctored the picture of their life. "It's extraordinary," he complained to Peggy Ramsay, "how, as people grow older and they have less to lose by telling the truth, they grow more discreet, not less." To Orton, indiscretion was the better part of valour. "He thought he was a very important writer," said Kenneth Cranham, Orton's friend, who played Hal in the first London production of "Loot." "He'd talk to you about his diary. He had a vision of this diary. . . ."

"I'm going up, up, up," Orton wrote a friend in March 1967; and the diary was a symbol of Orton's confidence in his new-found momentum. He was going to have an interesting life after all. For a while, even after he'd broken through, he wasn't sure. " 'Sloane' wasn't easy. It wasn't the overall critical success people think it was," Orton said. "I had to hack my way in." Although "Entertaining Mr Sloane" (1964) had succeeded in London, it had failed miserably on Broadway. "I must close now because I'm tearful and I must go out," Orton wrote to his American director, Alan Schneider, at the news the show was coming off after only thirteen performances, typically hiding his sadness behind a joke. "The air around Islington is like wine." The débâcle of the first production of Orton's second full-length play, "Loot," had left his career and his self-confidence in shambles. Orton stopped writing for a while. He threatened to quit the theatre. "I'm really quite capable of carrying this out," Orton warned Peggy Ramsay, just four months before Orton's play and his reputation were reborn. "I've always admired Congreve who, after the absolute failure of 'Way of the World,' just stopped writing. And Rimbaud who turned his back on the literary world after writing a few volumes." But "Loot" 's success liberated Orton. Before it, he had been promising; now suddenly he was major. His literary style and his life acquired a new amperage. He was on the top of his form, full of fun, and writing like the young master he knew himself to be. The buoyant outrageousness of Orton's comic style evolved mostly in the fecund last eight months of his life. In that time, besides the diaries, Orton wrote the ghoulish capriccio about faith and justice, "Funeral Games"; rewrote his first play, "The Ruffian on the Stair" (1963), and "The Erpingham Camp" (1965) for their stage premieres under the collective title "Crimes of Passion"; completed the screenplay "Up Against It"; and wrote his farce masterpiece, "What the Butler Saw." Orton's plays caught the era's psychopathic mood, that restless, ruthless pursuit of sensation whose manic joking announced a refusal to suffer. The diaries are a chronicle not only of a unique comic imagination but of the cockeyed liberty of the time—a time before the failure of radical politics, before mass unemployment, before AIDS.

Orton had long harboured fantasies of omnipotence. As late as 1961, in his novel "Head to Toe," Orton contemplated a new kind of writing "that would create a seismic disturbance" whose "shock waves were capable of killing centuries afterwards." In farce, Orton found a way of turning his aggression into glory. "To be destructive," he wrote, "words have to be irrefutable." And Orton's hard-won epigrammatic style achieved just that: "With madness as with vomit, it is the passer-by who receives the inconvenience." Orton's diaries make explicit his desire to drive an audience crazy with pleasure. "Much more fucking, and they'll be screaming hysterics in next to no time," he writes on

March 26, 1967, making a note to hot-up "What the Butler Saw." To be a "panic" is the aspiration of all great comedians, an encounter that exhilarates as it infantilizes an audience. Orton's comedy personified this instinct for anarchy and, in "What the Butler Saw," even invoked the traditional jester's symbol for it: the penis. Farce plays on a common recognition of insecurity and creates the illusion of mastery. Orton's obsession with the penis, on- and offstage, tried to turn his fears of inadequacy into a spectacle of potency and control.

" 'I'm from the gutter,' I said. 'And don't you ever forget it because I won't.' " Orton saw himself as a mixture of "truculence and charm" and recorded the impact of his studied toughness. He had lived through a lot and came across as a cool customer. On her first meeting with Orton, Peggy Ramsay recalls, "I was very hard on him because he was talented. He had this lovely detachment." And in her letter to the English critic Harold Hobson a few months later, urging him to attend the opening of "Entertaining Mr Sloane," Ramsay's admiration for Orton's toughness comes through:

> This play came to me in January and I thought it extremely talented and asked to meet the author. A young man called and I was much struck with him. I frankly told him that I was uncertain about the advisability of selling this play in case the critics might label it "Pinterish." He replied that I must do anything I wished and that he could easily manage if I didn't sell it, because he was living on £3. 10s. p.w. National Assistance, and had been doing so "ever since he came out." He then went on to tell me that he had been six months in Wormwood Scrubs for a series of minor thefts and that it had been remarkably good for him. When I asked if he intended going back to crime, he said certainly not, if it was possible to earn a living in any other way.
>
> Finally, I decided to get the play done quickly at the Arts. . . . In the meantime, I've been trying to help the author with money, but he firmly and tactfully says it's quite unnecessary and that he "can manage." I even offered him a TV set as a present, but he said he was quite all right without one!
>
> I'm much struck with a young man who doesn't want to exploit

people, who is prepared to live on £3. 10 p.w., who doesn't whine, or tell a hard luck tale.

With success, Orton continued to build up his reputation for hardness. To the *Evening Standard,* Orton drew another comparison besides wit between himself and Oscar Wilde: "I didn't suffer the way Oscar Wilde suffered from being in prison. But then Wilde was flabby and self-indulgent. There is this complete myth about writers being sensitive plants. They're not. It's a silly, 19th-century idea. I'm sure Aristophanes was not sensitive." He had himself photographed bare-chested with arms akimbo in stark and shadowy angles, glowering into the camera with a hard man's steely gaze. Orton worked at being both well-built ("I shall be the most perfectly developed of modern playwrights if nothing else") and well-hung. In the famous photo of Orton reclining in a desk chair with his crotch looming up in the foreground, Orton had stuffed his swimming trunks with toilet paper. "He looked tight and tough," the actor Simon Ward recalled. "Joe's hair was like a little tight skullcap. He walked very erect, his buttocks clenched, the pelvis thrust forward. There's only one way you can walk when you carry yourself like that—a cross between an automaton and a sailor's roll."

Orton's swagger, like his characters' strutting dialogue, presented an image of power that betrayed inadequacy. Says Detective Truscott in "Loot," for instance: "How dare you involve me in a situation for which no memo has been issued." As the diaries show, when faced with situations which make him feel "weak" or out of control—the enervating rows with Halliwell, the depressing opening of "Crimes of Passion," his mother's funeral—Orton sought to test and to confirm his strength in the anonymous dangers of the public lavatories. The tongue-in-cheek title of the diaries suggests that Orton was aware, on some level, of the comic strain of always having to appear big. The diaries contain many examples of Orton's detached amusement at himself. "Perhaps you better find yourself a different writer," he tells the Beatles' management brazenly, when the Fab Four stand him up at a meeting to discuss the possibility of writing their next film. But Orton spoils the startling hard-nose effect with a slapstick exit. "Left almost tripping over the carpet and crashing into the secretary who gave a squeal of surprise as I hurried past her. This I never mention when retelling the story. I always end on a note of hurt dignity.''

Orton's celebrity protected him from feeling humiliation. Every failure—his day trip to Libya, the Beatles' rejection of his screenplay, the fiasco of the *Evening Standard* award—could be turned to his advantage. But his search for invulnerability dominates his life as well as his stage laughter. Orton's notorious practical jokes—the defacement of ''dull, badly written books,'' and letters written in the spirit of oafish English middle classery and signed under the name of ''Edna Welthorpe (Mrs)'' —are defensive, albeit hilarious, pranks. The mischief is aggressive, but the culprit is invisible, the works of a trickster with a strong rage and a weak ego. Orton pasted an anonymous quotation on the back page of his ''Loot'' scrapbook: ''I was not nearly so sure of myself as I should have liked, and this made me present a brassy face to the world and pretend to be more hard-boiled than I was. . . . I developed a mocking, cynical way of treating events because it prevented them from being too painful. . . .''

The landscape of Orton's London is bleak: a soiled world of loss, isolation, ignorance, and bright decline. ''I'm a believer in original sin,'' Orton said. ''I find people profoundly bad and irresistibly funny.'' Public lavatories were often the setting where his point was proved most outrageously. ''No more than two feet away,'' Orton writes in the diaries, as seven men grope each other, including him, in a loo, ''the citizens of Holloway moved about their ordinary business.''

But if Orton relished the humor at his incidental encounters, his sense of sadness also comes through strongly in the diaries. He records the poignancy of a derelict singing ''Once I had a secret love.'' And two aged, out-of-work actresses touch him with buoyant small talk about their decrepitude. ''It was a very sad scene,'' Orton writes, of a tactic he himself used in his plays, ''because it was played in such a cheerful way.'' Likewise, the diaries sparkle with fun during a time when his mother dies, his father is hit by a car and goes blind, and his relationship with Halliwell (and Halliwell himself) is cracking up. ''He thought, planned, waited, and waiting, plunged into dreams,'' Orton wrote, summarizing his life before success so accurately that he'd repeated it both in ''Head to Toe'' and ''The Boy Hairdresser'' (1960). Now that the dreams had come true, Orton still couldn't banish his sense of foreboding. Happiness was rare enough in their life for Orton and Halliwell to have much faith in it. As he wrote in his Tangier diary:

> Kenneth and I sat talking of how happy we both felt. We'd have to pay for it. Or we'd be struck down from afar by disaster because we were, perhaps, too happy. To be young, good-looking, healthy, famous, comparatively rich *and* happy is surely going against nature. . . . I hope no doom strikes.

"Outcasts always mourn," Wilde wrote for his epitaph, and Orton's furious hilarity always contains a sense of loss. "I'm not in favour of private grief," says Fay in "Loot," which mocks the rituals around death. "Show your emotions in public or not at all." In Orton, grief translates as aggression: and sadness is never far beneath the lethal wit he showed both onstage and off it. "Joe had those absolutely black eyes with no expression in them at all," says Peter Willes. "I attribute it to unhappiness."

Orton had a long history of regrets. In "Head to Toe" he dramatized his condition as lost in an alien world, imprisoned in a country that confounds him and where his survival is uncertain. "I feel a great need of knowledge," says Gombold, Orton's fictional spokesman. And later: "He passed through each degree of despair that prisoners suffer." Orton was trapped by the deprivations of his working-class Leicester background, the first of four children in a family where there was never enough money or attention to go around. He had failed his eleven-plus; failed as an actor after RADA; failed for a decade as a writer; failed in the eyes of society to be a responsible, even normal, citizen. His laughter got even for these sources of humiliation: his credulous parents, the sexual guilt, the social stereotyping, the double-binds of authority in which his identity was discounted. "He'd suffered an awful lot from people's ribaldry about camp," says the novelist Penelope Gilliatt, who befriended Orton in 1965 when she was the drama critic for the *Observer*. "He was furious. He lived a lot of his life in a state of cold, marvellous, funny fury."

The diaries are full of Orton's percolating rage. "There's no such thing as a joke," Orton says, in one particularly instructive passage of the Tangier diary, on May 25, 1967, after he faced down the judgmental glare of a heterosexual couple with a bravura display of outrageousness. ("We've got a leopard-skin rug in the flat and he wanted me to fuck him on that, only I'm afraid of the spunk you see, it might adversely affect the spots of the leopard.") Onstage, Orton deployed his wit to the same end: to put distance between himself and the things that oppressed him. "If you could lock the enemy in the room and fire sentences at them . . ." Orton wrote in 1961. By 1967, his salvos were disarming the public, and the enemy was within.

"When Joe sent me 'Sloane,' he spoke of it as 'our play,' " says Peggy Ramsay. "The first time he came to see me, Joe didn't produce Kenneth. But the second time he said, 'Can I bring my friend?' And never at any stage was Kenneth not there." Orton dedicated "Entertaining Mr Sloane" to Halliwell, and Halliwell, too, talked of "a genius like us." This continued to be the pattern through Orton's struggles of 1965 and 1966. Orton wrote to Halliwell from New York, nervous about the Broadway reception of "Sloane": "I'm not hopeful of success. But we never were, were we." And when the original production of "Loot" faced its first audiences, Orton's distraught letters home to Halliwell register a tone of dependence and concern that are not in the diaries. "The play is a disaster," Orton wrote Haliwell on February 9, 1965, from its first tryout in Cambridge. "There were hardly any laughs for Truscott. The audience seemed to take the most extraordinary lines with dead seriousness. . . . I shall have to do some surgery. I can't come back Wednesday. Can't you ring me? It's all so dreadful. I've already had two rows of nerve-wracking proportions. I've said to [Peter] Wood that I'm not a commercial writer and perhaps he understands now why it's impossible that I should ever be a 'national humourist'. . . . I'm going to try and get back before the weekend, but I can't leave with it in this state." And from Oxford, the news was no better, but Orton's tone had the same solicitousness. "Do try and hang on doing something if you get too fed up without me," Orton wrote, signing off "Love, Joe." "I'll get back as soon as humanly possible. I'm not gallivanting about down here. It's the most depressing few weeks I've ever lived through."

But when Orton's luck changed, so did his relationship with Halliwell. "Joe had only one overwhelming relationship allied to loyalty, and that was Ken," said Peggy Ramsay. "He didn't care a damn about anybody else." Orton remained loyal in his fashion to Halliwell; but once in the public gaze, he couldn't bring himself to acknowledge the collaboration that made his success possible. Orton had cured himself of many of the culture's deliriums, but not its romance of self.

History is not kind to those sacrificed to someone else's art. Emma Hardy was seen as a vituperative, no-talent ninny; Vivien Eliot as the loony baggage the great poet was lumbered with, and Halliwell as a "middle-aged non-entity." They were all silent partners to admired artists, and they all had literary ambitions of their own. They stuck with their literary marriages in part because the other partner fulfilled a dream and in part because they had helped to fulfill it. But their collaboration became an alienation. This was especially true of Halliwell, who had worked a lifetime to create art but whose great creation was Orton. Halliwell supposed that with Orton's success some residual kudos would come to him. But Halliwell had to share Orton with a new lover —the public. "If he belongs to the public," Emma Hardy wrote to a friend about marriage, counselling not to expect gratitude, attention, or justice, "years of devotion count for nothing." Halliwell found himself forced into a position of being at once invisible and unwanted. "I hated Halliwell. No, I disliked him, he wasn't important enough to hate," says Peter Willes. "I put up with Halliwell the way one does with authors' wives if you want their work. . . ."

Halliwell was experiencing the desperation of many partners of the famous: discounted in public, they go quietly mad in private. "Everyone wanted to meet Joe—Emlyn Williams, Pinter, Rattigan," says Peter Willes. "I introduced Harold to Joe. Harold said, 'I couldn't believe he was so young.' Joe looked much younger than he was." But Halliwell looked old, and irrelevant. "They treated me like shit," Halliwell shouts in the diaries, hammering the wall after an evening with a new couple dazzled by Orton's name. "I won't be treated like this." Celebrity widened the scope of Orton's charm, which Halliwell had always envied. "God is on his side and fights for him and all people like him," says Halliwell's spokesman in "The Boy Hairdresser," of the way Orton attracted people. Orton's celebrity blinded people to Halliwell. "With Halliwell one always had to make such an effort," says Peter Willes. "He was just unsympathetic. It took enormous tact not to leave him out altogether." To get attention, Halliwell exaggerated both his importance and his actions; and made large and startling gestures, like Vivien Eliot who appeared at the first night of "The Rock" holding a placard that read: "I am the woman he abandoned." Halliwell didn't display a placard; but he did wear an Old Etonian tie to a swank cocktail party given by Peter Willes. That night Orton was delivering "What the Butler Saw" for Willes to read. If Halliwell couldn't win the approval of Orton's admirers, then hostility was something to build on:

> Went to Peter Willes' for dinner. When we got there he stared at Kenneth in horror. "That's an Old Etonian tie!" he screeched. "Yes," Kenneth said. "It's a joke." Willes looked staggered and wrinkled up his face in an evil sort of way. "Well, I'm afraid it's a joke against you then. People will imagine you're passing yourself off as an Old Etonian. They'll laugh at you." "I'm sending up Eton," Kenneth said. "Oh no!" Willes cackled with a sort of eldritch shriek. "You're pathetic! I mean it's disgraceful wearing that tie." "It's a joke!" Kenneth said, looking tight-lipped, a little embarrassed and angry. "People will know." "Not the people I meet," Kenneth said. "They'll think it's funny." "You're making people angry," Willes said. "I don't care," Kenneth said, laughing a little too readily. "I want to make them angry. . . ."

While in private he always acknowledged Halliwell's importance to his work, Orton completely edited Halliwell out of the public story of his success. "All you people who are mad on Joe really have no idea of what he's like," Halliwell said that same evening. But people weren't interested in Halliwell's version of events, only Orton's. Halliwell usually absented himself from the flat when Orton was interviewed. He was absent on the day Orton explained the origins of his mandarin style to "The Transatlantic Review." "I like Lucian and classical writers," Orton said, never mentioning how he'd come by such tastes. "I suppose that's what gives my writing a difference, an old-fashioned classical education! Which I never received, but I gave myself one.'' Orton also portrayed himself to the press as having been married and divorced. His comments about marriage were a disturbing projection of his fraught relationship with Halliwell. ''It just didn't work out. I mean, I was too young,'' said Orton, who'd moved in with Halliwell as a teenager. ''We drifted apart. Those kinds of marriages never last.'' And as late as June 9, 1967, two months to the day before he was murdered, Orton was insisting to the *Evening News* on a writer's need for freedom as the reason he'd never remarry: ''That's tied up with the possession thing, too. They have to be your responsibilities. . . .''

Scrupulously excluded from Orton's public world, Halliwell was beginning also to be excluded from Orton's social world. ''Joe was very protective of Halliwell,'' says Peter Willes. ''He wouldn't go anywhere without him. He didn't care if he gave a bad impression. It was 'take me as you find me.' '' But in the last weeks of his life, Orton had agreed to come without Halliwell to a party of showbiz luminaries given by Dorothy Dickson. Orton was killed within a week of the party, but Halliwell's distress was apparent before it. ''Ken came to see me while waiting to get a prescription of tranquillizers from Dr. Ismay filled,'' says Peter Willes, who helped organize the party, when Halliwell landed on his doorstep on August 7, 1967. '' 'You don't realize how Joe carries on at the thought of separating. You don't realize how dependent he is on me.' I couldn't wait to get Halliwell out of the flat. I felt I wanted to disinfect the place. I telephoned Joe and said, 'Listen, you can't leave Kenneth and come to the party.' It was quite a big decision because it was a grand party. That was the first time I knew for sure that I was talking to Joe on the telephone because Kenneth had just left my flat. Ken imitated Joe's voice on the phone—they sounded just alike—and you had to be careful. He wanted to find out what people were saying to Joe—anything that might possibly affect their life together.''

The famous leave around them shattered lives which are either overlooked or underplayed by biographers, or rewritten by the celebrities themselves. After Emma Hardy's death, Thomas Hardy burned her diary testimony entitled ''What I Think of My Husband,'' ghosted his own biography, and recast the barbarity of their relationship into fine poetry. Eliot sealed his past in silence by stipulating no biography in his will, while the estate continues to buy up and keep under wraps Vivien Eliot's correspondence. Orton never had time to rewrite his history. The diaries offer a rare, if unwitting, glimpse into the punishing dynamic of celebrity's self-aggrandizement. As Halliwell's suicide note implies ("If you read his diary all will be explained") the diaries were both an explanation *and* a provocation. Orton owned the future, the past, and now even Halliwell's suffering.

The diaries are not just a chronicle of the drama between them, but a prop in it. Orton and Halliwell lived in extraordinary physical proximity. Their room was sixteen by twelve. The space was so small that two people could not easily move about in it at once. The bulk of the diaries were written virtually under Halliwell's nose. They were kept in a red-grained leather binder in the writing desk where Halliwell could—and did—read their punishing contents. Everything about the diaries was provocative, a symbol of Orton's retreat into himself and away from Halliwell. The title, which emphasized Orton's singularity, was also a reminder that if Orton was somebody, by implication, Halliwell was nobody. Orton was the center of Halliwell's existence, but, as he could read, Halliwell was an increasingly minor—and frequently irritating—extra in the drama of Orton's eventful life.

Inevitably, Orton's memory is selective. Orton's accounts of Halliwell's depressions—the rows, the nagging, the brittle *hauteur*—are well documented; but the issues behind these scenes are kept very much offstage. "Halliwell felt he was excluded somehow and not valued," says Dr. Douglas Ismay, a G.P. with an interest in psychology to whom Peter Willes had sent Halliwell for help, and who gave Halliwell Tofranil and sympathy. "People didn't know he helped to write and edit some of the plays. He said that Orton was a much less well-educated person than he was and Orton drew on his know-how and grasp of English. He felt frustrated." Although Orton acknowledges Halliwell's critical acumen in the diaries, none of Halliwell's claims come into the debate between them. In Orton's version of his daily life, Halliwell is shown merely as an accoutrement. And by then, he was. But the Beatles' screenplay was based, in part, on their first novel (1953), when the only thing Orton could contribute to the collaboration was his typing. "The Ruffian on the Stair," which Orton polished for the Royal Court, was adapted from their novel "The Boy Hairdresser." "Sloane" was, according to Orton, "our play." Even Orton's wonderful gift for dialogue owed its power to collage, which was originally Halliwell's fascination. Halliwell had been completely taken over by the imperialism of Orton's fame. ("Must make it plain," Halliwell wrote to Peggy Ramsay, asking her to assess his collage murals, "this invite is not from J or anything to do with him or his Works. . . .") On that painful issue Orton remains mum in the diaries. According to Dr. Ismay, Halliwell "said that Orton thought he was a pain in his side, a nuisance who was interfering with Orton's success." Orton rarely states his feelings in the diaries. Instead, he signals his disaffection in small asides ("Kenneth quel moan") and throwaway snatches of sour conversation. "You look like a zombie," the diary reports Orton saying to Halliwell on April 23, never in print probing Halliwell's complaints too deeply. "He replied, heavily, 'And so I should. I lead the life of a zombie.' " Crying on the terrace of a Tangier restaurant, creating a scene at Peter Willes's home, threatening suicide, Halliwell's emotional pressure on Orton is as apparent as Orton's refusal to be moved by it. "The tranquilizers worked against too much yapping," Orton writes on the day of the "zombie" exchange.

But the diaries are also an extraordinary record of Orton's sexual adventures: his way not just of keeping count but of recapturing desire. "At one moment," Orton writes on June 11, "with my cock in his arse, the image was, and as I write still is, overpoweringly erotic. . . ." Halliwell hated Orton's promiscuity. "Halliwell was disgusted more and more with Orton's promiscuity," says Dr. Ismay. "The public lavatory theme was the thing that bothered him most." Orton insisted the trolling fed his work; but it also fed Halliwell's rage. "I'm disgusted by all this immorality!" Halliwell shouts at Orton, after the anticlimactic dinner of May 4 with Clive and Tom. "Homosexuals disgust me!" Promiscuity not only exacerbated Halliwell's sense of sexual guilt, but his sense of sexual inadequacy. Halliwell may have been the focus of Orton's affections, but never of his sexual desire. "Kenneth knew that Joe didn't reciprocate this romantic attachment in any way," says Peter Willes. "Joe had no feeling for him except protection and loyalty." But the issue of sexual prowess became an infighting point between them. When Halliwell loudly claims in front of the "Loot" cast that Orton isn't over-sexed, Orton takes umbrage; likewise, Orton is angered by Halliwell's bravado on the subject of Tangier rent boys:

> Kenneth said "Oh, all the boys will do anything." "They won't," I said. "There's a lot of things they won't do." It was irritating to be told by someone who likes being masturbated that the boys "will do anything. . . ."

The jibe about Halliwell's prowess precipitates the first of Halliwell's violent attacks on Orton.

Orton instinctively taunted the bogus; promiscuity was, on some level, a way of taunting and testing what he saw as Halliwell's illusion of their family unit. "The household they had was a fake household and Joe knew this," says Penelope Gilliatt. "Joe knew the fakery well enough to kick it about and endanger it as much as possible by staying out late, by promiscuity, by every means he could. To see how far he could drive Halliwell. I think Joe hated himself for accepting domesticity and carrying on with it." The diaries brought Orton's promiscuity off the streets and under their roof. The fact that Orton described these scenes with such humor and insight only compounded the problem. Orton was making a legend of something profoundly undermining to Halliwell. Orton was writing down these scenes—and relishing them in set pieces of conversation—while Halliwell was at the same time acting out his desperation to be loved. It was a dangerous game. Orton was not only flirting with death in the public lavatories, but with Halliwell at home. He and Halliwell had already explored the murderous parameter of Halliwell's self-loathing and possessiveness in "The Boy Hairdresser." They had already imagined their deaths in print: Orton's "beauty smashed forever"; Halliwell dreaming of one crazy act of revenge before killing himself—"When he went, he'd take others with him. . . . The last laugh had to be played correctly."

In their novel, the revenge is botched; in life, it wasn't. The diaries were the focus of both attacks on Orton. The first, in Tangier, took place while Orton was writing the diary, with Halliwell "hitting me about the head and knocking the pen from my hand." In the second attack, Halliwell's suicide note was placed directly on top of the diaries, directing police to them as an explanation for the bludgeoning and his own suicide.

The diaries pick up Orton's story just after the power in Orton's and Halliwell's relationship has shifted irrevocably in Orton's favour. Orton had the big bank balance, the big name, and the big future. All the calls and the letters were for him. Halliwell, who had been Orton's mentor, was now his employee. "When I said, 'What's your job,' " recalls Dr. Ismay of his first meeting with Halliwell, "he said, 'I'm a secretary.' Later it transpired that he was a writer." By the time of the diaries, Halliwell's resentments and frustrations had changed Orton's tone from one of comradely dependence to forbearance ("We got home, had a cup of tea, and it was smiles until bedtime"). In the diaries, Orton continually looks at Halliwell and finds him lacking. Halliwell's whining, his prissiness, his self-consciousness, his bombast are all noted in Orton's asides. And when Orton forthrightly defends Halliwell against the slander of being a "middle-aged non-entity," he is compelled to add: "Kenneth has more talent, although hidden. . . ."

There was nothing hidden about Halliwell's talent to Orton when they first met at RADA in 1951. Halliwell was twenty-five, imposing in his bravado and his baldness. Orton was eighteen, a raw kid who'd never spent two weeks away from Leicester. To him, Halliwell was promise incarnate. Halliwell had everything Orton envied and lacked: his own flat, a car, a library, an education. He also had a good line in literary chat. Halliwell spouted the kind of romantic idealism he put into his play about Edmund Kean, "The Protagonist": "This is the end to which my being has been directed: the acclamation of the world and nothing less." Halliwell preached the gospel of Art, at least until he became its victim. "He was an artist," he wrote in "The Protagonist" of Kean. "If a man must, by the very true nature of his work, live more intensely than others, may not extravagance be forgiven in him, which would be blameworthy in others?" Orton became Halliwell's acolyte. "When I spotted Orton in the RADA canteen queue, I'd been at the academy about three weeks," recalls Frank Whitby, who had met

Orton and his mother the previous year at a tryout for the Old Vic Theatre School. "I went across and reminded him of our meeting and congratulated him on getting into RADA. He immediately flashed a look over his shoulder, and there, looking at me with malevolence, was Kenneth Halliwell. Already, after one full term, Orton had exchanged maternal possessiveness for something that was to be lethal."

Halliwell's possessiveness and desire to control were the result of the traumatic abandonments of his childhood. Halliwell's mother died in 1937, when he was eleven, of a wasp sting on her finger while making breakfast. Up to then, according to J. P. Howarth, who was the Halliwells' lodger from 1933–7, Kenneth had been a "mother's boy" whose mother wouldn't let her taciturn husband touch him. "She pampered him. They talk of the silver cord—well, it would never have been severed between them." With her death, Halliwell "became introvert and very difficult to talk to." He and his father had little to say to each other. They lived as strangers under the same roof. In this sad atmosphere, Halliwell studied hard at the Wirral Grammar School and did well, earning Higher School Certificates in ancient history, Greek, Latin, and German. And then, in 1949, Halliwell came downstairs one morning to find his father lying dead with his head in the oven. With typical reticence, the father had left no note. Inevitably, after such overwhelming rejection, Halliwell, whose mother had expected great things from him, found refuge in grandiose fantasy. His mother had wanted him to be a doctor. His father quarrelled with him about his decision not to follow the academic path. But Halliwell had his heart set on the glory road, which would lead him nowhere.

" 'Tight' is the word that comes to mind for Halliwell," said Charles Marowitz, the director of the first London production of "Loot." "He was organizing his social persona so vigorously, so forcefully, that I never once saw him in repose. He could never unclench." Even as a teen-ager, Halliwell was grave. By the time he'd got to RADA, as his teachers' comments indicated, the strain of his defensiveness was already visible in the tension in his body, his voice, and his personality. Onstage, Halliwell was all perspiration and no inspiration. What came across the footlights was not strength but self-consciousness.

—I think a little more divine discontent with his own work might be welcome. . . .

—Seems to be unconvinced that acting is the expression of *emotion*. The result is that his approach is all mental—giving a tight, almost prim aspect to his work. . . .

—a strangely set and rigid student . . .

—sound work but really too boxed up . . .

Halliwell was older than most of the students, and his high-handed manner kept them at a distance. What Orton saw as intellectual authority came across to more sophisticated students as hapless insecurity. "He was a very affected little man," said Margaret Whiting, who won the Bancroft Medal for the outstanding performer of their year. "He had visions of grandeur. He was always in his little world of creative fantasy. He was so selfish and preoccupied about himself. Constant talking of self, ego, ambition. He was a great egotist." "Artistic temperament," Chesterton wrote, "is a disease that afflicts amateurs." Halliwell's tantrums, his conceit, his highfalutin pronouncements about art and other actors would in time be an example of Chesterton's point: "There are many real tragedies of the artistic temperament, tragedies of vanity or violence or fear. But the great tragedy of the artistic temperament is that it cannot produce any art."

All too aware of his threadbare resources, Orton saw Halliwell as a teacher, a father, and a friend. And Halliwell, an orphan, found in Orton someone willing to share his life and his dreams of glory. Orton was vivacious and charming; and, so they wrote in "The Boy Hairdresser," reconstructing the origins of their relationship, Orton "made him feel young." He also made Halliwell feel powerful: "he was in need of protection." Orton, as depicted in "The Boy Hairdresser," "was half-educated, half-baked, half-cut." And to educate Orton gave them both a mission and a bond. They were united in their desire to be special.

"I never was able to imagine myself as ordinary," said Orton. Orton got this idea from his mother, Elsie, who looked upon "her John" as the most gifted of her children. Elsie refused to admit the ordinariness of her life or her children. She was always in search of some indication of status: Players, not Woodbines; ham, not Spam; opera, not Gilbert and Sullivan. She wanted the best; but she had been shortchanged in life. Her family had no money, no education, no prospects. When Orton failed his eleven-plus, Elsie pawned her wedding ring, so Orton was the only boy on his Leicester estate of fifteen hundred to attend a fee-paying school. Typically, Elsie chose Clark's College, which offered a commercial curriculum, not the academic course she'd intended. In his plays, Orton mocked his mother's pretensions to propriety; but Orton worked to fulfill the generalized ambition he'd absorbed from her. At fifteen, before he'd even appeared in a play, Orton had dedi-cated his life, so he wrote in his teen-age diary, to the theatre. "He seemed a child that had missed out on a lot of love," said Joanne Runswick, who directed Orton in one of his early amateur theatricals. "I used to want to draw him to me because he used to go away, always apart. He was so apart." While at RADA, Orton came back to see Joanne Runswick, already fired with Halliwell's ambition to write. "He said, 'I want to write plays,' " she recalls. "I wanted him to make good, but I was a little worried. He was so tense about it, about becoming somebody." And so, too, was Elsie, who accompanied Orton to his audition at the Old Vic Theatre School in 1950. "After Orton had gone off to do his prepared pieces she began to talk to me," says Frank Whitby. "She babbled on about him. With her strong accent, one that I was not used to, and her old-fashioned clothes, she looked and sounded like a character out of an Ealing comedy. I remember her constant falling inflections at the end of each sentence. This 'dying fall' certainly had a depressing effect on me. . . ."

Although Orton came home for two weeks each summer, Elsie only started to correspond with Orton after his success. "You will be sur-prised to hear from your mother," she wrote, after "Entertaining Mr Sloane" 's reviews at the end of May 1964. "First of all I am very happy for you had a little weep to think you had done it at last . . . God bless you John look after yourself you have had your troubles now look forward and not back any more." Elsie was bowled over by Orton's celebrity and wasted no time in pressing its advantage. "It gave me great pleasure to brag about one of my sons my boss ask me if you belong to me since then they treat me very good can't do nothing wrong . . ."

Always in debt, Elsie frequently asked Orton to get her out of hock. He paid, and she made a show of looking out for his economic interests: "I can't believe months ago you were broke now you are better off than any one in all the family both sides . . . several people want to borrow your book but I won't let them have it let them buy one." Elsie waited eagerly to see her son on television and sent him clippings about him from the *Leicester Mercury*. "People want to know," she wrote on September 10, 1964, "why there is never any mention of your parents."

The reason was simple: home was with Halliwell. Orton's family had nothing to do with the bright talent being praised in the press. Orton not only glossed over his family in interviews, he left them out of his will, which named Halliwell as the sole beneficiary. Although Orton had been living with Halliwell since 1951, the family didn't clap eyes on him until 1964, when Halliwell, standing in for Orton, who was nervous of his mother seeing her pretensions lampooned onstage, escorted them to "Entertaining Mr Sloane." "Ken we all thought was a very nice chap," Elsie wrote Orton.

"If we could pool our resources, we could help each other," says Halliwell's spokesman in "The Boy Hairdresser." Orton's contribution, at first, was enthusiasm and attention. Halliwell exerted almost complete control over the relationship. Halliwell provided the food and cooked. And more than that, as Lawrence Griffin, who shared their first flat at 161 West End Lane, recalls, "Halliwell showed Orton what to wear, what to read, where to go." The price Orton paid for this largesse was loyalty. Halliwell, who called him "my pussycat," kept Orton on a tight leash. "Kenneth Halliwell didn't like John being away," Griffin says. "You could see Halliwell was jealous. John didn't bridle. It was useful. It was a base to go back to. He was like Sloane, a tease." Griffin was not the only one of Orton's acquaintances who saw the connection. "Joe was Sloane," says Peter Willes. "Ruthless, not immoral but amoral, and pragmatic." Orton followed the line of least resistance; and, like Sloane, was maneuvered into a situation he'd never bargained for.

"They had the idea they were going to be brilliant actors," says Griffin. "Sometimes I used to feel the odd one out because they practically convinced me they were so good. They looked upon themselves as very special." But when their acting dreams collapsed, Orton and Halliwell fixed on writing. Cocooned in their room and their dream of literary success, they began to write and make a study of literature. Orton projected their relationship into "Head to Toe," with Orton as the lost wayfarer Gombold and Halliwell as Doktor Von Pregnant who offers Gombold knowledge as a means of escape.

The Doktor talked constantly, continuing Gombold's educa-
tion.
"What's the abiding value?" he said one evening.
"Truth," Gombold replied.
"I have taught you nothing then," the Dokter said. "The rulers of whatever country you choose will designate as true that which is useful to them. Truth is relative, and always behind it stands some interest, furthering its own end."

"To escape unaided," wrote Orton, "had never occurred to Gombold." Nor had it occurred to Orton. After a while, their regimen of writing and reading became habit; and Orton, like Gombold, "never now mentioned escape. Study took the place of liberty; absorbed in acquiring knowledge, days, months, and years passed in rapid and instructive course." Orton's fictional characters "slithered to what they hoped was freedom." They didn't find it; and neither did Orton and Halliwell. For them success was freedom; and it completely eluded them. Nothing was published. Their hostility—in the form of the defaced books—landed them in an actual, not an imagined cell. In 1962, they were sent to separate prisons for six months. It was the first time Orton had been away from Halliwell for a sustained period of time. On summer holidays, Orton never stayed away longer than a fortnight. "I must get back to Ken," was always his explanation, according to Orton's sister, Leonie Barnett. Ken was also the reason Orton never returned at Christmas. "I can't leave Ken on his own." In jail, on his own, Halliwell grew depressed; and, soon after his release, he attempted suicide. But Orton learned something about himself that brought detachment and boldness to his writings: "Before, I had been vaguely conscious of something rotten somewhere; prison crystallized this. The old whore society really lifted up her skirts, and the stench was pretty foul." For Orton, the experience was a liberation. "Being in the nick brought detachment to my writing," he told the *Leicester Mercury*. "I wasn't involved anymore and suddenly it worked." Orton had passed beyond suffering. He now had nothing to lose. His laughter became dangerous. He had at last found a way to "rage correctly."

"I don't write fantasy," Orton said. "People think I do, but I don't." The diaries confirm this. Orton's comic world, with its monsters of power and propriety, was all around him. He heard his brand of daft pretension in passing street talk; and he lived the truth of farce's momentum. "My life is beginning to run to a timetable no member of the royal family would tolerate," he writes, as the traffic plan for his liaisons with Moroccan boys assumes farcical complications. Orton's complaint about traditional farce was that it was "still based on the preconceptions of half a century ago, particularly the preconceptions about sex. But we must now accept that, for instance, people *do* have sexual relations outside marriage. . . ." Onstage and off it, Orton practiced an unbuttoned liberty.

But it was not just the rapacity of his farces that mirrored Orton's life. Farce is ruled by the law of momentum: at a certain speed all things disintegrate. At speed, panic substitutes for reason, and characters are pushed beyond guilt and beyond their connection to each other. So it was with Orton and Halliwell. In the momentum of Orton's new celebrity, he could not properly register Halliwell's disintegration. In any case, probably neither of them had the inner resources to cope with such drastic changes in their relationship. Halliwell's persistent psychosomatic complaints—the tightness in his chest, the constipation— broadcast his sense of being trapped. Orton, on the other hand, was feeling the heady rush of his new freedom. "Kenneth v. Depressed," he writes on March 10, contemplating writing a joke play under an assumed name. "I was feeling merry." Orton was unprepared to concede anything to Halliwell's signs of unhappiness. In Tangier, desperate to win Orton's approval, Halliwell makes the mistake of posing as Orton's Pandarus:

We were hailed with "Hallo" from a very beautiful sixteen-year-old boy whom I knew (but had never had) from last year. Kenneth wanted him. We talked for about five minutes and finally I said, "Come to our apartment for tea this afternoon." He was very eager. We arranged that he should meet us at The Windmill beach place. As we left the boy, Kenneth said "Wasn't I good at arranging it?" This astounded me. "I arranged it," I said. "You would have been standing there talking about the weather forever." K. didn't reply.

Often their bickering takes on the crazy symmetry of Orton's farce double-binds:

"Are you going to wear your blue suit for the summer?" he said. "No," I said. "Then why did you have the trousers altered?" he said. "If you hadn't had them altered, I could've worn them." "But if you could wear them," I said, "they wouldn't've fitted me. That's why I had them altered." "And now they don't fit me," he said. "No," I said. "But if they'd've fitted you they wouldn't've fitted me. And as they didn't fit me I had them altered. And now I've had them altered they don't fit you."

The joke at the heart of Orton's farce mayhem is that people state their needs, but the other characters, in their spectacular self-absorption, don't listen. "Hum to yourself if you're sad," says the nurse in "Funeral Games," taking leave of the defrocked priest who is her patient. Orton's laughter invokes a world of no consolation; and, in private, Orton could give little to Halliwell. He was incensed on Halliwell's behalf over the "middle-aged non-entity" slur. He continued to try to get Halliwell's collages exhibited. And in the last week of his life, with Halliwell sinking into his final, fatal depression, he offered to take him to Leicester, a strange suggestion since Halliwell had never visited Orton's family and would again find himself only an appendage. As the diaries show, nothing, not even Halliwell's veiled threats of violence, could make Orton attend properly to Halliwell's anguish. On March 9, Orton writes: "Kenneth said, 'You're turning into a real bully, do you know that. You'd better be careful. You'll get your just deserts!' Went to sleep.''

"You're a quite different person, you know, since you've had your success," Halliwell tells Orton in the diaries. And he was. Orton was more confident. Halliwell, as they'd written in "The Boy Hairdresser," "preferred him wracked with hesitation, only at ease in a conspiratorial way." But now Orton's conspiracy for high jinks was with the public. It made him bolder, and, to Halliwell, more threatening. "Arguing about a Polaroid camera," writes Orton on July 26. "Kenneth says it's a waste of money. I want one. Conspicuous wealth, I suppose." Orton had his own money now, and, with it, the freedom to do what he liked. Their old style of making-do didn't fit his new life. Their room was no longer the haven it once was. Orton was increasingly lured away into the world where there were other people to listen to him and to laugh with him. "When I've taught you a little," says Dr. Von Pregnant in "Head to Toe," "You'll know as much as I do myself." That day had come. Halliwell had invented his Perfect Friend, only to watch his efforts win from the world an admiration he himself could never earn. In "The Boy Hairdresser," they'd imagined Orton's "charm become sinister." And from Halliwell's point of view, it had. Orton sneered at Halliwell's attempts to stand out (the Old Etonian tie, his safari suit); he mocked Halliwell's sexual passivity, and, more hurtful, he disrespected Halliwell's "wifely" role:

> Kenneth's nerves are on edge. Hay fever. He had a row this morning. Trembling with rage. About my nastiness when I said, "Are you going to stand in front of the mirror all day?" He said, "I've been washing your fucking underpants! That's why I've been at the sink!" He shouted it out loudly and I said, "Please don't let the whole neighborhood know you're a queen." "You know I have hay fever and you deliberately get on my nerves," he said. "I'm going out today," I said, "I can't stand much more of it." "Go out then," he said. "I don't want you in here. . . ."

"The *Daily Express* telephoned me and said 'Have you heard the news about Joe Orton?' " Peter Willes recalls, of how he learned of the death. "I thought Joe had been up to no good at the King's Cross cottages. My first thought was to ring Ken at the flat. I called. The police answered. That's when I learned Halliwell had killed him." Orton was a voluptuary of fiasco; and his death seemed a macabre echo of his plays. (Even Peggy Ramsay, terrified at having to identify the bodies, made a farce entrance: walking backward into their room.) Nobody, certainly not Orton, believed Halliwell capable of such an act of will. Orton had long ago begun to discount Halliwell's threats as yet another indication of his hectoring impotence. " 'When we get back to London we're finished!' " Halliwell snarls at Orton, in their bitter quarrel on June 27, a few days before leaving Tangier. " 'This is the end!' I had heard this so often. 'I wonder you didn't add "I'm going back to Mother." ' . . . It went on and on until I put out the light. He slammed the door and went to bed."

When he wasn't writing, Orton increasingly found ways to stay away from their flat. But he was adamant to Kenneth Williams that he'd never forsake Halliwell. Peter Willes concurs: "Kenneth thought he was losing Joe, but he never would have." In one sense, as the diaries show, Orton certainly couldn't continue to cohabit long in the atmosphere of cramped desperation and envy which Halliwell created around them. But Halliwell was the entire creative environment of Orton's adult life. Orton, like so many literary figures with unhappy silent partners, had persisted so long in the relationship not only out of loyalty to his partner but also out of advantage to his craft. Halliwell was not just Orton's editor and sounding board; he was his subject matter. Out of their melodramatic and tortured arguments about personal needs Orton got "What the Butler Saw." Orton was prepared to buy Halliwell off with a house. He encouraged Halliwell to take up other people and other interests. The only way to change Halliwell was to change his situation. But Halliwell wanted only Orton and their old world back. And that was lost.

"Events move in one direction and are cumulative," they wrote in "The Boy Hairdresser." From their calendar in mid-August, it was clear in just what direction their destinies were going. On the day they died, a chauffeur was set to take Orton to Twickenham Studios to discuss "Up Against It" with Richard Lester. The following day Halliwell was scheduled to see a bona fide psychiatrist at St Bernard's Hospital. When Dr. Ismay called in the psychiatrist, Halliwell told him he was "taking the matter far too seriously." But in the early hours of August 9, the prospect of Halliwell's left-over life drove him crazy. Halliwell beat out the brains that poked such wicked fun at the world, then took his own life. In murder, Halliwell was imitating *their* art. "Which is worse?" asks Halliwell's alter ego in "The Boy Hairdresser," before he attempts murder. "Evil to look back on, nothing to look forward to, and pain in the present." Death made them equal again, linking Halliwell finally and forever to Orton. In the anarchy of his farces, Orton took revenge for the fretfulness of his desires and his disillusion. Now Halliwell did the same. What is left to the world is Orton's evergreen laughter, and the last testament of the fierce, sad kingdom of self from which it came: his diaries.

MAX WALL

THE MONKEY KING OF COMEDY

MAX WALL DIED ON MAY 22, 1990. He was an isolated, sullen, feisty man who brought his sadness on stage and dumped the hostility that came with it hilariously in the audience's lap. Wall's act was a cunning turn, achieved with a physical prowess and an insolence forged out of the vagaries of a vaudeville life. "Max Wall, standing before you, ladies and gentlemen. Man's answer to the peacock," was how he began his act when I finally caught up with him in Adelaide, Australia, in 1976. Wall, a veteran of half a century of English music hall, a former contortionist, stood straight in his tight-fitting black coat, gray hat and slap shoes, smiling nonchalantly at the audience. He had a new set of false teeth, which made the smile incandescent and alarming. He was twelve thousand miles from London, and knocking them dead.

"Welcome, darling," he said, tipping his hat to the first latecomer and withering her with a tired glance. "No offense. Arts Theatre welcomes you. Monday to Saturday. Well-upholstered, plush . . ." He repeated the line every time another paying customer straggled in. The audience soon became insiders, convulsing as someone else tried to sneak into his seat. That night ten people arrived late. He spoke quietly. No patter. No sweet talk. "I do what I do. And I do it well." While he warmed up the audience, testing them, showing little bits of himself for their delectation, Wall acknowledged the piano player to one side of the stage. "He's a composer," Wall said. "While he's composing, I'm decomposing." The laugh, when it finally came, was one of shock. Wall was playing for keeps, going daringly near the knuckle, moving the audience from one plateau of laughter to another, never losing their interest or their affection. Wall didn't want his audience to escape into gales of laughter. He worked slowly. He dismissed his jokes. "I don't tell any of them 'cause I don't like them." Then he told the one about his wife being a religious cook: "Everything she cooks is either a sacrifice or a burnt offering." Big laugh. Wall declined it, undercutting it with a grimace at the material. He understood that humor is more often in the characterization than the joke. Wall didn't throw away jokes; he gave them away. "I'm being serious," he confided. "But I'll change in a minute. Marvellous stuff to come later."

Wall kept promising nothing and accomplishing everything. "Terrific self-confidence is beyond me. I could never have it," Wall said. But he had the chutzpah to try anything on stage. He played the trumpet. "We've all heard the late Louis Armstrong play the trumpet. Tonight you're going to hear me. You'll notice the difference." He stopped to observe his performance and praise it. "Notice the silence? That's my command of the audience." Later, while recollecting his failure on records, he added with a shrug: "In the end, all is silence." When a laugh didn't score, he'd give a languid wave of his hand: "Press people come and say the jokes are terrible. I know they are. . . . I could come out and say I'm happy working here. . . . You don't care. Not really. If you look into it deeply." In the pauses, Wall pulled a face. He had a broad forehead and a large chin and those teeth. He wasn't exactly a picture postcard, but you couldn't take your eyes off him. Wall's game was to relax the audience with sight gags and silliness, and then goose it with honesty. He referred to himself as a boy and then cringed at the word: "How much imagination can one man have!" And even his waning sexual powers came in for a laugh when he discusses going to a drugstore for some Vaseline. "I don't even know what I wanted the Vaseline for. Probably chapped lips. It'd have to be chapped lips. . . ."

Wall knew his craft and he knew it was artful. He teased the audience's idea of culture, which assumed art was grave. When he entered, Wall did fifteen seconds of pantomime as he waddled across the stage in his slapshoes. Later, he got a laugh by saying: "It was pure ballet. You applauded 'cause you thought I was working a bit." The audience laughed because at first it thought Wall's movement wasn't a dance and his statement bravado. But Wall knew it *was* ballet; just as he knew his material had touching overtones. "Some of my stuff's subtle. I don't understand half of it myself." Wall's performance was kinetic. He spoke with his body, with song, with language. "Nothing is important but the moment," he told the audience in one startling aside, and then savored every macro-second, packing it with delicious detail, enlarging the laughs until time itself was banished. Wall never pressed an audience. He stood before it and invited interpretation. In the middle of a story, his voice suddenly deepened into an articulate, BBC baritone, his arms struck a heroic pose, and he detoured from the punch line to ask: "Did you like that? It's Acting."

Wall knew how to make a perfect spectacle of himself. He didn't have what Chaplin called "that come-hither thing," but he was brave and unnervingly honest. At his finale, Wall rushed out mumbling nonsense sounds of gratitude. "Well, what does that all add up to?" he asked. "I suppose stalling." The audience expected the polite goodbye, but Wall was never polite. "Tonight, in my estimation, you've been fifty per cent." The line was breathtaking. Wall let his hostility dangle in the air for a split second and then added that he'd been fifty per cent, which added up to 100 per cent. He ended poignantly with a music hall coda: a song reminiscent of a time when clowns got their education in front of an audience instead of a camera.

> Now that the act is over
> Now that the act is done
> Thank you for your attention
> It's really been great fun
> I hope you'll be as happy
> Next time I call. . . .

I went to see him again the next night. He was giving the audience the same casual riff, the same illusion that each joke was newly minted in the tension of the moment. "Isn't it terrible you have to tell people you're acting," he said. The line got a laugh; but no one but Wall realized that this vivid performance was word perfect, a three-hour routine into which he breathed new immediacy each night. The joke was on the audience, as his standoffish delivery should have told us. In his sorrowful capering, Wall took his audience where only a great clown can: to the frontiers of the marvellous.

BARRY HUMPHRIES

PLAYING POSSUM

MARCH 8, 1989. IT'S 3 P.M., but the marquee above the Theatre Royal Drury Lane, the oldest and most venerable of London's theatres, has already been switched on. Passersby as far away as Covent Garden can pick out the sign's blinking red neon message: "Dame Edna's Second Coming—She's Back Because She Cares."

In England's rich and vicious eighties, "caring" was high concept that became high parody. Margaret Thatcher, caricatured on the cover of *The Spectator* as a Dame Edna look-alike, complete with pink diamanté glasses, assured the nation that the Tories cared. "Labour Cares" was the theme of the Opposition. And Dame Edna, always up to the minute, was repeating her 1987 revue, and raking in approximately a hundred and sixty thousand pounds a week from selling out the Drury Lane's twenty-two hundred and forty-five seats, because she, too, cared. "I mean that in a very caring, nurturing way," Dame Edna was fond of saying after delivering a particularly low blow. The maneuver was in keeping with the vindictive style of the times, and so was the title of Dame Edna's 1987 show, "Back with a Vengeance!" By the late eighties, revenge on liberalism was such a blatant part of the English political climate that maliciousness—Dame Edna's stock-in-trade—could be uninhibitedly flaunted. And Dame Edna was nothing if not uninhibited and illiberal.

Dame Edna had announced herself to the critics and the newspapers weeks before the opening of the 1989 show—"Back with a Vengeance! The Second Coming"—and had done it in her own inimitable style: "My gynaecologist, my numerologist, my biorhythmologist, my T'ai-Chi instructor, my primal scream therapist, and my aromatherapist all tell me that I will be at the height of my powers as a woman from March 9, 1989, for a strictly limited season.'' The press release, featuring a Russian Constructivist logo and a clenched fist full of gladioli, added, ''It's not so much a show, more a private audience. And since I'm writing my autobiography this could just be one of the last chances you have of seeing me before my millennium comeback. DO YOURSELVES A FAVOUR—See the Turn of the Century *before* the turn of the century.'' This was not a conventional press release, but then Dame Edna is not a conventional person. Dame Edna is, in fact, a theatrical phenomenon: the only solo act to play (and fill) the Drury Lane since it opened for business, in 1663, with Beaumont and Fletcher's ''The Humorous Lieutenant.'' The *Observer* named Dame Edna ''one of the idols of the 80s,'' and the public keeps faith with her. The 1987 ''Back with a Vengeance!,'' which ran nine months and played to capacity, had the third-highest advance in the history of London's West End—exceeded only by ''Phantom of the Opera'' and ''Chess.'' For the thirty-one shows in Dame Edna's 1989 season, the box office had six hundred thousand pounds in advance sales the day before opening. Television had won Dame Edna an even wider popularity and a new theatregoing audience. In the autumn of 1987, a seventh of the British Isles, or about eight million three hundred thousand people, representing 48.7 percent of the network share, tuned in to ''The Dame Edna Experience'' in prime time—at ten-thirty on a Saturday night—to watch Dame Edna, the supremo of narcissists, treat the celebrity guests on her TV talk show like audiovisual aids.

But Dame Edna's influence on the imagination of British culture is best registered by how she has been incorporated into some of the most cherished English institutions. Dame Edna has opened the Harrods Sale, turned on Regent Street's Christmas lights, played a cameo role in the long-running radio soap opera ''The Archers,'' and twice been a radio guest on that surest barometer of British success, ''Desert Island Discs.'' Dame Edna has sung in the Royal Albert Hall, when two thousand people in two nights heard her cantata ''The Song of Australia.'' A street has been named after her in Moonee Ponds, the suburb of Melbourne from which she hails. She is one of four Australians whose waxwork effigies are on display at Madame Tussaud's. And the College of Heraldry has drawn up Dame Edna's coat of arms, which bears the motto "I Share and I Care," with the heraldic symbols of crossed gladioli, a funnel-web spider, a blowfly, and the Sydney Opera House. "Dame Edna has been notionally advanced to GBE, so that she qualifies for armorial supporters," the *Times* of London reported in 1982. "They are a shark and a possum, both wearing butterfly glasses."

Dame Edna has also blitzed the commercial world. Between 1981, in a previous season at the Drury Lane, and 1989, Dame Edna's billing, while always monumental, underwent a subtle shift, from "housewife/superstar" to "megastar." She is now, like the celebrities of whom she is a parody, a multinational corporation of one, who franchises every last particle of her persona that the public will buy. And it will buy a lot. Dame Edna is a spokesperson for an airline and an electrical-appliance company. Her piercing singing voice, which sounds like an outback Jerry Colonna, is on tape cassettes doing both disco versions of rock-and-roll standards and her own golden oldies, like "Niceness," "The Night We Burnt My Mother's Things," and "Every Mother Wants a Boy Like Elton." There are mugs ("A Dame Edna Everage Beverage"), badges ("I'm into Edna"), and even imitation Dame Edna eyeglasses. These yellow plastic replicas of Dame Edna's "face furniture," complete with a star cluster sweeping up and over the rims, cram the joke-shop window across the street from the Drury Lane, while a behemoth green neon version of them flickers on the billboard above the theatre entrance.

Dame Edna's name is synonymous with surprise, and even with shock. As her former sobriquet "housewife/superstar" implied, Dame Edna is a celebration of contradictions: hilarious and malign, polite and lewd, generous and envious, high and low comic. But the most sensational of all Dame Edna's contradictions is that she is a he.

Dame Edna is the creation of Barry Humphries. Or, as the letterhead of his yellow stationery has it, "Barry Humphries is a division of the Barry Humphries Group." This is true. Dame Edna has taken on a visibility and a reality for the public which vie with, even subsume, Humphries' own public persona. A star is the impresario of himself, but Humphries is the impresario of his selves. The small print at the bottom of his stationery says, "The recipient is advised to preserve this memorandum as it could well become a very extremely valuable collector's item.'' This, too, is true. The fifty-seven-year-old Humphries is a prodigious comic talent. His co-presence in Dame Edna—a character so real to the English public that her autobiography, ''My Gorgeous Life,'' is being sold by his publisher, Macmillan, on its nonfiction list—incarnates the essence of the grotesque: the sense that things that should be kept apart are fused together. This style—what Baudelaire called ''the absolute comic''—also creates in an audience a paroxysm, a swoon, ''something profound, primitive, axiomatic, which is much closer to innocent life and absolute joy.''

I know the feeling. At Dame Edna's 1981 show, ''An Evening's Intercourse with Barry Humphries,'' I was blindsided by one of her startling observations and fell off my seat laughing. I can't account for the next two minutes of the show. I was on the floor.

Afterward, I determined to write about Humphries from the wings. I still have notes from our first backstage meeting, when I sat with him between acts and we talked as I watched an urbane Australian man of letters transform himself into Dame Edna, whom he has been sporadically impersonating since late 1955. ''There's something of the clown, something rather ritualized about the character,'' Humphries said, applying his carmine ''lippie.'' ''It's a clown in the form of an Australian housewife. It belongs a bit to the pantomime-dame tradition, though it doesn't exploit the pantomime dame, which is generally a rather sturdy man. The joke of the pantomime dame is the tension between the female of the clothes and the stocky footballer's legs and boots. The drag queen is the other extreme, really a man on the one hand mocking a woman and at the same time trying to titillate the audience. Edna is somewhere in between—closer, really, to character acting: a man playing a woman and making points about life.''

In the years since that first interview, Humphries has become more famous (the marquee announces ''The Almost Legendary Barry Humphries''), and Dame Edna's frivolity more majestic. But as I walk through the safety doors onto the vast Drury Lane stage, where the technical run-through is noisily in progress, neither the actor nor his creation is to be found. Backstage feels drab and mundane, but the props, scattered about the stage like so many jigsaw pieces on a gargantuan table, promise something bright and extraordinary. An Australian flag stretching the width of the proscenium is being battened down to be flown up in the labyrinth of catwalks and ropes. A cherry picker—a crane with a basket, which will lift Edna fifty feet above the stalls to sing her finale straight into the eyes of her balcony fans, whom she refers to as "the paupers"—is shunted off into the shadows. The basket itself, which usually hoists more earnest citizens, like firemen or telephone repairmen, has been turned into a kind of surrealist sculpture: its sides are now a dress of white organza, and its base is disguised with red, white, and blue crinoline and a pair of Edna's red size-9 high heels. Edna's magic wand, an electrified plastic gladiolus into which a microphone has been rigged, rests on the side of the basket.

The lightboard has been set up in the center of row J. Behind it, slumped in conversation on the greenish-gold seats, are two men: Humphries' producer-manager, a no-nonsense Australian named Dennis Smith, who joined forces with Humphries in 1979, when he was about to launch "An Evening's Intercourse"; and Ian Davidson, a comedy writer, whom I recognize from my 1981 visit to the Drury Lane. Davidson's name has come up in the credits of almost all Humphries' comic activities since the late sixties, when he directed some of Edna's sketches for "The Late Show," the BBC's unsuccessful attempt to catch the receding wave of satire before it washed out. A modest, quiet man who began as an actor, and, in the mid-sixties, performed with Alan Arkin and Barbara Harris in America at the improvisational Second City, Davidson is one of three men billed as providing "acceptable additional jokes."

"Periodically, Barry says, 'These topical lines are getting a bit tired, better have a think about them,' " Davidson explains, pulling away his *Evening Standard* to reveal a pad on which he has jotted a few droll notions for his friend. "Then we have a phone call about them. But Barry rings other people as well. It's not a sort of solo position I have, although quite often I do get things in." He was whispering comic ideas to Humphries back when I interviewed him in the middle of his 1981 Drury Lane season. "I like to hear what the public are saying at the interval," Davidson told me then, while Edna was slipping into the tennis outfit she was wearing that year. "I stumbled upon a quarrel between a couple. She was accusing the man of sighing. He'd obviously bought the tickets. She was drunk and took exception to the show. 'You're sighing.' 'I never sigh.' 'Don't be so combatative.' She put in an extra syllable. I told Barry. He thought it was funny, and that night Edna said, speaking of her own husband, 'Oh, Norm. I used to take Norm to the theatre, but he didn't enjoy it. And when I said, "You've been sighing," he'd say, "Don't be so combatative." ' Barry's got this sort of total recall. He just threw it in during a little lull. I went back after the show, and Barry said, 'Two people have had an unforgettable night.' "

A BBC television crew appears in the Royal Box, to the left of the stage, and begins setting up its equipment. Smith checks his watch. "She's late."

"She's probably on the phone," Davidson says, jotting something down on his notepad.

"Got anything?"

"Something for Les," Davidson says, meaning another Humphries character in the show—Sir Les Patterson, the well-hung Australian cultural attaché and author of "The Traveller's Tool," who is the star of "Les Patterson Saves the World" (1987), Humphries' latest venture into feature films. Sir Les, with his "enormous encumbancy," has his own special way of opening Dame Edna's revue, and Davidson has come up with an idea in keeping with the full moral authority of the character. " 'Catch-69,' " he says. " 'If you do this thing, you're wrong. If you do that thing, you're wrong. It's a Catch-69 situation.' That's a Les possible. If you get a funny idea, it could be used for Les or for Edna. Or it could end up as a notice in the foyer."

The show's P.R. agent, Lynne Kirwin, looks out into the auditorium from the corner of the stage. "Edna's just coming," she says, as if the falsetto voice somewhere up and to the left of the lights being tested in the Royal Box could leave any doubt.

Davidson says, "We always talk about Edna as though she existed. 'Edna could say this,' not 'You could say this.' As a character, she is separate from him."

Dame Edna stands against the balustrade of the Royal Box while the

TV crew presses microphones and recording machines up under her double chin. In high heels and hairdo, Edna is surprisingly large: around six foot four, with wide shoulders and very well-shaped and well-shaven legs—a kind of amazon of outrageousness. Her dress, a gaudy sunburst of colors, is matched by lensless glasses scalloped today with what look like variegated coffee beans. She stares out at the theatre dress circle, in front of which are the names of literary and theatrical giants, emblazoned in gold leaf: "Byron," "Dryden," "Garrick," "Sheridan," "Kean." "Dennis!" Dame Edna cries, in the high-pitched voice that is her calling card: "Wouldn't it be nice if Edna's name was added to those in front of the dress circle?" Dennis smiles and makes a note.

Dame Edna turns back to the task at hand, which is to talk to the TV presenter Cathy McGowan—herself a media star in the sixties, when she headed a popular music show, "Ready, Steady, Go." The interview starts, and Dame Edna, a master of media manipulation, goes to work. The character is in the voice, and its command never wavers. The mouth may twitch in mock anxiety at a probing question, the timbre may lower in a send-up of intimacy, but the swagger in Edna's falsetto is resolutely consistent.

"I feel I know you, Cathy. I do. That fresh little face has looked at me in black-and-white and color. And your natural coloring is gorgeous. It is! And what a survivor you are, aren't you? As fresh and lovely as you were in those old swinging sixties days. You were a famous television star then and I was just an ordinary Melbourne housewife. And look at me now . . . ha, ha! The young adore me. I can't analyze it. I don't analyze these things. But I struck a note with young people. There are a lot of Ednaboppers and Wannabe Ednas. Kiddies copy me slavishly, Cathy . . . as they did you in the old days. Remember the whole of London was filled with little Cathy look-alikes, wasn't it? Remember?"

"No," Cathy says, a little nonplussed to find the ball suddenly back in her court. "Can I ask you about the outfits you wear? Your clothes? I don't really recognize the designer, Dame Edna."

"No," Dame Edna says, her voice slipping into its confidential mode. "I don't think designers should be too recognizable. That means an extreme of style, and you can only wear it about once and it goes out of fashion. I like to wear something a bit like Her Majesty the Queen—a close personal friend." She turns to the camera—"Hello!"—then back to Cathy. "She's watching. She just rang me to tell me that. Actually, she faxed me. I've got a little fax in my purse. I'm one of the very few people with an in-purse fax."

"What did she say in the fax?"

"I'm not allowed to say. Our friendship would be at an end. But it was intimate. I can tell you that."

"Dame Edna, thank you so much for inviting me to the Royal Box."

"That's all right. This is the Royal Box. Where members of the Royal Family and very selected friends of mine come and watch my beautiful shows. And there's a lovely anteroom off it where they can have 'sambis.' Beautiful sandwiches. 'Sambis' is an Australian word for sandwiches. An old Aboriginal word. (It's not a very difficult language.)"

The lighting man is laughing so hard at Edna's flight of fancy that a lamp drops out of his hand. The crew sets up again. Dame Edna continues in full confidential flow: "There's a gorgeous mahogany little toilet there, too. Would you like to see that afterwards? Yes, many, many people have made themselves comfortable there."

Even after the camera is lifted off its tripod and the lights are packed away, Dame Edna is still holding forth in the Royal Box. In character, Humphries radiates what Charlie Chaplin, mourning its absence in his own music-hall performances, called "that come-hither thing." Dame Edna enjoys the exhilaration of the liberties she takes. Her pleasure is infectious. She's regaling the assembled about her special Australian ointment for stretch marks. "Ever seen a kangaroo with stretch marks? It contains an extract of a kangaroo's spleen. It does. You don't use too much of it. Princess Diana actually uses it. She said she was starting to develop a pouch. So follow the instructions."

Dame Edna seems amazingly actual. Whether watching her on TV or face-to-face, a person soon loses the sense that this is a man-as-woman, and accepts her as real. (So real, in fact, that Edna is impersonated at drag parties.) This sense of actuality is due in part to the rich coherence of her story, which Humphries has built up in public over the years, and in part to his own performance, which is so relaxed and vivid within the parameters of her monstrous character. Dame Edna compels belief.

(She won't reply to questions addressed to "Barry.") By maintaining Edna's persona, Humphries keeps the people around him playing his game. For both performer and public, it's an exercise in improvisation, but in this battle of wits the public is unarmed.

Dame Edna walks slowly down the back stairs toward the stage. She's a little ungainly on her pins, like an athlete in cleats on the concrete walkway from locker room to field. The stage is empty except for the drum kit of the three-piece band that accompanies the show. This is the first time since 1981 that Dame Edna has been on the Drury Lane stage—her 1987 show played the Strand—and she is all too aware of its history. "Guess what, possums?" her press release boasted. "I've just hired the most famous theatre on the planet." The boxes loom high and close above her. The space itself is expectant. Seats, lights, boxes, aisles all point toward center stage, where Dame Edna moves around, getting the feel of the Drury Lane's size and atmosphere. Dame Edna has a heavy-hipped, awkward, almost royal gait. She does not mince; her step has a thrust to it. "I like to acquaint myself with the empty auditorium," Humphries told me in 1981. "I make strange sounds, rather the way whales or dolphins do. I do a bit of vocal bouncing." Tonight, Dame Edna just comes to the front of the stage and starts confiding to no one in particular. "All you do is stand on the stage and talk to the people as though you were just talking on the phone," she says. "Just have a chat. People make such a fuss about it. I hate shows—don't you?—where you go and they're not talking to you, they're talking to each other. It's very rude."

From the shadows of the stalls Davidson answers back.

Dame Edna reacts. "Extremely rude," she says, "pretending the audience isn't there. Imagine if you rang someone up and they were talking to someone else all the time?"

Dame Edna does some more vocal bouncing and then looks down toward the lightboard, where Dennis Smith is standing. "How's the box office?"

"People were lining up until three-thirty."

"We should bring them coffee," Dame Edna says, strolling over in my direction. (I'm in the wings.) "Who are the people in the news, Ian?

Winnie Mandela. Has she been in the news? What's that film Dustin's done?''

" 'Rainman'!'' I shout, obsessed, like everyone else, with getting Dame Edna tuned up for the challenge of opening night.

" 'Rainwoman,' '' Dame Edna says, sharpish. "I was offered the part.''

Davidson lobs something up about Roy Orbison's death. "Little Roy,'' Dame Edna says. "One of the nicest albinos I ever knew.'' Dame Edna paces the stage in silence and then looks out toward her producer, who has moved to the front row. "What time are we starting the tech?''

"Seven-thirty.''

"Perhaps I should have a nibble now. Come into the dressing room.'' Dame Edna starts off the stage, and is met by Dennis Smith. As she passes me in the wings, she says to her producer, "Look at this mysterious figure.''

At the start of the technical rehearsal, the BBC newsreader John Humphreys comes up on a screen that has dropped down in front of the Drury Lane proscenium. His grave and measured voice, which over the years has brokered many a world calamity to the citizens of Britain, is broadcasting the latest jolt to the national psyche. "Sad news, I'm afraid,'' he says, putting down the phone at his elbow which keeps a BBC newsreader in instant touch with his correspondents on breaking stories. "We've just had confirmed reports that one of Australia's most famous men has died. Mr. Norman Everage, husband of world-famous actress Dame Edna Everage, passed away peacefully in London just about an hour ago. Norman Everage was a shy, modest man. He distinguished himself as a soldier in the Second World War and married Edna May Beazley in the forties. They had three children: Bruce, Valmai, and Ken. However, soon after Mrs. Everage, as she then was, made the first of her highly successful public appearances, her husband developed a urological disorder for which he's been undergoing treatment for a quarter of a century.''

Norman Everage never made an appearance in one of Dame Edna's shows, but Dame Edna had turned his prostate into legend. "Norm's prostate has been hanging over me for years," she confided onstage and in her autobiography, as the rolling joke of her browbeaten mate and their family changed with the times and with the rise of Edna's star. In "An Evening's Intercourse with Barry Humphries," Dame Edna told how Norm had to have his hands strapped to the sides of the hospital bed and was learning to knit with his mouth. "He's into oral socks," she explained.

Now another BBC reporter, Sue Cook, is pictured outside "the world's first prostate-transplant unit," interviewing doctors, nurses, and Dame Edna herself. The effect of seeing representatives of the real world incorporated into Dame Edna's fantasy is unnerving. But it's a confusion that Humphries relishes. For Dame Edna's autobiography, Humphries has chosen an epigraph from Benedetto Croce: "All history is fiction, just as all fiction is history." And Dame Edna makes a fiasco of history. Once, looking at a picture of Dame Edna amid the Royals, which stood on his dressing-room table, Humphries said, "That's a joke in itself." And so it is. Dame Edna's mere presence at public occasions calls the reality of society into question.

In the early days, Edna sometimes had to thrust herself into the paths of the famous, like Australian Prime Minister Sir Robert Menzies, for whom she waited with a photographer until he appeared outside London's Savoy Hotel. "I'm one of your electors," she said as he snubbed her. "You're doing a fine job." But, as the souvenir program celebrates in snapshot, the famous now flock to Dame Edna. She is shown variously meeting and greeting a gallimaufry of the celebrated: the Queen Mother, Princess Diana, Joan Collins, Joan Baez, Bob Geldof, Zsa Zsa Gabor, Larry Hagman, Charlton Heston, Joan Rivers, Jeffrey Archer, and Mary Whitehouse, Britain's self-proclaimed moral guardian, whose righteousness Dame Edna both voices and lampoons.

At the end of the BBC broadcast, the newsreader looks out at the audience and says, "We have confirmation that Dame Edna has cancelled all stage performances. No money will be refunded. And that's the news tonight."

The screen flies up. The musicians are soon in place, ready for Humphries to start running through the material. The pianist puts a pad beside her on the bench to jot down any tasty one-liners that Humphries may improvise and want to put into the act. Humphries strolls onstage wearing the head mike that fits under Edna's wig. He's in blue jeans, white socks, and sandals, an altogether unlikely Edna. He speeds through the prose portions of his act in double time: ''And so and so and so and so and so I feel a song coming on!'' In Edna's falsetto, Humphries launches into the boffo opening, a hymn to frivolity's refusal to suffer:

> A minute ago
> I was locked in my room.
> My life seemed pointless and hollow,
> Where before it was warm
> With the presence of Norm,
> And I thought ''Where he's gone I must follow.''
> I looked at the Valium, I considered the stove,
> I weighed up the stern moral issues.
> But the strength inside me grew
> When I was almost through
> My last box of Kleenex tissues.
> So I hope you'll all applaud my great achievement.
> I am here tonight in spite of my bereavement. . . .

When Dame Edna sings about the triumph of fame over grief, her bigheartedness always admits the spirit of revenge, an impulse that is never far from the aggressive wellsprings of comedy. It's a game that Humphries, too, has been known to play with his public. He told the Australian Press Club in 1978, ''In Melbourne I used to like sitting in a little Greek restaurant called Cafe Florentino at about eight-ten in the evening and seeing old Melbourne Grammar boys, contemporaries per-haps of our Prime Minister''—and himself—''hurrying with their wives down the stairs in order to attend one of my performances which I had absolutely no intention of starting for another three-quarters of an hour. The advantage, of course, of being a solo performer is that they can never start without you. And I think that is probably one of the few advantages, except it keeps me off the streets and fills my evening entertainingly.''

Now Humphries stops the song to adjust the arrangement with the band: "Be nice if we could add a note there. A little Kurt Weillish note: 'And now you know / I'm too much of a pro / To let *yoooou* down.' "

After the song, Humphries descends into the stalls and sits talking with us as the crew gets the next set in place. He is a more reserved presence than the ebullient Dame Edna. Edna's voice is tight and sharp, but Humphries' voice is breathy and light. Where Edna is garish, Humphries is suave. Where she is direct and downright rude, he is oblique and well mannered. Edna is unaware of what she projects, and her lack of awareness empowers the public to laugh at her; Humphries is knowing, and his knowingness keeps those around him at a distance and on the defensive. His smile is tired tonight, but the furrowed laugh lines around his mouth and his high, fleshy cheekbones give his face a dramatic—even youthful—definition. His eyes, when they focus on you, are bright and warm, and convey a very definite sense of authority.

Dame Edna's biases are there for the world to see, but Humphries is much harder to fathom. As one would expect of a comedian who treads so gracefully between insight and outrage, Humphries is a man of intelligence and taste. Dame Edna says the first thing that pops into her airhead, but Humphries listens. He is reflective, choosing his words carefully and well. Humphries has talked of the feeling of "allegiance to the fellowship of music-hall artistes," but his articulacy separates him from the old-timers whose glorious tradition he is carrying almost single-handed into the twenty-first century. Buster Keaton had two days of official schooling; Charlie Chaplin learned a new word a day; Bert Lahr built up his vocabulary by doing crossword puzzles. But Humphries, whose act combines lowbrow antics with a highbrow aesthetic, is both well educated and well-read, as the range of images and references in his conversation displays.

A stuntman and a stuntwoman are having trouble wiring themselves up for Humphries' most outrageous effect—the spectacle of paupers plummeting from a box seat. So Humphries turns back to me and begins talking. "My German Expressionist touch," he says of the stunt. "I like to produce this in the theatre, and I like to combine it with comedy. I was in the film society at university, and I deliberately disinterred a lot of German Expressionist films. I liked the kind of spooky, rather frightening effects that some of these actors produced in the movies. I very much liked the sense of melodrama and—what are they?—the *frissons.* I don't know why I liked shocking people. I think it just gave me a sense of identity. I guess it gave me a sense of power, too, because I felt rather powerless and swamped by—well, the dullness of Melbourne. Although I'm very fond of it, Melbourne is a transcendentally dull city. I was rather puritanical in those early days, and moralistic. Anxious to *show* people. Edna was conceived as a character to remind Australians of their bigotry and all the things that I found offensive. She was a rebuke. She was a silly, bigoted, ignorant, self-satisfied Melbourne housewife. They're still around. They're still there. Now they just wear a different uniform. They drive Volvos and occasionally swear. No one before me in Australia had looked at the suburbs and said, 'Here is the stuff of comedy.' It's only when Edna took on a life of her own, when she was invested *with a life,* that she turned the tables on me, in a way."

The stuntman yells down that they're ready, so Humphries hoists himself up and goes back onstage to work through "The Gladdy Song," which is the segue out of his *coup de théâtre.* "Now let's try and throw a few gladdies up to the paupers," Humphries says in an uninflected Edna voice, not lingering to act the words. " 'I don't think I can. But I will . . . uh . . . uh . . . uh .' " Humphries mimes the backhanded flip with which for a quarter of a century he has been heaving what Edna calls the Australian national flower at the audience. The drummer does a rim shot as each imaginary gladdy lands in the audience.

"What about me, Dame Edna?" the stuntwoman, sitting on the balcony railing, calls, waving.

"Oh, I don't think I can. Uh . . . uh . . ."

"*Aaaaaaah!*" The woman tips out over the box, dragging the stuntman with her. They dangle above the empty stalls like rock climbers rappelling a cliff.

"Can you see them?" Humphries asks, as the woman swings on wires and a halter concealed by her dress. "Will enough people see that?"

"Everybody and his dog will see that," Dennis Smith says.

The stuntwoman and the stuntman are hauled back into the box, and

Humphries continues running the lines. "You all right? What a miracle there was a rope ladder up there, paups! Heaven be praised."

"We love you, Dame Edna!"

"Oh, you move me when you say that, lemming. Wouldn't it be ghastly if that happened every night?" Even in rehearsal, the line gets a laugh from the crew.

"On first night at the Strand, they dropped out of the top box like that," Ian Davidson says. "Someone from the stalls—an intrepid man—ran up on the box below and climbed out on the ledge to help the woman. Thereafter, they had to have someone standing in the corridor to stop anyone trying to make a brave rescue. The man was terribly brave. The box wasn't as high as this, but it was still damned high. I can't imagine any other comedian who would have such a stunt take place in an auditorium—have such amazing, riveting attention taken away from him in that way. It all rebounds to Edna's benefit, but even so . . ."

The smoke machine starts working, and the cherry picker moves onstage. "I see. That's good," Humphries says. "Tell me, have you got nice color on that? Are there flashing lights? Great blasts of color?"

Humphries, whose first ambition was to be a painter, thinks visually, and his shows make striking stage pictures. In the past, he has tried to shoot gladioli into the balcony with a cannon, fielded people's shoes from the stalls in a butterfly net, pulled a rip cord on his dress that turned its front into a Union Jack. But in having Dame Edna rise fifty feet above his audience at the finale of "Back with a Vengeance!" Humphries has topped himself. "It's a parody of the Assumption as though painted by Murillo or perhaps a late-Venetian master," he says.

Humphries locks himself in the basket as the crane begins to work through "Shyness," Edna's last song. As he has instructed, the cherry picker moves him slowly downstage and then thrusts him out and up over the stalls. Just the sight of Humphries suspended in air makes those of us in the audience laugh. The machine judders. Humphries grasps the rails. "There's terrible lurches down there," he says in his own persona, and the word "lurches" reverberates in the sound system. "Hello, paupers!" Humphries says in Edna's brightest falsetto. "I feel like Edna Poppins up here. I do. I hope I don't do anything involuntary. Be it on your heads if I do.''

Even without costume and disguise, Humphries in Edna's voice whips up the tired crew and the scattered audience as the band builds to the song's climax. And when Dame Edna says, ''Was it good for you, too, possums?'' down below all of us shout ''Yes!''

A strange lassitude fills the theatre the next day, in the final hours before the opening. Humphries' dresser, Katie Harris, has turned a costume trunk into a table—a kind of altar of artifice, on which many of the disembodied features of Humphries' characters are on view. The table holds Dame Edna's natural wisteria wig, her rings and diamanté bracelets, Sir Les's fluorescent-green socks and his brown-and-white platform shoes, whose soles are stamped ''Made from genuine dead kangaroo.'' There is also a box of black-and-white publicity postcards of Humphries in bow tie, with one eye hidden under the brim of his fedora and the other eye glaring up at the viewer. ''I look like a minor Surrealist painter in that,'' he says.

Humphries, who has described himself as ''an Aussie *arriviste,*'' is a dandy. He has a deep knowledge of *fin de siècle* Europe and the aesthetes who pushed the envelope of individualism. Over the years, Humphries has affected the dandy's advertisements of impertinence and leisure: the monocle, the walking stick, the silk polka-dot cravat or bow tie, the long hair. In his Dimitri Major tailored suits and his Jermyn Street shirts, he cuts a fine, colorful figure. Through Dame Edna, Humphries allows the audience to share and to excuse the dandy's thrill at bad taste and his aristocratic pleasure in giving offense. Through Dame Edna, he vents both the dandy's insolent superiority and his rebellion against the rigidities of the workaday world, using wit to bend the world to him. Through Dame Edna, Humphries' progress in English and Australian society has been impressive. Even Prince Charles, an Ednabopper of long standing, comes occasionally to Humphries' house in Hampstead for dinner.

Humphries takes his mail and sits down at his dressing table, where his makeup and brushes have been laid out as meticulously as instruments in an operating theatre. Aerosols of hair spray and deodorant, pots of makeup, a polishing pen for Edna's nails, a bottle of Lea & Perrins Worcestershire sauce (the finishing touch to Sir Les's ruffled tuxedo shirt) are ranged against the back mirror. At his right hand is a small palette for blending the makeup; at his left is Sir Les's snaggle-toothed denture. A white towel has been placed in the center of the dressing table, and on it are three sable brushes and two Hudson's Eumenthol jujubes. To the left of the makeup but no less important to Humphries' backstage ritual is the telephone.

Humphries is reading through the stack of mail. A woman in Black-pool writes to complain that she's been upset for two days over Dame Edna's mockery of bereavement. A single parent in Surrey giggles along in Edna's idiom ("gladdies," "possums," "nice"). Someone has cut out an ad for the show and scrawled across it, "Take that shit off your face and do some work you lazy bugger." And Margaret in Bourne-mouth wants six hundred pounds, to redecorate her flat: "Dearest darling Dame Edna, will you be my Fairy godperson and grant my tiny little wish."

Humphries himself is hardly ensconced in luxury. The dressing room consists of a small changing room and a large, dingy waiting room with a sofa bed, two chairs, and a table on which bottles of soft drinks and mineral water have been set out for opening night. Bouquets from well-wishers have been arranged around the room, but nothing can renovate its drabness. There is not a picture on the wall, not a new lick of paint. The sense of color, texture, fun which so distinguishes Humphries' performances onstage is entirely absent from the gray room, as if all energy and imagination were being saved for the front of the house. But the barrenness and boredom that the dressing room exudes provide the climate that feeds the exasperation that Humphries turns into outra-geousness. "I'm always conscious of the desert inside Australia, of the vacuum," he has said. "Sunday afternoon in Melbourne, the exquisite boredom. The exhilarating depression. Neat houses. Somewhere down the street there's a Celica being cleaned; otherwise no sign of life. That appeals to me in a terrible way. But I feel, too, there's a decadence, among all the health and the prosperity." Edna is a product of a subversive imagination that sees itself as "sinking artesian wells into the suburban desert, drawing up composite portraits." The notion pleases him. "I'm in the boredom-alleviation business, aren't I? This art is meant to be an antidote to boredom," Humphries says, speaking as much for himself as his audience.

Humphries has described himself as "self-educated, attended Melbourne Grammar School." The man who would become a dandy of delirium traces the origins of his rebellion to the oppressiveness of the city's poshest educational institution—the one that the upwardly mobile Humphries family chose for their firstborn son, and to which he was admitted in 1947, at the age of thirteen. Humphries was not happy with the choice and has spoken of the move from his friends at Camberwell Grammar School as "a great bereavement." The trauma has never been forgiven by Humphries or forgotten by Melbourne Grammar. In 1953, Humphries was sensationally banned from the Old Melbournians association for his irreverent sculpture "Old Fool's Tie": a bottle of beer with a Melbourne Grammar tie knotted around it. He was eventually welcomed back, and made an equally sensational return to the fold at an Old Melbournians night in his honor in 1971: he entered riding on a camel.

Dame Edna owes her paternity in part to Humphries' fierce disgust at the blinkered conformity of the school and its masters, whom he has called in print "picturesque ignoramuses." Humphries says, "I became attracted to the modern school of painting—that is to say, the modern school as it was in the second decade of the twentieth century. The Dadaist movement, and, later, the Surrealist artists, fascinated me very early. I was familiar with the works of Picabia, with the writings of Salvador Dalí, with most of the works of the French nineteenth-century writers. I knew all about Cubism, and was, indeed, painting in a Cubist style. So that I was, in fact, very precocious in my reading before I was thirteen." Already a talented painter in oils, Humphries had been introduced, through the influence of a Camberwell art teacher, Ian Bow, to "the exhilaration of eccentricity" and the ravishing thought of "what a marvellous liberating thing it must be to be an artist, to be able to escape from the humdrum world of mathematics, compulsory sport, gymnasium, cold showers, boxing, and all these terrible imperatives of a boys' school." When Humphries was five and his mother asked him what he wanted to be, he answered, "A genius." But Melbourne Grammar put no premium on originality. "It's significant that very, very few people of any artistic sensibility at all emerged from the school after the war," he has said. "But out of a kind of rebellion against the school system I developed certain techniques, which have been very useful in my subsequent artistic life—certain forms of rebellion and anarchy, certain artistic methods."

Humphries also hated the school uniform, which draped his dreamy artistic persona in a navy-blue serge version of a thirties business suit and turned him and the rest of the luckless internees of the school into "double-breasted, tie-pinned parodies of Ronald Colman or the Man from the Prudential." This later seemed to Humphries a self-fulfilling prophecy. "Most of my contemporaries at school entered the World of Business, the logical destiny of bores," he has written. The school's motto was "Pray and Work," but it was to sport and the homogeneity of attitude which games instill that the school seemed dedicated. Humphries was not, and never would be, a team player. "I hated sports. I still do," he says. His aversion to physical exercise earned him the nickname Grannie at Camberwell and Queenie at Melbourne Grammar.

Humphries' sport was frequenting second-hand bookshops—especially one on Bourke Street, whose owner, a Mrs. Bird, called him Mr. Humphries and imbued him with an enthusiasm he still holds for the "curdled late Romantics," like Ann Radcliffe, Monk Lewis, Charles Robert Maturin, Byron, and Mary Shelley. Even rummaging in the dusty shop among stacks of old volumes had maverick overtones for Humphries, because his parents insisted he have new books. "Schoolboys generally didn't go into secondhand bookshops," Humphries says. "One was discouraged from 'dirty books'—that is to say, books that other people had owned. It was a very hygienic society. Hygiene was a great god."

As a child, Humphries dreamed of being a magician. "The big advantage of being a magician," he says, "was that you could make people disappear." But at Melbourne Grammar he discovered that if he couldn't make the school disappear, his laughter could keep the people in it at bay. Humphries found himself in the dandy's dilemma: at once dominated by and attempting to dominate convention. In this delicate situation, wit was the acceptable face of insolence, and his school years were spent in the learning of effrontery. He recalls of his small circle of friends, "We sat in a rebellious and probably rather irritating little group at the back of the class, drawing attention, wherever possible, to areas of ignorance in the schoolmaster. These were considerable, I need hardly say." He acted out what he calls his "dandiacal rage" in caricature both of the teachers and of himself. "I had always drawn, particularly caricatures," he has said. "I used to do caricatures of teachers on the blackboard. So when they entered the classroom they could see themselves up there on the board to the amusement of others. I found I had a gift for amusing my schoolmates, which, in a way, protected me from bullies. If you could make them laugh, they wouldn't hit you."

A renegade reputation requires courage, and Humphries, a churchgoing and well-bred young man, had to summon it up. "It didn't come naturally to me," he says. "One had to impersonate a brazen person. One had to act as if one were courageous." He was emboldened by the sure knowledge that "I had absolutely no desire to be like *them,* whatever happened—*them* were these boys in school uniforms." Humphries grew his hair long. "By modern standards it wasn't long. But it was certainly long for the school, where they insisted 'Long hair is dirty hair.' I later had that translated into Latin—'Crines longi, crines foetidi'— and called it the motto of the school. There was such a strong emotional feeling about long hair. It aroused such primitive revulsion that I knew I was on the right track."

Although he bucked the system, he could not always beat it. He became the subject of scandal and concern when his ruse for avoiding sports was uncovered. Humphries had appeared in soccer gear and had his name ticked off, and had then slipped away to the lavatories, where an accomplice brought him his school uniform to put back on. "This went on for over a year," Humphries says. "One day, there was a tap on the door. It opened, and the captain of the school was standing there. He said, 'The game's up, Humphries.' I'll never forget those words. I was caned. It sometimes pleases me to think that this schoolboy, only a couple of years older than I was, who unmasked me so brutally and punished me so mercilessly, is now a traveller for a cheap brand of port. I think Dame Nature, as Edna would call it, has a way of settling some of these accounts.'' The humiliation was compounded by the headmaster, who called Humphries into his study and said, ''I hope you're not turning pansy?'' Humphries says, ''I hadn't the *faintest* idea of what he meant, except that it was rather threatening. There was no way to formulate a reply to it.''

Humphries' way of dealing with his anger was then, as it is now, to perform a kind of psychic jujitsu—to ''throw people'' by using the force of their attitude to defeat them. Having been labelled effeminate and made to attend soccer matches in the name of school spirit, Humphries sent up both injustices by sitting with his back to the playing field and knitting.

The older generation of clowns to whom Humphries is a legitimate successor took their urgency from poverty; Humphries took his urgency from privilege. They wanted a way into the mainstream; Humphries wanted a way out of it. ''The word art never entered my head,'' Chaplin wrote, speaking of his time in music hall, before it did. And Keaton was equally matter-of-fact: ''I never realized that I was doing anything but trying to make people laugh when I threw my custard pies and took my pratfalls.'' The Old Guard were inspired by business, not art. Humphries was inspired by art, not business. Even at grammar school, he felt a special kinship with the Dadaists and their subversive gestures of unreason. ''I was instantly fired with admiration,'' he says of his first exposure to them, in William Gaunt's ''March of the Moderns.'' ''It seemed to me that even though these stunts had oc-curred forty years before, they still produced a *frisson* that was the kind of artistic performance I aspired to.'' Humphries wanted to create his own ''ferocious Dada jests.'' He helped to form the Art Club and to start a Dadaist faction, which organized a sculpture exhibition at the school. The forces of authority won the first round against Humphries' aspiring anarchy: the Dada sculptures were judged too subversive and were withdrawn. But Humphries' gift for provocation, so carefully held in check in his Melbourne Grammar days, was unleashed on the world when he took up his infamous residence at Melbourne University, between 1951 and 1953.

''The only Australian who ever understood the Dada principle of *provocation,*'' Robert Hughes wrote in ''The Art of Australia'' (1966), "was the actor Barry Humphries, who organized two Dada shows in Melbourne and (before leaving for England in the late fifties) performed a number of gratuitous public acts whose ferocity and point might have pleased Tristan Tzara." The Dada exhibitions and the pranks made a legend both of Humphries' desire to shine and of his sense of displacement. "It was important to emancipate oneself from this suburban milieu, because it was so seductive and oppressive," Humphries says. "You thought it was inescapable. It was so disturbing. I had absolutely no idea of what I would do in life. I remember a friend of mine had a printing press. I had a visiting card made with my name on it. He said, 'We better put occupation.' I said, 'Put "Dilettante." ' A very effective card to have. In fact, it didn't entertain me very much to be a dilettante. I became a specialist."

The first Pan-Australasian Dada Exhibition, in 1952, announced Humphries' expertise at creating a panic. "I had packages printed up called PLATITOX—really just sawdust in packages," Humphries recalls. "It was a 'poison' to put in creeks and streams to kill the platypus, which is a very much protected, loved, endearing indigenous Australian animal. In fact, if I were to be given a chance to save a platypus, at some risk to myself, I would probably attempt it. So why have an exhibit that offers a pesticide to destroy these animals? *Because* everything was in its place in Australia. On the package it said in small print that it was also rather good for Aboriginals. Aboriginals didn't exist: in a way, one was led to believe that they lived a long way away and were dying out anyway, which was terribly sad, but there it was. This was all part of the tyranny of niceness and order. I didn't want to *overthrow* order. I just instinctively wanted to give it a bit of a *jolt,* so that people could see it."

"Pox Vobiscum" was the motto of Melbourne University's Dada group, which put on the second exhibition, in 1953. Members of the public who strolled into the lounge of the Student Union and were surrounded by the sound of diabolical laughter counterpointed by a record rigged to repeat, from "South Pacific," "And you will note there's a lump in my throat / I'm in love, I'm in love, I'm in love . . ." soon got the splenetic message. Humphries had filled a pair of Wellington boots full of custard and titled it "Pus in Boots." Under the title "Her Majesty's Male," Queen Elizabeth II was shown with five-o'clock shadow. In both exhibitions, the punning titles of many of the works disabused art of its gravity and proclaimed Dada's faith in life as a joke: "Yes, We Have No Cezannas," "Roof of the Cistern Chapel," "Portrait of James Juice," "Christopher Fried," "Erasmus-Tazz," "My Foetus Killing Me," "Puree of Heart." Humphries created a series of works that rotted and smelled, in order to satirize the notion of genteel art collecting. He produced "Shoescapes" from old shoes, "Stinkscapes" from lambs' eyes, "Cakescapes" from cake pressed between glass to create a kind of Jackson Pollock abstraction. To a local newspaper he explained, "Here are the artistic media which best express the multifaceted image of Australian life—cake, shoes, and tomato sauce. From footwear, custard, and chutney you can create the Old Masters of the future."

"Dada shows its truth in action," Tzara said. Inevitably, Humphries and the Dada group were drawn toward performance. Their Dada revue, "Call Me Madman" (1952), achieved notoriety. The furor was caused not by the blanks being fired over the audience's head, or by the din of the orchestra playing combs, bottles, and gongs, or by the spectacle of Humphries dressed as a nun and singing "I Wish I Could Shimmy Like My Sister Kate." What made the front page of the Melbourne *Sun* was the finale, "The Indian Famine." A missionary sat across a table from his wife, played by Humphries minimally disguised in a dress over his suit. The table was piled high with cauliflower, cake, and raw meat. "It looked like a harvest festival," Humphries recalls. The missionary read aloud statistics of a recent famine. As each horrific figure was announced, the wife laughed and repeated, "I don't care, I've got plenty of food, lots of food. And they've got nothing." Humphries says, "The point was crudely moral in order to dramatize public indifference to these kinds of catastrophes and to provoke respectable undergraduate audiences into some kind of irrational behavior, some kind of demonstrative feeling."

Humphries succeeded all too well. As the missionary's broadcast of statistics grew louder, so did the wife's hysterical laughter. They started throwing food at each other, and some food found its way into the audience. The audience started hurling the food at the actors, who, in turn, threw it back at them. A food fight had begun. "We had an audience of affluent Australian university students throwing perfectly good food about the auditorium while statistics about the current famine were being broadcast over the amplifiers at them—an act therefore of total anarchy," Humphries explains. "The satirical intention is very apparent in all this. It eluded the audience, however, who stormed the stage, after my blood. I remember hiding in the broom cupboard under the stage." The Dada group was banned from ever again using the Student Union theatre.

Humphries also started making a spectacle of himself. He cultivated his myth. "I was entertained by the idea of slightly fictionalizing myself," he says. His tailored suits, his still longer hair, his mauve ink (an affectation acquired from reading Ronald Firbank) heralded the dandy's intention of inhabiting a world of his own. Humphries gathered around him a group of women he dubbed "hoydens" and "doxies," one of whom was Germaine Greer. "He would dress them up as schoolgirls and passionately kiss them in the street," the Australian critic Clive James reports in his essay "Approximately in the Vicinity of Barry Humphries." "Until the police arrived, whereupon birth certificates would be produced."

And so began a series of legendary pranks, in which Humphries moved "from a visual vocabulary to a theatrical one." In one notorious escapade, Humphries had an accomplice, John Perry, dress as a blind man and take a seat in a non-smoking compartment of a Melbourne commuter train. As Humphries has described it: "Perry was reading Braille. How anyone in a non-smoking compartment of a commuter train could have mistaken a piano roll for Braille, goodness knows. John was reading a piano roll. He had dark glasses and his leg was in a cast. He aroused an enormous amount of curiosity and pity, I should think, on the long journey into town. So when, at a certain stop, in came a rather garishly dressed, long-haired youth, smoking gold-tipped cigarettes between the wrong fingers, and reading a foreign-language newspaper—very foreign-looking—immediately they looked. First of all, I'd given them plenty of time to feel compassion and admiration for this man. Then in comes another figure, smoking in a non-smoking compartment, reading a *foreign* newspaper, long hair. So another emotion takes over. Then the foreign person looks down at the blind man and, as he's about to get out of the train a couple of stops later, unleashes a volley of foreign-sounding gibberish, grabs the Braille, tears the paper, kicks at the blind man's leg, and tears off his glasses and throws them on the floor. Then he gets off the train. The commuters were invariably transfixed with horror. No one ever pursued me. Mind you, I ran as fast as I could. People tried to comfort John Perry. He would always say 'Forgive him.' It was also very funny to do, and very hard not to laugh. It's a bit hard to say what effect the stunt was meant to have, since it was meant to amuse us, a kind of outrageous public act.''

The pranks turned life into ''a mini-spectacle with me as the audience,'' Humphries says. They also gave him a ''theatrical thrill,'' which he explains as ''changing people's lives slightly by making them the witness to some rather remarkable and absolutely inexplicable thing that could not happen in real life.'' It was a dangerous sport, but one Humphries experimented with after he'd dropped his university studies (law, then liberal arts) and joined the repertory theatre on the Melbourne University campus, in the mid-fifties. The actress Zoë Caldwell was part of the same repertory and got caught up in Humphries' masquerade. ''He used to do a very strange thing,'' she says. ''He would pretend to be a spastic, a genuine spastic. People would pity him. It's still in Dame Edna—he pushes responses in people. But they're responses we should feel ashamed of. He forces you to feel emotions. I was his sister. That's what he cast me as. It wasn't my idea of a swell night out. We'd go to a restaurant and ask for tea. The waitress would bring the tea, and he'd take the milk and pour it on his head. The girl was trying to keep her patience. Then Barry would pour the sugar on the floor. He did the whole thing, never stopped. Watching people pity him and pity me, I knew what he was after—false sentiment. He wanted to see what reactions people had to disability. Barry forced you to look at the ugly and the monstrous. He was trying it out. The genesis of what he wanted to trap—bogus emotion, denial, what we all do— was there. I think he wanted to trap it and say 'Look, look what you do.' And so he's outrageous. At parties, he used to sing:

> 'Lasso that spasso
> And beat him till he's sweatin'

Lasso that spasso
I'm a'hangin' on to this here cretin.'

"People would say 'How cruel,' or 'Oh, Barry!' That's the response he wanted. He was trying to provoke and entrap their sentimentality. I see this in Edna Everage, only now Barry makes people laugh. He didn't make people laugh much at the time. He's now wonderful as Edna because he's so free, as if he's found exactly what's right for him.''

"You can come in, John." Humphries is dialling a number, speaking to my reflection in the left-hand corner of his dressing mirror. "They want me to close the Prince's Trust performance. Frank Sinatra, Sammy Davis, Jr., Kiri Te Kanawa, and Liza Minnelli will be on the bill, too." He puts down the telephone and turns to face me: relaxed, excited, already watching Edna's persona go by. "I have to come on late, because of my show. I suppose I'll do 'My Public' and change the lyrics. But what about them? I don't know too much about them!"

"Well, Sammy Davis is black, one-eyed, and Jewish."

Humphries' eyes drift away into thought. He mumbles a snatch of song: "I'm better off than Sammy." And then, with a clap of high-pitched laughter, he turns back, beaming: " 'I may be overtired and fluish / But at least I'm not one-eyed and black and Jewish.' Dare I sing that? They'd never allow it on television!"

The phone rings. "Hello, Stephen." Humphries launches into a description of a dress he saw in a Parisian revue which he wants Stephen Adnitt, his designer, to copy. "It had mirrors on it. Actually around the neck. A kind of V neck or yoke of mirrors. They were rather chunky tiles, almost. No, but you can imagine what happened when the lights hit them, because they were separate and moved with the fabric a bit. They sent these rays straight out into the audience."

Edna began life, in the mid-fifties, dressed from secondhand clothing shops. And as she has progressed in confidence and class, so have her costumes. Humphries' ever-changing satire on modern manners is inevitably a satire on modern fashion. Over the last twenty years, Dame Edna has become a clotheshorse of many colors. She herself explained the transformation to London's *Sunday Telegraph* in 1987: "As late as the early 1970s, I was still really dressing like a tourist, buying off the peg in Oxford Street. I wore a tweed overcoat which may have come from C. & A.; white vinyl Courrèges-style boots, a hangover from the 1960s; and a felt hat in autumnal colours.'' But since the late seventies, when she declared herself a superstar, Dame Edna has been in the vanguard of fashion, exploiting the punk leather look, the denim look, the tennis look. For her cantata ''The Song of Australia,'' she wore a dress that opened in front to reveal the Australian coat of arms lit up, flashing a kangaroo and an emu holding a shield. Offstage, a stagehand pulled a string, and a cape unfolded behind Edna like wings, adding decibels to the applause. After Princess Di attended the Cannes Festival in a puffball dress, Dame Edna had one made up, complete with a Windsor Castle hat bearing a flag that could be run up on the turret, and little corgis on the brim. Dame Edna has also attempted (and failed) to crash the Royal Enclosure at Ascot wearing a behemoth hat in the shape of the Sydney Opera House, with a shark-infested bay as the brim.

''And, Stephen,'' Humphries says, ''also remember on the bill are Liza Minnelli, Sammy Davis, Jr., Frank Sinatra, Kiri Te Kanawa—I have to excel them *all*.''

Dennis Smith and the stage manager, Harriet Bowdler, come into the dressing room. Humphries sings Smith the lines about Sammy Davis, Jr. ''In superb taste,'' says Smith, who bears a handful of opening-night telegrams and a memo about the charity performance.

Humphries goes into the bathroom to freshen up. The pre-opening orders to the ushers from the Drury Lane stage sound through the loudspeakers in Humphries' dressing room. ''They've adjusted the speakers,'' Bowdler says. ''Barry gets most upset if we play a theatre and the show relay doesn't come back to the dressing room. He likes to hear the audience.''

''He often says 'Listen to them,' '' Katie Harris says, scuttling into the dressing room with Sir Les's padding.

Bowdler says, '' 'Is it a nice crowd?' he'll say. 'Who's out there?' He likes to know people are waiting. Sometimes he just needs to know they're waiting.''

Humphries comes out of the bathroom and sits on the edge of the sofa bed, which has been made up in the waiting room. ''I think I'm going to have a ten-minute nap, John." He pulls down the coverlet. "It'll go all right tonight, don't you think?"

> *"Your attention please, ladies and gentlemen. Contrary to the television broadcast you have just seen, we have received word that a world-famous woman is speeding to this theatre under police escort in the Ednamobile. The management have little doubt that if this proves to be Dame Edna and that she has indeed decided to keep faith with her devoted public and give you a show tonight, the generous-hearted men and women of goodwill in this audience will give this courageous woman and widow a standing ovation rarely witnessed in the annals of the British Theatre."*

A crash of cymbals. A spotlight. And there, at the front of the stalls, is Dame Edna, in her widow's weeds. "Hello, possums!" she shouts, waving and smiling and vaulting up the stairs to the stage in her slightly bowlegged gait. "Hello, darlings. Hello, possums." She beams as she crosses the stage.

"I'm glad I stepped onto the stage now, possums. I am. I am. When I first heard that Norm had been axed by the Big Rupert Murdoch in the sky, I phoned up my shrink in L.A. Dr. Marvin K. Schadenfreude, M.D. I share him with little Elton John, little Michael Jackson, and big Sylvester. I said, 'Doctor, what am I going to do?' And he said, 'Let it all hang out, Edna.' I said, 'That's what Norm did. And look where it got him!' He said, 'Time is a miracle healer. Only Time can heal.' And he was so right. Because that was—what?—four hours ago. And already I'm feeling *marvellous*. I am."

He was born John Barry Humphries, in the Melbourne suburb of Kew, on February 17, 1934, the first of Eric and Louisa Humphries' four children. Although it would be wrong to consider Edna merely Humphries' alter ego, it would also be wrong to consider her just "this woman you inhabit," which was Graham Greene's description. Edna originated as a totem of Humphries' sense of displacement both from his milieu and from his parents. "I invented Edna because I hated her," he said. "I suppose one grows up with a desire to murder one's parents, but you can't really go and do that. So I suppose I tried to murder them symbolically onstage. I poured out all my hatred of the standards of little people of their generation.'' As a comic caricature, Edna allowed Humphries to turn the infuriating fears of his parents against them.

Edna is, among other things, a son's disturbing view of his mother. Edna talks but never listens. She asks questions only to double-bind her interlocutors. She is a queen of control. ''You're tired. You're over-excited,'' she says, turning fiercely on her infantilized audience. ''There'll be tears before bedtime!'' What Edna claims about herself and what the audience perceives about her are different matters. She is ''approachable'' and devastating, ''nice'' and devouring, ''caring'' and callous, ''intimate'' and detached. She contains a son's envy of his mother's power to be at once the agent of joy and the means of eradication.

Louisa Humphries looked on her son with bemusement. ''Where did you come from, Barry?'' she used to say to him when he was a child. ''We never knew where you came from.''

''My mother would very frequently express surprise at me, which reinforced my adoption fantasy,'' Humphries says. ''My father became very successful. I didn't see a great deal of him. He was always very, very busy.'' Humphries pictures Eric Humphries—a third-generation builder, whose father immigrated to Australia from Lancashire—as surrounded by the drawing boards, set squares, drawing pins that were the tools of his trade and the source of the increasing wealth that helped him move from Oldsmobile to Buick and on to Mercedes in the fifties. ''My mother was a distant figure as well,'' he says. ''I think she had a period of illness. I think she was sent away for a bit. It might have been as little as a fortnight, but it seemed months to a child.''

The Humphries family lived in a two-story neo-Georgian cream brick house in Camberwell, the most fashionable new suburb of Melbourne, on the Golf Links Estate and looking down Marlborough Avenue. Outside, in the spacious world of herbaceous borders and rolling lawns, Humphries sensed an ''unneighborly feeling.'' His parents didn't fraternize much with the neighbors. ''It was thought not altogether 'nice' to know people very well,'' Humphries says about the general ''lack of intimacy,'' which also prevailed in the world inside his house. By the age of six, Humphries was withholding his deepest hurts from his parents. "I was puzzled even then by the mysterious lack of rapport which seemed to have grown up between parents and child."

The incident that prompted this recollection was a schoolyard quarrel at the detested South Camberwell State School ("I still drive past in order to see if I can revive my hatred of the school: I do so without any difficulty"), which Humphries briefly attended before entering Camberwell Grammar. "Once, a whole crowd of bullies set upon me in a corner of the arid and ashen playground, because I had a toy submarine they envied," he recalled. "They'd seized handfuls of gravel to pelt me, and in self-defense I threw a handful back at them and was immediately reported for throwing stones to Miss Jensen, the woman in charge of our class. Miss Jensen preferred to take their testimony against my own, and she threatened to take me to the headmaster. Waiting to see the headmaster, I was placed in a corner of the classroom, in front of everyone, with a note on my back. 'I am a bully,' said the note. 'I am a bully.' So I was subjected to this humiliation, and after that I broke down and confessed that in fact I had been culpable—when, of course, I knew I hadn't really—to avoid the ultimate vengeance of a confrontation with the headmaster. This filled me with very uncomfortable feelings for many, many years. I've often thought to this day of taking some form of revenge upon Miss Jensen if she is still alive, some kind of incomprehensible vengeance—to find her in some place of retirement and inflict upon her some mild punishment, some bewildering punishment. It would make me feel better."

Humphries found impersonating Edna "very therapeutic and liberating." He says, "I was finally more comfortable as Edna, because I was more heavily disguised. I could relax in the character. It was like a girl who suddenly discovers she has a career in prostitution. On the one hand, she suddenly thinks, 'Oh, I've got a job.' And, on the other hand, 'Well, actually, it's a job my parents aren't going to be too happy about.' "

Humphries' parents were vociferously disapproving of their son's vocation. "A man does all he can for his kids and what does he get for it?" was the beginning of one of Eric Humphries' familiar litanies, which his son put verbatim into one of his lesser caricatures, the successful businessman Colin Cartwright. "Things were going well for *him* professionally," Humphries says of his father. "Then, suddenly, I seemed to be what Vance Packard called the 'slip generation,' the one who was going to blow it all. I shared his anxiety but didn't let on. What, indeed, would I be? I was tortured with wondering. It certainly couldn't be anything I was good at or enjoyed—it had to be something else." At first, his parents boycotted his shows, and, even with his success, Louisa refused to see her son perform his priapic Sir Les Patterson. "Only later did my father come," Humphries says. "He went to a theatre in Melbourne. The box-office lady said to me, 'Oh, your father's such a nice man.' I said, 'When did you meet him?' She said he'd come in that morning. He wanted to buy all the tickets in the theatre and give them to his friends. He was very surprised to learn they were sold out. He was convinced no one would come."

To his mother Humphries was, according to him, "guilty of letting down the side, a frequent crime." An elegant woman, Louisa was adored and spoiled by her husband, whose preoccupation with his business left her ruling the roost at home. "My mother wasn't a particularly warm woman," Humphries says. "She had artistic qualities that were *all* suppressed." Louisa was judgmental and could make her disapproval felt. When Humphries told her he had met the Queen after a command performance at the Palladium, she replied, "I hope you were wearing a nice *suit*." Humphries wasn't. "She had a very oblique way of paying you a compliment, always very recondite," Humphries says. "It didn't seem necessary to inform her that I was wearing a dress." But, even before acting and Edna, Humphries had difficulty in making his mother see him for himself. She once asked him to return the gift of a pair of earrings he'd bought her. "This was a very wounding experience for a child," he says.

The problem of being properly accepted remained an issue between them in his adulthood. Humphries tells of returning from London to Melbourne to show off to Louisa his newborn son Oscar, the first child of his now dissolved third marriage, to the painter Diane Millstead. "She had not met her grandson," he recalls. "As I arrived home, I noticed my mother listening to the transistor radio. I came forward to present my son to her, and she was cautioning me, 'Listen! Listen!' It was a typical Australian disc jockey on a phone-in program. He happened to be talking about me. Was I good for Australia or not? It was generally felt that I was doing Australia a great disservice by my impersonations—particularly that of Sir Les Patterson, this anachronistic figure. My mother was saying, 'Shhh . . . shhh . . . listen!' People were ringing up and saying things like 'Well, I haven't seen one of Barry's shows, but from what I've heard it's a disgrace.' This disc jockey by impugning my patriotism was inflating his own reputation. My mother said, pointedly, 'You see? That's what they think. That's what they think of you!' I was so incensed that I should come home and my mother should be listening to this rubbish, and not dismissing it, instead of greeting me and her grandson, that I went into another room. I telephoned the radio station as Edna. I got through using the voice of Edna. I said that this was Dame Edna and I was on a brief visit to Australia and I was listening to the program about Barry Humphries and I heartily agreed with these women. I said, 'Not only do I agree with what these women said about Barry Humphries but I happen to know that Barry Humphries' mother thinks *exactly* the same.' ''

Dame Edna is out of widow's black now and into iridescent celebrity red. ''Eat your heart out, Tina Turner!'' she shouts, unveiling the short, fringy dress in which she hymns her dead husband, her public, and her professionalism. The audience is in a party mood. Someone hidden in the shadows of a box throws a chartreuse-and-yellow card, and it lands with a clatter at Edna's feet. She kicks the missive offstage, and Harriet Bowdler retrieves it. ''I LOVE YOU,'' it reads. ''Hays, known as 'Hayseed' from Kentucky. 1st bloke in 1st box on left.''

Edna, too, is talking of love: ''I love to hear laughter. I call it Vitamin L, what an essential part of our spiritual diet it is, isn't it, possums? Norman and I—oh, how we used to love to laugh. We were always playing little jokes on each other. And it's not easy, is it, playing jokes on institutionalized loved ones. Huh. But every April Fools' Day we had a little jest with each other. I remember last April the first . . . hah! . . . We pretended to Norm . . . hah! . . . he was going to be discharged from the hospital. Ha, ha! Isn't that gorgeous? You could do that with a loved one. The matron helped, too. She packed his little case so he could watch her doing it out of the corner of the mirror above his page-turning machine. He's had 'The Thornbirds' open at the same page for the last seven years. (Who hasn't?) Anyway, they got him into his dressing gown, and he shuffled down to the front of the hossie, where they had an ambulance ticking over. And just as Norm was about to fall into the ambulance . . . hee, hee . . . *it whizzed off down the driveway!* Ah, ha, ha! . . . He fell flat on his face in the gravel. And all the doctors and nurses leant out the windows and said, 'April Fool!' . . . Ha, ha! . . . I wish Norm could have laughed at that. Oh, dear . . . oh, but I'm a lucky, lucky woman, because I was born with a priceless gift. 'What gift is that, Dame Edna?' I hear you saying. The ability to laugh at the misfortunes of others. And, you know, that keeps me cheerful twenty-four hours a day, it does!''

Edna frequently criticizes Humphries in public and in the press. (In her autobiography she writes, ''BARRY HUMPHRIES. Still my manager, but under solicitor's thumb. His contributions to our show getting smaller by the year.'') And Edna's putdowns about his lack of talent only add to his legend and his mystery. In explaining Edna to the public, Humphries does what all dandies do: he obscures his depths and his roots. ''If England is the Motherland and Germany is the Fatherland, Australia is certainly the Auntieland,'' he told his friend the actor-writer John Wells. ''I had a lot of aunts, all very nice, but they were there, all the time. So I was pretty good at giving an impersonation, certainly, of a kind of synthesis of these women. And also of their obsession with domestic detail, seeing the whole world, really, through the venetian blind of the kitchen window: seeing everything in terms of household arrangements, cleanliness, all that stuff. These people who managed to live comfortably and happily in such a narrow world that they could get by without ever having read the Muirs' translations of Kafka, that they could be perfectly happy and well entertained without dipping into 'Cardinal Pirelli.' ''

There were few books in the Humphries house. ''My mother was a great student of *The Australian Women's Weekly*,'' Humphries says. The family's tidy and comfortable home was as free from dirt as it was from the infection of ideas. ''There were just standard books,'' Humphries recalls. '' 'The Family Doctor,' an encyclopedia bought from a travelling salesman. Very few novels. My uncle—my mother's brother-in-law —had been in France during the First World War. He had a lot of books and gave me some. My father bought me whatever books I wanted, although a copy of D. H. Lawrence was seized by my mother.'' Humphries also had two great-uncles who painted. ''They did very large pictures of the River Nile at sunset and of lions in their lair,'' he says.

It was not only the deadly tedium of the Melbourne suburbs that so powerfully affected Humphries but the silence inside his own house. ''It was quiet. Only at my insistence was a gramophone obtained,'' he says. ''I started collecting records seriously as a boy.'' Music partly answered Humphries' ''hankering for somewhere else.'' He says, ''In the early Melbourne days, sitting in Camberwell wondering what I was going to do when I grew up, I was mostly listening to English music: Vaughan Williams and Delius in particular, romantic 'pastoral' music.'' The family's brown Bakelite radio also abetted Humphries' yearning for ''moister climates,'' by bringing him into contact with British music-hall comedians and the notion that people told jokes for a living. This discovery occurred when Humphries was about ten, and laughter seemed to hold out to him a power comparable to his fantasy of being a magician and making people disappear. Humphries says, ''I wanted to exercise power over people. I wanted to control their access to me.'' In a mock novel about ''an androgynous and eldritch child'' named Tid, Humphries wrote, in 1961, ''Tid's main thing was trying not to be seen. You can't imagine how hard this job was. He just wanted ladies and men to accept the fact that he wasn't there.'' At the end, Tid becomes King. Humphries wrote, ''Tid hides in the world and is King of it.''

''It's true,'' Dame Edna says, scanning the front rows. ''There are such a lot of lovely young folk here to see me. The young *adore* me. And please, youngsters, remember everything you see tonight. Will you promise Edna? Please? Your grandchildren are probably going to want to know about this experience. They are. This could be your only interesting anecdote.''

Dame Edna sees herself as the world's role model. She is, she says, into "M"'s, including matrimony, motherhood, and monogamy. Dame Edna has always been true to Norm in her fashion. As she sang in "Why Do I Love Australia?":

> Why do I love Australia?
> Why does it grab me so?
> Life was so sunny and informal
> When my husband Norm was normal
> And my career was in embryo.

Dame Edna treats her children with the same combination of sentimentality and neglect. "I think my famous softness really took a big leap forward when my first bubba came along," Dame Edna writes in "My Gorgeous Life," and she recalls returning to her roots in Moonee Ponds and going through the postures of parenthood while looking at the pencil marks of her children's heights still on the doorframe. "My lovely hazel eyes prickled with tears as I looked around."

Humphries himself is a much-married man. In *Who's Who* he does not acknowledge his first marriage—to a classical ballerina, Brenda Wright, in 1955, when he was twenty-one. He married, he told the press, "much too young," and in 1959, after he was divorced, he married another dancer, Rosalind Tong, whom he'd met during the run of a children's play he co-wrote and starred in—"The Bunyip and the Satellite." Humphries' second marriage, which produced two daughters—Tessa, in 1963, and Emily, in 1965—lasted nearly twelve years and ended with Rosalind's leaving a packed suitcase for Humphries at the stage door. Humphries told the Sydney *Daily Mirror* in 1982:

> I was enjoying all the razzle-dazzle of success. After leaving the theatre at night, instead of going home, I'd find myself going to a pub, then on to a club or party. I got to the stage where I hardly bothered to look at my watch.
>
> I don't reproach Rosalind at all for what she did. I reproach myself. We were together for nearly twelve years, and when it was over, I was deeply unhappy for a long time.

For a few years after his divorce from Rosalind, Humphries declared himself a bad matrimonial bet and swore off the institution. "For a long time I was an impossible person to live with," he told English *Vogue* in 1976. "I'm fine as far as work is concerned, but I'm bad at other things, like returning phone calls and making breakfast. The traditional wife has her uses—but I wouldn't want to live with anyone who wanted to be just a wife. Anyway, after unsuccessful relationships, one gets a bit tense, a bit wary."

But in 1975 Humphries met Diane Millstead, whose paintings he had admired in a Melbourne gallery, and in 1979 she became the third Mrs. Humphries. "Diane claims I used to be a terrible womanizer before I met her," Humphries said in the *Mirror*. "I prefer to say I was very, very fond of female company." The marriage produced two sons— Oscar, in 1981, and Rupert, in 1982—and its share of headlines. At the beginning of their marriage, Millstead referred to Humphries in the press as "the sex symbol of the Eighties," but when the marriage ended, in 1989, she was calling him "a champion mattress tester." In June 1990, Humphries married Lizzie Spender, the actress-playwright daughter of Stephen Spender.

"Isn't it a spooky thought," Dame Edna says, pursuing the idea of family and children, "to think that one day in the twenty-first century your little grandbubbas will be huddled around your gnarled and knotted kneecaps? You'll be leaning on your Zimmer frame and they'll look up to you and they'll say, 'Oh, Nana, Nana, tell us again that lovely story of the night, that historic night at the Theatre Royal Drury Lane (now a supermarket) . . . tell us about the night you went to see Saint Edna.' "

Dame Edna scowls at the audience for laughing at the notion of her as a canonized model of nurturing self-sacrifice. "Please! Don't laugh. I've had a tipoff. I can't tell you who told me, but he's Polish, single, and lives in Italy. That's *all* I can say." But later, after her monologue has meandered through accounts of her "regular exploratories" and her Swiss financial advisers, Dame Edna returns to her latest claim for herself as a mother. "I'm an upmarket Mother Teresa. I am. I am. And Mother Teresa comes to see me, too. Every time she comes to London. She comes to London once a year, for the Harrods Sale. It's not—no, it's not for the merchandise. She just loves sleeping in the street. She *loves* it. She said to me, 'Edna, those Knightsbridge gutters have got the edge on Calcutta.' She came backstage with her little program, holding a little gladdy she'd caught. And I said, 'Did you enjoy it, Tess, tell me?' And she said, 'Edna, I came out of your show feeling another woman!' ''

Dame Edna is spinning a yarn about a letter she has received from a woman in Shepherd's Bush who has been to one of her shows. ''She said, 'I was the woman sitting in the first six rows that you chose that night . . . as you always do . . . choose a woman . . . to do the nude cartwheels onstage.' '' Dame Edna paces the stage and looks down into the front rows. ''And now the mood has completely changed, hasn't it? I don't know what you'd call it. Blind terror, I think, don't you? I think these yups want to be up with the paups, don't you? *I think they do.* But don't you be nervous. Please. Supposing I chose, for argument's sake, *YOU!* In the third row—as I almost certainly will. Hello? What is your name? You. Yes. Yes. What is your name?''

''Emma,'' says a middle-aged blonde, faintly.

''Hello, Emma,'' Dame Edna coos. ''Have you done much nude-cartwheel work? Don't worry, Emma. We've found audiences prefer an amateur nude cartwheelist, they do! They have a way of falling over which is vulnerable and—well, strangely appealing. So don't be nervous, Emma. Don't scratch your eczema, Emma. Because you will not know that you're doing these cartwheels, Emma. Do you know why? You'll be in deep shock, Emma. You will. Because whenever we women are very, very frightened, our bodies do a funny thing. We secrete an enzyme at the same time. So you'll not only be in your birthday suit endeavoring to do cartwheels, and failing. But you'll be secreting an enzyme at the same time. I hope that's reassuring.''

Dame Edna began as a less strident voice from the back of the Union Theatre Repertory Company touring bus taking ''Twelfth Night'' on one-night stands through Victoria in 1955. It was Humphries' first year as a professional actor. He was twenty-one. Having dropped out of Melbourne University two years earlier, he had been earning his living by working at E.M.I. as, variously, a wholesale record salesman and a breaker of recently obsolete 78s. "This latter chore," he says, of days he spent in a windowless room in an "inane frenzy," destroying piles of Mahler, Sibelius, Debussy, and the Ink Spots, "produced a more acute form of nervous exhaustion than I had experienced in my less compulsive Dadaist activities, though it bore an ironic resemblance to them." Humphries' Duke Orsino, on the other hand, was less than smashing. "He wasn't a swell leading man," says Zoë Caldwell, who played Viola. "Clearly, he didn't concentrate. He couldn't stay in a role. You thought, 'He can't possibly be an actor.' But I knew he'd be something. He had such an extraordinary mind. As Orsino, his legs were too thin. When he came on, he got a laugh."

To entertain themselves from one country town to another, the cast sang songs, told tales, and recited verse. Humphries' party piece was Edna, who had "the unmistakable voice of the genteel Melbourne housewife," he says, and who was also "a flashback, really, to my earliest university days and late school days, when with a group of friends we formed a Melbourne Dada group . . . in which we attempted to ridicule the fellows who we felt were terribly stuffy—and, indeed, we were quite right in thinking so." Edna allowed Humphries to show off his gift for caricature and his desire to shine. "I found that I had a good falsetto voice, and I invented a character to go with it—a female character, because, you see, every night, when the curtain fell on 'Twelfth Night,' the local lady mayoress or the ladies' committee would invite this distinguished cast from the city of Melbourne to what was called a bun fight: cups of tea and wonderful cakes such as only Australians seem able to make—plates of lamingtons and iced vovos and butterfly cakes all stuck together with cream and cocoa. They used to give little speeches about how wonderful 'Twelfth Night' was. I had a knack of anticipating some of the ladies' speeches very, very well as my funny little character in the back of the bus."

Edna was encouraged by the company's resident writer-director, Ray Lawler, whose "Summer of the Seventeenth Doll," in the late fifties, was the first Australian play to win international fame and, along with Humphries' characters, sound a new theatrical note of Australian self-awareness. Humphries recalls, "When it came to be time for the annual revue, 'Return Fare,' which Lawler was directing, Ray said, 'Why don't you write a sketch for that character you did in the bus? What's she called?' I plucked a name out of the air: 'Edna,' I suggested, since I'd once had a kind of nanny called Edna, of whom I was very fond. I said, 'Her name is Edna, and she comes from Moonee Ponds.' I thought, I daren't say Camberwell, or my mother will think it's based on her. Indeed, Edna is more of a Camberwell character than she is a Moonee Ponds character. Moonee Ponds was a suburb of Melbourne I'd never been to, at the time. 'Well, if I write a sketch for this character,' I said, 'who will play Edna? Will I do the voice from offstage?' Ray said, 'You do it yourself.' 'Can't Zoë be Edna?' I asked. He said, 'No, you be Edna. Do it like a pantomime dame.' ''

On December 19, 1955, Edna Everage made her stage début. She wore no wig, no eyeglasses, and no makeup. "She had shortish brown hair, which was in fact my own longish hair combed down," Humphries says. "She wore a hat, a voluminous skirt, flat shoes, and sockettes, and carried a rather large handbag. She looked somewhat gauche and nervous and spoke in a high, genteel, less vigorous and confident way than she speaks now. She was, after all, someone who had merely strayed from the kitchen onto the stage." The sketch was called "Olympic Hostess"—a title as up to the minute as Edna's palaver. The 1956 Olympic Games were to be staged in Melbourne, and already there were advertisements in the local newspapers asking for fifteen thousand beds to put up the athletes. In the sketch, Edna attempted to offer her Moonee Ponds home for the Games, an opportunity not so much for hospitality as for house pride. "There were not many traditional jokes in this piece," Humphries has written. "The real jokes turned out to be her lovely home itself."

There's our bedroom, one—then there's the lounge and dining room. If you open the double doors—little Kenny—that's my youngest—always calls them the reindeer doors because of the sandblasted reindeers on the glass—if you open the double doors it's a lovely big room. We pushed back the Genoa velvet couch and rolled back the burgundy Axminster squares for Valmai's twenty-first, and the young people had the time of their lives.

"You could hear the whoosh of laughter," Humphries says of the audience's rapturous shock of recognition. Even the cast was surprised by the sketch's impact. "No one had really talked about Australian houses before," Humphries has said. "Since my father was a builder, and the creator of a number of substantial Melbourne houses, in jazz moderne with manganese bricks, or Spanish Mission with the barley-sugar columns and little grilled windows, I was interested in houses. I found that I'd discovered something I could write about, not by putting the telescope to my eyes and trying to write something in the manner of Coward or Alan Melville, but by just looking through the venetian blinds onto my own front lawn. So Edna was born. Edna Everage as in 'average,' husband Norm as in 'normal.' "

Until Edna's début, Humphries had been "the boy in the rep who was worst at learning his lines and was getting smaller and smaller parts." Edna's success made him the star of the revue. Humphries ended up getting an eighteen-month engagement in revue at the Phillip Street Theatre in Sydney. "I found, to my great pleasure," Humphries says, "that the 'Olympic Hostess' sketch was popular there and that Mrs. Everage was by no means unknown in New South Wales." But Humphries had no ambitions for the character. Having discovered her, he promptly put her in mothballs. Edna made her Sydney début in 1956, in "Mr. and Mrs.," but she didn't appear onstage in Melbourne again until 1958, when she was seen first in Peter O'Shaughnessy's "Lunch-Hour Theatre Revues" and later in the "Rock 'n Reel Revue."

"In Australia, before me, most comic stereotypes were kind of rural people, hayseeds, hillbillies," Humphries says. "There seemed to be no Australian comedians who actually tried to reproduce *as accurately as possible,* without the use of jokes, or even funny names, something intrinsically funny in the way that *most* people really did live. In refrigerators. In appliances. In the problems of parking the car. It was just a sort of fresh interpretation of ordinary life. Whereas before, when you were identifying with Lucille Ball or Bob Hope or the Marx Brothers, you had to go through a very quick series of transpositions. First, you had to translate from the American into the English or Australian idiom, and *then* get the joke." In Edna's case, the joke was at the Australian front door.

Edna was the doyenne of philistine denial. She feared the penetration of anything: germs, ideas, certainly sex. "Although my childhood was in the midst of—at the very heart of—niceness and decency and cleanliness and comfort," Humphries has written, "I perceived the little dramas of Australian suburban life: the war against stains and creepy crawlies and the mysterious Outback; the knowledge that we didn't really live in Bournemouth or Wimbledon, but on the ghostly periphery of Asia with no traditions or even ghost stories to palliate our fear." Edna barricaded herself in the trivia of daily life. She gave her listeners detailed baking recipes. She lectured the audience on home hygiene: "A drop of disinfectant in your kiddy's schoolbag could save a lot of heartache. A Pine-O-Cleen rinse makes your rubbish bins safe to live with." She hymned the contents of her medicine chest: "Calamine lotion. Milk of magnesia. Laxettes. Aspros. Band-Aids (flesh-tint). Bicarbonate of soda. Golden eye ointment. Raleigh's Ready Relief . . ." Her fear of infection betrayed a mind without a thought—with just the echo of brand names and the rhythms of their advertising slogans.

For Humphries himself, there was no advertisement like self-advertisement. Edna gave Humphries the license to make a spectacle of himself. And he did. "Barry Humphries is, perhaps, the most gifted clown in Australia," said Humphries' bio in the 1958 program for the "Rock 'n Reel Revue." By 1959, Australian society had taken both the character and her creator to its heart, and that summer Humphries set off to test his talent in the more competitive arena of English theatre. Dame Edna, in her chapter about the Australian leave-taking in her autobiography, recalls that Mother Teresa subsequently told her that true happiness comes from renunciation. "I began my Life of Renunciation years ago," Dame Edna writes. "I decided to renounce Obscurity." It was a big roll of the dice for both Edna and her creator. Humphries' arrival in London was noted in one paragraph of the *Evening News* with the headline "A STAR HERE?" "That question mark haunted me for years," Humphries says.

"Excuse me," Dame Edna says, breaking off her monologue in "Back with a Vengeance!" to take the twenty-two hundred and forty-five paying customers sternly into her confidence. *"Paupers, stop leaning for-*

ward. I've told you a squillion times! There was a tragedy here the other night. We've kept it out of the papers, but I have to tell you what it was. A pauper woman—a paupess, actually—plummeted . . ." Having invented a word and reinforced it by alliteration, Edna continues to dazzle the audience with her effortless juggling of pun, innuendo, and irony, which unobtrusively plants in the audience's imagination the notion of someone falling out of the balcony. "She was leaning forward—it's so steep up there—she was leaning forward to get a chockie off the lap in front of her. At least, that's what we *assume* she was doing. She was fumbling for a hard one, Emma, when she came out. She wrapped her chops around the back of a seat, the toughest hard one she's ever experienced. They had to put her in a plastic bag and take her away. I laughed. I laughed compassionately. I did."

"A number of people prophesied success for me who saw me on my home ground, where I *knew* I was funny," Humphries says of his move to London. "There's nothing better than seeing a comic who thinks he's funny. If he's not entirely sure that what he's saying is amusing, or if his anxiety gets the better of him, he's not doing himself justice." And anxiety was the mood of Humphries' life as he struggled to get a theatrical foothold in London. "Barry was absolutely broke," says his compatriot Ian Donaldson, a professor of English literature and also an Old Melbournian, who hung out during the early, insecure years in the louche atmosphere of Humphries' Notting Hill basement apartment, with other artistic Aussie expats, like the painters Arthur Boyd, Sidney Nolan, and Francis Limburner. In order to audition by day, Humphries took a job in an ice-cream factory by night. "I didn't work there very long, but it was my only experience of factory work," he says. "It was a hellish experience, and sort of Dadaist as well. At first, I was working on a conveyor belt. It was Chaplinesque. Because of my maladroitness, I was put with the morons. I wasn't *allowed* to work on the conveyor belt, because I kept dropping the ice creams. I was put in a room where a group of us sat around an enormous plastic drum throwing damaged ice creams into it. I felt I smelled rather of raspberry ripple when I went to auditions."

Five months after arriving in England, in June 1959, Humphries landed a small part. He played the madhouse keeper in "The Demon Barber," a musical about Sweeney Todd, at the Lyric, Hammersmith— far from the West End. Humphries' own characters fared less well. His desiccated Melbourne ghost, Sandy Stone, made a brief appearance on British television upon his arrival. "I don't think anyone made anything of it at all," Humphries says. Edna seemed to arouse even less interest. If his prospects appeared to be dim, his intellectual life took on a new amperage. He seized his London days with manic energy. His appetite for England and all things English filled his unemployed hours. "He was extraordinary," Donaldson says. "He fitted in immediately. He knew London. He knew about various writers and artists who we thought were dead. He said they were living in basements and attics. He knew the right pubs to drink in, the right people to talk to. He established this extraordinary network—still not getting employment but becoming known and being seen as someone of extraordinary knowledge who was also entertaining."

"In London, it was a question of finding a voice that people could actually hear and wish to listen to," Humphries says. London seemed like the Big Table at which he was not allowed to sit. "People are talking and you're outside" is how he characterizes the feeling. "You sort of tune in. You think, 'I want to come in on this, but I have to wait until the moment.' "

Humphries goes on, "I've suddenly discovered that England is really a province of Australia. And so I needn't have been frightened all those years ago. If I'd gone straight in . . . But I wasn't ready." Although he soon got work in the West End, appearing as Sowerberry in Lionel Bart's "Oliver!" (1960) and, later, in his "Maggie May" (1964), he did not get much satisfaction. "I think Barry's mood in London when I met him was bad," says Peter Cook, who was then at the height of his celebrity both as an entertainer in "Beyond the Fringe" and as an impresario of outrageousness, who owned substantial shares in the satirical magazine *Private Eye* and was the proprietor of the Soho comedy club The Establishment. "I feel sure that he was certain he was very talented. I don't think he liked being in a minor part in 'Oliver!' Why it took Barry so long to become established—and, indeed, adored—over here, I don't quite know. I think in those early years, he was feeling a bit embittered." Cook, who was a fan of some records Humphries had made—especially those featuring Sandy Stone—but who had never seen him perform, generously threw Humphries a lifeline, asking him to do a three-week season at The Establishment in 1963, for a hundred pounds a week. "Big money," Humphries recalls of his Establishment gig, in which Sandy Stone and a timid Edna made their theatrical débuts in England. "*Very* big money. As soon as I got there, though, I felt a little uneasy. The shape of the room was long and narrow. The audience wasn't close to me, and it wasn't an experienced cabaret audience, either. The huge success of satire and 'That Was the Week That Was' on TV had led them to expect a certain kind of humor—very topical and often very witty and very irreverent about British institutions. My kind of rambling regional monologues, which depended for their effect not on jokes or on impersonations of political figures, were really unsuitable for that kind of place. They wanted Harold Macmillan. They didn't want Glen Iris, Melbourne."

In the annals of The Establishment, according to Peter Cook, no turn went down worse. "The stoniest of stony silences," Cook says. "*Nobody* found Barry remotely amusing. There were about three or four people who thought, This is very, very funny. Mainly, John Betjeman, John Osborne, and me. I felt ashamed of my fellow-Londoners for not appreciating him." In "My Gorgeous Life" Dame Edna turns this punishing memory of humiliation into hilarity by blaming her actor-manager, Humphries, for the disaster. He, she claims, went on *before* her, and emptied the room. "I had a bit of a weep afterwards," Dame Edna writes. "Barry had gone home in a huff, the worse for a few sherries I'm afraid. This was the lowest ebb in my career, but I have described it honestly and courageously. I was hurt at the time and my confidence was badly shaken, but I decided to have a few tough new clauses written into my contract with Mr H. I also vowed that if I ever found success outside my native land, I would remember this incident."

And Dame Edna has remembered it. As the title of the present show admits, Dame Edna embraces her celebrity with a vengeance. And, like Humphries, Edna deals with her corrosive sense of envy by becoming the envied. She revels in her distinction in the same way and for the same reason that all the programs of Humphries' twelve one-man shows contain encomiums of his genius and photographs of him with the cultural icons of his era. "Barry Humphries is the first Australian Satirist, he is also one of the funniest men in the World, if you don't think so, then it's your loss," Spike Milligan wrote for Humphries' second one-man show, "Excuse I" (1964), adding, under his name, "(being of sound mind)." On the same page is a photograph of the young Humphries with another licensed trickster, Salvador Dalí. Humphries' insistence on his comic and intellectual pedigree belies his long, sometimes hurtful struggle to have it validated.

"Barry first came to my attention at The Establishment," says the New Zealand–born cartoonist Nicholas Garland, who collaborated with Humphries on the sixties cult cartoon "The Adventures of Barry McKenzie," which ended up as two feature films. "The act was a failure, but we were all *enormously impressed* by Barry. We all began talking to each other in this preposterous parody of Australian. He instantly became somebody you rated. He was immediately subsumed into our culture, into our vocabulary, into the way we spoke. But it was a struggle for Barry. The English have plenty of eccentrics, plenty of people pretending to be Oscar Wilde and wearing their hair long. It took a while for Barry to get the measure of this." With a leg up from Peter Cook, Humphries was soon playing with the big boys. He crashed the cliquish Shrewsbury set that ran *Private Eye,* appearing in the magazine's columns both in the Barry McKenzie cartoon and as its astrologer, Madame Barry. He was cutting comedy tracks like "Old Pacific Sea," "Chunder Down Under," and "The Earl's Court Blues." He was doing character work for Joan Littlewood's Theatre Workshop, in Stratford East, as well as appearing in the West End. (He would make seventeen appearances in the West End in the subsequent decade, including a leading role in "The Bed-Sitting Room," with Spike Milligan; a memorable Long John Silver—"I'm going to take a peep round the poop"—in a Christmas production of "Treasure Island" at the Mermaid Theatre; and Fagin in a revival of "Oliver!") He was also tapped to join BBC-TV's "The Late Show" wits in 1964–65. Humphries was promising but not established. His frustration was beginning to show. He was on the page, on the stage, on records, on TV, and on the bottle.

"I remember Barry at a Boxing Day party doing something that I'd never witnessed before," says Peter Cook, who enjoyed bending an elbow with Humphries. "I think you have to reach another level of drunkenness to achieve it. I did the normal thing of falling down drunk, but Barry upstaged me by falling upstairs. I don't know how he did it." Between the mid-sixties and the early seventies, when he swore off the sauce, Humphries drank so heavily he nearly died from it. By the power of his charm and his humor, he managed to conceal much of his drunken desperation. "I remember sitting in a taxi with a Harrods bag on my lap that had a half bottle of whisky in it and looking at the queue of heroin addicts outside Boots the Chemists in Piccadilly Circus with contempt," he is quoted as saying in a recent biography by Peter Coleman, of the time he now characterizes as "when I was ill and mad." "They were addicts and I was something else. I was, if you like, a genius out of luck. I was a sensitive person. I just drank alcohol like all the best people, like Dylan Thomas, like Scott Fitzgerald, like Malcolm Lowry, like John Barrymore, like Tony Hancock. I belonged to the aristocracy of self-destruction."

"There is a woman here tonight," Dame Edna says, peering over the footlights. "A woman who intrigues me. *You!* In the middle of the second row, with a little thoughtful look on your face. Hello, darling. Did you see me peeping at you?"

"Yes," says a thin voice from row B.

"I saw you peeping at me, too. You'd be a foolish woman if you weren't, wouldn't you? Swivelling your head like the kiddie in 'The Exorcist.' What's your name?"

She's Margaret from Hornchurch.

"I don't know Hornchurch very well, but there are some lovely homes down that way, aren't there? Do you live near any of them, do you? Margaret? What type of a home have you?"

"A detached home."

"Oh, lovely," Dame Edna says. "Hear that, paupers? A detached home. It's a foreign language to them, Margaret. Have you made it nice inside? I . . . think . . . you . . . have, Margaret. I think you have. You can redecorate, can't you, Margaret, quite inexpensively. A little bit of emulsion. A little bit of paint. To make a beautiful home, I

think that's serious money, as the yuppies would say. And yet . . .
you've saved on clothes, haven't you, Margaret?''

Dame Edna likes to disconcert her audience. In previous shows, she
has asked for, and received, shoes from the audience for her inspection.
She has coaxed four people onto the stage to cook a barbecue and then
left the paying customers alone in front of two thousand people while,
with consummate daring, she made her exit for a costume change. She
has insisted that her audience sit still for a Polaroid picture to remember
it by. ''You could feel the audience posing,'' Ian Davidson says, recalling
the preposterousness of someone trying to photograph an entire audience. ''A little picture would come out, and Edna would say, 'It's not
very good of *you.*' '' Dame Edna has also pulled a flashlight from her
purse and trained it on the critics, trying to make them identify themselves—a job made easier by a sign saying ''Critic'' which dropped
down over their assigned seats.

''What color carpet?'' Dame Edna is asking Maud from Chingford.
''Beige? Good heavens, she's been to the same remnant sale as you,
Margaret. Any pictures on the wall? No pictures. No little pictures on
the bedroom wall? Sounds delightful. And you're delightful, Maud.
(You're going to adore this woman when she's onstage in a minute.)
Maud has gone beige now! Not yet, darling, no, but *soon*! So soon, that
if I were you I'd start tensing up now.''

Dame Edna is maneuvering the audience to join her onstage as extras
in her epic. ''Did you ever see my wonderful show 'The Dame Edna
Experience'?'' she says. ''Emma, did you see it? It was marvellous,
wasn't it, Emma? (Emma's getting a bit more animated by the minute
there.) Did you see it at all, my TV series? Did you, Maud? Lovely. I tell
you what I started doing. I was just talking to friends like Charlton
Heston, Larry Hagman. And then it proved too popular. They said they
wanted me to do another series this year. I said *I will.* But I said I want
real people. I said this time actually I want non-entities. I want . . . I
want women like you, Maud, as a matter of fact. Whose chances of
becoming a celebrity are—ha, ha—let's face it, darling, *nil.*''

Edna was damed spontaneously, on camera, by the Socialist Australian
Prime Minister Gough Whitlam. Happy to hitch his then popular public

image to Edna's rising star, Whitlam made a guest appearance in the final scene of "Barry McKenzie Holds His Own" (1974), the second successful film collaboration of Humphries and the director Bruce Beresford. "Did you know the Prime Minister and I once slept together?" Edna says to her nephew Barry McKenzie as they approach Sydney Airport and a hero's welcome at the end of their adventures in Central Europe. "It was at the Opera House, during the second act of 'War and Peace.' " The joke was cribbed from Ronald Firbank's play "The Princess Zoubaroff," but the finale was wholly original, a surprise even to Humphries. Edna came out of the plane and fell into the Prime Minister's arms, and Whitlam said, "*Dame* Edna. Arise, Dame Edna." Thereafter, she was Dame Edna. "In a sense, Edna takes directions from herself, not me," Humphries says. "If the character seems to be developing that way, I generally go with it. I don't allow the puritan conscience to arise in me and say, 'What is she doing being a famous person when she should be back in Melbourne telling them what's wrong with their bathroom fittings?' "

Dame Edna declared herself a superstar. It was a smart career move. The mutation in Edna's character occurred in the mid-seventies, by which time the West had become accustomed to parody display and celebrity rule. Of Edna's evolution into superstar, which gave her a universal focus and turned her quickly into a piece of cross-cultural folklore, Humphries says, "I noticed that Barbra Streisand was starting to make pronouncements on things. They were views on poetry and art. These people who were traditionally philistine were not meant to excel in intellectual pursuits or matters of alternative religions. So Edna caught the wave that her countrywoman Germaine Greer had helped to generate, and started doing some fancy surfing. It was originally a conscious parody of what these other people were saying. For instance, Streisand came out and said that her favorite picture was Edvard Munch's 'The Scream.' That played right into Edna's hands. She said it was her favorite picture, too, and she'd had it made into dinner mats. Also, when these stars started to talk about being 'very private people,' Edna leaped on that. It was only people who were *fiends* for publicity who ever said it. As she became more famous, she adopted the postures of modesty. So she became a kind of cipher and also a megaphone for the styles and affectations of the period, which changed very rapidly. You had to be very up-to-date.''

In the program, Edna identifies herself as Housewife, Megastar, Investigative Journalist, Social Anthropologist, Children's Book Illustrator, Film Script Assessor, Diseuse, Swami, Monstre Sacré, Polymath, and Hard-nosed Literary Agent, specializing in radical women's issues. (Her bio photograph shows Dame Edna posed with the book ''Sexual Harassment: A Pictorial History.'') ''More and more, I find with Edna that you can throw anything into the cauldron, and somehow it's just Edna's new shape,'' Humphries says. ''That's how she's developing today.''

''Bring on my talk-show hostesses, please,'' Dame Edna says, suddenly Lady Bountiful dishing out compliments to the show's four chorus girls, the Lesettes, and promises of BMWs and world trips to the audience.

This is the moment that the audience has feared and been thrilling for, the moment in which Humphries, in a sense, recapitulates in the audience his childhood terror of being wiped out. Such is the power of Humphries' control of an audience and Dame Edna's tyrannical charisma that, no matter how far away they sit, all members of the audience feel a quiver of terror that Dame Edna will choose *them*. Humphries says, ''I've taken to holding out these bribes—'Now, my next big major prize-winner is . . .'—if there looks to be a difficult, recalcitrant member of the audience. I prefer the doubtful ones.''

''So,'' Dame Edna says, ''without any further ado . . . I feel the excitement mounting. . . . And so I would like to invite to your ovation a very special person that I noticed almost as soon as I stepped on the stage tonight. Let's hear it for Maud from Chingford.''

With the entire auditorium straining to see her, and the boom of some two thousand deeply relieved people clapping at the sound of her name, Maud is finally coaxed out of her seat and up the stairs at the side of the stage into Dame Edna's waiting arms. ''Hello, darling. Hello, Maud. How nice to see you,'' Dame Edna says, giving her a big hug and a big smile. ''You delightful woman. You are absolutely delightful. And what lovely, lovely happiness you radiate, too. You do. Hairdresser's this morning, Maud?''

"No," says Maud.

"I didn't think so for a moment. However, never mind." In the moment between the uplift of Edna's compliment and the sting of her putdown, Humphries winks at Maud to disown the laugh and relax her fear.

"Barry's got the audience so well drilled that they all laugh at the same time," Ian Davidson says. "They're a solid mass. And they all turn to their partners to seek confirmation. You can see this. I've sat in the box and watched the audience. Between the moment of laughter and when they turn for corroboration, there is a moment of audience blindness. The audience isn't looking at the stage. You can do things in that moment. Barry usually smiles and winks at his victim."

Maud is ushered, laughing, offstage to be dolled up for the talk show. Dame Edna turns back to her audience. "And now my Hornchurch pilgrim, MARGARET! Here she is!"

But Margaret isn't budging.

"Come on, Margaret. Come on. Wait a minute. What's the matter, Margaret, darling?"

"I would prefer not to come," says Margaret.

"What? Mmn."

"I would prefer not to come."

"No?" says Dame Edna. "But the audience would love you to come. And to be branded a spoilsport would be horrible, Margaret. Wouldn't it be ghastly? Leaving the theatre, people spitting on you. I mean . . . I think the little bank manager next to you is trying to discourage you, isn't he, darling? Is he? You're the first woman who's ever rejected my offer, Margaret. Isn't that sad? I hope it doesn't bring you *terrible luck* for the rest of your life. What is Margaret's seat number? Ah, yes, yes. You would have—you would have won the BMW. Ha, ha. I'm so sorry. Never mind. Some people are killjoys, aren't they? It's a lovely opportunity to meet an understudy. A woman who we've spoken to before and she's longing to come up and join me. And what an ovation she'll get when she does. It's the lovely EMMA!"

Emma, tonight's erstwhile nude cartwheelist, gets a big hand and is greeted by Edna with fulsome praise for her "little outfit." Says Dame

Edna, "I think you've paid me a great compliment coming straight from work to my show."

The audience creases up. Humphries gives Emma the wink and rounds on the uproarious crowd. *"Please! Don't be so rude! Have your manners just flown out the window?"* To which the answer, happily, is yes.

"Now let's hear it for Dame Edna's seminal, pivotal, mold-breaking, and revolutionary TALK SHOW!"

In conventional talk shows, the host listens while the guests talk, but with Dame Edna, who assumes that the guests are there for her amusement, the formula is reversed. They have to listen hard while *she* talks. Rarely is she bested. Dame Edna once probed former Prime Minister Ted Heath about his homes and the names of his Spanish staff. "I have a cleaning lady called Purificación," said Dame Edna. "And I have another Spanish helper, called Contracepción."

Said Mr. Heath, sharpish, "How do you get the two to work together?"

TV viewers had the unusual sight of Dame Edna laughing out loud at repartee that beat even her to the draw.

The show tries to exploit Dame Edna's confusion of reality and the credulity of the viewing public. "Most upmarket London penthouses have very highly trained Filipino staff," Dame Edna said in one show. "Mine is no exception. Except the little woman who smilingly Vims my vanitary unit is my next guest. She's the former First Lady of all Filipinos. Yes. IMELDA MARCOS!"

"Imelda Marcos" entered to studio-audience applause, took a bow, and began walking toward Edna. "She's wearing my shoes!" Dame Edna said in horror, blowing a whistle she had taken from her purse. A barking mastiff bounded across the set and chased the stand-in offstage. In Dame Edna's first series of shows, "Charlton Heston" appeared in a wheelchair at the top of the set's steep and dangerous staircase. "It's just a bad sprain," he said. Dame Edna sent a nurse to help him. "Heston" and the nurse proceeded to tumble down the stairs. So real did the stunt look that Humphries' other guests, who could see "Heston" only on the monitors, were terror-stricken. The real Heston subsequently received thousands of get-well letters until he appeared on the show the following week in one handsome piece. Other public figures have met similar disasters. "Kurt Waldheim" appeared at the top of Dame Edna's stairway only to be dropped through a trapdoor. And "the Duchess of Kent," on her entrance, was snared in a booby trap and swung from her heels as Dame Edna signalled for a station break.

Dame Edna gives her non-celebrity guests a much gentler ride. Dressed as a nun, an Edna look-alike, a punk rocker, and a showgirl, the guests cram onto Dame Edna's postmodern sofa like so many dummies on a ventriloquist's knee. Dame Edna gets them to nod and respond while she pretends to ask for some collective wisdom about her wayward daughter, Valmai. "She shoplifts now, she does," Dame Edna says, keeping her guests captive with the cold intensity of her eye contact. "She goes into some of those Bond Street shops. She steals things. Puts them in her panty hose. Particularly frozen chickens when she's in a supermarket. Of course, the store detectives can smell those barbecued chickens when she goes out. Because she's a human microwave. She thinks she's an art collector. She thinks she's Peggy Guggenheim. That name ring a bell? She collects primitive art. New Guinea sculpture. Do you know much about New Guinea sculpture, Maud?"

"No," says Maud, running the gamut of her dialogue for the evening.

"You're missing nothing, darling. It is grotesque. It's mostly wooden willies."

And, with the notion of penises firmly planted in the audience's mind, it's a quick segue to the Gladdydämmerung that has been Edna's traditional spectacle of mayhem since the mid-sixties. "There's nothing more holy," Dame Edna said in "An Evening's Intercourse," "than massed gladioli." And, from the audience's delight, so it would seem. "It's gladdy time," says Dame Edna, frog-marching her accomplices downstage to the footlights. "There's some glads I want you to throw one at a time *gently* into the audience. Don't forget to let go. The Flinging Nun. It's gladdy time, a very beautiful moment in my famous show. Gladdy time. I mean, what other show . . . Could you imagine Barry Manilow doing this? Or Stevie Wonder?" Dame Edna throws a gladdy over her shoulder. *"Not in a million years! Not in a million years!"*

Dame Edna propels each gladdy higher, until the audience is watching gladioli fly up to boxes three tiers high.

"What about me, Dame Edna?" calls a woman from a fourth-tier box.

There's a drumroll. Dame Edna backhands the gladdy up to her. It falls short of its target. Another drumroll. Another try. The gladdy arches up past the follow spot. The woman reaches for it, and, with an ear-piercing scream, topples out of the box.

People beneath her shriek and scatter as she holds on and clambers up.

"Has anyone got a blanket?" Dame Edna shouts, and then she passes down a blanket from the stage. There is a moment of pandemonium. Panicked theatregoers are cowering by the exit doors. Four stalwart members of the audience hold the gray blanket beneath the woman, bracing themselves to catch her.

"Heaven be praised! There was a rope ladder in that box," Dame Edna says. "Oh, wouldn't it be ghastly if that happened every night!"

Harriet Bowdler, the stage manager, turns to me. "He'll probably be in a good mood for the rest of the show. He enjoyed it. They look silly."

"Up, up, up! Hold your gladdy by the end of the stem for maximum gladdy thrust. And when I give the word—there we are, darling—up, up. What a beautiful sight!"

The audience sings "The Gladdy Song" with Dame Edna, and, at her command, stands and trembles the gladdies. The evening is almost over, but not before the proper benedictions and the absolution of applause. The guests are sent back to their seats with appropriate gifts: Camembert, Nivea cream, Steradent, a jar of Vaseline, a pair of Norm's Y-fronts, along with flowers and bottles of champagne. Before Edna's Assumption, there remains the blessing of her disciples. Maud, who is the last to leave the stage, is asked to bow her head. "Isn't it pathetic that this is the highlight of her life?" Dame Edna confides to the audience. And then she waves a gladiolus over Maud's head and recites:

> Lucky possum that you are,
> You are now a mini-star.

A big fish in a tiny pond,
Thanks to my magic wand.
Timid once, now you are bolder
Since Edna's gladdy
Touched your shoulder.
Go forth now, be kind and true,
Like Dame Edna was to you.

Soon dry ice is filling the stage with smoke, and Dame Edna's apotheosis is in its full magnificent swing. She has saved the most spectacular stage picture for last as she rises on the hydraulic lift high above the audience, singing about her shyness. No one in the audience wants Dame Edna shy. Everyone wants her as loud and vulgar and daring as she always is. Everyone wants her never at a loss, but filling life with the articulate energy of great clowning:

Yet, I must confess that I've felt
slightly better since
You've helped me sublimate my grief-stricken reticence.
So . . . now . . . goooodbye.
I've got my act together and my head held high,
So high.
I'm a merry widow with a roving eye,
Yet I get so terribly shy
When the time finally comes for me to say
Was it good for you, too, possums?
And goooodbye. . . . Good night.
Darlings.

The cherry picker deposits Dame Edna back onstage, and the din of applause and bravos continues over her bows. But she can't sit still for an audience even in its adulation. Dame Edna is twisting to a samba beat, blowing a carnival whistle, waving to her paupers. Her need for attention is no smaller than the audience's need for joy. Dame Edna doesn't want to leave the stage, and the audience doesn't want her to leave it. Even when the curtain falls, Dame Edna is still a presence. A spotlight lingers on her hand, which plays near the floor in front of the curtain. Behind the curtain, Dame Edna is on her stomach, gesturing into the noisy void. She begins by giving the audience a wave—"almost a caress," says Humphries—and ends by almost giving it the finger.

Outside, after the show, people linger under the dark-blue columns of the Drury Lane's portico. Maud from Chingford is exiting with her armful of gladioli. A young man within earshot says, "There's Maud. There's the star of the show."

She nods in his direction and walks slowly down the marble steps into the chill of the London night.

JACKIE MASON AND MORT SAHL

WORKING THE ROOM

Outside, it was over-coat weather, but inside at the Golden, where "Jackie Mason: Politically Incorrect" is currently moored, the air-conditioning was on—a sure sign that a comedian was in residence. By a comic's logic, people must be comfortable to receive uncomfortable ideas. Mason's arena consisted of a red podium, white stars projected on an aquamarine cyclorama, and an American flag tucked into the left-hand corner of the stage— none of which, when the time came, he ever used or referred to. Mr. Mason entered to the strains of "Living in America" and proceeded immediately to launch himself at the first rows. "This is a very interest-ing show, Mister," he said, pronouncing it "Mistuh." "Are you a homosexual?" At first glance, Mason is a chipper sad sack. He walks with a kind of sailor's roll, his potbelly preceding him by a few inches and housed under a natty gray double-breasted suit. This show of refine-ment is belied by his diction, which moves in and out of thick Yiddish inflection, turning "work," "words," and "girls" into "woik," "woids," and "goils." A small man with a big mouth, Mason stands before us in his sartorial propriety spilling out the impropriety of his doubts. "If you've got AIDS, you can come into this country," he says. "If you've got fruit, you can't." His sad, sunken eyes look out quizzi-cally. "Do you understand this?" he says, and he repeats the phrase frequently throughout the evening, his bafflement releasing howls of laughter from the audience, most of whom, in today's earnest, politi-cally correct climate, are afraid to admit the ambivalence of their hearts.

We live in a noisy republic. American democracy is always reinventing itself, and the air is loud with lamentation about change—either too much or too little. Change means loss, and loss is an uncomfortable feeling. And so Americans complain, and Mason, in particular, is in the avant-garde of the kvetching. In earlier, imperial times, Americans were obsessed with being winners; now, in our present sour moment, we're obsessed with being victims. And Mason is here to remind us that the empowered white middle-class majority feels victimized. "People today are being persecuted by minorities," he says, and his combative comedy insists on promoting, not silencing, the loud diversity essential to democracy. Mason, a former rabbi from a family of rabbis, uses the stage as his bully pulpit. Behind his shtick, which is sometimes vulgar but always funny, is a fundamentalist disgust at the world's fraud, wickedness, hypocrisy, and inhumanity—a disgust that gives him a curious aloofness and intensity. There are no morals; there are no standards; and now, worse luck for comedians, there are no more stereotypes.

Mason is no great comic mind, but he's a canny technician. His jokes, even when their conclusions are dubious, promote thought and tap into society's discontents. He presents himself as an ordinary Joe awash in the new relativism and double-teamed by hectoring activists. "Every time two homosexuals get together, there's a parade," he says. Mason's gripe is with liberal guilt, which he sees no reason for shouldering. On the issue of Louis Farrakhan's claim that the Jews were the slave owners of the world, Mason shrugs wearily and says, "Jews came from Kiev. When did they have slaves?" He goes on, "Every decent person wants equality for all people," and he admits that without political upheaval blacks wouldn't have made the advances they did. But, he adds, blacks have burned down their own neighborhoods. "When Jews start a fire," he says, "we know what to do. Every fire shows a profit." To Mason, the white establishment has as much backbone as a soufflé. He turns its timorous backpedalling into hilarious Milquetoast davening: "I don't know how I became a heterosexual. I'll try to get over it. I'll see what I can do about it. It's not definite. Just because I have it doesn't mean I'm stuck with it. I know I could get over it. Gimme a chance."

Even though the full house, on the night I saw the show, was poleaxed with pleasure, the critics have more or less mugged it. "There's something they see in me that's a menace, a revolution, a fear, a panic—I dunno what,'' Mason told me, with the bewilderment that figures as much in his offstage persona as in his professional one. ''They didn't even review me as a comedian. They reviewed me as though I were a problem.'' The problem is not his but theirs. Theatre is the proper arena for the illiberal as well as the liberal. When you're in the dark, facing the stage, surrounded by the laughter of others, repressed feelings can be coaxed out into the open. This can be both terrifying and thrilling, and you can see the panic and the elation on the faces of Mason's audience. Its members frequently laugh with their hands over their mouths, as if shocked at what Mason has called out of them. They are quite literally ''beside themselves,'' exhilarated at having the weight of their apologetic correctness momentarily lifted by Mason's outland-ishness. ''The only person you can fire is a white Protestant American Gentile,'' he says.

Comedy's anarchy is currently abused by a mimetic fallacy; that is, a feeling among certain segments of the society that jokes, like TV vio-lence, kill people. (On this issue of people's imitating behavior they see on TV, Mason also has a few words. ''You ever walk to the window after watching 'Superman' and say, 'I think I'll go to Pittsburgh'?'') Jokes don't kill people; what they kill is certainty, and activists can never forgive funnymen for this. To those hungry for progress, doubt is as welcome as modesty in a whore; but, while faith is nice, doubt gets you an education. And there's something to be learned about America's secret heart from listening both to Mason and to the response of his audience. He is not chic, he is not an intellectual (unless studying psychology in college counts), but he knows about middle-class guilt and about the inhibiting fear of public humiliation. ''Freedom of speech is now in reverse,'' he says in his show. ''People are panicky to express themselves, because they feel guilty. They're nervous. They're jumped on as soon as they say anything that could be implied as prejudice, even if it's ridiculous. But blacks are free to express themselves. They made a picture 'White Men Can't Jump.' Everybody enjoyed it. But if you made a picture 'Shvartzers Can't Fly'?''

Mason is skeptical about affirmative action. ''How come there's no affirmative action for Jews?'' he asks the audience. ''Fifteen years ago, Jews couldn't get into medical school.'' And he goes on, ''In order to compensate for the sins of the past, they are lowering the mark to make it easier for blacks and Hispanics to get into college. If a Jew wants to get into medical school, he needs an 89.9 average. If you're Hispanic, thirty-two is enough. If you're black, two. I'm not against affirmative action. If you have affirmative action for blacks and Hispanics so that they can go into medical school with a lower mark, why shouldn't there be lower basketball nets for the Jews?'' It's Mason's contention that much of what is called discrimination is simply cultural difference. ''There never was a Jewish hockey player thirty years ago,'' he says. ''If they applied the same measurement to the Jews as to the blacks, you could claim it as a civil-rights problem. It has nothing to do with civil rights. The simple fact is that a Jew doesn't become a hockey player because he doesn't *want* to be a hockey player. When a Jew sees sticks flying around, he knows it's not for him. He could get hurt. As soon as sticks are flying back and forth, a Jew looks for a Gentile and says, 'Listen, Mister. That's for you.' A Jew not only doesn't stay in the rink —he doesn't even watch it from the front row. A Jew knows in case of an accident he doesn't want to be even near it. He stays in the back with binoculars.''

At intermission, the people next to me were deep in discussion about Mason's act. ''What's his cause?'' a young man asked. Mason's cause— any authentic comedian's cause—is intellectual freedom. ''Is democracy only for candidates?'' he says, setting his sights on President Clinton at the beginning of Act II. ''Does he have a right to lie to you, and you don't have a right to mention it?'' All genuine comedy is politically incorrect: challenging assumptions, testing limits, crossing boundaries, disabusing the public of its most firmly held beliefs. Mason ends the evening by spelling out the comic mission: ''The purpose is to commemorate the right to talk freely.'' The ordinary citizen can't and won't risk this, so we pay people like Mason a king's ransom to act out this dream of freedom for us. Mason doesn't really have a second act, but it hardly matters. The show's announced theme shifts to more generalized topical observations about the state of the nation, and the amperage of danger and dyspepsia drops accordingly. Mason is best when he uses the language of the man on the street to report on the big issues of state— especially the national-health-care proposals. To hear the audience laugh at Mason's imitation of public misunderstanding is to see how badly the government has communicated its policy. "There's not one guy who understands this program," Mason says, and he proceeds to act out a typical discussion. " 'How will it work?' 'You go into the doctor's office, and . . . as soon as the doctor sees ya, then all of a sudden that's it.' 'Who's gonna pay for it?' 'Whoever has the money.' 'Where will the money come from?' 'It'll come from . . . the people . . . who have it.' " Mason also teases, among many things, New York's inept Indian taxi drivers (" 'You know this city?' '*I* know this city.' *Calcutta* he knows") and Clinton's doublespeak about marijuana. "I smoked it, but I didn't inhale." Mason holds out his small hands and clucks. "Let's be honest. Would you put a pastrami sandwich in your mouth if you didn't want to swallow?"

"Mort Sahl's America" brings one of the innovative funnymen of the fifties and sixties back to New York from L.A. after a seven-year absence. Sahl doesn't so much have an axe to grind as he has a living to grind out. He is, as he tells us, an odd-job man on the lecture circuit and at the movie studios, where he rewrites films ranging from Robert Redford's "Ordinary People" to Sydney Pollack's "The Firm." Suntanned and sharp-eyed, Sahl bounces onto the Theatre Four stage in a red V-neck sweater and blue button-down shirt, promising us news of politics and of the war between the sexes (he's recently divorced but dating again), and delivers neither, really, but he does it with enormous laid-back charm. This is the man who characterized three generations of sexual politics in a single joke, which is still one of my all-time favorites: "In the fifties, you had to be a Jew to get a girl. In the sixties, you had to be a black to get a girl. In the seventies, you had to be a girl to get a girl." At the beginning of the show, an announcer rolls Sahl's credits, letting us know that Bill Clinton has called him "the Will Rogers of his generation." Rogers twirled a rope; Sahl spins yarns about the rich, famous, and corrupt. He tells how his friend Woody Allen said that Sahl's humor had changed his comedy and his life. Then he tells of seeing Allen recently at the Russian Tea Room and sending the maître d' over with the line "Tell him the man who changed his life would like to see him." Allen, in this account, embraces Sahl, saying, "Can you change it *back?*"

Sahl is sharply intelligent but too witty to be vulgar, and this is too bad. He doesn't punch the heart of his audience so much as flatter its head. His gig is more a series of cocktail-party set pieces than a show. "Comedians are out to lunch," he says. "They think comedy is to help you escape from the truth rather than highlight it." Sahl is certainly not escaping, but he's not attacking, either; he's vamping. His America turns out to be talk shows, movie studios, cocktail parties, and Presidential banquets, with an occasional detour into the Warren Report. In fact, he reads verbatim a snatch of Earl Warren and the then Representative Gerald Ford interviewing a barman, Curtis LaVerne Crafard, who had worked at Jack Ruby's Carousel Club before he was seized by F.B.I. men as he hightailed it out of town the day after the Kennedy assassination, saying, "They're not going to pin this on me." In the interview, Warren asks him what he did before he was a bartender. "I was a master sniper in the Marine Corps," Crafard says. Warren's next question is "What kind of entertainment did they have at the club?" It's the one pure moment of political comedy in a show that otherwise bears out one of Sahl's best quips: "An intellectual in show business is like the smartest bear in the zoo."

PETER COOK

BEDAZZLED

THE LEGEND OF A GREAT comedian dies with him. He lives in the moment, passing time with a generation or two, whose deliriums he identifies and sends up. The culture, too, dies a little death, and loses part of that promise of delight which is each funnyman's gift to us. Peter Cook was a comedian's comedian, who died, too young, at fifty-seven, on January 9, 1995, of a gastrointestinal hemorrhage. "Oh, God, the fucker's dead. There's a hole in the universe" is what Cook's former sidekick Dudley Moore thought when he got the news. Cook and Moore, along with Alan Bennett and Jonathan Miller, were part of the famous revue "Beyond the Fringe," which blasted the parochial shackles off English humor in the early sixties; they went on together to create the beloved (and much imitated) working-class palaver of "Pete n' Dud" and their scatological yobbo counterparts "Derek and Clive." "Pete's wife, Lin, called me about one in the morning to tell me he'd died," says Moore, who called it quits with revue sketches and with Cook in 1977. "I kept waking up afterward with this terrible sense of dread. So I phoned his home just to get his answering machine and to hear his voice."

When Cook was sober, his voice was elegant, polite, conventionally upper middle class; but his comic voice—the flat, reedy, nasal drone, with its bizarre phraseology, which he projected onto a series of preoccupied working-class and lower-middle-class obsessives—is what almost single-handedly took British comedy into fresh, bracing territory. "He was the greatest creator of comic material that I've ever come across," says John Cleese, one of the Monty Python team, who aped Cook's discoveries. "It was almost discouraging. Whereas most of us would take six hours to write a good three-minute sketch, it actually took

Peter three minutes to write a three-minute sketch. I always thought he was the best of us, and the only one who came near being a genius, because genius, to me, has something to do with doing it much more easily than other people." In his life, Cook sometimes came face-to-face with this kind of praise. In 1979, the BBC broadcaster David Dimbleby asked Cook how he felt about being "probably the funniest Englishman since Chaplin." Cook thought about it; then, in his bland trademark twang, he said, "Well, this is no time for false modesty."

Cook's blessing and his burden was that as a teen-ager he came into British public life with his comic skills almost fully formed. He had already worked out his major comic maneuver: to combine the suburban with the surreal. He was amazingly fluent and freewheeling. The first sightings of Cook were decidedly sensational. He was tall, sinuous, and exceedingly charming. His combination of wit and aloofness made him catnip to both sexes. "There was something almost Firbankian about him," the Australian comic Barry Humphries, whom Cook helped to get a foothold in Britain, recalls. "He had the English public-school boy's habit of tossing back a forelock. He was one of those English people you can't quite reach. He was all the time joking. He never spoke seriously about anything for a second, so one didn't get near him."

Cook wasn't comfortable in the world, and he lived in a climate of mockery. At his public school, Radley, Cook had written a few farces; one was called "He Who Laughs." "It might be described as a posthumous work," he explained after he was installed at Pembroke College, Cambridge, where he became president of the Footlights Revue. "It was put on after I left, and I never saw it myself." Jonathan Miller first saw Cook—"an astonishing, strange, glazed, handsome creature producing weird stuff the like of which I'd never heard before"—in the Footlights Revue. "I remember the first time I was shot upright in my seat by him," Miller says. "He was playing some person in a suburban kitchen concealed behind a newspaper. He didn't say a word. But all eyes were drawn to him. Then he rustled the paper and simply said, 'Hello, hello! I see the *Titanic*'s sunk again.' One knew one was in the presence of comedy at right angles to all the comedy we'd heard." Dudley Moore was also impressed by the crazy logic and the sophistication of Cook's material. Moore remembers Cook at eighteen writing a sketch about a one-legged man auditioning for Tarzan. Cook, whose father was a colonial diplomat, played an appeasing film director. "I've got nothing against your right leg," the director says. "The trouble is, neither have you."

Cook's imagination, like his language, had the habit of taking absurdist turns, which impressed the old pros as much as the Young Turks. As an undergraduate, Cook contributed his comedy material not just to university revues but to well-known comedians, like the beaky, high-camp Kenneth Williams, who used Cook's routines for the bulk of his hit revue "Pieces of Eight" (1959). In one memorable sketch, which perhaps foreshadowed the most famous of Cook's gallery of demented sad sacks (the rumpled and wacky E. L. Wisty), Williams entered with a box, sat on the stage, and confided, "I've got a viper in this box. It's a viper. It's not an asp. It's a viper." The line quickly became a comic catchphrase. Even before Cook himself was a public figure, his comic voice—the banal monotone—was being widely imitated. "He must have left Cambridge in the summer of 1960, and I arrived in October," Cleese says. "His presence was still very much alive. Everybody was doing him. When I was doing the 1962 Footlights Revue, dear old Trevor Nunn, who was directing it, would sit down in the rehearsal breaks and do Peter Cook sketches. So we knew Peter's voice, and some of his material, before we'd ever set eyes on him."

Cleese, along with most of the theatregoing public on both sides of the Atlantic, set eyes on Cook during the five-year run of "Beyond the Fringe" on the West End and Broadway. "It was the funniest thing I've ever seen," he says. "And it remains that." According to Jonathan Miller, Cook contributed "a larger part of the script than anyone else." What distinguished him, Alan Bennett says, "Was this effortless facility to improvise." In "Beyond the Fringe," Bennett had to follow one of Cook's solo spots. "It was supposed to go on for eight minutes," Bennett recalls. "And he would go on for twenty. Of course, it was wonderful stuff." Cook's monologue was a virtuoso bit of improvising; the thrill was in watching him ride the crest of that improvisational wave and remain elegantly on top of his material. The monologue began famously:

Yes, I could have been a judge but I never had the Latin, never
had the Latin for the judging, I just never had sufficient of it to get
through the rigorous judging exams. They're noted for their rigor.
People come staggering out saying, "My God, what a rigorous
exam—" And so I became a miner instead. A coal miner. I
managed to get through the mining exams—they're not very rigorous, they only ask you one question, they say "Who are you?"
and I got seventy-five percent on that.

Even in the sketches that were written collaboratively, Cook's scorn
for oafishness and his fierce, ironic understatement make his contributions easy to spot. In "Civil War," a sketch about what to do in case of
a nuclear attack, Cook hectored the audience in his best pukka posture:
"Get right out of it—get right out of it—If you're out of it you're well
out of it, if you're in it you're really in it. If you are caught in it when
the missile explodes, for goodness' sake don't move, stand absolutely
stock-still—not under a tree, of course—that could be extremely dangerous."

Cook has been dubbed "a master of satire" by the British newspapers,
but satire wants to create a seismic disruption, and Cook was no instinctive disturber of the peace. "The idea that he had an anarchic, subversive view of society is complete nonsense," Jonathan Miller says. "He
was the most upstanding, traditional upholder of everything English and
everything establishment." Alan Bennett concurs: "He wasn't interested in satire at all. He was interested in being funny. I think he didn't
like some of the harder-edge stuff, because it wasn't funny enough. He
wasn't particularly into making any points. The thing that was political
was his imitation of Prime Minister Macmillan. Nobody had ever done
that on the stage before. When Macmillan came to the show, everybody
knew he was there, so it was quite funny to begin with. But then Peter
just started going for him; and he went on and on until the audience fell
nearly totally silent. It never bothered him if he lost the audience. He
was immune to embarrassment."

Cook's humor was not so much a shrewd method of attack as an
ingenious style of retreat. His characters kept the public (and him)

captivated and at a distance from deep emotion. Talking about psycho-analysis, and about the quest to "find" oneself, he told the New York *Times* in 1973, "I have a feeling that what I'd find I wouldn't like in the least, and nobody else would, either." There was a strange inconsistency between Cook's debonair façade—the part of him that Miller calls "the handsome paragon"—and the nervy, threadbare characters who inhabited him and were a barometer of some deeper impoverishment. As early as 1959, in one of his first interviews, Cook spoke of the appeal of these characters. "Sometimes I think of old men who live alone in single rooms," he said. "I see them listening to their portable radio sets and charting news bulletins, which then take on great importance in their pathetic little lives. They become amusing, not because one pokes fun at them, but because they make unimportant things seem important and base their lives on false premises." Cook didn't so much invent the characters as let the characters take him over. "It was like somebody was speaking through him," Alan Bennett says. And Miller adds, "I never knew Peter to be funny in his own voice. He was an interesting, amiable, pleasant, home-counties Tory. Quite suddenly, this other voice would speak through him, and then he would be taken possession of, sometimes for two or three hours at a stretch." In later years, as Cook's appetite for alcohol increased and he became more chaotic, his friends frequently found that the only way to be with him was to enter his fantasy. "There wasn't any ordinariness there," Bennett says. "There wasn't any just sitting around chatting. He'd go off into some riff or other. He was always performing."

But in the salad days of the sixties Cook was a kind of Sun King of Comedy, with a court of followers. No contemporary British comedian seized his moment with more generosity or ventilated English life with more raffish assurance. He used his newfound power and prestige to turn over the comic soil of Great Britain. Cook owned sixty-six percent of Britain's satirical magazine *Private Eye,* which he also helped to edit, and for which he invented the cartoon-bubble cover and such popular features as "True Stories" and "Mrs. Wilson's Diary." At *Private Eye,* where he was called Cookie by the editor, Richard Ingrams, and was known in print as Lord Gnome, Cook was very much the centerpiece. "I was sometimes appalled by the immoderate laughter that greeted all of Peter's *mots,*'' Humphries, who was still an upstart outsider, says. Humphries saw clearly that at the magazine the caste system of public school had been extended into real life. "It was run by the prefects, who were Cook, Ingrams, and Willie Rushton. And the fags were people like Tony Rushton, Willie's cousin, who did the layout, and Barry Fantoni, who contributed feuilletons. Occasionally, ravaged schoolmasters, like Claud Cockburn and Malcolm Muggeridge, were let into the prefects' study."

In 1961, Cook and a partner bankrolled The Establishment, billed as "London's First Satirical Nightclub"; characteristically, he drew a comparison for the press between his Soho "satirical venue" and Berlin cabaret, "which did so much to stop the rise of Hitler and prevent the outbreak of the Second World War." The Establishment is where such bright new comic lights as John Bird, Eleanor Bron, and John Fortune got their education in public; where Frankie Howerd had his spectacular renaissance; and where Lenny Bruce made his English début. It was also where Barry Humphries introduced Edna Everage to the British public. "It was courageous of Peter to put me there," says Humphries, whose housewife superstar was voted one of the idols of the decade by *The Observer* at the end of the eighties. "I don't think I did as well as I could have. I mystified people. Not many people turned up." Still, Cook backed Humphries and gave him a leg up into *Private Eye* by persuading the cartoonist Nicholas Garland to let Humphries write the text to the Barry McKenzie comic strip, a saga of a beer-swilling Aussie innocent, which became a cult satire of London high life and the subject of two feature films. "Peter's generosity was unusual in a profession notoriously self-seeking and fraught with petty jealousies," Humphries says.

By the mid-seventies, Cook's successful partnership with Dudley Moore was foundering. Cook, who had been the leader of the pack after "Beyond the Fringe," could still spin wonderful yarns, but his comrades in comedy had started to outpace him. Moore was getting interested in Hollywood movies, Bennett was writing West End plays, and Miller was directing theatre and opera all over the world. Cook, by contrast, was treading water. He began to drink; and those who, like Humphries, sometimes drank with him got another impression of his cavalier persona. "Peter was pretty well topped up most of the seventies and eighties," Humphries says. "He had too much of a sense of cosmic joke to ever reveal self-pity. I got the feeling of sorrow—sorrow about the end of the Dudley Moore alliance. Peter felt enormous frustration. I think rage is not an exaggeration."

Cook joked about his lack of ambition. "I suppose I have some regrets," he once said. "But I can't remember what they are." At other times, he was defiant: "I don't give a toss if people say I haven't fulfilled my promise." The real problem was that Cook's special kind of intellectual high jinks had nowhere to go. "He hated doing anybody else's words," Moore says. "He couldn't remember anybody else's words." Cook was a miniaturist. His gift was for the dead word, the daft deconstruction of logic, the surrealist aside. "Ideally, I like two at a time on the stage—and a four-minute duration of dialogue," he said in 1959; and his literary horizon never really expanded much farther than that. But within those parameters Cook could make huge, ineffable moments out of his characters' tiny minds. ("Oh, the same thing happened to me, Dud," Pete moans. "Knock, knock, knock at the window. Who's there? Bloody Greta Garbo! Wearing a see-through shortie nightdress. I said, 'Ged off!' ")

Cook had many cameo performances in movies, none of them particularly distinguished. "After his great stage and TV successes, he had nowhere to go, because basically the way up was via film," says Cleese, who, with Graham Chapman, wrote the 1970 film "The Rise and Rise of Michael Rimmer," in which Cook had the lead. "And although he was a great sketch performer, he wasn't a very good actor. I would suspect that it was something to do with the fact that he wasn't very comfortable with his emotions, and as an actor you have to be able to access your emotions. In the milieu where he grew up, emotions were kept very much out of the way, and were regarded as these occasional nuisances that surface and complicate life. And, as far as writing was concerned, he never got interested in writing longer pieces—in the problems of structuring a full-length thing." Cook did write a few movies. One of them, "Bedazzled" (1967), was his version of the Seven Deadly Sins, and had Raquel Welch cast as Lust—or, specifically, Miss Lillian Lust. "He didn't want the film to be called 'Bedazzled,' " says

Cook's friend the humorist Martin Lewis, who produced "The Secret Policeman's Other Ball" (1982), in which Cook was featured in many skits with the Python people. "He wanted it to be called 'Raquel Welch.' I inquired why, and he said because he fancied the marquee saying, 'Peter Cook and Dudley Moore in Raquel Welch.' He said, 'For some reason, the distributors didn't see the point.' "

Cook and Moore were magisterial in their mischief. "It was ideal," Cook said of their partnership. "I doubt if I will ever do anything better." The lanky Cook and the pint-size Moore cut a memorable comic silhouette. They sparked and amused each other with what John Bird calls "a spontaneous combustion of comic invention," and their legacy of liberating cut-and-thrust is visible in other contemporary British comic double acts: Mel Smith and Griff Rhys Jones, Stephen Fry and Hugh Laurie, Jennifer Saunders and Dawn French. In "Good Evening" (1973–75), a two-man show that toured around the world, with stops on Broadway (four hundred and thirty-eight performances) and the West End, the sludge of Pete and Dud's bluff discourse—the know-it-all versus the sycophant—made a hilarious spectacle of their ignorance and credulity. In one sketch, "Gospel Truth," Peter, dressed as a shepherd, is being interviewed by Dudley for the Bethlehem *Star* about the birth of Jesus:

> PETER: Yes. Well, it's quite simple, really . . . er . . . basically what happened was that me and the lads were abiding in the fields.
>
> DUDLEY (*writing*): Abiding in the fields . . . yes . . .
>
> PETER: Yes . . . mind you, I can't abide these fields . . .
>
> DUDLEY: No?
>
> PETER: I mean, look around you—they are unabidable fields.
>
> DUDLEY: Yeh . . .
>
> PETER: I'd say these are about the most unabidable bleeding fields I've ever had to abide in.
>
> DUDLEY: Yeh . . . I'll abide by that. (*Dudley laughs at his joke. Peter is unmoved.*) No . . . no . . . my apologies . . . You were abiding in the fields? . . .
>
> PETER: . . . and we were watching our flocks by night.

DUDLEY (*writing*): Watching our flocks by night . . .
yeh . . .

PETER: Yes . . . cos that's when you have to watch 'em, you
know, that's when they get up to all their rubbish.

In the ravings and songs of "Derek and Clive" Cook took the opportunity, according to Moore, "to do things that were very extraordinary
—very obscene things that we couldn't do on a regular basis." He adds,
"He wanted to scare the shit out of me, and now and again he did."
The first "Derek and Clive" record, which had "Warning, must not be
played to miners" stamped across it, is an exercise in liberty, and even
in the most stolid adult heart it can still inspire a vulgar sense of infantile
exhilaration. "Cook, even when drunk, elevated scatology to a lyrical
plane," Barry Humphries says. One Derek and Clive song, about a man
afraid to jump from a burning building, is set to a seventeenth-century
Christian chant. The crowd sings:

> Jump, you fucker, jump.
> Jump into this 'ere blanket
> What we are holding
> And you will be alright.
> He jumped. Hit the deck.
> Broke his fuckin' neck.
> There was no blanket.
> Laugh? We nearly shat.
> We have not laughed so much
> Since Grandma died
> Or Auntie Mabel caught
> Her left tit in the mangle.
> We are miserable sinners
>
> Filthy fuckers
> *Aaaahrsoles!*

By 1977, Moore and Cook had stopped performing together. "There
was nothing more to be done," Moore says. Moore wanted to change

the direction of his career ("I didn't want to do sketch material anymore. I wanted to do material where I could act"), and Cook, it seemed, couldn't change. In 1973, during the Australian tour of "Good Evening," Cook, who had been served with divorce papers by his first wife (he was married three times), began going onstage drunk. "I couldn't understand why for four or five days he was blitzed out of his mind, not apologizing for it and not aware, it seemed, of what chaos he was causing," Moore says. Over the years, with the success of "10" and "Arthur," Moore's celebrity grew; Cook's declined. "Greatly to his credit, he didn't resent the fact that Dudley had taken off," Alan Bennett says. "Dudley can't write. Peter could, and all the sketches were written by Peter. And then Dudley took off and made a fortune in Hollywood." But Moore admits to some "disease" between them over the last twenty years. In private, Cook may have denied any envy; but in public the tone of his quips told another story. "Perhaps if I had been born with a clubfoot and a height problem, I'd have been as desperate as Dudley to become a star," he said. Increasingly, drink became a problem. In the early seventies, a thirteen-week gig as a BBC live-talk-show host was cancelled after the first show, when Cook rose to greet his first guest, Kirk Douglas. Instead of asking "How are you?" Cook asked, "Who are you?"

Cook was a familiar figure on the Hampstead High Street, trudging to the supermarket in colored sneakers for his cigarettes and booze, his lithe figure now potbellied, his fingers nicotine-stained, his hair dyed blond. To Jonathan Miller, he seemed "a swollen, smoked, rather spirit-logged figure." Miller remembers that one day during this phase his wife, Rachel, spotted Cook. "Oh," she said. "Peter's gone prematurely orange."

By then, Cook had married his third wife, a Chinese woman named Lin Chong, who lived apart from him. "It was probably the first time he'd experienced a fairly ordinary, decent sort of love," Dudley Moore says. "Peter wasn't mad about women; he was a bit of a misogynist. He used to sort of adopt an attitude of the suburban working-class person who rather grumblingly accepts the fact of a woman in his household— 'Yes, dear, yes.' " This attitude may have been what drove his previous wives, Wendy Snowden and Judy Huxtable, to treat him with disdain. Humphries, who found Cook somewhat "henpecked" at home, recalls, "It was always quite a surprise, when one rather idolized him, to hear someone speaking to him as though he were a kind of fool, or even a cuckold."

When I met up with Cook at his dishevelled Hampstead mews house in the late eighties, to interview him for a book on Dame Edna, his shaky hand was spiking his morning coffee with Scotch; the sound of the doorbell sent him lurching to the window to peek out in case it was the tax collector, to whom he owed, he said, seventy thousand pounds. Last year, though, Cook made a scintillating appearance on a TV show called "Clive Anderson Talks Back," in which he performed as four guests—a judge, a soccer manager, a seventies rock star, and a biscuit quality controller. "The tragedy is that he was really getting his life under much greater control," John Cleese says. "He was looking much better. He was trimmer. Then he lost his mother, and he slipped back into drinking."

The news of Cook's death came as no surprise to Moore. "We all expected it," he said. "He was ingesting everything." Four years ago, Cook was warned by doctors to stop drinking. "He really loved drink more than he loved life," Cleese says. "At some point, he almost took the choice that he would rather live a shorter time and drink. That was the great sadness, because his close friends—and, latterly, I counted myself as being very, very close with him—made some feeble attempts to say something. He responded not in an unfriendly way but by slightly changing the subject, and also with a slightly humorous defiance."

Defiance was always part of the ironic game that Cook played with the English public. "One of the ways of avoiding being beaten by the system is to laugh at it," he said. He lived quietly, by his own defiant standards, lobbing his little jolts of joy and fury into the community when the voices came to him. Like all great comedians, he understood his gift well enough to know that he couldn't reliably control it. When you're hot, you're hot, as they say, and when you're not, you're not. His life made a spectacle of both sides of that equation: the glorious transformation and the punishing demoralization. He was resigned to his doomed contentment. As one of his characters, the restaurateur Sir Arthur Strebe-Greebling, owner of the Frog and Peach, puts it, "Oh, yes, I've learned from my mistakes and I'm sure I could repeat them exactly."

PART 2
PLAYWRIGHTS

OSCAR WILDE

RUNNING WILDE

On February 14, 1995, nearly five hundred people crowded into the south transept of Westminster Abbey in London to dedicate a diamond-shaped pane in the new stained-glass east window to the Irishman Oscar Wilde. The ceremony marked the centenary of Wilde's great comic triumph "The Importance of Being Earnest," which premièred at the St. James Theatre in 1895, a year that also saw the beginning of his tragic downfall. Four days after the play's opening, Lord Queensberry, the father of Wilde's twenty-four-year-old boyfriend, Lord Alfred Douglas, left his famously misspelled calling card at Wilde's club, insulting him as a "posing Somdomite." What began on March 1 as a libel action brought by Wilde, the most celebrated playwright and pundit of his age, ended on May 25 with Wilde becoming its most celebrated pariah. The master was reduced to the martyr, and sentenced to two years of hard time for his homosexual activities. Except for the poem "The Ballad of Reading Gaol," published in a private edition and under his prison cell number, C.3.3, Wilde never wrote again. When he died, at forty-six, in France, on November 30, 1900—stripped of his name, his family, his fortune, his library, and most of the fashionable English and French society which he'd entertained with his presence and his pen for nearly a quarter of a century—there were only fifty-six people at his funeral.

Wilde is very much our contemporary. "He belongs to our world more than to Victoria's," concludes Richard Ellmann in his massive biography of Wilde—a view with which Wilde, in a lifetime of self-promotion as an apostle of the New, heartily concurred. "The future is what artists are," Wilde once wrote, and of all the writers of the last

century he best foreshadowed the brilliance and barbarity of the individualism of our own era. Wilde's persona and his laughter—the twin
vehicles of his masquerade of equipoise—made a haunting myth of the
coming century's intoxications: fame, glamour, pleasure, and self-destruction. He is, as Ellmann says, "one of us" not so much because he
championed women's rights or prison reform as because he was famous
before he'd achieved anything; because he refused to suffer; and because
he was betrayed by his romantic imagination.

As Wilde knew, he was his greatest creation. He was an ungainly six
feet three (his feckless older brother, Willie, was six feet four); he was
unathletic (he walked with an "odd elephantine gait") and unhandsome
("The plainness of his face," the actress Lillie Langtry said, "was
redeemed by the splendour of his great, eager eyes"). Wilde used the
charm of his genius to make himself and his mischievous ideas irresistible. "I altered the minds of men and the colours of things: there was
nothing I said or did that did not make people wonder," he wrote to
Lord Alfred Douglas from prison, in a fifty-thousand-word letter later
published as "De Profundis." "I awoke the imagination of my century
so that it created myth and legend around me: I summed up all systems
in a phrase, and all existence in an epigram." In this, as in so much of
his writing, Wilde was exactly right—and exactly wrong. The mind he
most spectacularly altered was his own.

Wilde grew up in a climate of fierce expectation, nurtured by the fame
of his physician father, William, an eye and ear specialist, and the
vainglorious dreams of his celebrated mother, the poet Lady Wilde,
who liked to be known by her nom de plume, Speranza, and who,
although her great-grandfather was a bricklayer, claimed Dante as her
ancestor. At her knee, Wilde learned the gospel of attainment: "God
alone *is*; Man is *becoming*," she said; she also said, "The *Wildes* are
destined for celebrity and pinnacles." Her son made a production of her
notion of perfectability. By the time he came down from Magdalen
College, Oxford, in 1878—he was twenty-four and had earned a
double first in Greats—he had already worked out the personal theatrics
that allowed him to crash not just English society but English consciousness. He hired a voice coach to eliminate Irishness from his accent. ("I

want a natural style with a touch of affectation," he told his teacher.) He turned to theatre *costumiers,* not tailors, for the dramatic sartorial outline that was bound to make a proper spectacle of him. "Success," Wilde wrote after he'd achieved some, "is a science. If you have the right conditions, you get the results." The first condition of fame is, of course, to be talked about. (The Latin root of "fame" means "rumor.") Once in London, Wilde set about creating what he called "the fiction of position." He surrounded himself with "beautiful people," a phrase that he coined. He wanted stardom, was starstruck: he often wrote poems to his favorite performers. (Later, always with an eye to the main chance, he would send them his verse dramas.) He was briefly the secretary to the actress Lillie Langtry, and he travelled to Folkestone to strew lilies at the feet of Sarah Bernhardt. With his flattery and his fine mind, Wilde soon won the allegiance of Bernhardt, Ellen Terry, Henry Irving, and Madame Modjeska, who was bemused by his social precocity. "What has he done?" she asked. "He has written nothing, he does not sing or paint or act—he does nothing but talk. I do not understand."

Wilde gave himself the title "Professor of Aesthetics," and fanned the flames of controversy with his stunts (arriving at a party with a snake around his neck) and his sass. "I have come to dine with you," he told William Spottiswode, striding uninvited into Spottiswode's Grosvenor Square drawing room. "I thought you would like to have me." It took Wilde two years to establish his name and his act in London. "My art was to me, the great primal note by which I had revealed, first myself to myself, and then myself to the world," he wrote later, adding, "I was a man who stood in symbolic relations to the art and culture of my age." Indeed, Wilde thrust himself into that position. In a sense, he was the first performance artist. He treated the world as a figment of his imagination, and everyone in it as an extra in his epic. "One should either be a work of art, or wear a work of art," he said famously. Wilde's wit always had the last word, and the best one; his extravagant persona, seen against the backdrop of stolid Victorian respectability, was a sendup of the dullness and Philistine vulgarity of Victorian life. "Everything Oscar does is a deliberate trap for the literalist," Henry James said. Wilde opposed the cult of utility with his own cult of beauty, and held himself up as a model of being, not doing. He used himself and his aphorisms to force society to think against itself. He was a militant disguised as a fashion plate, flaunting the grave authority of the era's muscular Christianity with the light touch of his pagan frivolity. He was, as in Stanislavsky's definition of acting, "living truthfully under imaginary circumstances."

Having successfully invented himself as a dandy of detachment, Wilde proceeded to take his production on the road, first on a series of lecture tours, begun in 1882, that made his name in America, and, later, when his literary performance had caught up with his public one, through stage surrogates of himself. There was Lord Illingworth in "A Woman of No Importance" ("He is *myself*," Wilde said); Lord Goring in "An Ideal Husband" ("He plays with life," says the stage direction. "He is fond of being misunderstood"); Algy in "The Importance of Being Earnest." In the meantime, he entered into a marriage of inconvenience with Constance Lloyd, fathered two sons (Cyril, 1885; Vivyan, 1886), accepted the editorship of the monthly *Women's World,* and set himself up in a Tite Street town house. The house—full of light, its walls yellow, its woodwork and dining-room furniture white—was designed, like Wilde's persona, to banish Victorian sombreness. Wilde's sudden burst of literary activity—his reputation was vast, but his literary life, in terms of real productivity, lasted less than ten years—began in the late eighties, and corresponds almost exactly with the period of his homosexual awakening. A man, Wilde wrote, "may commit a sin against society, and yet realize through that sin his true perfection." And, "What the paradox was to me in the sphere of thought, perversity became to me in the sphere of passion." The fierce pleasure and guilt of Wilde's "feasting with panthers" gave him something intense to express and made his game with society more dangerous and exciting.

So Wilde, who tried to keep up the façade of respectable married life while trolling in Soho for trade, became a man of masks. "It is not wise to show one's heart to the world," Wilde wrote to a friend, in 1894. "As seriousness of manner is the disguise of the fool, folly in its exquisite modes of triviality and indifference and lack of care is the robe of the wise man. In so vulgar an age as this we all need masks." Dissimulation was for Wilde first a style, then an aesthetic, and, finally, a destiny. His deluxe persona and his laughter incarnated the equanimity and the invincibility of perfect individualism: "One who is not worried or wounded or maimed or in danger." Wilde, of course, was all of these, and disguised it. He preached dissimulation in his criticism ("Decay of Lying"); he dramatized it onstage ("Bunburying"); and he practiced it in life. Wilde saw life as "complex and relative," and his literary pronouncements express his need to disabuse life of its certitudes: "To have a style so gorgeous that it conceals the subject is one of the highest achievements," he wrote. This and countless epigrams like it were the outward manifestations of his manic defensiveness: a show of mastery to reverse his fears—fears of, as he put it, "failure, disgrace, poverty, sorrow, despair, suffering, tears even, the broken words that come from the lips of pain, remorse that makes one walk in thorns, conscience that condemns." Wilde needed big magic to contain his anguish, and as a result he was caught in a perpetual performance of his brilliance. "To become a spectator at one's life," Wilde said of his role playing, "is to escape the suffering of life."

Suffering, it seems, is what Wilde pitched his entire being against. "I shunned sorrow and suffering of every kind. I hated both," Wilde wrote later, from prison. "I resolved to ignore them as far as possible, to treat them, that is to say, as modes of imperfection. They were not part of my scheme of life. They had no place in my philosophy." Wilde chose to submerge himself in Beauty and Pleasure; and to use his intellectual power to transmute his sense of doom into a playful sense of paradox. In "The Importance of Being Earnest," he laughs his pessimism off the stage:

> ALGERNON: I hope to-morrow will be a fine day, Lane.
> LANE: It never is, sir.
> ALGERNON: Lane, you're a perfect pessimist.
> LANE: I do my best to give satisfaction, sir.

The prowess of Wilde's wit allowed him to live "where sorrow was not allowed." In his first term at Oxford, when Wilde read Walter Pater's "Renaissance" ("that book which had such a strange influence over my life''), he had been struck by ''how Dante places low in the Inferno those who willfully live in sadness.'' Wilde's university friends had dubbed him ''O'Flighty,'' which teased both his middle name— O'Flahertie—and his grandiosity. But the nickname was more prophetic than they knew. Flight became Wilde's modus vivendi. Even the name he used in exile, ''Sebastian Melmoth,'' borrowed from the hero of his great-uncle's Gothic novel ''Melmoth the Wanderer,'' invoked the notion of perpetual retreat.

What was Wilde running from? The charisma of Wilde's comic image has blinded even his most sagacious biographers from the darkness of his childhood. Ellman writes that ''Wilde seems to have had an untroubled upbringing,'' but this is simply to take Wilde at his public word. In ''De Profundis,'' he wrote of inheriting from his parents both a great name and a great place in the intellectual history of his time; but his destiny, as it played out, also points to an inheritance of doom—a tendency toward self-destructiveness—that both parents, despite their manic activity, passed on to their sons. When Oscar was born, Speranza, in the course of recounting her blessings to a friend, proclaimed eerily, ''Life has such infinite possibilities of woe.'' Wilde's sister, Isola, died at the age of ten, and the family doctor noted the twelve-year-old Oscar's ''lonely and inconsolable grief.'' An atmosphere of loss fed the Wilde household's frantic energy. Speranza had been drawn to Sir William Wilde by his attainment and his celebrity, but in marriage and family life, the wiry, restless Sir William proved considerably less vivacious. Speranza once wrote to a friend:

> He has a strange, nervous, hypochondriacal home nature which the world never sees—only I and often it makes me miserable. My husband so brilliant to the world envelops himself in a black pall and is grave, stern, mournful and silent as the grave itself. Although I have my high-spirit and have long warred bravely against this gloom, yet at length his despondency has infected me and now I am nearly as gloomy as himself. This is bad, so tell me how to keep up the bright vivid nature I once had, which made all things possible to me—when I ask him what could make him happy he

answers *death*. . . . His whole existence is one unceasing mental activity.

Sir William, who is rarely acknowledged in Wilde's public utterances, is mentioned significantly in Constance Wilde's correspondence with their son Vivyan, after Wilde's imprisonment. "Try not to feel too horribly about your father," she wrote. "Remember that he is your father and he loves you. All his troubles arose from the hatred of a son for a father." Sir William, a great womanizer, was a source of humiliation for Oscar and his family. He fathered two illegitimate daughters and was the subject of a notorious sexual-harassment scandal in which the plaintiff, Mary Travers, was granted a farthing for her honor, and Sir William was charged with paying the substantial two-thousand-pound court costs. On the other hand, Wilde idealized Speranza. ("She was one of the great figures of the world," he said, with no irony, adding elsewhere that she "intellectually ranks with Elizabeth Barrett Browning, and historically with Madame Roland.") She, like her husband, was a whirlwind of activity (thirteen books, three children); but would often, as Wilde put it, "dip into pessimism." She characterized her moods as "black, bleak, and unutterably desolate," and, like her son after her, chose action as the antidote to anxiety. "I want excitement. Excitement is my genius," Speranza wrote. "I should like to range through life—this orthodox creeping is too tame for me—ah, this wild rebellious ambitious nature of mine."

So Wilde grew up a product of both privilege and neglect, like the baby left in a handbag at Victoria Station in "The Importance of Being Earnest." Despite Speranza's flashy talk, she was, according to a close acquaintance, "most inconsistent and in many ways foolish"; her protestations of love to her children and her presence were at odds, leaving Wilde with a sense of being at once empowered and unloved, idealized and unlovable. Even when Wilde was a thirteen-year-old public-school boy, a letter home to Speranza is strategically pitched to elicit a reaction by appealing to her greatest passion—her literary career. "Don't please forget to send me the *National Review*," Wilde wrote, about the paper in which she had a poem. And, "You never told me anything about the publisher in Glasgow, what does he say . . . ?"

"A mother's love is very touching, of course," Wilde observed in "A Woman of No Importance." "But it is often curiously selfish. I mean, there is a great deal of selfishness in it." When Wilde edited *Women's World* he gave his mother work; in his criticism, he gave his mother credit (or risked her hectoring: "Why didn't you name *me*? Me who holds such a historic place in Irish literature," she wrote after one of his reviews). When she moved to London in 1879, Wilde even made appearances at her Sunday salons. ("Desperate affairs," Shaw said.) Oscar fulfilled his mother's dream of literary greatness to such a degree that she joked, "I must now pose as 'The Mother of Oscar' "; but she never attended one of her celebrated son's celebrated plays.

In order to project the perfection that Wilde's mother and later he preached, Wilde had to kill off large areas of feeling in himself. "The world's a graveyard," Wilde wrote in "The Duchess of Padua." "And we each, like coffins, within us, bear a skeleton." Conquest, not intimacy, is what Wilde sought in his pursuit of fame and pleasure, and fame conferred a sense of invulnerability that made Wilde indifferent to the suffering of others. "I forgot that every little action of the common day makes and unmakes character," he said. Wilde's spiritual atrophy was, as he wrote, "foreshadowed and prefigured in my art." Wilde's fairy tales, written in the mid-eighties, admit both the deadliness of his self-involvement and his longing for redemption. There is "The Fisherman and His Soul" (he pursues pleasure—the mermaid—and "takes no care of his craft"); "The Happy Prince" (he is golden, seated on a pedestal, but with a lead heart); "The Remarkable Rocket" ("I am made for public life," says the vaunting Rocket, who turns out to be a dud); and "The Selfish Giant" (walled up inside his arid garden with a sign that reads, "Trespassers Will Be Prosecuted," he insists, "My Garden is my own Garden. I will allow nobody to play in it but myself").

In the novel "The Picture of Dorian Gray," written in 1891, when Wilde had embarked on his subterranean sexual journey, Wilde's spiritual anxiety found a more complex metaphor. "My own personality has become a burden to me," says the beautiful Dorian, another enchanted person who is not free. As most readers will know, Dorian hides the painting of his unspoiled youth because the portrait is "the face of my soul," and "constantly calls me to judgement," and although Dorian's public image is unblemished, the painting—like some moral barometer —becomes increasingly grotesque. The image of corruption is so shameful that Dorian kills the portrait's painter to prevent him from seeing how horrible it has become. Then he slashes the canvas and kills himself. "Withered, wrinkled and loathsome," Dorian is unrecognizable when his body is discovered. But his portrait is miraculously whole, and his painted face restored to its "exquisite youth and beauty." "The moral is this," Wilde told the *St. James Gazette* in 1890. "All excess, as well as all renunciation, brings its own punishment." But the novel's imagery seems to imply something else. Through his suicide, Dorian puts an end to his "false face" and redeems his soul. The masquerade through which Wilde turned himself into an art object was a kind of stultifying dance with death. "Sometimes I think the artistic life is a long and lovely suicide," Wilde said. "And I am not sorry that it is so." Without knowing quite how, Wilde wanted to put an end to his performing self.

The war inside Wilde between redemption of the soul and the imperialism of the self—"the fierce misery of those who live for pleasure" —was tested in the courts. "He had grown reckless, hardened and conceited," André Gide wrote of Wilde in 1894. The next year, absenting himself from the rehearsal of "The Importance of Being Earnest," Wilde, with Lord Alfred Douglas in tow, met up with Gide in Marrakech, and Gide found them "the most compromising people in the world." He found Wilde's brazenness disconcerting, and called him "the most dangerous man of modern civilization." Wilde's tragic downfall, when it came, is put down to many things: his vanity; the viciousness of the middle classes whom he'd teased so brilliantly over the decades, and who sat in judgment over him during the three trials; his rebellious challenge to the sexual hypocrisy of the age. Actually, homosexuality was no news in London in the eighteen-nineties; the police had a list of twenty thousand male homosexuals.

Seamus Heaney, in a dedication to Wilde at the centenary celebration, fit Wilde into this radical heroic mold: "In a reckless tactic that prefigured the non-violent politics of the century ahead," Heaney said of Wilde's courtroom performance, "he provoked the violence of the system and suffered it in order to expose it."

Although Wilde kept up his public show of nonchalance during the trials—"Have no fear, the working classes are with me, to a boy"—he exhibited no such equanimity or righteous militance in private. He likened his destiny to the progress of an ox to slaughter, which prompted G. K. Chesterton to observe, "Any ox that is really sacrificed is made sacred." And, of course, Wilde's canonization has more or less come to pass. But, at the time, Wilde was panic-stricken, and there was something unconscious at play in Wilde's puzzling inability to save his own skin. "Poor Oscar! Why did he not go away when he could?" Max Beerbohm asked. Certainly Lord Queensberry expected Wilde to flee. "I will not prevent your flight," he told him. "But if you take my son with you I'll shoot you like a dog." Even Wilde's counsel, Edward Clark, "hoped and expected that he would take the opportunity of escaping the country." Wilde's dithering and his stubborn refusal to flee to France expressed the suicidal nature of his struggle. His inability to act was exacerbated by Speranza, who, always conscious of the dignity of the Wilde name, threatened to withdraw her love if he left the country. "If you stay, even if you go to prison, you will always be my son," she said. "But if you go, I will never speak to you again." The playwright Hugo von Hofmannsthal sensed something of this huge psychological battle when he wrote, "He walked towards his catastrophe with the same steps as Oedipus; the seeing-blind one."

At the libel trial, Wilde began by using the full authority of his wit to face down Lord Queensberry's counsel, who took the court through Wilde's "Phrases and Philosophies of the Young" in an attempt to paint him as a corrupter of youth. Here, for instance, is the exchange over Wilde's aphorism "If one tells the truth, one is sooner or later to be found out":

WILDE: That is a pleasing paradox, but I do not set very high store upon it as an axiom.

COUNSEL: Is it good for the young?

WILDE: Anything is good that stimulates thought in whatever age.

COUNCEL: Whether moral or immoral?

WILDE: There is no such thing as morality or immorality in thought. There is an immoral emotion.

In the end, when Queensberry produced several male prostitutes (whom he paid five pounds a day for their testimony) and proved the facts of his claim, the libel action collapsed. Wilde was removed to Holloway Prison to await trial under Section 11 of the Criminal Law Act of 1885, which stated that "any male person who, in public or private, commits, or is party to the commission of, or procures or attempts to procure the commission by any male person of, any act of gross indecency with another male person, shall be guilty of a misdemeanor." Wilde's subsequent two trials (the first ended in a hung jury) precipitated what Henry James called "an earthquake—social, human, sexual." It was the watershed event that brought an early *fin* to the *siècle*.

When asked why he stayed to face the music, Wilde said, "Because it was more beautiful to do so." For an aesthete like Wilde, the catastrophe was yet another example of life imitating art. "I was never really tempted to kill myself," Wilde said; instead, he let the court destroy the burden he had unconsciously dreamed of murdering—the persona of Oscar Wilde. Self-indulgence and fame had trivialized him. "The supreme vice is shallowness," he wrote in "De Profundis"; and in becoming shallow, Wilde had sinned grievously against his profound nature. The trial both dramatized this predicament and offered Wilde a possibility to regain control over the best part of himself. "For each man kills the thing he loves," wrote Wilde in "The Ballad of Reading Gaol," who had made a myth of his adoration of himself. He also compared himself to his two favorite fictional characters, Balzac's Lucien de Rubempre and Stendhal's Julien Sorel: "Lucien de Rubempre hung himself. Julien Sorel died on the scaffold. I died in Prison."

Near the end of his life, in exile, drinking too much and strapped for funds, Wilde sat over dinner in France with two loyal English friends— Robert Ross, the man who first seduced him, and Reggie Turner, the journalist and wit who lived mostly abroad. "Oscar told us that he had had a horrible dream the previous night—that he had been supping with the dead," Robert Ross wrote. "Reggie made a very typical response. 'My dear Oscar, you were probably the life and soul of the party.' This delighted Oscar, who became high-spirited again, almost hysterical." The joke went to the heart of Wilde's spiritual journey. Wilde, who outlived his sister, his brother, and his ex-wife and in a sense himself, had stopped running from loss, and had learned to embrace it. "Sorrow, then, and all that it teaches one, is my new world," he wrote from prison. Through suffering, Wilde had grown. He had lost his name, but he had found himself. Wilde's sense of omnipotence—that imaginary world, which, W. B. Yeats observed, he inhabited without self-mockery, and which separated him from others—had been breached by pain; and Wilde had come to terms with the reality of losing it. "I have learnt in prison cells to be grateful," he wrote in "De Profundis." "That, *for me,* is a great discovery. I have learnt gratitude—a new lesson for me— and a certain amount of humility as regards myself." Comedy was no longer part of Wilde's arsenal of self-defense. "I am no longer the Sirius of comedy," he wrote in prison. "If I write any more books, it will be from the library of lamentation."

In a sense, all Wilde's laughter was a lament. His trial and imprisonment deprived Wilde both of his subject—himself—and of his object— the admiring gaze of the public. After prison, what he saw in the public's eyes was not love but loathing. ("While I can sit at ease with the poor, I could not with the rich; for me to enter a first-class carriage containing other people would be dreadful," he wrote after his release.) Comedy is about confidence; and, now that Wilde allowed himself to acknowledge fear, the fear showed. He was no longer funny, though he claimed not to be distressed about his inability to write. "I wrote when I did not know life, now that I know the meaning of life, I have no more to write," he told an old acquaintance who encountered him in Paris. "I have found my soul. I was happy in prison because I found my soul."

In our pagan age, the depth of Wilde's spiritual struggle does not touch the heart or move the imagination as much as the injustice to his talent. We want the stimulation of his mind; but he wanted the salvation of his soul. He engineered a kind of redemption in his downfall—which was, in a way, his greatest achievement. The rest of Wilde's life was not happy, but it was not shallow. It's Wilde's revelation of suffering, not of genius, that makes his story at once so heartbreaking and so compelling. "Like a many-coloured humming top," wrote G. K. Chesterton, "Wilde was at once a bewilderment and a balance. He was so fond of being many-sided that among his sides he even admitted the right side. He loved so much to multiply his souls that he had among them one soul at least that was saved. He desired all beautiful things—even God."

HAROLD PINTER

NIGHT SWEATS

Harold Pinter is the
pathfinder of postwar English drama. No modern British playwright has
been more controversial, more imitated, more influential, or more
published. Since Pinter's London début, in 1958, with his first full-
length play, "The Birthday Party," he has written at last count twenty-
six volumes, including plays, screenplays, and poems, and has also
directed and occasionally acted for the stage. He has been a mentor to
such highly original and varied dramatists as Heathcote Williams, Joe
Orton, and David Mamet. Besides his own body of work, he has generated a mountain of critical studies and doctorates filtering his ambiguous
images through any number of ideological lenses. Such is the vastness of
this academic enterprise that there is even a journal devoted exclusively
to Pinter studies. This year alone, Pinter has performed in the successful
West End revival of his "No Man's Land"; directed David Mamet's
"Oleanna," which is soon to transfer to the West End after a sold-out
run at the Royal Court; and had his film version of Kafka's "The Trial"
released. And last week, at the resourceful Almeida Theatre, in Islington, he opened his first full-length play in fifteen years, "Moonlight."

"I have no aim in writing other than exploring the images that come
into my mind," Pinter said in 1988. "I find some of those images really
shocking, so they shock me into life and into the act of writing." In
public, Pinter is sometimes intemperate and hectoring, but in his writing he remains a poet, open and unjudgmental of the images served up
by his unconscious, and courageously waiting for their mysterious arrival. This is not a happy situation, and he has had to learn to live with
uncertainty. When a play finally does materialize, the anxiety of the
unknown is inevitably part of the drama and the structure. "My charac-

ters tell me so much and no more," he said in his earliest and clearest account of his method, in the *Sunday Times* in 1962. This murky imaginative territory of unresolved and probably unresolvable feeling yielded an extraordinarily fecund early period. There was "The Birthday Party," "The Caretaker" in 1960, and "The Homecoming" in 1965, followed by an impasse that was announced, 1975, in "No Man's Land" —a place, as one character says, "which never moves, which never changes, which never grows older, but which remains forever icy and silent"—and that was finally broken, in 1978, by the more direct narrative of "Betrayal." After that, Pinter, styling himself as an activist, managed a series of increasingly slighter, less convincing polemical finger exercises ("Mountain Language," "Party Time," "The New World Order"). And then, in the playwright's sixty-third year, "Moonlight" suddenly happened—a gift that bears out W. B. Yeats's dictum "We make out of the quarrel with others, rhetoric; but out of the quarrel with ourselves, poetry." Grief-stricken and furious, "Moonlight" lays an ambush of language and imagery to catch the unspoken and unspeakable sorrow that surrounds a dying man's sad little wish to be loved. "Moonlight" is a big, brave play, as dramatically compact and as emotionally searing as anything Pinter has written.

Moonlight is the apt shadowy, mercurial ambience for Pinter's characters, who exist in an unstable state of half-openness, moving perpetually between the seen and the unseen, sleep and wakefulness, outer and inner life. Pinter resists interpretation, and so does David Leveaux's expert production. "The play works as a direct appeal to the unconscious," Leveaux says. "One must try one's best to remove the anxiety of interpretation or intellectual obfuscation for an audience. Otherwise, the air is too noisy for an audience collectively to receive things at the level at which they need to be received. What Pinter is trying to show is the most intensified form of reality, as opposed to a kind of metaphorical reality." Accordingly, Leveaux's stage pictures have a limpid, suprareal quality. Even Pinter's stage directions hint at magic realism: "Fred in bed. Jake in to him." "Enter" would suggest that the characters were coming *from* somewhere. The surreal is also implied elegantly in Bob Crowley's minimal set, which offers the audience a world that is literally divided—by a painted piece of white gauze that extends from

the large gray upper chamber of the stage, where the sixteen-year-old
Bridget (Claire Skinner) first addresses the audience ("I can't sleep,"
she says, a sleepwalker announcing the restlessness of the play's other
uneasy souls), to the floor below, separating the bunk bed of a son's
sleeping quarters from the more substantial brass bed of his dying
father.

"Moonlight" is a haunted play that begins and ends with a haunting.
Bridget, in bare feet and a white cotton nightgown, stands before us in
the half-light, willing herself to be quiet for her parents' sake. She
sounds a new note in the usual furious hubbub of Pinter's plays: an
innocent, who speaks without guile. "They need to sleep in peace and
wake up rested. I must see that this happens," she says. "It is my task.
Because I know that when they look at me they see that I am all they
have left of their life." Although Bridget talks of her parents, they
hardly ever mention her name, and the lilies placed downstage in a vase
hint at a far greater loss, which the audience only gradually understands.
She is the manifestation of a catastrophe of which her dying father,
Andy, and his wife, Bel, can hardly speak. She is dead. ("I want to put
my cards on the table about one thing," Pinter told David Leveaux.
"There are many things I don't know about the play, but I have a strong
feeling Bridget is dead.") Just how or why she died we never know. But
she brings glimpses of the shadow world that grows closer for Andy
with each beat of the play. Bridget, as her family says, is the one who
understands. In one gorgeous monologue, she talks of journeying
through "fierce landscapes" into a sheltering jungle. "I can hide. I am
hidden," she says, in a speech that suggests the father's fantasy of solace.
"The flowers surround me but they don't imprison me. I am free.
Hidden but free. I'm a captive no longer. I'm lost no longer. No one
can find me or see me. I can be seen only by eyes of the jungle, eyes in
the leaves. But they don't want to harm me."

Shame, which has its root in a word for "cover," is what sends the
dying Andy (and all Pinter's characters) scurrying into nervy defensive
maneuvers, those famous and still potent Pinter evasions, put-ons, and
put-downs, with which they attempt to face off the prying eyes of the
world. "Where are the boys? Have you found them?" are Andy's first,
punishing words. Played with rueful, bullying brilliance by Ian Holm

(returning to the stage after fourteen years), Andy is shamed both by the memory of loss and by the fact that his sons will not come to his deathbed. He is unwanted as a parent, and unreachable as a husband. Andy's impotence is overwhelming. He says later, fumbling in the moonlight for a nightcap: "No fags, no fucks. Bollocks to the lot of them." Pinter's dialogue marvellously subverts each clinched emotional moment, moving by turns from pain to mockery and on to corrosive rage as Andy tries to manufacture a sense of potency from the dross of his humiliation. "Where are they?" he says. "Two sons. Absent. Indifferent. Their father dying." Bel (played superbly by Anna Massey, with sad-eyed sangfroid) reminds him that they were good boys, who helped her do the dishes. "The clearing of the table, the washing-up, the drying. Do you remember?" The question allows Holm, who played Lenny in the original production of "The Homecoming," and who knows how to drive a Pinter line hard to its lethal payoff, to swoop down on her like a bird of prey:

You mean in the twilight? The soft light falling through the kitchen window? The bell ringing for Evensong in the pub round the corner? [*Pause*] They were bastards. Both of them. Always.

The invective at once admits and conceals hurt not just about the children but about the absence of intimacy between Bel and himself. Mockery is their oxygen and their substitute for passion. Pinter invokes the word "mockery" in the first five minutes of the play and, in the next hour and a quarter, proceeds to demonstrate all its penetrating guises: sometimes killing grief ("You're not a bad man," Bel says to Andy. "You're just what we used to call a loudmouth") and sometimes causing it ("Think of the wonder of it," Andy says. "I betrayed you with your own girlfriend, she betrayed you with your husband and she betrayed her own husband—and me—with you! She broke every record in sight! She was a genius and a great fuck"). Andy's onslaughts are beaten back by Bel, who gives as good a low blow as she gets. "She's probably forgotten you're dying," she says to Andy when he complains that the girlfriend isn't there to console him. "If she ever remembered."

But words can't reach Andy's sons, the bedridden and perhaps dying Fred (Michael Sheen) and the caustic Jake (Douglas Hodge). They won't talk to him, or even mention his name except to viciously belittle his memory. "Oh, your father? Was he the one who was sleeping with your mother?" Fred says to Jake. In their suffocating and unrelenting send-ups, Pinter magnifies Andy's spiritual isolation. No claim of the father is allowed to stand unmocked. The public admiration of Andy as a civil servant is a source of his sons' private ridicule. They call him The Incumbent. Andy's value as a provider, and even his paternity, are turned upside down. The terror behind this manic subterfuge reflects Andy's volatile temperament. "In all your personal and social attachments the language you employed was mainly coarse, crude, vacuous, puerile, obscene and brutal to a degree," Bel says at one point. "Most people were ready to vomit after no more than ten minutes in your company." Andy's sons are victims turned victimizers. They show no remorse and offer no reconciliation. In the play's penultimate moment, Bel finally makes the call to her boys. Jake picks up the phone and says, "Chinese laundry." "Your father is very ill," Bel says softly, her eyes brimming with tears. Jake hands the phone to his brother. "Chinese laundry," he says. The silence that follows is noisy with a lifetime's unspoken regret and fury. Family is refused a place in the boys' reality, and the only way to reach them is to live within their fiction. "Do you do dry cleaning?" Bel says, finally. The harrowing and brilliant scene ends with Jake, having hung up, bending over the phone and shouting, "Of course we do dry cleaning! Of course we do dry cleaning! What kind of fucking laundry are you if you don't do dry cleaning?"

The play's sense of grief is all the more immense for being unspoken. There are no words for the kind of loss Pinter is talking about—only intimations. At one point, late in the play, under the cover of darkness, Andy inhabits the shadowy space usually occupied by Bridget, who materializes briefly in his empty bedroom, and talks to himself. "Ah darling," he says, filling the silence with heartbreaking remorse. "Ah my darling." In this brief and eloquent moment, we feel a hurt beyond repair. Bel appears in the moonlight. They look at each other and turn away: a dumb show of the unbreachable and infuriating separation from others which the play's final moments incarnate. As Bridget tells one last story, all the characters are set out in a tableau of disconnected angles. Bridget confides a dream in which she is invited by, perhaps, her parents to come to a party but is told to come when the moon is down:

> When I got to the house it was bathed in moonlight. The house, the glade, the lane, were all bathed in moonlight. But the inside of the house was dark and all the windows were dark. There was no sound. [*Pause*] I stood there in the moonlight and waited for the moon to go down.

When the moon finally does vanish, Andy will be dead. Meanwhile, Pinter leaves us with a final image of abandonment and total disconnection. The sense of separation is cavernous.

"Moonlight" is Pinter's most satisfying play since "The Homecoming," and ranks among his major works. It will bring Pinter yet greater glory. But what is so cunning and so courageous about the play is that it's a testament not only to the audacity of his terrific talent but to the frightful price he has paid for it. Many interpretations of the play will follow. For me, it's a magnificent map of individualism's dead heart; and, for those who know how to read it, "Moonlight" shows where the bodies are buried.

MIKHAIL BULGAKOV

THE LONE WOLF AND THE RUSSIAN BEAR

When a novelist discovers the theatre, he takes a ravishing but flighty mistress. The theatre can break your heart. No modern writer suffered for his theatrical passion more than Mikhail Bulgakov (1891–1940), who emerged in the mid-nineteen-twenties as one of Moscow's finest playwrights only to lose his heart's delight to the caprice of the state. The Bolsheviks showed the bourgeoisie their ass; but in his 1926 hit "The Days of the Turbins," which dramatized the Bolshevik Revolution from the point of view of the Whites, not the Reds, Bulgakov showed them his face. He paid a price for not toeing the Party line. In 1926, his diaries and the typescript of his novel "The Heart of a Dog" were seized by the secret police. By 1929, all productions of his five plays had been banned and public readings of his work prohibited. Bulgakov wrote to Maxim Gorky that he had not a kopeck, not a play, not a job offer, not a line in print. He signed off one letter that year ruefully, "Yours until the grave (which is not too far off)." To a writer, Bulgakov said, "not being allowed to write is tantamount to being buried alive." In a gesture typical of the pugnacity, bravery, and dopey perseverance that characterized his nervy nature, Bulgakov wrote a letter to the Soviet government admitting "deep skepticism about the Revolutionary process" and asking "Am I thinkable in the U.S.S.R.?" He cited as evidence his clippings album, which contained three hundred and one references over a ten-year period, and noted, "Of these, three were complimentary, and 298 were hostile and abusive. These 298 reflect, as in a mirror, my life as a writer."

Demanding that he be allowed to leave Russia or that his "virtuoso knowledge of the stage" be put to use, Bulgakov sent seven letters to various Soviet leaders. Only one replied. On April 18, 1930, just as Bulgakov was lying down for a postprandial nap, Joseph Stalin telephoned him. Stalin (who was to see "The Days of the Turbins" fifteen times in the next decade) listened, and then gave the nod to the famous Moscow Arts Theatre and secured Bulgakov a job as assistant director and, subsequently, occasional actor and adapter. But what began in hope ended in hate. Bulgakov's hilarious unfinished roman à clef, "Black Snow," which offers, among many pleasures, the only extant poison-pen portrait of the Moscow Arts Theatre's co-founder, Konstantin Stanislavsky, and his Method, is a testament to both his passion and his pain. Between the beginning of his employment by the Moscow Arts Theatre and his death, Bulgakov wrote five plays, four opera librettos, a biography of Molière, and two novels, including his masterpiece, "The Master and Margarita," but in his lifetime only his adaptation of Gogol's "Dead Souls" and a blighted run of his play "Molière" reached the public. The novels had to wait until 1965 to be published. And now, fifty-five years after Bulgakov ceased work on "Black Snow," the satiric message in the bottle has happily washed up for the first time on our shores, in a faithful, svelte adaptation by British playwright Keith Dewhurst, and has been decoded by the marvellous Surrealist imagination of Britain's boldest young director, Richard Jones, at the Loeb Drama Center, in Cambridge, which houses Robert Brustein's American Repertory Theatre.

On opening day, with fifteen minutes to go before the end of the last rehearsal, the director, an unprepossessing thirty-nine-year-old, stood, in a blue work shirt, checking his watch and waving his hand over the large model of the Moscow Arts Theatre, which was positioned at the side of the stage and allowed audiences to imagine not just what it looked like but, by its variously lighted windows, in what rooms the play's conversations were taking place. "Could we have some more snow?" Jones asked someone on the lighting board. "It should snow on the theatre." Snow, with its associations of purity and chill, was an apt metaphor of the contradictions in Bulgakov's enormous literary endeavor. Black snow, referring to the blood of a murdered man from which the would-be playwright in the piece gets his title, was an exact correlative of the violence done to Bulgakov's creative life by the

M.A.T., which he called "the graveyard of my plays." Jones turned back to the stage: a shallow white box stretching the forty-foot width of the proscenium, it exaggerates the cramped quarters and the few emblematic objects (chaise longue, books, clock) of Bulgakov's writer-spokesman, Maksudov, into a dreamlike De Chirico corridor where the words that fill his mind are scrawled not just on paper but on the floorboards and the walls around his writing table. Jones, who admits to "being obsessed by pictures of Meyerhold's work," is also devoted to staging a kind of playful kinetic theatre that embraces Meyerhold's rebellion against the grave immobility of Stanislavsky's naturalism, in which, Meyerhold wrote, "the actor has no need of the juggler's art, because he no longer 'plays' but simply 'lives' on the stage." Jones matches Bulgakov's originality with a startling stylization that yokes the familiar and the strange. For those who have followed Jones's sensational, award-winning productions in Europe (David Hirson's "La Bête," Stephen Sondheim's "Into the Woods," Corneille's "The Illusion"), the sharp angularity and daring artificiality of Antony McDonald's fine set bear all the characteristic Jones thumbprints. Giddy with rage, Bulgakov fiercely distorted his backstage portraits into caricature, which turned his skepticism into high style. Jones's scenic distortions match this literary aggression with weird Expressionist stage pictures, whose absence of depth broadcasts the triumph of surface over psychology, the extraordinary over the mundane, satire over sentiment. Some farsighted American city fathers looking for world-class theatre should just give Jones an auditorium (plus an administrator) and let him get on with what he does best, which is being brilliant. His productions shine with inventiveness, and "Black Snow" is no exception.

Robert Brustein, who has given a home to such varied talents as Robert Wilson, Andrei Serban, and Peter Sellars (Sellars directed his first professional show at the A.R.T. while he was a senior at Harvard), is responsible for luring Jones to Boston. Brustein himself arrived fourteen years ago, from Yale, and has been fighting the good fight for a challenging, eclectic theatre in a town that has traditionally been a tryout stop for Broadway and has proved itself notoriously unreceptive to the progressive theatrical arts. David Wheeler's Theatre Company of Boston, founded in 1963, had a shelf life of twelve years. The Charles

Theatre Company also had a few seasons. Now that the Huntington Theatre does the commercial staples of Stoppard, Shaw, Gilbert and Sullivan, and American musicals—the last a form of entertainment of which Brustein is not overfond (although his office trophies include a plaque that reads, "American Express Applauds George Gershwin, Jerome Kern, Cole Porter, and Robert Brustein")—the A.R.T. is free to pursue a more radical path, which Brustein has outlined in such books as "The Theatre of Revolt," "Reimagining American Theatre," and "Who Needs Theatre." During the last rehearsal of "Black Snow," Brustein, a tall, mustachioed sixty-five-year-old, lurked in the back of the theatre, an éminence in two tweedy shades of gris. "We've built up a subscription audience of more than ten thousand," he said. "It's a great audience. Adventurous. Vocal. The median age is thirty-four, one of the youngest in the country. We consider the audience the final actor in the production."

"Tom," Jones said, peering over the square wire rims of his glasses up at the light board. "Could you just pulse it to see if the snow works?"

"We play to ninety-two percent capacity," Brustein said, losing concentration as the snow finally descended with the proper density.

With that, Jones declared himself finished with rehearsal. He grabbed two festively wrapped opening-night presents and marched up the raked aisle to the back seats, where we huddled. "I can't imagine what the American audience will make of this," he said, the edges of his mouth rising to a smile. "There's no sexual relationship in it. The main relation is between a man and his work. I don't think you can imagine that in an American play, really."

"Richard Jones to the Donut, please!" The loudspeaker was calling the director to the reception area at the side of the dishabille theatre. Boxes of promotional literature lined the side walls, and a crate of dead beer bottles seemed to have taken up permanent residence under the stairway.

"Russians are very special, aren't they?" Jones said. "They talk a lot about 'soul.' When I was there, they'd say these kind of really spiritual things. They'd sort of look at you and say, 'I see you have the eyes of a poet.' It would completely floor you. That's partly why Russian things are so hard to assimilate in this culture. I think it's hard for an American actor to fantasize himself into the very Russian frame of mind. 'Either I write this novel or I commit suicide.' As long as he can create, he can live. It's a critical thing. Americans are used to saying what they feel.''

"It's like what Philip Roth said," Brustein piped up. "In the Soviet Union, nothing is allowed and everything matters. In the United States, everything is allowed and nothing matters."

While many plays about theatricals mine the hilarity of actors' narcissism ("Hay Fever," "Noises Off," "The Seagull"), Bulgakov's is unique in taking the audience comically into what Chekhov called "the haze" of a writer's life. Here concentration warps time and space, and the rumpled solitary is visited by weird apparitions and overheard voices, to whom he unabashedly talks and which he tries to chronicle. "Bulgakov's a great imaginist," said Jones. "For that reason, he has to be a good writer for the theatre." Jones embraces Bulgakov's visionary spirit, and his theatrical sleight of hand powerfully conjures the no man's land between the heaven of a writer's imagination and the hell of his inadequacy. Maksudov enters, "white" with fatigue. His books burst into flame. His writing table glows white as he reenters the world of his failed novel to salvage it as a play. "They've come out of the pages," Maksudov says of the characters of his novel, with whom he can't bear parting. "But if I write down whatever I see in the box it will not fade. The people will not run away from me." Maksudov trails his characters like Chekhov's Trigorin, "not knowing what I'm writing half the time." We are immediately submerged in the tumult of his mind: gunshots, the magnified sound of the ticking clock and the scratching pen, the shock of real sunlight and real voices. But when an excerpt of Maksudov's novel gets him a contract with the "Independent Theatre" (read Moscow Arts Theatre), he happily trades the lacerations of the soul for the frustrations of collaboration. To Maksudov, as to so many before and after him, the theatre is an answer to the novelist's silent prayers both for applause and for company.

"For the first time in my life I am beholding a reader!" Maksudov says of the M.A.T.'s dramaturge. The theatre promises Maksudov both the irresistible, sensual thrill of his words incarnated and a public whose responses he can see. A novelist rarely sees his readers take pleasure in his work, or walk out on it. But in the theatre the encounter with the public is as immediate and dangerous as a stolen kiss. Bulgakov teases the Moscow Arts Theatre's messianic dedication to art (portraits of the greats of Western literature are interspersed with those of the theatre's artistic team), while showing Maksudov's delight at the flamboyant, temperamental characters and power plays that make the place a hot-house both of wonder and of waste. Jones brilliantly depicts the would-be playwright's poignant first glimpse of the backstage world as the actors take their bows upstage to a volley of applause. And when the playwright encounters Ivan Vasilyevich (a.k.a. Stanislavsky), Jones engineers an automated cat that darts across the stage like an electronic hare at a dog track, pulling down Vasilyevich's curtain and adding another delicious touch to the fiasco of their first meeting. In Bulgakov's portrait, Stanislavsky, here shrewdly sketched by the A.R.T. veteran Alvin Epstein, is a hypochondriacal, vindictive windbag with a distaste for gunshots and a knack for steering a script into shallow waters. He wants Maksudov, for instance, to change his crucial scene from a shooting to an offstage stabbing. "The government aren't going to pat me on the back for letting Strizh rake the theatre with gunfire, are they?" the great director says, referring to the hated putative director of Maksudov's show, whom Ivan Vasilyevich later successfully undermines. Stanislavsky's Method aspired to create the new actor who would mesh easily with the new Marxist-Leninist man, liberated from the bad old habits of the past in order to call into being a new, disciplined, enlightened inner self. "A real artist must lead a full, interesting, varied and exciting life," Stanislavsky wrote in "An Actor Prepares." "He must be an ideal human being . . . capable of reaching the high points of his epoch . . . of reflecting the spiritual cravings of his contemporaries." The revolution that Stanislavsky wanted was internal and posed no threat to the state.

But in Bulgakov's argument the M.A.T., which in 1936 withdrew his "Molière" after seven performances—despite five years of rehearsal and twenty-two opening-night curtain calls—because of a bad review in Pravda, was a real threat to the writer's freedom. "In your play," Vasilyevich says to Maksudov, in a line tweaking the M.A.T.'s institutional temerity, "you must not pray to God but to art." Maksudov, like Bulgakov himself, invests his self-expression with an almost religious zeal. "I have been the one and only literary wolf," Bulgakov wrote to Stalin, about his refusal to tailor his plays along Soviet ideological lines. "Whether a wolf dyes his fur or has it clipped, he will still look nothing like a poodle." "Black Snow" bears satiric witness to the stifling of an author's literary freedom by the vainglorious demands of management. Ivan Vasilyevich's interminable études during rehearsal (including an amusing exhibition of how someone in love rides a bike), his time-wasting demand for specious rewrites, and his love of theatrical anecdote try Maksudov's patience just as they did Bulgakov's. When Stanislavsky took over rehearsals of "Molière" in the fourth year, Bulgakov was spitting spiders to his diary: "In the presence of the actors, he began to tell me all about the fact that Molière was a genius, and how this genius ought to be depicted in the play. The actors licked their lips in glee and began to ask that their parts be made larger." Bulgakov fought like fury to keep "the capacious cup of my patience" from overflowing. The joke in "Black Snow" is that Maksudov never gets his play performed. "If you could act," the exasperated Maksudov tells the histrionic Lyudmila, who keeps interrupting with her shows of temperament, "you wouldn't need a Method!" The process takes over, the pages fly up, and Maksudov is finally brought down. The evening ends in fine satiric symmetry. Having begun with a botched suicide over his failed novel, Maksudov finally achieves suicide with his unproduced play. Playwrights will know the feeling.

"The genuine grotesque," Stanislavsky wrote, "is the best kind of art." Bulgakov's theatrical gargoyles require a bold, distinctive, comic playing that can establish a character in quick strokes and fill it with personality. The A.R.T. can't quite flesh out "Black Snow" with uniformly accomplished comic cameos. But Derek Smith, as Maksudov, gets the naïveté, if not the dyspepsia, in the writer's beleaguered nature. Candy Buckley, as a telephonist and typist extraordinaire, and Patti Allison, who, as Ivan's old aunt, dodders across the stage carrying a pug whose face has a droll similarity to her own, rise to just the right level of outrageous comic attack. Having outlasted Stalin's purges, the K.G.B., and *Pravda,* "Black Snow" will survive the blinkered local Boston press, who missed the fun of it. But no matter. The smart A.R.T. audience got it. Another production of "Black Snow" (with an American adaptation by Keith Reddin) is scheduled in the spring at Chicago's Goodman Theatre. The literary wolf is here for keeps.

TENNESSEE WILLIAMS

FUGITIVE MIND

Tennessee Williams wrote in his "Cahiers Noirs," "*I, I, I!*—a burden to be surrendered." But until his accidental death, at the age of seventy-one, in 1983 (he choked on the cap of a pill bottle), Williams never stopped taking his moral temperature and weighing the increasing psychic cost of his drive to be great against his desire to be good. "The plays, with a little discernment, prove to be as naked as the best confessions," Elia Kazan, who first directed many of the best of them, wrote in a memoir. Williams, the most autobiographical of American playwrights, began by making a romance of himself and ended by recording the atrophy of his soul. His drama offers a unique view of American individualism, bearing witness to both the brilliance and the barbarity of the one big idea of the American experiment—what Whitman called "the destiny of me."

Williams pushed himself and his fugitive heart to the limit: he calculated his life to be "work and worry over work, 89%; struggle against lunacy . . . ten percent . . . and friends, 1%." What he called his "nearly blinding preoccupation with an effort to outrun time in the completion of what I hoped would be a major body of work" took its toll. Williams wrote eight hours a day for forty years. He wrote in spite of his analyst's warnings that he was burying himself in his work ("I was bored not writing. I began to cheat"); and, inevitably, cut off from friends and from the ordinary life around him, he felt adrift. He destroyed himself for meaning. "For love I make characters in plays," he said. He wrote more than seventy plays, fifteen movies, two novels, two volumes of poems, and countless short stories and essays. Trapped in what he called his "little cave of consciousness," he was compelled to explore and to try to unify his "irreconcilably divided" nature. "The process generally parallels a mood I am in," he said. "If I have a problem, I invent people in parallel circumstances, create parallel tensions. It is my way of working out problems."

"Tennessee," Tallulah Bankhead said to Williams, "you and I are the only constantly High Episcopalians I know." It was a good joke, and a telling one. Williams's legend of excess—part of the romantic rebellion that first his plays and later he himself acted out for the public— disguised the latent spiritual longing that informed his life and much of his work. Born on Palm Sunday, 1911, he was a religious man—a kind of righteous pagan, who, like Shannon, the defrocked priest in "The Night of the Iguana" (1961), saw himself as "a man of God, on vacation." Williams was born and reared in an Episcopal rectory, in Columbus and then in Clarksdale, Mississippi, where his beloved grandfather the Reverend Walter Dakin was minister. "My grandfather was very, very High Church," Williams said. "He was Higher than the Pope." The Reverend Mr. Dakin was the only positive male figure in Williams's growing up, and was an important influence. (Williams bequeathed the revenues from all his plays to the minister's alma mater, the University of the South at Sewanee, Tennessee.) In his "Memoirs," Williams recounts a religious brainstorm when he was sixteen, in which "the grace of God touched me." He believed in prayer ("Help me, dear God, to find what I need," he wrote in a 1943 diary); kept images of the Virgin Mary by his bedside; and was converted briefly to Catholicism in 1969. "Faith is in our hearts, or else we are dead," he wrote in the collection of his plays which he presented to the priest who converted him. And in his "Cahiers Noirs," an entry entitled "My list of synonyms" gives his definition of truth as "the possibility of a God, unseen, unknown and unknowable, but without which—take it away!" Intimations of his spiritual longing can be glimpsed sometimes in the titles of his plays ("Stairs to the Roof: A Prayer for the Wild of Heart That Are Kept in Cages"; "Two Acts of Grace"—the original title of "The Night of the Iguana") and sometimes in his hunted characters, damned in their skin, who carry both his sense of corruption and his hope of salvation.

Williams's emergence as a playwright coincided with his embrace of romanticism. The dutiful narrator of "The Glass Menagerie" (1944),

Tom Wingfield, is accused of being a selfish dreamer ("Self, self, self is all that you ever think of!") and evolves into a symbol of the romantic ideal—that "long delayed but always expected something that we live for." Wingfield's escape from his troubled family lays the groundwork for Williams's subsequent romantic image—haunted, isolated, doomed to a life of wandering and of relentless pursuit of his poetic vision. Alma Winemiller's valedictory salute ("a gesture of wonder and finality") to the crouching stone angel that dominates the public square in "Summer and Smoke" (1945) was Williams's hard-won, emblematic farewell to Christian self-sacrifice and his hello to romantic self-aggrandizement. Alma, who has also grown up in the shadow of a rectory, abandons it for the Moon Lake Casino—"where anything goes"—clutching a package of pills, whose prescription she calls "the telephone number of God." Alma is the first of many Williams women—Stella, in "A Streetcar Named Desire" (1947), for example, and Rosa delle Rose, in "The Rose Tattoo" (1951)—to be liberated by appetite from the prison of manners. This unlearning of repression has its male corollary in Williams's memorable celebration of the primitive—Stanley Kowalski in "Streetcar"; Alvaro Mangiacavallo in "The Rose Tattoo"; Val in "Orpheus Descending" (1957). By the early fifties, as Williams confesses in "Camino Real" (1953), he feared he had been betrayed by his romantic imagination: "As you approach middle life you are apt to meet an impasse, to lose your way in the dark woods." And Williams *was* lost. His plays shift from self-exploration to self-justification. Daring to imagine for himself a new kind of Heaven, he had made only a new kind of Hell. "I can't be the better part of myself anymore," he wrote in 1957.

"Sweet Bird of Youth" (1959), currently being revived at the Royal National Theatre, in London, picks up Williams's story at the panicky moment of the hardening of his spiritual arteries. In "Sweet Bird of Youth," the most underrated of his great plays, two self-confessed monsters, Chance Wayne and the Princess Kosmonopolis, a.k.a. Alexandra Del Lago, act out the division in Williams's warped heart between being big and being good. The sense that time is running out on the Princess's career and, as his name implies, on Chance's opportunity is what gives the play its peculiar giddy climate of frenzy. Richard Eyre's vivid but unsubtle production—what might be considered an acrylic version—nonetheless allows us to see the grandeur of Williams's writing and to appreciate how much of America's competitive ethos he explores in his idiosyncratic meditation on the monstrous. "I'm a peculiar blend of the pragmatist and the Romanticist and the crocodile. The Monster," Williams said in 1973. The notion of monsters crops up first in "Cat on a Hot Tin Roof" (1955), when Maggie admits that in her struggle to survive she has mutated, "gone through this—*hideous—transformation*—become—*hard! Frantic!—cruel!*" And in "The Night of the Iguana," the last great play in the Williams canon, the monster—the eponymous iguana—is literally at the end of its tether under the veranda of Maxine's Costa Verde Hotel, trying "to go on past the end of its goddam rope," Shannon says. "Like *you!* Like *me!*" The iguana is eventually freed; but Williams never was. "Sweet Bird of Youth," set on Easter morning, is a kind of resurrection play—a daydream of atonement, in which Williams faces up to the sin of his separation from others and the dilemma of lost goodness.

The word "monster" has its root in the contrary notions of marvels and warnings; and "Sweet Bird of Youth" probes the ambiguities between achievement and destruction. "We are two monsters, but with this difference between us," the Princess, a movie star on the run from the imagined failure of her Hollywood comeback film, says to Chance, her young "pitiful monster," who is attempting a comeback of his own, by blackmailing her into being his ticket to theatrical fame and fortune. "Out of the passion and torment of my existence I have created a thing that I can unveil, a sculpture, almost heroic, that I can unveil, which is true." Here Clare Higgins's husky voice and ravaged face invest the Princess's panic and vanity with a compelling ferocity. Dazed and demented, the Princess sprawls on the silk sheets of the hotel double bed, squinting at her gigolo through cracked eyeglasses. "Well," she says, in a line resounding with a lived sense of rapacity and loneliness, "I may have done better, but God knows I've done worse." Higgins isn't always so successful at finding the humor in the Princess's knowing detachment—partly because she lacks a star's deadly imperialism, and partly because there's no chemistry between her and Robert Knepper, who, as Chance, hasn't a whiff of sex or loss about him. This results in some strange readings. "Monsters don't die early," the Princess says, hectoring Chance. "They hang on long. Awfully long. Their vanity's infinite, almost as infinite as their disgust with themselves." Higgins punctuates these cauterizing lines with a wiggle of her hips.

"Sweet Bird of Youth," which dramatizes Chance's twenty-four-hour return to the Gulf Coast town where the legend of his youth began and where it will end, is full of mordant commentary on the soul's decay. "The age of some people can only be calculated by the level of . . . rot in them," Chance says to the Princess. "And by that measure I'm ancient." The cavernous darkness that fills the stage at curtain rise is the perfect ambience for the immensity of shame they're in retreat from. Anthony Ward's monumental louvred bedroom shutters, which reach from floor to ceiling, make the point as spectacularly as Williams's poetry. The characters long to be redeemed from their dead hearts. "Once I wasn't this monster," the Princess says to Chance, surprised to find herself feeling "something for someone besides myself" and momentarily looking to him for salvation. "Chance, you've got to help me stop being the monster that I was this morning, and you can do it." She is a big winner in the American sweepstakes who is terrified of losing; he is a big loser who is terrified that he'll never win. She is trying to hide from the memory of achievement; he is trying to manufacture achievements to hide in. Together, they are a kind of psychological composite of Williams. "Somehow we Americans have never stopped fighting," Williams said, in 1958, of the corruption brought on by the fever to win. "The very pressure we live under, the terrific competitive urge of our society brings out violence in the individual. We need to be taught how to love. Already we know only too well how to hate."

"Sweet Bird of Youth" is really Chance's story, but the play's flawed structure skews the focus. In an attempt to give a larger dimension to Chance's relationship with his beloved childhood sweetheart, Heavenly (who has to be sterilized because of his betrayal), and to give more coherence to Chance's ultimate fate—his castration by the henchmen of Heavenly's draconian father, Boss Finley—Eyre has boldly assembled his production script from seven drafts of the play. The retooling is generally effective (although giving the role of Heavenly to Emma Amos, who is neither delicate nor believable, cancels out much of the narrative gain). Eyre deserves enormous credit for having mounted three major Williams revivals since he took over as director of the Royal National Theatre, in 1988. "I think the neglect of Williams by the British theatre, let alone the American theatre, has been absolutely shameless," he told me. "I deeply underrated Williams. I didn't see him in the way that I do now, as a moralist and the best writer of English prose in the theatre of this century." The prose *is* wonderful; but, having tampered with the script, Eyre is oddly timorous about adapting Williams's stage directions, and, as Williams instructed, allows Chance and the Princess to speak their long arias to the audience, and not to each other. This may be Williams's scenic way of indicating the isolation of two major-league narcissists, but it bogs down the play's momentum. As if to recoup it, the production mistakes agitation for desperation.

But there is no mistaking Williams's dream of salvation. At the finale, the Princess, forced by Chance to call a Hollywood gossip columnist on his behalf, learns that her film is a hit. In that instant, she is reborn Alexandra Del Lago, "redeemed" by fame to her former invulnerability. She immediately forgets about Chance. Her vainglorious volte-face is hilarious and lethal. The kingdom of self is reasserted, and the monstrous invoked once again. "I climbed back alone up the beanstalk to the ogre's country where I live, now, alone," she says to Chance, who refuses to be part of her entourage and to leave with her, despite Boss Finley's threats on his life. The parade has passed Chance by, as the Princess reminds him. "Chance," she says, "you've gone past something you couldn't afford to go past; your time, your youth, you've passed it. It's all you had, and you've had it." Chance, who has been notoriously irresponsible—he arrives in town unaware of his mother's death or Heavenly's operation—now owns up to his dereliction. He stops running, and chooses not "the spurious glory" of the Princess— the kind of fame he first glimpsed as a Broadway chorus boy in "Oklahoma!"—but the Christian glory of self-sacrifice. In Eyre's production, Chance's pill-popping and manic behavior make his decision to stay and face down his tormentors more resigned than heroic. "Something's got to mean something," Chance says, in a line unfortunately cut from Eyre's production. The castration—what Williams referred to in a letter to Kazan as "the quixotic, almost ridiculous choice, to stay and atone''—is a kind of leap of faith: an expression of Williams's own longing to reclaim his belief. Eyre's production emphasizes the sacrificial nature of the act by having the Boss's men advance on Chance with torches. While Chance's back is to us, his arms shoot out from his body as if he were crucified; and as the lights fade he falls backward with his pelvis thrust upstage at the approaching mob.

Salvation was easier for Williams to create in his plays than in his life. Drugs, drink, and dementia eroded much of his power of penetration and organization in the particularly chaotic period between 1964 and 1969, which he called his "Stoned Age." After that, what remained to him was his "left-over life," a gradual attenuation of friendships and of energy. "I feel like a sinking ship," he wrote his new agent, Bill Barnes, in 1973, "but things have a habit of going on." When his plays could no longer find a receptive audience, Williams put himself and his moral drama directly before the public. Asked to explain his conversion to Catholicism, he said, "I wanted to have my goodness back." But he never really regained it. "To the world I give suspicion and resentment mostly," he wrote in 1980, in the introduction to his collected short stories. "I am never deliberately cruel. But after my morning's work, I have little to give but indifference to people. I try to excuse myself with the pretense that my work justifies this lack of caring for almost everything else. Sometimes I crack through the emotional block. I touch. I hold tight to a necessary companion. But that breakthrough is not long lasting. Morning returns, and only work matters again." Williams's particular poignancy is that he saw the light but didn't want it enough.

❖

"Have finished 'The Caller,' " Tennessee Williams wrote in a postscript to a friend in August 1944, referring to "The Gentleman Caller" —a play that he had also worked up as a movie treatment and unsuccessfully pitched while he was on the MGM payroll doing rewrites for, among others, Lana Turner. "No doubt it goes in my reservoir of noble efforts. It is the last play I try to write for the now existing theatre." Seven months later, in March 1945, "The Gentleman Caller," retitled "The Glass Menagerie," was produced. It became a watershed event and was the first of Williams's dramas to win a wide public. In its personal lyricism, "The Glass Menagerie" marks the theatre's evolution from polemical thirties social realism (what Williams called "the exhausted theatre of realistic conventions"), and perhaps even the transformation of the nation's collective unconscious from war-effort sacrifice to postwar self-involvement. The play, which celebrates its half century this month, with Frank Galati's fascinating production at the Roundabout, is the most transparently autobiographical of Williams's works, and dramatizes the central psychic struggle of his life: building, as he wrote in a 1941 poem, "a towering pillar of my blood / Against the siege of all that is not I." Williams had survived a brutal and indifferent father, a misguided mother, the tragedy of a beloved sister who was eventually lobotomized, a long apprenticeship, grinding poverty, his homosexual awakening. He emerged, at the age of thirty-four, as the great playwright of his time, and, indeed, of the century. After "The Glass Menagerie," which made a legend of his literary emergence, Williams spent the rest of his life vainly trying to survive his fame.

"What a dark and bewildering thing it is, this family group," Williams wrote of his "haunted household," whose members he transformed into the Wingfields onstage. In Loy Arcenas's set, the Wingfield home is surrounded by scaffolding, as if the dingy walls were in danger of collapsing. The gray floor and the gray back wall elegantly reflect Mimi Jordan Sherin's moody light and the novelty of John Boesche's projections. (Williams's script originally called for projections, but they are rarely used.) Before the play begins, the back wall is dominated by an image of Williams as the big theatrical cookie he became: mustache, a cigarette holder in one hand, a page of dialogue in the other. Although the projected images are subtly employed, they have the cumulative effect of drawing the eye away from the immediacy of events onstage and leaching intensity from the scenes. But the image of the celebrated author is particularly apt for a play that boldly announces both Williams's power as an artist ("Yes, I have tricks in my pocket, I have things up my sleeve") and his romantic literary persona: haunted, restless, alone ("I would have stopped, but I was pursued by something"). Williams's theatrical surrogate is the narrator, Tom Wingfield (the droll and dreamy Zeljko Ivanek), to whom Williams gives his own first name and both his initials. The Williams family motto was "Know Your Opportunity—Seize It," and "The Glass Menagerie" dramatizes Williams's panicky attempt to do just that. "I'm planning to change," says Tom, a would-be writer, who longs to be free. Tom needs some big magic—the magic of an escape artist he's seen who managed to get out of a coffin without removing a nail. "Get me out of this two-by-four situation!" Tom says. At work in a St. Louis shoe warehouse, he is a wage slave lumbered by tedium, and at home he is a dutiful son lumbered by a possessive, puritanical mother, Amanda, and a shy, crippled sister, Laura. Tom is obsessed with his own momentum ("I am *about to move!*"), but domestic responsibilities threaten to stall his pursuit of self. "Self is all that you ever think of," says his long-suffering mother, who lectures him to "overcome selfishness." The play, in making a case for romantic individualism, acts out the self denied (the martyred Amanda), the self repressed (the pathologically shy Laura), and finally, in Tom's ruthless emergence as a writer, the self affirmed.

"The Glass Menagerie" is dominated by the absent father ("a telephone man who fell in love with long distances"), and in most productions his photograph faces the audience throughout the evening—a permanent reminder of the family's sense of being both abandoned and stranded. Here the father is only occasionally recalled in the projections. The result is a lowering of the play's emotional temperature. In real life, Williams's father, the womanizing and fractious C. C. Williams, a travelling salesman, certainly made the family blood boil. Williams wed Edwina Dakin, a beautiful chatterbox, in 1907; but until 1918, when Edwina and her children moved to St. Louis, the family lived with her father, a minister, in a series of Episcopalian rectories in Mississippi, with C.C. visiting a few times a month. "The Glass Menagerie" documents the family's traumatic sense of dislocation after they moved from Mississippi gentility to the anonymity of St. Louis. It was the first time that C.C. had cohabited with the family, and the first time that Edwina, now thirty-four, had had to cook. Isolated and flummoxed by their circumstances (the Williamses moved nine times during the first few years), the family floundered. They retreated, like the characters in "The Glass Menagerie," into fantasy worlds: Williams's sister, Rose, into psychotic isolation; Williams himself into his writing; and Edwina into a daydream of Southern aristocracy.

"You lost belief in everything but loss," Williams writes in the poem "Cortege," about his childhood. This same rueful sense of desperation is superbly conveyed by Julie Harris as Amanda. "Things have a way of turning out so badly," she says, her reedy voice registering heartbreaking exhaustion at the collapse of her plans for the hapless Laura (Calista Flockhart). Harris brings to the part an affecting delicacy and a shrewd dramatic intelligence. She doesn't force herself on an audience. She lets the play speak quietly through the character. Her Amanda is neither a monolithic puritan (Williams's view of Edwina) nor a deluded fool. Instead, as filtered through Harris's gentle and compassionate heart, Amanda is a decent woman whose confused vitality exhibits both resourcefulness and a kind of heroism in the face of terrible circumstances. Harris finds a sweetness in Amanda's possessiveness. Her hands don't so much clutch as flutter affectionately around Tom—patting, smoothing, caressing. She's never funnier than when pushing her agitated, dreamy son ("Man is by instinct a lover, a hunter, a fighter") into a chair so that she can talk her notion of sense to him. The arc of Harris's anger is carefully plotted, reaching its powerful apogee after Tom forgets to inquire about the gentleman caller's marital status. (He's engaged.) "Don't let anything interfere with your selfish pleasure! Just go, go, go—to the movies!" she shouts at Tom. "Go, then! Then go to the moon—you selfish dreamer!"

Tom's rebellion takes the form of action, but Laura's takes the form of paralysis: she's frozen, both by anger at her mother's expectations for her and by fear of her repressed sexual fantasies. When Tom arrives with Jim O'Connor (well played by Kevin Kilner, as a kind of hulk of hopefulness), Laura won't go to the door. "Why have you chosen this moment to lose your mind?" Amanda says. Laura finally lets them in, but she can't look at her guest or, later, sit at the table with him. These exquisite and excruciating moments are well staged by Galati, who uses Kilner's size (he's six foot three) to make Laura seem as small and brittle as one of the glass figurines she collects. "Look how big my shadow is when I stretch!" O'Connor says, when they are alone; and the shadow he casts is as enormous as his credulity. Laura's face is lit by the flickering glow of a candelabra. As Flockhart skillfully plays the scene, Laura is coaxed out of herself into a sudden beautiful moment of intimacy, which is just as abruptly snuffed out when Jim explains that he's spoken for.

"We can't say grace until you come to the table!" Amanda calls out to Tom at the start of the play. But they don't. Later, when the gentleman caller arrives, Amanda again mentions grace. "I think," she says, "we may—have grace—now." And they do. Laura and Jim briefly break through their solitude and make some spiritual connection. But the enduring grace that the play dramatizes is the power of the narrator's imagination to transform the blighted lives of Williams's family into beauty. "I feel that God should walk into this mellow kitchen of mine with drawn sword and just wordlessly chop my head off because I have been too fortunate compared with the female members of my doomed house," Williams, in California in 1943, wrote to a friend. His guilt and his glory coalesce in the finale of "The Glass Menagerie," which turns loss into legend. "Now that we cannot hear the mother's speech, her silliness is gone and she has dignity and tragic beauty," the stage directions say. Even Laura smiles. "Blow out your candles," the narrator says. Laura blows out the candles. "And so good-bye . . ." In that gesture, the romantic playwright becomes God, remaking the universe to his own requirements. "The Glass Menagerie" ends not with "good night" but with "good-bye." Onstage, Williams made, if not quite peace, then a kind of truce with his past. In life he never could.

TONY KUSHNER

BEYOND NELLY

$$H$$IGH ON A HILL IN DOWN-
town Los Angeles, the thirty-six-year-old playwright Tony Kushner
stood watching an usher urge the people outside the Mark Taper Forum
to take their seats for the opening of "Angels in America," his two-part
"gay fantasia on national themes." It was the première of the play's
long-awaited second segment, "Perestroika," which was being performed, together with the first part, "Millennium Approaches," in a
seven-hour back-to-back marathon. "I never imagined that this was
going to come out of sitting down in 1988 to write what was supposed
to be a two-hour play about five gay men, one of whom was Mormon
and another was Roy Cohn," Kushner said. "The level of attention
that's being paid to the plays is completely terrifying." On the first day
the Taper opened its box office for Kushner's twin bill, it took in thirty-
two thousand eight hundred and four dollars, far exceeding the previous
record in the theatre's distinguished history; and just last week "Millennium Approaches," which ran for a year at the Royal National Theatre
in England, won the London *Evening Standard*'s award for best play.
Driving to the Taper for his opening, Kushner said, he had thought, If I
have a fiery car crash, the play will probably be really well received and
no one will dare trash it, and it would be this legendary thing. Now
Kushner was experiencing the actual rush of first-night terror: he
couldn't feel the pavement under his feet. "I feel like I'm walking on
some cushion, like dry sponge," he said. "Unsteady. Giddy."

Every playwright has a ritual for opening night. Some playwrights
walk. Some drink. Some tough it out and watch from the back of the
theatre, silently coaxing the players over every production obstacle.
Kushner takes himself away for a Chinese meal; in the case of this

doubleheader, he'd need two meals. He had already taped his opening-night ticket into his journal. He'd fitted himself out with a lucky ceramic lion given him by his mother and with a medal of the Virgin Mary from Majagure, in what was formerly Yugoslavia. He had one more thing to do. "Once the curtain goes up, I sing 'Begin the Beguine'—it's the longest pop song without a chorus," he explained, shouldering a blue backpack. "I have to sing it *well* from start to finish. If I can get through the whole thing without fucking up the words, it's going to be O.K." I left him to it.

Inside the seven-hundred-and-forty-two-seat auditorium, the Taper's artistic director, Gordon Davidson, shmoozed with the first-nighters like a rabbi with his congregation. Over the twenty-five years of Davidson's stewardship, the Taper has generated a prodigious amount of theatre work, some of which has invigorated Broadway and off-Broadway. Although the local press likes to bite the hand that feeds it, and periodically snaps at Davidson, no other American regional theatre approaches the Taper's record. Recently, Davidson and his theatre seem to have had a second lease of creative life, giving George C. Wolfe's innovative musical "Jelly's Last Jam" its first production and staging Robert Schenkkan's "The Kentucky Cycle," which was the first play to win a Pulitzer Prize without being put on in New York. With "Angels in America," which Davidson workshopped, and into which he has already sunk a million three hundred thousand dollars of the theatre's budget, the Taper is poised for another scoop. Davidson worked the room, handing out butterscotch candies, as is his opening-night custom, and smiling the smile that has launched a few hundred shows but none more brazenly ambitious or better produced than Kushner's. The occasion felt more like a feeding frenzy than like a first night. Robert Altman was there, checking out the play as movie material. A good proportion of the New York theatre's high rollers seemed to be there, too, eager to get a piece of Kushner's action: JoAnne Akalaitis, of the Public Theatre; Rocco Landesman, of Jujamcyn; the Broadway producers Margo Lion and Heidi Landesman; and a host of critics, including Frank Rich, of the *Times,* and Jack Kroll, of *Newsweek.* As the houselights dimmed, Davidson found his seat and glanced at the copy of "Moby-Dick" that Kushner had given him as an opening-night present. "I felt it was appropriate for the occasion," Kushner's inscription read. "It's my favorite book, by my favorite writer, someone who spent years pursuing, as he put it in a letter to Hawthorne, 'a bigger fish.' "

Just how big a fish Kushner was trying to land was apparent as the lights came up on John Conklin's bold backdrop of the façade of a Federal-style building, leached of color and riven from floor to ceiling by enormous cracks. The monumental design announced the scope and elegant daring of the enterprise. It gave a particular sense of excitement to the evening, and bore out one of Kushner's pet theories. "The natural condition of theatre veers toward calamity and absurdity. That's what makes it so powerful when it's powerful," he said before he decamped to Chinatown. "The greater the heights to which the artists involved aspire, the greater the threat of complete fiasco. There's a wonderfully vibrant tension between immense success and complete catastrophe that is one of the guarantors of theatrical power." From its first beat, "Angels in America" exhibited a ravishing command of its characters and of the discourse it wanted to have through them with our society.

Kushner has not written a gay problem play, or agitprop Sturm und Schlong; nor is he pleading for tolerance. "I think that's a terrible thing to be looking for," he told me. Instead, with immense good humor and accessible characters, he honors the gay community by telling a story that sets its concerns in the larger historical context of American political life. "In America, there's a great attempt to divest private life of political meaning," he said. "We have to recognize that our lives are fraught with politics. The oppression and suppression of homosexuality is part of a larger political agenda. The struggle for a cure for AIDS and for governmental recognition of the seriousness of the epidemic connects directly to universal health care, which is connected to a larger issue, which is a social net." Set in 1985, at the height of the Reagan counter-revolution, "Millennium Approaches" maps the trickle-down effect of self-interest as Kushner's characters ruthlessly pursue their sexual and public destinies. Louis, unable to deal with illness, abandons his lover, Prior, who has AIDS; Joe, an ambitious, bisexual Mormon Republican legal clerk, abandons his dippy, pill-popping Mormon wife, Harper ("You, the one part of the real world I wasn't allergic to," she tells him later); and Roy Cohn, in his greed, is faithless to everybody. "There are no angels in America, no spiritual past, no racial past, there's only the political," Louis says, in one of the idealistic intellectual arabesques meant to disguise his own moral and emotional quandary, which Joe Mantello's droll characterization both teases and makes touching. Louis invokes Alexis de Tocqueville, and it's Tocqueville who put his finger on that force of American democracy whose momentum creates the spiritual vacuum Kushner's characters act out. "Thus not only does democracy make every man forget his ancestors, but it hides his descendants and separates his contemporaries from him," Tocqueville wrote. "It throws him back forever upon himself alone and threatens in the end to confine him entirely within the solitude of his own heart."

This isolation has its awesome apotheosis in the dead heart of Roy Cohn. "Hold," Cohn barks into the phone—his very first word. Turning to Joe (Jeffrey King), whom he's singled out as a potential "Royboy," he says, "I wish I was an octopus, a fucking octopus. Eight loving arms and all those suckers. Know what I mean?" This is a great part, which calls out of Ron Leibman a great performance. Roaring, cursing, bullying, jabbing at the air with his beaky tanned face and at the phone with his cruel fingers, he incarnates all that is raw, vigorous, and reckless in Cohn's manic pursuit of power. "Love; that's a trap. Responsibility; that's a trap, too," he tells Joe while trying to set him up as his man inside the Justice Department and spell out the deep pessimism behind his rapacity. "Life is full of horror; nobody escapes, nobody; save yourself." With his rasping, nasal voice swooping up and down the vocal register, Leibman makes Cohn's evil incandescent and almost majestic. ("If you want the smoke and puffery, you can listen to Kissinger and Shultz and those guys," he confides to Joe at one point. "But if you want to look at the heart of modern conservatism, you look at me.") Cohn is the king of control and the queen of denial. He tells his doctor when he learns he has AIDS, "Homosexuals are men who in fifteen years of trying cannot get a pissant anti-discrimination bill through City Council. Homosexuals are men who know nobody and who nobody knows. Does this sound like me, Henry?"

But Cohn's hectoring gusto doesn't overwhelm the piquancy of the other stories. Kushner's humor gets the audience involved in the characters, and the play works like a kind of soap opera with sensibility, whose triumph is finally one of design rather than depth. Kushner doesn't impose personality on ideas but lets ideas emerge through careful observation of personality. He listens to his characters and, with his percolating imagination, blends the quirky logic of their voices with their hallucinatory visions. Prior (played by Stephen Spinella) dances with Louis in a dream. In her lovelorn grief, Harper (Cynthia Mace) fantasizes herself in the Antarctic, and later Joe comes hilariously alive, stepping out of a pioneer tableau, during Harper's vigil in the Diorama Room of the Mormon Visitors' Center in New York City. Ethel Rosenberg, who owed her execution to Cohn's single-handed, improper intervention with the presiding judge, appears at Cohn's bedside. These hauntings are sometimes dramatized as projections of parts of the self that have been murdered in order to survive. "Are you a ghost?" Prior asks Louis as he sways in the arms of his guilty lover to the tune of "Moon River." "No," Louis says. "Just spectral. Lost to myself." The final, ambiguous image of "Millennium Approaches," which brings the play to a halt, if not to a conclusive end, is the appearance of an angel to Prior while he languishes in his sickbed. "*Very* Steven Spielberg," Prior says as the set parts and the angel (Ellen McLaughlin) swings down on wires, to proclaim him prophet and tell him tantalizingly that his great work is about to begin. With the help of jets of smoke, Pat Collins's evocative lighting, and the strong directorial hands of Oskar Eustis and Tony Taccone, the audience is brought bravoing to its feet. The production is far superior in every scenic and performing detail to the celebrated English version.

"Perestroika" is the messier but more interesting of the two plays, skillfully steering its characters from the sins of separation in the eighties to a new sense of community in the embattled nineties. Though "Perestroika" should begin where "Millennium Approaches" breaks off, it opens instead with an excellent but extraneous preamble by the oldest living Bolshevik, bemoaning "this sour little age" and demanding a new ideology: "Show me the words that will reorder the world, or else keep silent." Kushner can't keep silent; but, while his play refuses ideology, it dramatizes, as the title suggests, both the exhilaration and the terror of restructuring perception about gay life and about our national mission. The verbose angel that appears to Prior now turns out in "Perestroika" to be the angel of death or, in this case, stasis. She takes up a lot of time broadcasting a deadly simple, reactionary message of cosmic collapse. "You must stop moving," she tells Prior. "Hobble yourselves. Abjure the Horizontal, Seek the Vertical." But, once the characters get back on the narrative track of the plot, "Perestroika" finds its feet and its wisdom.

The real drama of "Perestroika" is the fulminating, sometimes funny battle the characters wage in trying to deal with catastrophic loss. Here, as in "Millennium Approaches," Cohn, the fixer, is shrewdly placed at the center of the argument. Cohn will not accept loss, always stacking life's deck to maintain his fantasy of omnipotence. "I can get anyone to do anything I want," he tells his black male nurse, Belize (played with panache by K. Todd Freeman), before picking up the phone to blackmail an acquaintance for the drug AZT. "I'm no good at tests, Martin," he tells the acquaintance. "I'd rather cheat." And later, with his stash of AZT in a locked box in the foreground, he crows at his nurse like a big winner: "From now on, I supply my own pills. I already told 'em to push their jujubes to the losers down the hall." All change requires loss, and Cohn's power is a mighty defense against change. His emptiness is colossal. Significantly, Cohn dies mouthing the same words that introduced him in "Millennium Approaches." Kushner shows his other characters growing through an acceptance of loss. "Lost is best," Harper says, refusing to take Joe back after his fling with Louis, and going with the flow of her aimlessness. "Get lost, Joe. Go exploring." Prior, too, has finally wrestled control of his life and what remains of his momentum from the Angel of Stasis. "Motion, progress, is life, it's— modernity," he says, unwilling to be stoical. "We're not rocks, we can't just wait. . . . And wait for what? God." His task is to make sense of death and, as he says, "to face loss, with grace."

Part of this grace is humor, the often heroic high-camp frivolity that both acknowledges suffering and refuses to suffer. When Cohn brags to his nurse, "Pain's . . . nothing, pain's life," Belize replies, sharpish, "Sing it, baby." Kushner uses laughter carefully, to deflate the maudlin and to build a complex tapestry of ironic emotion. He engineers a hilarious redemption for the politically correct Louis, who is forced by Belize to say Kaddish over Cohn's dead body in order to steal the remaining AZT to prolong Prior's life. Louis prays with Ethel Rosenberg's ghost over the body, and they end the Hebrew prayer with "You son of a bitch." And at another point in his emotional turmoil Prior turns to Louis and accuses him of having taken a Mormon lover. "Ask me how I knew," Prior says. Louis asks, "How?" Prior rounds on him: "Fuck you. I'm a prophet." Even Cohn gets off a cosmic joke, making a last-minute appearance from Purgatory as God's lawyer. "You're guilty as hell," he growls at the Deity. "You have nothing to plead, but not to worry, darling, I will make something up."

"Perestroika" ends by celebrating community, not individualism, auguring with eerie serendipity the spirit of the new Clinton era. Even the monstrous Cohn is acknowledged as a fallen victim by the brotherhood. "The question I'm trying to ask is how broad is a community's embrace," Kushner says. "How wide does it reach? Communities all over the world now are in tremendous crisis over the issue of how you let go of the past without forgetting the crimes that were committed." In the play's epilogue, which jumps to 1990, Kushner confronts the audience with the miraculous. Prior has lived four more years. He sits in Central Park in animated conversation with his friends. Then, turning the conversation up and down at his command (Kushner's homage to the ending of "The Glass Menagerie"), Prior steps out of the play world to talk directly to us. It's an extraordinarily powerful (if haphazardly staged) moment, in which the community of concern is extended by the author to the human family, not just the gay world. "Bye now," Prior says. "You are fabulous, each and every one, and I love you all. And I bless you. *More life.* And bless us all."

Backstage, Kushner stood dazed and rumpled among a crowd of well-wishers. "I've been working on this play for four and a half years," he said. "Tonight, a whole era in my life comes to an end. It's been an incredibly strange ride." His exhaustion and the happy fatigue of the cast members, who lingered in doorways, seemed to bear out part of Kushner's opening-night message, which was pinned to the stage-door bulletin board. "And how else should an angel land on earth but with the utmost difficulty?" it read. "If we are to be visited by angels we will have to call them down with sweat and strain, we will have to drag them out of the skies, and the efforts we expend to draw the heavens to an earthly place may well leave us too exhausted to appreciate the fruits of our labors: an angel, even with torn robes, and ruffled feathers, is in our midst."

Kushner and the excellent Taper ensemble had made a little piece of American theatre history on that cloudless California night. "Angels in America" was now officially in the world, covered more or less in glory. It was a victory for Kushner, for theatre, for the transforming power of the imagination to turn devastation into beauty.

❖

Tony Kushner wrote "Perestroika," the second part of "Angels in America," in what he describes as "an incredible eight days I spent at the Russian River, in Northern California, in April of 1991, ten months after my mother died." The play was a tape-measure job—three hundred pages, five acts—that would take six hours to perform. After finishing the epilogue, Kushner threw his belongings in his car and set off down through the Napa Valley toward San Francisco. Almost immediately, life began to imitate the play's marvels and resonances. "When I got in the car, this magical thing happened," Kushner told me the day before he jetted off to watch the London production of his superbly expanded and polished final product (it had been reworked in collaboration with its director, George C. Wolfe, and the New York cast of "Millennium Approaches"), at the Royal National Theatre, and five days before the same version opened on Broadway. "I turned on the radio, and the first thing that came on was 'American Pie.' I started to lose that station, so I switched to the next station. It was Simon and Garfunkel, singing 'America.' Then a group called, I think, the Black Crowes, singing the song 'She Talks to Angels.' Then I switched to a classical-music station that was playing Mozart's bassoon concerto, which was one of my mother's practice pieces. That was amazing. Really amazing." When Kushner got to San Francisco, he installed himself and his humongous manuscript in a café on Market Street and called his friends. "For the entire evening, people came by," he said. "It was a huge party. I ran up this immense bill on bottles of champagne. It was worth it. I really didn't know if, especially after my mother died, I'd ever finish the play, which bracketed my mother's death, and contains it—a form of mourning and a form of not letting go."

"Perestroika"—the word is the Russian for "rebuilding"—dramatizes the work of mourning: the struggle to embrace both loss and change. The play is immense in its wisdom of the heart; every line sings with hurt and humor. Although Kushner has cut the playing time and the number of pages by half, the five-act structure remains intact, parcelled neatly around two intermissions, and is crucial to Kushner's vision of the play's metaphor. " 'Perestroika' doesn't have that classical cadence, that one-two-three punch—a beginning, a kickup, and a bang," he says. " 'Perestroika' doesn't rise and fall in the same way. It's iambic pentameter: 'this and then this and then this and then this and then this.' It's epic. You experience each act very much as an installment of a journey, and you feel, I hope, that at the end you've arrived at a huge place. It's very tricky. For me, the bulk of it—the epic nature of it—becomes part of what it's about: this incredible struggle I feel people have to wage in order to be able to change themselves."

At the end of "Millennium Approaches," all the characters have come to grief and to stalemate. The Mormon wife, Harper, has lost her bisexual lawyer husband, Joe Pitt. Hannah Pitt, Joe's mother, has sold her house in Salt Lake City to move to New York. The defiantly macho Roy Cohn has contracted AIDS. Prior Walter, also suffering from AIDS, has been abandoned first by his lover, Louis, and then, apparently, by his senses, as an angel crashes through the ceiling of his apartment at the finale to announce that Prior is a prophet and she is the messenger. But of what? In "Perestroika," the angel turns out to be an angel of stasis, part of the forces of entropy creating the climate of collapse which Prior either has to join or reject. She carries a red-and-gold "Tome of Immobility, of respite, of cessation." Suspended above Prior and somersaulting occasionally to make a point, the angel (the strong-jawed, fierce-eyed Ellen McLaughlin) is the voice of retreat in the face of overwhelming loss. "Forsake the Open Road," she tells him, sounding like a retrograde Walt Whitman. To Kushner, who is staunchly agnostic, the angel "embodies the longing for a cosmic regression which is so profound that it becomes deeply reactionary and destructive." For the new production, Kushner has cut a lot of the cosmic flimflammery from the début version of "Perestroika" (which was at the Mark Taper Forum, in Los Angeles), and, by showing Prior to be as puzzled as the audience by the angelic visitation, has made it more dramatic. Prior wants to know if the angel is there to damn or save him. "In the Judeo-Christian tradition, the Day of Wrath is both the day of wrath and the coming of the Kingdom of God," Kushner says. "The honey of Heaven may or may not come. You don't get the answer. You get an absolute maybe." Is Prior a prophet? Or is the visitation a dream? In his quandary, Prior (played, by Stephen Spinella, with a poignant and ever-increasing comic command) bolts from the angel. "He is running, he thinks, in defiance of the angel's command to 'be still,' " Kushner wrote in his notes to the director of the English production, Declan Donnellan, "and of course in the process is running himself to death." Prior and all the characters in "Perestroika" teeter on this delicate, terrifying balance between resignation and action. Choice is made harder because the characters have been abandoned both by God and by ideology. A note of historical confusion is sounded in the prologue by the oldest living Bolshevik, Aleksii Antediluvianovich Prelapsarianov, who in the play's first beats raises the question of change. "The Great Question before us is: Can we change? in time? And we all desire that change will come," he says. His old eyes hidden behind sunglasses, Aleksii goes on to scold the audience about "this sour little age," and warns: "If the snake sheds his skin before a new skin is ready, naked he will be in the world, prey to the forces of chaos. . . . Have you, my little serpents, a new skin?"

At the beginning of "Perestroika," the skins of all the characters are by no means thick. They evade the excruciating pain of loss by an obsession with fantasy or with flesh. Harper is distracted by grief. "I'm stuck," she says. "My heart's an anchor." ("What I love in the character," Kushner wrote in his notes to the director, "is that she is both very brave and amazingly inventive in her avoidance, she creates spectacular routes of escape and then unravels them because she knows they're untrue.'') Marcia Gay Harden gives Harper's poetry and pottiness fine definition as she acts out her anguish by chewing down a tree at the Botanic Garden arboretum and, later, spending hours at the Mormon diorama at the Visitors' Center in New York, looking at "The Great Trek," because the main figure reminds her of Joe. "When they push the buttons he'll start to talk," she tells Prior, who is there to learn more about angels. "You can't believe a word he says but the sound of him is reassuring. It's an *incredible* resemblance." Cohn, now pasty and shrunken as he lies in a hospital bed, still wields his furious power as a bulwark against change. He dies, significantly, echoing the words with which he's introduced in "Millennium Approaches." "A nice big box of drugs for Uncle Roy!" he shouts on the phone, blackmailing someone into getting him some AZT. "Or there'll be seven different kinds of hell to pay!" In a perfectly modulated and unforgettable performance, Ron Leibman, with his tongue darting out and with bloodshot eyes shrinking to beads of hate in his gnarled face, turns the bedridden Cohn into a kind of iguana of invective. The hectoring generates a self-hypnotic sense of power, which cuts Cohn off from his loss. "Tough little muscle," he says of his heart. "Never bleeds."

Prior, on the other hand, is full of raw, contradictory feelings, still imagining Louis's return and confessing to feeling "lascivious sad." Louis, for his part, is just plain lascivious. He assuages his guilt by submerging himself in appetite. "What he wants from Joe is the sort of impossible, cost-free salvation Joe seems to offer," Kushner writes. "To get this, Louis has to submit to Joe—politically, sexually, psychologically." As Louis, Joe Mantello has continued to extend the subtlety of his marvellous characterization, and superbly savors the self-loathing in Louis's sexual narcotics. Louis forces himself to connect with Joe Pitt, his ideological opposite, as a kind of penance. "The nose tells the body —the heart, the mind, the fingers, the cock—what it wants," he says, licking Joe's cheeks in one of the most extraordinary seduction scenes I've ever seen, "and then the tongue explores, finding out what's edible, what isn't, what's most mineral, food for the blood, food for the bones, and therefore most delectable." Louis puts his hand down the front of Joe's pants, pulls it out, and smells and then tastes his fingers. "Chlorine. Copper. Earth," he says, and makes his move. Joe falls in love with Louis. This is one of Kushner's major discoveries in the rewrite, and allows him to extend their relationship beyond political squabbling to the play's more central issue: Where do love and justice meet? "I mean you say law isn't justice and justice isn't morals," Louis says in the middle of one of their bouts of lovemaking, "but really, who if not the right is putting the prude back in Jurisprudence?" David Marshall Grant makes Joe at once sweetly expansive in love and obtusely closed down in life. When, late in the play, Louis and Joe square off against each other over Joe's ghostwriting of reactionary legal decisions, Joe continues to bleat, "It's law, not justice, it's power, not the merits of its exercise, it's not an expression of the ideal, it's . . . ." And there's an ugly fight, in which Louis gets bloodied. "It's literally having blood on his hands that makes Joe get it," Kushner wrote in his notes.

The black nurse, Belize, is the character who mediates between the living and the dead, and between Louis and Prior. As Belize, Jeffrey Wright comes into his own in "Perestroika," stamping the character with a distinctive, camp combination of fury and fun. When Cohn boasts, "Pain's . . . nothing, pain's life," Belize counters, "Sing it, baby." Belize is the play's moral bellwether. He tips off Louis to Joe's ghostwriting and to his relationship to Cohn, and it's also Belize who recognizes in Cohn not just the "polestar of human evil," as Louis calls him, but a fallen gay brother. "A queen can forgive her vanquished foe," Belize says. "It isn't easy. . . . Forgiveness. Which is maybe where love and justice finally meet." He engineers an epiphany of love and justice by getting Louis to say Kaddish over Cohn's dead body while he steals Cohn's AZT to prolong Prior's life. In this exquisite scene, Kushner manages to act out both anger and atonement by having Louis and the ghost of Ethel Rosenberg finish the prayer, saying in counterpoint, "You son of a bitch."

For most of the characters, the play's arc leads to an acceptance of loss and to a new kind of strength in solitude. "Sometimes, maybe lost is best," Harper tells Joe, who returns on the rebound from Louis. "Get lost, Joe. Go exploring." She hands him her Valium stash and exits from their symbiotic relationship into a hard-won, clear-eyed independence. In an airplane on the way to San Francisco, she thinks of the hole in the ozone layer and has a vision of dead souls floating up "like skydivers in reverse, limbs all akimbo, wheeling and spinning." The departed clasp hands and form a web that repairs the hole. "Nothing's lost forever," she says in one of Kushner's most gorgeous speeches. "In this world, there is a kind of painful progress. Longing for what we've left behind, and dreaming ahead."

Prior, too, has fought his way to a spiritual place. He climbs a neon ladder to Heaven and confronts a congress of angels, the Council of Continental Principalities. "We live past hope. If I can find hope anywhere, that's it, that's the best I can do," he tells them, finally rejecting the "Tome of Immobility" and able to receive the gift of the dead, which is a renewed sense of life. "I want more life," he says. Prior becomes strong enough to accept his isolation and his death. "This is my life, from now on, Louis. I'm not getting 'better,' " he says. Louis declares his love for Prior and asks to come back, but Prior, while acknowledging love, also acknowledges that some hurts are irreparable. "You can't come back," he finally tells Louis. "Not ever. I'm sorry. But you can't." Mourning has led him to a new way of being. "To face loss. With grace. Is key, I think, but it's impossible," he says.

There's comparable gallantry in the passionate restraint of George C. Wolfe's production. Wolfe inherited "Millennium Approaches" when the script was frozen, after its successful London and Mark Taper productions, but here, in reimagining "Perestroika" for Broadway, he has been free to impose his swift, unfettered intelligence on the material. As a result, the play is tighter, sharper, more scenically and emotionally streamlined than "Millennium Approaches." Robin Wagner's set is simpler and more effective; and Jules Fisher, the maestro of the lighting board, shapes an array of subtle and suggestive moods.

Just before the epilogue, Hannah Pitt (the formidable Kathleen Chalfant), whose rigidity has lost her the allegiance of her homosexual son but who learns tolerance through her friendship with Prior, takes leave of him in the hospital, promising to come again. "Please do," Prior says, invoking Tennessee Williams: "I have always depended on the kindness of strangers." Hannah, who has no self-pity and doesn't seem to know the famous line, rounds on Prior, saying, "Well, that's a stupid thing to do." It's a big laugh, but it's also telling. Not since Williams has a playwright announced his poetic vision with such authority on the

Broadway stage. Kushner is the heir apparent to Williams's romantic theatrical heritage: he, too, has tricks in his pocket and things up his sleeve, and he gives the audience "truth in the pleasant disguise of illusion." And, also like Williams, Kushner has forged an original, Impressionistic theatrical vocabulary to show us the heart of a new age.

At the finale, which jumps forward four years, to 1990, with Prior still alive and chatting happily with his "family"—Louis, Belize, Hannah—beneath the angel at the Bethesda Fountain in Central Park, Kushner takes another leaf from Williams's book. He lets Prior stop-start the vivacious chat the way Tom Wingfield does in "The Glass Menagerie." "The world only spins forward. We will be citizens. The time has come," Prior says to us, turning upstage and then, almost as an afterthought, turning back to deliver the ineffably moving envoi. "Bye now," he says. "You are fabulous creatures. And I bless you: *More life. The Great Work Begins.*" And on that note of blessing—at once elegiac and adamant—the characters take leave of us. But, long after the ovation is over, we retain their sense of life and struggle and miracle. In the strict sense of the word, we *are* all fabulous—"the subjects of whom stories are told." And Kushner, in his bighearted and almost reckless bravery, has told a great story. There will be those who will regret the subject matter, or the length, or the cosmic folderol. But the carping hardly matters. "Perestroika" is a masterpiece.

EDWARD ALBEE

SONS AND MOTHERS

For one terrible moment at the beginning of "Three Tall Women," the pretension that has sunk so many of Edward Albee's theatrical vehicles in his middle years looms menacingly on the horizon. "It's downhill from sixteen on," says one of the women, a middle-aged character called B, who takes care of a rich, imperious, senile old bird called A and is herself a connoisseur of collapse. She goes on, "I'd like to see children learn it—have a six-year-old say 'I'm dying' and know what it means." But then, as we and the old lady settle into the demented fog of her remembering and forgetting, it becomes apparent that Albee has found his way back to the sour and passionate straight talking of his early, best plays.

The last great gift a parent gives to a child is his or her own death, and the energy underneath "Three Tall Women" is the exhilaration of a writer calling it quits with the past—specifically, the rueful standoff between Albee and his mother, the late Frances Cotter Albee, who adopted him only to kick him out of the family home, at eighteen, for his homosexual shenanigans and later to cut him out of her sizable will. The play has earned Albee, who is sixty-six, his third (and most deserved) Pulitzer Prize, but the writer's real victory is a psychological one—honoring the ambiguity of "the long unpleasant life she led" while keeping her memory vividly alive. Far from being an act of revenge or special pleading, the play is a wary act of reconciliation, whose pathos and poetry are a testament to the bond, however attenuated, between child and parent. "Three Tall Women" bears witness to the son's sad wish to be loved, but with this liberating difference: the child is now finally in control of the parent's destiny, instead of the parent's being in control of the child's. Here, in a set whose Empire furniture, mahogany parquet, flocked blue bedroom wallpaper, and resplendent silver tea service emphasize the iconography of privilege, and not the clutter of decline, sits the ninety-two-year-old A, a fragile, white-haired replica of Albee's mother. A is a spoiled, petulant, demanding, bigoted, manipulative old bat. "*I'll* fix him" she says of her absent son, her quicksilver emotions veering suddenly from tears to a hatred that includes B and a twenty-something female lawyer, C. "I'll fix *all* of 'em. They all think they can treat me like this. You all think you can get away with anything." A's transparent impotence makes the once horrible hectoring now merely laughable. But she is still a potent amalgam of dyspepsia and decrepitude. A former beauty (Albee's mother was briefly a model), A was protected first by the fortune of a face and then by a fortune. Her narcissism and her isolation are spectacular. "You take people as friends and you spend time at it, you put effort in, and it doesn't matter if you don't like them anymore—who likes anybody anymore?—you've put in all that time, and what right do they have to . . . to . . ." she says, her thoughts, like her life, evaporating disconcertingly before her eyes.

Act I paints the landscape of A's old age—the humiliations of incontinence, memory loss, confusion, and regret—and is dominated by the huge, heroic performance of Myra Carter. Ms. Carter, who is sixty-four and is new to me, gives one of the finest performances I've ever seen on the New York stage—an enormous feat of memory, energy, and observation. "I've shrunk!" she says, overwhelmed by the confusions, real and imagined, that beset her. "I'm not tall! I used to be so tall! Why have I shrunk?" Carter hits every vowel and consonant of Albee's words, filling each one with lucid thought and wonderful music. She growls, squawks, cackles, whimpers, rages through the torrent of emotion and memory that's called out of her by the two interlocutors. A's life turns out to have been a series of punishing losses: a sister who became a drunk; a mother who, when she moved into her daughter's home, became an enemy; a son who became a stranger; a husband who became first a philanderer and then a victim of cancer. Carter's face is still beautiful, and it lights up intermittently with childlike delight, even sweetness, which reminds us of the charm that A's former good looks exerted on the world, and mitigates the emptiness of the shallow life she describes. "I was . . . well, I was naked; I didn't have a stitch, except I had on all my jewelry. I hadn't taken off my jewelry," A says, giggling, about a crucial episode of her early marriage, when "his pee-pee was all hard, and . . . and hanging on it was a new bracelet." Her husband wants a sexual favor that the well-mannered A can't and won't perform. She continues, "Well, it started to go soft, and the bracelet slid off, and it fell into my lap. I was naked; deep into my lap. 'Keep it,' he said and he turned and he walked out of my dressing room." She weeps at the memory, which sounds the first note of her husband's emotional retreat.

The ballast to A's dementia is provided by B, the droll and delightful Marian Seldes, who moves like a slow loris around the stage, her shoulders hunched as if lumbered with the weight of both her own and A's boredom with old age. "And so it goes" is her recurring catchphrase, which announces the giddy zone of resignation and detachment that she inhabits. "In the morning, when she wakes up she wets—a kind of greeting to the day, I suppose," she tells C, translating her irritation into little dollops of snideness to make it bearable. "The sphincter and the cortex not in synch. Never during the *night,* but *as* she wakes." B exists to register the old woman's existential anguish; and the inflexible C is there to broadcast moral horror. Albee is less successful with C, who is meant to be callow but—in the first act, at least—is just a poorly written prig. A lawyer sorting out A's unpaid bills, C (played by Jordan Baker) behaves more like an intemperate and insensitive teen-ager than like an employee. A, who is full of antique phrases like "Don't you get fresh," is also full of the ancient bigotries of her class. These draw implausible reactions from C. A's recollection of Irving Thalberg as "a real smart little Jew" prompts C's dopey outrage: "I'm a democrat." And, later, when A talks about "colored help" knowing their place ("none of those uppity niggers, the city ones"), C explodes in dismay, "Oh, Jesus Christ!" Her tone soon becomes predictable, and the character loses a purchase on the audience's imagination, which is focussed on A and on what she sees, at the end of Act I, as her inheritance of hate. "I think they all hated me, because I was strong, because I *had* to be," A says, rationalizing her self-involvement. "Sis hated me; Ma hated me; all those others, *they* hated me." She goes strangely silent after the speech. And Albee brings the curtain down with B and C realizing that their employer has had a stroke.

In Act II, by an ingenious coup de théâtre, "Three Tall Women" expands from a parental cameo to a vista of decline. At curtain rise, A is still collapsed in bed but now has an oxygen mask over her face. B and C seem to have dressed up for their bedside vigil in period high fashion— B in pearls and an elegant gray frock with a full, pleated fifties skirt, and C in a layered ankle-length cream chiffon dress that evokes the twenties. Then, as B and C bicker about death, and the conversation drifts to the absence of a living will and why A didn't write one, A herself, in an elegant lavender dress, walks in from the wings. "I was going to but then I forgot, or it slipped my mind, or something," she says. The moment is electrifying. The body in the bed turns out to be a manne-quin. In this theatrical fillip, Albee goes from a familiar external reality to a bold interior one. B and C are now projections of A, who speaks rationally for the duration of the play, responding from different stages of her life. Albee's wonderful invention allows him both to incarnate A's narcissism and to lift the play from characterization to meditation. What we get is a kind of Cubist stage picture, where the characters are fragments of a single self. The device is at its most eloquent when the son appears, in preppy clothes and clasping freesias, to sit by his coma-tose mother in a dumb show of devotion. The characters circle him:

C (*Wonder*): I have children?

B (*None too pleasant*): We have one; we have a boy.

A (*Same*): Yes, we do. I have a son.

B (*Seeing him, sneering*): Well, fancy seeing you again. (*Sudden, and enraged, into his face*) Get out of my house!

In this terrifying and terrible moment, the son doesn't react. In fact, he never speaks. B, the voice the son heard when he was growing up, berates him as "filthy," but A, from the distance of her dotage, begs for tolerance. "He came back; he never loved me, he never loved us, but he came back. Let him alone," she says, adding later, "Twenty-plus years? That's a long enough sulk—on both sides." Lawrence Sacharow, the director, stages these lines impeccably and with awful authenticity. The boy's muteness is a metaphor for the inconsolable gap between parent and child. It's also another of Albee's cunning dramatic maneuvers: the child is forever outside the narcissistic parental embrace—seen but not heard.

The son's leave-taking ("He packed up his attitudes and he *left*," B says) is just one of a litany of losses that A and her former selves pick over in this fugue of hope and hurt. Inevitably, the play becomes a dance of A's defensiveness, as her psyche struggles to idealize itself. "I . . . will . . . not . . . become . . . you. I will *not*. I . . . I deny *you*," C says to A, who, in turn, is unrepentant and rejects their versions of life: "I'm *here*, and I deny you *all*; I deny every *one* of you." In this landscape of loneliness and heartache, C, at the finale, asks about the happy times. "I *know* my best times—what is it? happiest?—haven't happened yet. They're to *come*," she says. "Aren't they? Please?" B can't agree, preferring her own middle age: "It's the only time you get a three-hundred-and-sixty-degree view—see in all directions. Wow! What a view!" But A has the final say, which is pitched, sardonically, like the happy ending of a Restoration play, with the characters joining hands to face the audience. With B and C on either side of her, A speaks her notion of the happiest moment in life. "When we stop. When we can stop," she says, and, as they together breathe and exhale for the last time, the lights fade to black. At the beginning of this gorgeous final speech, A catches herself lying about her age—a sweet vanity that Albee pays off with a joke. "Give a girl a break," she says to B. And that, finally, is what Albee's "Three Tall Women" does for his mother. The mute young man in the play can now, in his own middle age, give her the gift of his words, and make something beautiful and enduring about both her privilege and her neglect.

SIR TERENCE RATTIGAN

UNTUTORED HEARTS

W<small>HEN</small> S<small>IR</small> T<small>ERENCE</small> R<small>AT</small>-tigan (1911–77) was seven, he conceived the notion of being both a playwright and a confirmed bachelor. "Wives can be an awful handicap to writers," he explained to his mother. "They are constantly telling their husbands to do this, fetch that, and ordering them from the house." Rattigan attributed his subsequent homosexuality to the atmosphere of repressed hostility in his genteel household, where his father, a philandering diplomat, kept up the appearance of marriage to his beloved, unhappy mother. Rattigan's father had wanted him to follow the paternal footsteps into the diplomatic corps, and, in a way, Rattigan did. Onstage and off, he was the most politic of playwrights, discreetly transforming the turmoil of his homosexual life into stylish, affecting heterosexual form. From the late thirties to the mid-fifties, a string of hits—"French Without Tears," "The Winslow Boy," "The Browning Version," "Separate Tables," "The Deep Blue Sea"—made him the most successful commercial playwright of his day. He believed that the playwright owed the public a story. He honored feeling, not ferment. His tales of upper-middle-class life had no political, polemical, or ideological residue. "From Aeschylus to Tennessee Williams, the only theatre that has ever mattered is the theatre of character and narrative," he said. This attitude, which for a while made Rattigan the last word on the West End, eventually turned him into a dead letter.

"Perhaps I should have stayed and fought it out," Rattigan said in an interview shortly before his death. "I just didn't have a chance with anything." In the face of the New Wave's radical hyperbole about theatre, Rattigan stuck to his conservative guns. "The successful creation of living characters upon the stage," he wrote, "has always been, is now, and will remain a higher achievement for the dramatist than the successful assertion of an idea, or series of ideas." Out of step with the egalitarian momentum of the welfare state, Rattigan was damned by the theatre's Angry Young Men as much for the suburban audiences that flocked to his plays as for his apolitical success. By the beginning of the nineteen-sixties, he was out of fashion; and by the end of the sixties he was out of English theatre's critical discussion altogether. "It's all very well to dislike one's plays, but they ought to be disliked for a better reason than that they're out of fashion," Rattigan said at the end of his life. "I always thought that justice would one day be done to me."

And now, sixteen years later, London's small (three-hundred-seat), influential Almeida Theatre has given Rattigan's emotional and dramatic subtlety its due in a stunning revival of "The Deep Blue Sea" (1952). The play has been mounted twice in London over the last eight years without a ripple, but the Almeida has made waves by shrewdly enticing the filmmaker Karel Reisz to tackle it. Reisz, who has coaxed some of the finest performances from actors like Albert Finney ("Saturday Night and Sunday Morning"), Nick Nolte ("Who'll Stop the Rain?"), James Caan ("The Gambler"), and Meryl Streep ("The French Lieutenant's Woman"), has cut the play's period excesses, polished the well-cast performances to a shine, and focussed his Czech outsider's sharp eye on the play's dark, unsparing exploration of the ferocious tension between passion and English manners. Now that history has put paid to the delirium of ideology, Rattigan's intelligence and quiet audacity are more easily seen. The revival, which will transfer to the West End after its sold-out eight-and-a-half-week run, signals a rise in Rattigan's fortunes. Ridley Scott has bought "The Browning Version" for the movies, and Peter Hall is planning a revival of "Separate Tables" this spring. Reisz's production does for "The Deep Blue Sea" what Hall did for Harold Pinter's "The Homecoming" and Lindsay Anderson did for Joe Orton's "What the Butler Saw"—gives the British a perfectly poised, many-layered, exemplary production, which so deftly illuminates the author's style and content that the play's stature as a postwar master-piece is incontrovertible.

Rattigan has gained an unlikely champion in Reisz, whose "Saturday Night and Sunday Morning" helped put him and boulevard gentility on the shelf. The film not only ushered in the new era of working-class actor heroes (Finney, Peter O'Toole, Tom Courtenay)—performers who before the Education Act of 1944 would never have got to drama school—but brazenly ignored upper-middle-class life, which was outside the experience of three-quarters of the British public. Reisz is my next-door neighbor and friend, so I dropped in to find out what, exactly, had attracted him to Rattigan. "He's extraordinarily unflinching about the human heart," Reisz said, over tea in his study. "There's a lot of feeling but no sentimentality. It's a very subversive view of eros. The play completely attacks the accepted assumptions about romantic love, marriage, the way the sexes relate. To Rattigan, perhaps because of his homosexuality, there is always the pursuer and the pursued. There is always a power imbalance in sexual relationships. There is never a mutuality of desire and affection."

This shaming fact is what drives Hester Collyer to try to gas herself in "The Deep Blue Sea." "Finished—Freddie" are her first words as she regains consciousness after her botched suicide attempt (a reimagining of the suicide of Rattigan's former lover, who left him for a younger man). Hester, an upper-class vicar's daughter who has bolted from her seven-year marriage to a respected judge for a ten-month fling with a former RAF fighter pilot, has come down in the world. This descent, echoing that of a winded nineteen-fifties Britain, is underlined by her dingy rented rooms, which have been converted from grander Victorian days, when they were part of a single house. In Penelope Wilton's marvellous interpretation, Hester is a sharply intelligent, strong-willed woman of sensibility (she paints), who is trapped and humiliated by an obsession that seems, in Rattigan's words, "too strong for her to resist." Her obsession is Freddie, a sporty chap who has gone off on a golfing weekend and forgotten her birthday. The discrepancy between the immensity of Hester's need—she fairly leaps at Freddie, like a bass to a lure, when they finally kiss and make up—and the inadequacy of Freddie's affection has brought her to this pretty pass. She is caught in a desperate equation of passion that won't factor out, and she knows it. "Zero minus zero is still zero," she says of Freddie's feelings for her. Hester tries to force affection, but it can't be returned. As she confides to her landlady, Mrs. Elton (Sandra Voe), here blessedly stripped of the period de rigueur working-class comic stereotype, "When you're between any kind of devil and the deep blue sea, the deep blue sea seems very inviting."

The suicide attempt brings the return of Hester's husband, Sir William, who stands before her not as judge but as a kind of bleeding wound, a decent English gent of cultivated mind and untutored heart. In Nicholas Jones's touching, beautifully modulated performance, William Collyer—a man who incarnates convention—is bemused by Hester's unconventional behavior. He puts a suave face on hurt. He can't express his feelings. This doesn't so much cancel them out as magnify their inarticulate power. Sir William is kind, reasonable, and rich, and he wants her back. He has everything to offer but intimacy. Their scenes together punish and burn as they try to steer a safe course between affection and disappointment. What, Collyer asks, does Freddie give her? "Himself," Hester explains. But sex can't quite speak its name. "There are polite words and impolite words," Hester says about the ineffable liberation of sexual abandon. "They all add up to the same emotion."

All Rattigan's characters are trapped within the limits of their psychological makeup, none to more surprisingly poignant effect than the pukka Freddie, who rightly observes, "My sort never gets a hearing," and whose boyish narcissism is cleverly captured by Linus Roache. The best of Freddie's life is behind him. ("He loved 1940," Hester says.) Drinking has blighted any future as a test pilot, and Freddie can't seem to find a place for himself in peacetime Britain. In Freddie, still waters run shallow. "God, how I hate getting tangled up in other people's emotions," he says to a friend after discovering Hester's suicide note. Unlike Sir William, Freddie knows the limitations of his heart and isn't so empowered by wealth or position as to delude himself that he can satisfy Hester's enormous emotional needs. Her possessive demands only magnify an inadequacy that he well understands and that infuriates him. At first, he tries to reason Hester out of their relationship: " 'A' loves 'B'—'B' doesn't love 'A,' or at least not in the same way. He wants to, but he can't. It's not his nature. . . . demands are made on him which he can't fulfill." Finally, in the face of Hester's hysterical clinging, Freddie quits her, saying, "Hes, this is our last chance. If we miss it, we're done for. We're death to each other, you and I.'' And he's right.

Rattigan passes no judgments and offers no cures. He evenhandedly makes each character's case, while wringing the situation of every nuance of hope and desolation. Hester's abandonment, the smug curiosity of a pompous neighbor (William Osborne) who comes for Freddie's clothes, Sir William's spurned patriarchal offer of safe harbor, Freddie's tentative final return as he probes between the lines for a way back to Hester before going to certain death as a test pilot in South America keep the audience focussed on theatre's most elemental and hard-won issue: what happens next. Rattigan adds oxygen to the heat of his drama with a mysterious lodger—Mr. Miller, a disbarred foreign doctor who ministers to Hester, casting both a cold eye on English manners and a warm heart on her struggle to reclaim her life. Here Reisz has departed boldly from Rattigan's notion of Miller, which gave him a ''slight German accent,'' and has opted for someone completely foreign—the wonderful Polish actor Wojtek Pszoniak, famous for his roles in Andrej Wajda films. In his droll glances and his reflective stillness, Mr. Pszoniak, giving a good imitation of Reisz himself, adds great power to the emotional and moral stakes of the play. He is a model of philosophical detachment, and conveys Miller as someone who has the courage of his own solitude. His speeches have been made more monosyllabic, and add to the aura of a man who has learned to live with heartbreak. Miller, dismissed by others in the play as ''a bloody riddler'' and ''a callous phony,'' is the voice of the author's steely pragmatism. ''I cannot live without hope,'' Hester says to Miller. He pauses a moment and replies, ''Then you must learn. Without hope, there is no despair.'' Reisz ends his version of ''The Deep Blue Sea'' with one gorgeous theatrical fillip. ''The only purpose in life is to live it,'' Miller tells Hester in the simplified penultimate scene. And Hester finds the courage to let Freddie go and to survive the night. She lights the gas fire and, with gaslight flickering on her body, packs Freddie's raincoat into a valise. In a bit of invented business, she pauses to inhale Freddie's scent off the coat. In this last beat, the memory of sensuality is what remains.

LILLIAN HELLMAN

HELL ON A SHORT FUSE

ANGER WAS LILLIAN HELL-
man's oxygen. She began life quarrelling with the world, and she ended
it, notoriously, quarrelling with Mary McCarthy over whether there
was anything true in her writing, even the "and"s and "the"s. She
went to her eternal reward with the only reward she ever sought—
being on everybody's mind. Hellman's anger called the world to attention and insured that her presence was felt. "There's a place where
everybody wants to be insulted, and Lilly knew where it was,"
Hellman's lover and boon companion for her last twenty-one years,
Peter Feibleman, said a few hours before the official opening of "Cakewalk," his play about their relationship—freely adapted from his 1988
memoir "Lilly: Reminiscences of Lillian Hellman"—in the American
Repertory Theatre's production at the Loeb Drama Center, in Cambridge, Massachusetts. "Lilly could look at a man and know where the
place was and act on it. The insult always came before the compliment. I
used to watch and laugh. She was setting her hook; and, once the hook
was in, it stayed in. People thought immediately that she knew more
about them than anyone else ever had, including themselves. In some
cases it was true, but in many cases it wasn't. It was just that she knew
how to perform it."

In "Cakewalk," Hellman's performing self is inhabited by the formidable Elaine Stritch, who bristles with her own kind of irascibility and
brilliance. Stritch is a heaven-sent stand-in for Hellman. She is rough
and tough, but part of the fierce intensity she brings onstage is a sense of
woundedness and a refusal to capitulate to it. "Cakewalk," which takes
its name from the high-stepping dance competition, delivers the pranc-
ing, competitive Hellman. "There's a piece in the *Times* today—'the

three great living American playwrights, Williams, Miller and Albee'—
no mention of me—I'm not dead yet, but I'll have to prove it,'' she says
on the phone to Feibleman, dubbed Cuff in the play, inviting herself to
stay with him in New Orleans. The facts are less lovely and more
interesting. Feibleman remembers Hellman ''walking around her living
room like a termagant in a whooshing rage, saying 'I've got to get back
on top. I don't know how I'm going to do it. There are people who can
stand to be forgotten, and there are people who cannot. I cannot.' ''
Hellman mastered her envy by becoming the envied, and this accounts,
in part, for her slightly preposterous public insistence on herself as the
grande dame of American letters. She turned her tyrannical temperament into a legend of truculent integrity. After her plays could no
longer captivate an audience, she dramatized herself in four books of
quasi-autobiography, which, beginning in the late sixties, found her
both a new public and a new fame.

''The jump from thinking in dialogue to thinking in prose is enormous,'' Feibleman says. ''It's like asking a sculptor at the end of his life
to take up painting.'' His play pays proper respect to Hellman's discipline and her appetite for work, but her transformation from queen of
drama into drama queen is full of ironies. In many of her plays, much of
the crucial action takes place offstage. In her books, though, Hellman is
always center stage. With dialogue as shrewdly stilted and sensational as
that of a thirties thriller, Hellman portrays herself as a woman of action,
at pains to show *and* tell. She tells Sam Goldwyn to stuff it. She stands
up to the House Un-American Activities Committee—a decent gesture
that in her retelling, as Mordecai Richler has written, reduces the
McCarthy era to ''Lillian Hellman saying no to the resounding sound of
her own applause.''

''Cakewalk'' is an anecdotal play: the first act covers one summer in
the sixties, when Feibleman and Hellman hooked up on Martha's Vineyard, and the second canters through scenes from the next twenty-odd
years of their cooking, squabbling, loving, travelling, and being there for
each other. Feibleman generally steers away from the big, slightly incredible gestures of legend, and instead brings us news of the private
Hellman and the insecurity behind her fractiousness. Hellman's real
bravery is shown here in the ordinary business of making a good day for

herself, and in surviving, half-paralyzed and blind at the end of her life, in a body she had always hated. "Lillian divorced herself from her body at the age of five," Feibleman told me, explaining what he calls in his memoir her "outraged heart of childhood." He went on, "She was outraged at the misfortune of her face. In her generation in the South— she was born in New Orleans in 1905—if a woman didn't have money or looks she'd had it. Lillian looked in the mirror and thought, I have to go my own way. It was beyond the belief of the specialists at Mass. General that she didn't know where her liver, her lungs, or her heart was. They thought she'd been mentally affected by her strokes. But she hadn't. She just took no interest in her body. It was her enemy. She loathed it because it didn't get her anything. She got the body's pleasures with her mind, not her body."

The old are rarely embraced. This emotional deprivation, which is part of the poignance and terror of decline, is also a large part of Hellman's drama. She was forever maneuvering to be massaged, hugged, kissed, and slept with. The longing of the flesh for contact is palpable and punishing in "Cakewalk," and more should be made of it. "If you touched Lilly, she glowed," Feibleman told me. "Lillian was sexy when she was dying. There was a kind of burning out of bones. That's what it felt like." One of the play's most powerful and shocking moments occurs near the finale, when the decrepit and blind Lilly, in her wheelchair, turns to Cuff and tells him to shut the door. Cuff does as he is told. "I want to know," she asks finally, "if we're ever going to go to bed together again." Cuff says no. Seduction was central to Hellman's Southern character. She seduced with her plays, with her prose, with her fine cooking, with her abusive and her courtly banter.

In his memoir Feibleman recounts discovering Hellman in her hospital bed stroking a young guitar-playing doctor's leg. In the play, however, the doctor merely strokes the guitar. It's a missed opportunity both in the script and in Ron Daniels' uncharacteristically sluggish production. But Stritch is sexy. She throws her long legs and her one-liners flirtatiously around the stage, insinuating Hellman's game of intellectual slap and tickle, from which, as Jules Feiffer says, "you came away convinced that you were Nick and she was Nora." And, of course, Hellman was Nora—having been Dashiell Hammett's lover and the model for Nora Charles in "The Thin Man." In "Cakewalk," the smart talk smacks of William Powell and Myrna Loy meeting cute.

Hellman was, as the play says, "crotch-jealous." Much of the pathos and humor of the script focusses on the old battle-ax badgering, manipulating, even hiring a detective to spy on Cuff as he sorts out his hectic sexuality. When she's caught red-handed by Cuff, Lilly goes into high dudgeon. "You've upset me terribly—just imagine!—*accusing me of hiring a detective to spy on you.* It's unspeakable of you," she says. "I'll call you back when I get over the pain you've caused me."

Cuff narrates the events, moving in and out of the action to update the story and to do Hellman's special pleading. "You will have to explain the past," Lilly tells Cuff. In this production, John Slattery, as Cuff, doesn't seem either to age or to acquire the irony that comes with age. The amperage of his and Lilly's appeal for each other therefore loses much of its charge, and makes for a battle of wits in which one player is mostly unarmed. Cuff remains a guarded character, less effective than Lilly at displays of dissimulation. Lilly believes the lies she tells, but Cuff can't quite reach that level of self-delusion. The character seems fearful of admitting his own nature, which is too bad, since the facts of Feibleman's life are the stuff of good drama.

By the time Hellman took up with Feibleman, in 1963, when he was thirty-three, he had published two novels, had had a play on Broadway, and had been taken to Hollywood by his stage director, Joshua Logan. His first film earned him a production deal and a nervous breakdown. "If it hadn't been for Lilly, I think I would have ended up in an institution for a while," he told me. "Lilly stopped it. She put me to work. You never, never want to lose somebody who has done that for you. It's a huge thing. It's a big, big thing." Not, evidently, big enough to be properly dramatized. Although the play admits Feibleman's bisexuality and Hellman's rapacity, "Cakewalk" never quite fesses up to the emotional trade-offs in their unlikely bond. Feibleman makes only a glib flourish at his own extraordinary personal history. His father, who published some fifty books of metaphysics, was the head of the philosophy department at Tulane. His mother had been sexually mutilated after her mother caught her masturbating as a young girl. "If your mother can't have an orgasm—as my father told me when they divorced, in my teens—then older women become very sexually attractive, because somewhere you want to give it to your mother,'' said Feibleman, who by the age of ten not only had met Henry Miller, William Faulkner, Sherwood Anderson, and Paul Robeson at his parents' liberal New Orleans salon but had been in a ménage à trois that included the family gardener and the gardener's girlfriend. ''I had a kind of con act,'' he says. ''I was a ten-year-old child pretending to be a ten-year-old child. I was anything but innocent. And when I met Lilly for the first time, when I was ten, she called my shot. She was the first person to see me. And I recognized the con in her. It was recognition.'' But almost none of Feibleman's turbulent and revealing psychosexual complexity gets into the character of Cuff or into the drama of his romance with Hellman. A rewrite could easily remedy this glaring absence. Feibleman got a mentor and a passionate mother; Hellman, who had seven abortions during her rollicking life, got, as the play says, ''the closest thing to a child I'm ever going to have.'' Each assuaged the other's sense of inadequacy, and each needed the other to fulfill his or her destiny— literary for Feibleman and carnal for Hellman. Their connection, as the play poignantly shows, transcended their limitations.

''Cakewalk'' begins with an image of an osprey, a bird of prey whose name, the author informs us, means ''bone-breaker.'' And at the end the bird is projected larger and larger on a scrim as the lights fade on Lilly, standing on the beach in all her unrepentant contrariness—part monster, part master storyteller—chain-smoking in her Blackglama mink. ''Well, we got through it, that's the main thing—we came out fine in the end, didn't we?'' Lilly says in the play's last line, repeating a refrain in their relationship. In his memoir Feibleman answers in the affirmative. In the play, Cuff is mum. Feibleman, who disagreed with Hellman's publishing ''Scoundrel Time'' and with her suing Mary Mc-Carthy, nevertheless stayed the course, and was rewarded for his loyalty as both ''son'' and ''lover'' with Hellman's Martha's Vineyard house and half her royalties. Even in ambivalence, he is loyal to her literary memory, maintaining that Hellman is ''the only woman in the history of the world to become an internationally famous playwright.'' This says more about the patriarchal structure of theatre than about the quality of Hellman's plays. ''The Little Foxes'' and its more interesting sequel,

''Another Part of the Forest,'' are her only outstanding works, and at the end even Hellman had given up beating the drum for her drama. ''I don't basically have a theatre imagination,'' she told the *Los Angeles Times* in 1980. But the drama of her soul is another matter; and here Feibleman, with a bit more moxie, might have a terrific play. To pull it off, he'll have to forgo the romance of literary life—the swagger about discipline, fear, artistic temperament—and show the audience the impoverishment that such literary obsession hides. In prose and in public, Hellman knew how to exploit the moment and how to give it the illusion of significance. But both her work and her life were betrayed by an imagination that to the end mistook being visible for having a vision.

ALAN BENNETT

MADJESTY

ALAN BENNETT'S "THE
Madness of George III" begins just after the monarch loses the colonies
and just before he loses his mind. This landscape of loss and retreat is
distinctively Bennett territory. Nobody else sings Britain's postimperial
blues with quite such sad-sack and intelligent hilarity. "I see England
now in grammatical terms," a character in Bennett's "The Old Country" (1977) says. "Almost as a tense, a mood. The optative. Would that
this were so. Would it were different." England's future is conditional;
and Bennett, who keeps a fastidious distance from life's hurly-burly, is
sensationally tentative. He makes a patchwork of his winded society
from scraps of anecdote and overheard conversation; his nervousness
with plot betrays an imagination that, like the society itself, has lost faith
in the promise of coherence or of greatness. Since Bennett first announced the brilliance of his performing self to the British, at the age of
twenty-seven, in "Beyond the Fringe" (1961), his owlish presence—
the quiff of blond hair drooping above horn-rimmed glasses—has been
the face of endearing disenchantment which has launched a thousand
quips, winkling out drollery from disappointment and folly from hope.
"I think sexual intercourse is in order," says the upwardly mobile wife,
Joyce Chilvers, to her podiatrist husband at her moment of vindictive
social triumph in Bennett's film "A Private Function." As a performer
and a playwright, Bennett strikes a deep chord in English life not so
much by the stories he tells as by the voice he tells them in. His
characters emit either the squeak of pinched expectation or the high-
camp bravado of threadbare privilege. He is a master of mood and social
detail, the Turgenev of the English lower-middle class. Shy and her-
metic, Bennett is a man of abdications, whose comic tone sounds the

true note of stalemate and resignation in English society. This sense of limitation takes the form of irony, and Bennett is expert at deploying it as a kind of hedged bet against loss. "Irony is inescapable," he writes in "The Old Country," meditating on England, and on a habit of mind that so deeply divides the dour English from their optimistic American cousins. "We're conceived in irony. We float in it from the womb. It's the amniotic fluid. It's the silver sea. It's the waters at their priest-like task washing away guilt and purpose and responsibility. Joking but not joking. Caring but not caring. Serious but not serious." But the ambivalent tone is conspicuously absent from the rich royal trappings and the vigor of court life in "The Madness of George III"; here, for once, the irony resides not in the body politic but in the king's body.

Nicholas Hytner's elegant production, originally staged by the Royal National Theatre in 1991 and now on an American tour (it is currently at the Brooklyn Academy of Music), begins with a flourish of royal power. The King and his court materialize at the top of a flight of stairs that extends the width of the stage. Behind them is a fathomless blue sky —a horizon as hopeful and abundant as England's imperial dream. The royals descend, and four pages in red livery begin to move backward in our direction. The effect is swift and startling. In an instant, the formality of George III's court life and the fiction of position are established. Then, as now, the citizen must never turn his back on the sovereign; and the rituals that reflect power also confer power on those who take part in them. "What royalty wants nowadays is deference without awe," Bennett says in the play's introduction. "Though what they get more often than not is a fatuous smile, any social awkwardness veiled in nervous laughter, so that the Queen moves among her people buoyed up on waves of obliging hilarity. How happy we must all seem! Such tittering would have been unthinkable at the court of George III." The stakes of court politics in 1788 were made higher by the fact that the sovereign, and not Parliament, held the power of ministerial appointment. And on that constitutional difference Bennett hangs the drama of his tale. "We live in the health and well-being of the sovereign as much as any vizier does the sultan," William Pitt says of the dilemma posed by the King's mysterious debility. Can the King be brought to his senses and his patronage legitimatized in time for Pitt and his government to be saved? It's a race against the clock. By the end of the first act, the King has descended from majesty into madness, his decline a threat to Pitt and the Tories and a renewal of hope for Charles James Fox and the Whigs, who conspire to gain power through their allegiance to that "oversized turbot," the Prince of Wales, who they argue should replace the demented monarch. Bennett skillfully turns court life upside down. Act I, which begins with a show of deference, ends with a show of elimination as a page scrutinizes the King's chamber pot. It is not blue skies but the King's blue urine that dominates center stage.

When life offers Bennett a plot, he clings to it like Ishmael to a coffin. Much of his best work is based on anecdotes provided from his own experience, as in his memoir "The Lady in the Van," or by others, like the actress Coral Browne, who inspired his TV film "An Englishman Abroad." "The Madness of George III" is essentially a historical anecdote, which gives Bennett the fascinating narrative arc of his story, and which he transforms by the power of his wit and his marvellous writing into a kind of lunatic capriccio that bears out Joe Orton's famous adage, "With madness, as with vomit, it's the passer-by who receives the inconvenience." The King spits in the face of his beloved Queen Charlotte; he tries to strangle the Prince of Wales; he strikes his faithful servant and sends him sprawling. He abandons the throne for a restraining chair. His juddering speech slips from sense to scatology that has its own haunting, deracinated logic:

PITT: Would Your Majesty not prefer to sit?
KING: Stand-stand-stand. Can't sit-sit-sit shit-shit-shit.

As the King, Nigel Hawthorne, who in his periwig has the stolid, swank outline of a Romney portrait, misses no melodramatic moment in his tour-de-force delineation of the monarch's decline from potent ruler to incontinent wretch. "Doc doc doc doctors doctortures doctormentors doctalk doctalk talk talk talk talk," he says, words spewing out of him at a pace that skews his body as well as his soul. Hawthorne, who demonstrates a charming sense of command and cunning, adroitly plays both the curious and the cruel sides of the King. It's a tremendous performance, and, like madness itself, has the strangely unsettling effect of seeming to take place in a vacuum. As the King says, "I was the verb, the noun and the verb. Verb rules; subject: the King. I am not the subject now. Now I am the object, the King governed, the ruler ruled. I am the subordinate clause, the insubordinate George." The King, whether sane or demented, doesn't listen in an ordinary way, and inevitably this difference affects the stage life of the other characters, who are merely satellites in his wayward orbit. Nonetheless, Selina Cadell, as a Teutonically twittering Queen Charlotte; Clive Merrison, as Dr. Willis, the no-nonsense Northerner who attempts a kind of behavior modification with the King; and Nick Sampson, as the foppish Prince of Wales, make particularly strong impressions. Sampson gets to deliver some of Bennett's most delicious high-camp lines. "I want to be doing, not dangling," he says about waiting for kingship. "To be heir to the throne is not a position; it is a predicament."

A little stage madness goes a long way, and Bennett wisely reverses the King's fallen fortunes in Act II. The King regains his senses and his figures of speech and all the "hey hey"'s and the "what what"'s that invite auditors but not answers. The monarch's recovery allows both the King and Bennett to give the world the satisfying back of their hand. The King, promising to be the soul of reconciliation, prepares to embrace his sons. "Love," he says. "That is the keynote." But when the Prince of Wales unctuously inquires, "How is Your Majesty?" the King shoots back, "Fat lot you care!" It's a great joke, and announces the return of volatile family normality. The King's body has cured itself. The doctors, who have diagnosed his ailment, variously, as "flying gout," "rheumatism in the head," and "simple dementia," are pissed on from a royal height. "You fashionable fraud," the King says to one doctor, showing him and the others the door. "Go and blister some other blameless bugger, what what." Bennett, whose play refuses to push the metaphorical connections between the state of the King's health and the state of the nation, can't resist a joke about modern medicine. As the King moves briskly through the matters of state, he is handed a piece of paper by Pitt and suddenly stumbles toward the restraining chair. "Fasten me in," he says. The court and the audience hold their breath. It's a bill from the doctors. "Is it any wonder a man goes mad? Doctors. Thirty guineas a visit? And travelling expenses. For six months of torture. They would make a man pay for his own execution. What? What?"

Notoriously wary, Bennett never trusts life to serve up a through line or a happy ending. In the penultimate scene, the King and the Queen are in their bedchamber, and the Queen wonders out loud if perhaps the King's sexual fidelity and the repression of his appetites didn't lead to his madness. "No life is without its regrets," the King tells her, sounding a characteristic Bennett note. "Yet none is without consolations. You are a good little woman, Mrs. King. And we have been happy, have we not?" At that moment, for an instant, the King's body seizes up and he starts to stutter, a foreshadowing that there are bad times just around the corner. The King suffered from a metabolic disorder called porphyria, which caused chemical changes in the nervous system, and in the American production Bennett has cut a short and jarring scene that jumped forward in time to explain the modern medical research. Instead, he allows George III the full, devastating irony of a robust and happy ending. The King arrogantly dismisses his "healer," Dr. Willis, before ascending the staircase and walking, to the regal pomp of Handel's music, into the blue horizon. "Presume not I am the thing I was. I am not the patient," he says in the play's last lines. "Be off, sir. Back to your sheep and your pigs. The King is himself again." But, of course, he wasn't. He had another seizure in 1801, went insane in 1810, and died, deaf and blind, in 1820.

In the play, once the King has temporarily regained his sanity his loyal servants are dismissed: "Forget what you have seen. Majesty in its small clothes." Unfortunately, the modern British audience cannot so easily forget what it has seen. Too much light has been let in on mystery. Bennett's history lesson may stay on the surface of eighteenth-century life, but its popularity is a barometer of just how deep the play taps into modern Britain's disenchantment with the prowess of its leaders and its dishabillé monarchy. On the street where I live, in North London, is a poster whose message somehow always avoids being plastered over: "What do you call somebody who doesn't own the property they live in, avoids poll tax, pays no rent, and expects the taxpayer to foot the bill? Your Majesty."

ARTHUR MILLER

DEAD SOULS

"THERE ARE NO SECOND acts in American lives," F. Scott Fitzgerald wrote. He was wrong. There are no intermissions. According to the wacky American notion of progress, a writer who achieves greatness must never rest and must always be surpassing himself. Arthur Miller's "Broken Glass" arrives at the Booth Theatre fifty years to the month after Mr. Miller's first play, "The Man Who Had All the Luck," was produced on Broadway. But for the last thirty years Miller has been generally cold-shouldered by the critics, who are put off both by what they perceive as his old-fashioned storytelling and by the high moral ground from which he seems to speak. Tennessee Williams, Miller's contemporary, met a similar critical fate, and actually contemplated leaving America to settle in Australia, because he felt he had been "professionally assassinated Stateside." Williams roamed the world, working at his literary task, but Miller, now seventy-eight, has sat tight at his Roxbury, Connecticut, farm, still pondering America's deliriums, still writing, still insisting on putting himself before a public. Miller, like Williams, deserves the right to be heard, but in the current chilly commercial climate such opportunities are few and far between. When I spoke with him a few weeks ago, Miller was sniffing turbulence in America, and this made him more hopeful than he had been for years about having a discussion with an audience. "This turbulence is directing people's attention toward *real,* rather than purely stylistic, questions," he said. "In other words, what the play is saying to them, what its intellectual and emotional meaning is. They want an answer. It's a good moment, because there's an openness, an openness for some kind of answer."

"Broken Glass" takes its name from the anti-Semitic mayhem of

Kristallnacht, in 1938, but it is also a reference to the unspoken tyrannies imposed on each other by Sylvia and Phillip Gellburg, who are the central figures of this short, discursive, but compelling play. In the story of a woman's sudden hysterical paralysis late in her long, devoted marriage to a go-getting Jewish businessman, Miller has found a metaphor for the cycle of blame that has infected and seems to have stalemated modern life—a proliferating tribalism that separates communities and individuals from each other with an irrational, often righteous fury that is at once a mask and an admission of fear. "Broken Glass" is a contemplation of this private and public sense of retreat. "It's dealing with ethnic nationalism in a way," Miller says.

Although Miller sets out his story as a kind of medical thriller—with a local G.P., Dr. Harry Hyman (the charming David Dukes), sensing some hidden meaning in Sylvia's paralysis and in her obsessional anguish over newspaper reports of Jewish humiliation—he is not writing a case study. He is aiming for something much more ambitious: an anatomy of denial.

The fine-boned and beautiful Amy Irving makes Sylvia Gellburg's bewildered sadness vivid. "I can't describe it," she tells her sister Harriet about the numbness that has come over her limbs. "It's like I was just born and I . . . didn't want to come out yet. Like a deep, terrible aching." Irving is a compelling amalgam of regret and rage, whose delicate femininity hides a ferocious will. She is probably too young for the part, but she's such an expert actress that those large almond eyes radiate a sense of longing and loss which makes an audience instantly believe in the suffering and the envy that eat at her soul. Almost her first words to her husband, as they discuss Dr. Hyman's prognosis, are an apology. "I'm so sorry about this," she says.

No sooner has an audience heard Sylvia's apology than it is confronted with her muted fury, as Phillip brings news of their son, Jerome, a West Point graduate who, according to his father, "could be the first Jewish general in the United States." Phillip (played with a prickly and brilliant edginess by Ron Rifkin) sets great store by such small Jewish encroachments into Gentile territory, and is transparently proud of his offspring. Sylvia's gladness is tinged with resentment—a resentment that finally punctures his dutiful solicitude. "I said I'm here,'' Sylvia says to her husband as the conversation drifts toward the shallows of their marriage. "I'm here for my mother's sake and Jerome's sake and everybody's sake, except mine, but I'm here and here I am.'' Amy Irving chokes down the bile in these punishing words. Sylvia can't face her disgust at herself any more than she can face down her husband. Her private sense of humiliation is projected into her obsession with the public humiliation of the Jews. Except on this issue, she exudes a weird kind of contentment in her doomed state.

Sylvia's condition puts her beyond any hope of change, and therefore beyond any responsibility. She is suddenly excused from life: a victim who has in every sense lost control of her life and whose illness paradoxically shifts the balance of power in the relationship. Sylvia's paralysis is not just a humiliation but a threat, which explains Gellburg's own agitation as he vainly tries to get her to walk. "What are you trying to do?'' he says, shouting over her collapsed body. The illness gives Sylvia an authority that she couldn't otherwise command. There's even a change in her tone of voice. "What I did with my life!'' Sylvia tells her husband later. "Out of ignorance. Out of not wanting to shame you in front of other people. A whole life. Gave it away like a couple of pennies—I took better care of my shoes.''

Gellburg is devoted to his wife, but idealization is not intimacy. Gellburg has not had intercourse with Sylvia in twenty years. Her paralysis is external; his is internal. At the core of the standoff between the Gellburgs is the issue of sexual impotence, another awful by-product of fear. The Gellburgs never examine the fear, but sidestep the dangerous personal areas of rancor and embarrassment in silence. "I don't know,'' Sylvia says, of the great vacancy that is her life. "I guess you just gradually give up and it closes over you like a grave.'' Gellburg lets work close over him. "I kept waiting for myself to change. Or you,'' he tells her, in desperation. "And then we got to where it didn't seem to matter anymore. So I left it that way. And I couldn't change anything anymore.'' Gellburg's paternalistic control and his periodic violent outbursts (we learn that he once hit her with an overcooked steak and, on another occasion, that he threw her against a staircase for looking at French postcards) are attributed to his sexual inadequacy. He, in turn, attributes it to Sylvia's early refusal not to have a second child. "You didn't want me to be the man here," he says. She blames her disenchantment on Gellburg's early refusal to let her go back to the accounting job she loved when they first met. And so it goes: a sediment of hate and anguish and injustices which calcifies two souls who began their marriage with nothing more than a sincere desire to be decent to each other. The cycle of blame, with its litany of long-harbored recrimination, spews out of them and pushes them farther into their entrenched positions. They're both right, and they're both wrong. What's true is the psychological dynamic, in which blame becomes a way of not dealing with unacceptable feelings. Dr. Hyman says as much at the climax of the play, when Miller, in his best speech, brings together the public and the private denial to which their lives bear witness. "*Everybody's* persecuted," Hyman says. "The poor by the rich, the rich by the poor, the black by the white, the white by the black, the men by the women, the women by the men, the Catholics by the Protestants, the Protestants by the Catholics—and of course all of them by the Jews. Everybody's persecuted—sometimes I wonder, maybe that's what holds this country together! And what's really amazing is that you can't find anybody who's persecuting anybody else."

Sylvia finally moves out of their bedroom. It's a painful and devastating decision, all the more so for being a quiet one. Gellburg buries his head at her feet. "Do you want to kill me?" he shouts toward her wan, stoic face. And, of course, as the play's last beat illustrates, Sylvia unconsciously does. Gellburg has projected his sense of death—the self-loathing that Dr. Hyman describes as "this 'Jew, Jew, Jew' coming out of your mouth"—onto her. She's paralyzed by his fear, and he by hers. "I want my wife back," Gellburg tells Dr. Hyman after collapsing in a fury at having been snubbed by his pin-striped boss (the superb George N. Martin). It's a plea that Ron Rifkin makes as poignant as it is tragic. Bedridden, he begs for forgiveness from Sylvia, who is in the wheelchair beside him, asking her to stand. "I would do it but I can't!" she says. Gellburg leans across the bed toward her as his heart seizes up and his straining face turns beet red. As he falls dead, Sylvia finds her balance and stands.

"Broken Glass" is haunting and psychologically unsettling. In the Gellburgs' symbiotic relationship, Miller shows people living on death as well as on life, and dramatizes the impossibility of intimacy in a relationship without equality. These are the punishing mysteries of our lives, which is why both in New Haven and in New York, where I saw the play, the audiences listened with rapt attention. "To me, the greatest pleasure is to see the audience sit there and nobody's moving," Miller told me. "They're listening with such complete attention, and there are no theatrical goings-on. Now, you have to fight for that. You have to fight for that calm. That represents a reflectiveness I want, and, of course, that kind of reflectiveness is dangerous in a theatre that is all hyped up, that thinks it cannot exist unless somebody is full of jokes or screaming or yelling."

The heart is a foreign country; and "Broken Glass," while it's not a particularly elegant map, still leads an audience through emotional territory that everyone negotiates at his peril. What is distinctive about the play is not its structure, which is schematic; or John Tillinger's direction, which is crisp; or Santo Loquasto's set, which is lacklustre; but it is Miller's hard-won knowledge of the deviousness of the unconscious. "Broken Glass" is a brave, bighearted attempt by one of the pathfinders of postwar drama to look at the tangle of evasions and hostilities by which the soul contrives to hide its emptiness from itself.

EUGENE O'NEILL

SELLING THE SIZZLE

"O'NEILL" MEANS "CHAMpion" in Gaelic. Once Eugene O'Neill had decided to turn his grief into glory as a playwright, at the advanced age of twenty-five, he was hellbent on greatness. "I want to be an artist or nothing," he wrote to Harvard's George Pierce Baker, applying to Baker's famous playwriting class in 1914. By 1916, with "Bound East for Cardiff," the first of a series of six one-act plays about his early life at sea, O'Neill had broadcast his desire both to shine and to transform American drama from what he called the "showshop" mentality, whose commercial compromises had destroyed his father's great acting gifts, into an arena where the new century's language and life could be seriously displayed and dissected. "My soul is a submarine. My aspirations are torpedoes," O'Neill confessed in his 1917 poem "Submarine." The torpedoes soon found their mark. In 1920, "Beyond the Horizon," which is almost unreadable today, won O'Neill his first Pulitzer Prize; and by 1922, with "Anna Christie," whose three-year gestation was O'Neill's longest labor of love up to then, he had collected his second Pulitzer. He pronounced himself "the Hot Dog of the Drama."

And he was. Courting his art with the same fierce, reckless dedication with which he once courted oblivion, O'Neill bushwhacked his way through the morass of old showbiz assumptions. He was the first to stage the life and the idiom of the American lower classes; the first to put an American black man onstage as a figure of complexity and substance; the first to adapt the innovations of European drama to America; the first to challenge the soullessness of the century's materialism; and the first American playwright to insist on working as an artist. "I determined I would never sell out," O'Neill said. He kept on his writing desk a cautionary photo of his famous father, and in 1934, at the height of his fame, he withdrew from public life to work on a cycle of eleven plays, whose title, "A Tale of Possessors Self-Dispossessed," is indicative of the "cultural gas" with which his work and his ego were increasingly inflated. He later wrote to an eager Broadway producer, "My poverty-stricken years of past are proof enough that there is no danger of my street-walking along Broadway. I simply ain't that kind of a girl."

Well, a girl can change her mind, and on the subject of "Anna Christie" O'Neill did. "The fact is 'Anna Christie' is the stalest of all my plays—stale from much use, and stale because it is the most conventional playwrighting of anything I've done, although its subject matter was damned unconventional in our theatre of 1921," O'Neill wrote in 1941, contemplating Ingrid Bergman's taking Anna—the first of O'Neill's many whore-mothers—on the road. "It is a play written about characters and a situation—not about characters and life." "Anna Christie" and "The Iceman Cometh" have the same autobiographical origins, in Jimmy the Priest's bar, on Manhattan's Lower East Side, where O'Neill and a handful of other characters who appear in both plays steered into their skid. In this sense, both plays are ghost plays, reflecting aspects of O'Neill's hauntedness. What separates them is twenty years of craft, success, and overweening resolve "to howl: Imagination, Beauty, Daring, or bust." After "Anna Christie," O'Neill worked at a ferocious pace, creating as many clunkers ("Welded," "Dynamo," "Marco Millions") as classics ("Desire Under the Elms," "The Hairy Ape," "The Emperor Jones"). His bold experiments in pursuit of "tragic expression in terms of transfigured modern values and symbols" didn't so much strip life down as wear it down. The masks of "Lazarus Laughed" and "The Great God Brown," the five-hour "Strange Interlude," and the six-hour retelling of the fall of the House of Atreus in "Mourning Becomes Electra" amply demonstrate O'Neill's confusion of grandiosity with greatness. So his outbursts against "Anna Christie" have to be taken with a substantial dose of salt and with the knowledge that between the twenties, when he began his major work, and the mid-forties, when Parkinson's disease forced him

to put down his pen, he had progressed from America's theatrical
Jeremiah to its Gargantua.

O'Neill claimed of "Anna Christie," "I couldn't sit through it without getting the heebie-jeebies and wondering why the hell I ever wrote
it. . . ." He would remember quick enough, and be glued to his seat
into the bargain, if he could watch the sparks fly between Natasha
Richardson and Liam Neeson as they burn with regret and desire in the
Roundabout Theatre's Broadway revival. From the distance of seventy
years, the play, which foreshadows O'Neill's major themes but does not
labor them, is appealing in its modesty and potent in the playing of its
romantic passion. Richardson and Neeson are a particularly thrilling
matchup, and it's the chemistry of their contest that Richardson wanted
to talk about in her dressing room an hour before the opening; it
brought a shine even to her hooded left eye, which was swollen with
conjunctivitis.

In real life, Richardson resembles O'Neill's first-draft concept of
Anna, in which she was imagined to be from England rather than from
the Midwest, and was high-toned, not low-down: "Anna is a tall, blond,
fully developed girl . . . built on a statuesque, beautifully-moulded
plan. . . . her expression is alert, mobile, intelligent. Her wide blue
eyes betray anything of the dreamer. They shine with an eager, wistful
light." This is Richardson's second time around in the role, which has
attracted a number of charismatic, independent, and compelling performers, like Greta Garbo, Ingrid Bergman, and Liv Ullmann. A
woman of pedigree and passion, Richardson can amply hold her own in
such stellar company; she is one of those actresses by whom a generation marks its progress. Nearly three years ago, at London's Young Vic,
she scored a resounding triumph as Anna in a production whose casting
of her Swedish barge-captain father, Chris Christopherson, and her Irish
sailor sweetheart, Mat Burke, left large areas of their emotional landscape unexplored. The New York production certainly rectifies the
imbalance.

"When I first read the play, I knew it was written for Liam Neeson.
It's just written for him. Not just physically, but you'll see," she said,
her husky voice filled with expectation. "I felt the play could go on to a
whole other level—a deeper level of passion, of humor, of anger and

despair. I wanted to do it with Liam and with an actor playing the father who was not frightened of it emotionally. You can't fake these parts. You need enormous technical capacity, but you also have to be prepared to open yourself up emotionally. A lot of English actors are inhibited in this area. Liam's forty. He's a man, but he's still got vulnerability. I was afraid I might get stuck in the way I did the play before. But one of the great joys of working with Liam and Rip Torn''—he plays the father— ''is that a lot of stuff that I'd never imagined started to come out.'' Richardson cited as an example a powerful moment in the fourth act, when Burke returns to confront Anna, whose confession of her sordid past has sent both her long-lost father and her newfound love off on benders:

> BURKE: Tell me it's a lie, I'm saying! That's what I'm after coming to hear you say.
> ANNA: A lie? What?
> BURKE: All the badness you told me two days back. Sure it must be a lie! You was only making game of me, wasn't you? Tell me 'twas a lie, Anna, and I'll be saying prayers of thanks on my two knees to the Almighty God!
> ANNA: I can't, Mat.

''I used to say the 'I can't, Mat' terribly flat,'' she said. ''Now, with Liam, I have to make a conscious choice. He's so attractive, such a powerful presence, that it makes it very easy to fall in love with him. Now I really think about lying. Can I lie? Maybe I will. Then I realize I have to tell him the truth. So it raises the stakes for the character in terms of her courage. In fact, it brings my entire game up.''

No amount of exposure to Neeson's performances in films like ''Husbands and Wives'' and ''Leap of Faith'' or Richardson's hyperbole can quite prepare you for the actual encounter with him. This is his Broadway début, and, at six foot four, he towers above the rest of the cast like a kind of sequoia of sex. His amalgam of sensuality and sensibility sends an electrifying charge through an audience. When he washes up on Christopherson's coal barge after surviving five days at sea, the audience sits where Anna stands: eyeball to eyeball with a force of nature. He compels immediate attention and belief. He *is* a stoker. He *is* catnip to women. He *has* seen the world and loved the journey. His presence is so riveting that it can make you forget the vulgarities of the play's melodramatic structure and the cuts of the director, David Leveaux, which get Burke incongruously out of the water and onto center stage without so much as a helping hand. Not since Brando tossed meat up to Stella in "A Streetcar Named Desire" has flesh made such a spectacular entrance. Brando's Stanley was predatory and cruel. Neeson's Burke is gentler—a combination of boyish pugnacity and play- fulness. With fists as big as ham hocks and eyes as shrewdly watchful as a cat's, Neeson seems to have stepped right out of O'Neill's earliest notes for the character: ". . . his eyes dark and handsome, merry with a reckless good-nature; the white teeth of his self-indulgent, sensual mouth flashing in a smile tantalizing in its self-assurance. His laugh is rollicking, devil-may-care and infectious." Neeson, who hails from Bal- lymena, in Ireland, gets his tongue naturally around the rhythms of O'Neill's prose and gives it an unusual gaiety and grace. "Whisht, now, me daisy! Himself's in the cabin. It's wan of your kisses I'm needing to take the tiredness from me bones. Wan kiss, now!" he says. Anna, whose adolescent rape turned her to prostitution and to a hatred of men, "every mother's son of 'em," may momentarily spurn Burke, but the audience is well and truly ravished. The play is a potpourri of immigrant sounds, and such is the technical mastery of Torn, Richard- son, and Neeson that the collection of vernacular speech—Swedish, Irish, North American—makes an articulate case for one of O'Neill's most vaunted claims: that he was "a bit of a poet, who had labored with the spoken word to evolve original rhythms of beauty where beauty apparently isn't."

"Anna Christie" serves up the whole romantic soufflé. There's love at first sight. "It is dreaming I am?" Burke says when he comes to his senses and claps eyes on Anna's face, now relaxed and purified from her ten-day stay on the water in her father's barge. We know this because O'Neill lays it on with a lot of symbolic and, at the Roundabout, "non- toxic"—as the lobby sign calls it—fog. "It makes me feel clean," Anna says. What we're looking at is a walking, talking Christian symbol of redemption. Mat sees Anna's halo almost at once: "That fine yellow hair is like a golden crown on your head.'' Anna was ''a nurse girl'' before she became a hooker, and her first instinct when she sees Burke, whom she describes as ''a big kid,'' is to give him succor, feeding him with the glass teat of a whiskey bottle. But what really gives oxygen to O'Neill's fantasy and life to his dialogue, which in lesser hands might teeter on cliché, is the enormousness of need which Richardson and Neeson winkle out from behind the words. Raw longing draws them toward each other with a gorgeous, sometimes furious compulsion. When Anna elbows Burke away, she really belts him. There's a physical brazenness in their playing which conveys the gravity and the punishment of their romantic agony. Burke pushes the full weight of his broad forehead against the barrel of Anna's drawn gun. ''Let you shoot, I'm saying, and be done with it! Let you end me with a shot and I'll be thanking you, for it's a rotten dog's life I've lived the past two days since I've known what you are. . . .''

Anna was one of O'Neill's earliest projections of the abandonments of his own childhood. O'Neill, like Anna, had been given up to the care of strangers, and had been shunted off to boarding school from the age of seven. He, too, had found himself rootless and lost and exhausted from the struggle to survive. Anna is a repository for all these ancient and inarticulate wounds. ''If you'd even had been a regular father and had me with you—maybe things would be different!'' Anna shouts at Chris, who doesn't want her to marry her sailor, and whose bewildered possessiveness is well caught by Rip Torn. If ''Anna Christie'' is not the most articulate metaphor of O'Neill's own emotional abuse, the love triangle, in which Anna is trying to heal her family wound while making a new family, provides O'Neill with terrific set pieces that show off the originality of his dramatic instincts. In Anna's powerful confession, all of Richardson's fiery independence and keen critical intelligence are on display. She misses no nuance of anguish in Anna's ruined innocence, and moves effortlessly from sadness to brave cynicism. ''Will you believe it if I tell you that loving you has made me—clean? It's the straight goods, honest! Like hell you will! You're like all the rest!'' And when Burke grabs a chair and is about to beat her, Richardson's almond eyes close and she tilts her head slowly back against her chair to receive the pain—resigned to yet another blow, which will be no more brutal or capricious than what fate has already meted out to her. It's a memorable moment, and is topped only by their fourth-act reunion. On his knees, bent over his mother's crucifix, Burke takes a long time making Anna swear her true love: "And may the blackest curse of God strike you if you're lying. Say it now!" She does, and then another thought dawns. "Is it Catholic ye are?" says Neeson, turning O'Neill's ingenious twist into a scene of genuine comic complexity.

If Neeson's and Richardson's instincts for their material are unerring, David Leveaux's direction is not always so sure. He is at his best in the fine filigree work with his major actors, but is sloppy in other aspects of production detail. He gets the show off to a rocky start by jump-cutting it directly into exposition—a choice made on grounds of economy but at the expense of really establishing the particular end-of-the-line atmosphere of the place. Jimmy the Priest's bar, a haven for the losers in the American sweepstakes, exuded a very special kind of calm, an entropy that was itself a by-product of the society's new momentum, and O'Neill spelled this out in "The Iceman Cometh." ("No one here has to worry about where they're going next, because there is no farther they can go. It's a great comfort to them.") Although Anna brings a sense of exhaustion into the dive—"Gee," she says, "I sure need that rest! I'm knocked out"—John Lee Beatty's set, with its walls of creosoted pine planks and its makeshift downstage bar, whose array of bottles gives no sense of the serious cheap drinking that the script indicates, never quite clinches the sense of place. It's an ill-judged space, and its atmospheric implications are even more confused by a barman (Barton Tinapp) who seems to be working a Madison Avenue bistro instead of a bedrock saloon. Mr. Leveaux, who keeps an intelligent eye on the dynamics of the scenes, is not so vigilant about his sets. I was once an ordinary seaman, and no amount of special pleading can convince me that a Persian rug (albeit a threadbare one) is appropriate on the floor of a coal barge.

Still, Leveaux elegantly manages the final, controversial "happy ending" in a tableau of proper English irony. As fog billows out over the thrust stage, and the old salt Chris turns away from the new couple to look out to sea, Burke takes hold of Anna's wrist, but Anna is turned away from him, gazing upstage into a gray horizon. The light at the end of any O'Neill tunnel is always an oncoming train, so he was particularly stung by the critics' cries of cop-out at ''Anna Christie'' 's finale. ''It would have been so easy to have killed them off—one, two, or all three —so tragically easy!'' O'Neill wrote to his English publisher, Jonathan Cape. ''But realistically false—theatrical! They wouldn't have suicided, or murdered, or done anything at all but make exactly the pitifully humorous gesture in the direction of happiness I have allowed them to make.'' At one time, O'Neill thought of titling the play ''Comma,'' because ''the happy ending is merely the comma at the end of a gaudy introductory clause.'' He had no faith in happiness, and he didn't manage much of it onstage or in life. But, although he meant the play to be as tentative as a comma, the undisputed power of Richardson and Neeson, ably supported by Torn and a brief, welcome appearance by Anne Meara, as the captain's softhearted squeeze Marthy, turns the evening into an exclamation mark.

ARNOLD WESKER

HAND TO MOUTH

In THE HALLWAY OF AR-
nold Wesker's North London house is a framed letter from George
Bernard Shaw to the playwright who, at the time of the postmark—
June 10, 1949—was an impoverished seventeen-year-old amateur actor
from the East End, too poor to pay the fees for the Royal Academy of
Dramatic Art. "Take care to make your lines heard," Shaw told
Wesker, who had written for advice about how to play Marchbanks in
"Candida." "Leave the rest to luck." And luck—both the luck of
talent and the luck of changing times—was with Wesker, at least in the
first decade of his long theatrical career. The welfare state, which
transformed the landscape of English life after the war, also transformed
its theatre. The world of work and of working-class culture became the
focus of much contemporary drama. At the age of twenty-four, Wesker,
who had by then turned playwright, caught this new wave, first with
"The Kitchen" (written in 1957, produced in 1959), and then with a
series of autobiographical plays that are now set texts on the English
A-level syllabus: "Chicken Soup with Barley" (1958), "Roots" (1959),
"I'm Talking About Jerusalem" (1960), and "Chips with Everything"
(1962). Wesker gave opinionated voice to the struggles and dreams of a
class of people who a decade earlier, if they inhabited the English stage
at all, were there only as comic caricatures. Wesker is responsible for
eight volumes of plays, two volumes of essays, and one famous theatre
anecdote. "Shut up, Arnold," said the director John Dexter, who
staged all of Wesker's famous early work, including "The Kitchen,"
"or I'll direct this play the way you wrote it." The Wesker-Dexter
collaboration resulted in a string of influential productions throughout
the sixties. But by the mid-seventies the times and Wesker's luck had

changed. In 1971, the Royal Shakespeare Company's production of Wesker's "The Journalists" was scuppered when the actors refused to perform it. Then, five years later, Zero Mostel, the star of Wesker's "The Merchant," topped this spectacular collapse by dying after the play's first out-of-town preview. "If he'd stayed alive, I'd be a millionaire," Wesker says. There followed, in 1981, the dismal "Caritas," a tale of a barmy immured nun, at the National Theatre. Wesker found himself increasingly embattled and out of the critical discussion, but he has continued to pronounce himself to the English, even if they are not now so keen to hear what he has to say. (His earnings, according to him, come largely from foreign productions.) Stephen Daldry's current exciting revival of "The Kitchen," at London's Royal Court Theatre, where it was last staged in 1961, the year Daldry was born, pays proper honor to the innovations of the play and the playwright, and brilliantly illustrates the conundrum of English political theatre, which, while paying vehement lip service to the workers, rarely shows them at work.

"The Kitchen," which is Wesker's most frequently performed play (it ran for more than a thousand performances in Buenos Aires and for three years in Budapest and Warsaw, among other places), is the first modern English play to make a spectacle of people at work. Until the late fifties, English theatre was interested more in those eating the meal than in those making it. The reckless momentum of the kitchen captures the contemporary deliriums of speed, pleasure, and productivity. "It's a wonderful metaphor, isn't it?" Wesker says, and he's right. The momentum is also theatrically liberating: action stops rhetoric (especially Wesker's). The stage pictures restore the visual and the physical to theatre's game of show-and-tell, which has too often become merely a game of tell-and-tell. It's a sad fact of modern theatre that the prowess of the acrobat, the mime, and the juggler have been lost to the stage, and that the repertory of movement has been reduced largely to standing, sitting, and crossing to the liquor cabinet. Here the bustle and din of a working kitchen become a kind of three-ring circus where the chefs, cleaners, and waitresses are the performing workhorses and where movement is meaning. In the mayhem of this closed and captivating world, life is ruled not so much by behavior as by the clock and the compulsion of output—in the case of the Tivoli Restaurant, about two thousand meals a day. In "The Kitchen," the staff members mime their individual chores, and their actions at first seem at odds with the realistic environment but grow increasingly mesmerizing. Wesker conceived his inspired metaphor in 1956, while working in Paris as a chef at Restaurant Le Rallye, on the Boulevard des Capucines. "It is like working in a large room with an enormous blast of hot air buffeting you about," Wesker wrote in his diary that year. "Occasionally one has to scream. I do. I cry out aloud 'Shoot the bastards, don't serve them!,' in English. No one understands; so much noise hardly anyone hears. Five flames thrusting themselves with venom among the stones in iron ovens. Sometimes I feel they must explode. Force and fire cannot happen like that without something giving way." Onstage, Wesker re-creates the thrill and the punishment of the kitchen's mounting frenzy and lets them shape his play's structure and the final vision of disintegration.

"The Kitchen" offers a field day to ambitious directors. It launched Ariane Mnouchkine's career in France and Koichi Kimura's in Japan (this year, Kimura is mounting his fourth production of the play, and he has commissioned Wesker to write the book for a musical of it), and gave the playwright Jack Gelber a showcase for his directorial talents in his fine New York production with Rip Torn in 1966. Now Stephen Daldry has used the play as a vehicle for strutting his flamboyant stuff and solidifying his reputation as one of England's most exciting showmen. Daldry and his designer, Mark Thompson, have built a gorgeous set over the stalls of the Royal Court (eliminating almost a third of the theatre's three hundred and ninety-five seats), so the dress circle and a jerry-built grandstand on what is usually the upstage area of the proscenium stage now look down on the kitchen as if on a bull ring. It's an extraordinary sight. The oblong space, with its horseshoe of chrome counters, its *bains-marie,* its serving pots covered with dish towels, its neatly stacked piles of platters and plates, its black-and-white tiled floor, turns the theatre into an arena, emphasizing the essential nature of the play as contest.

"The Kitchen" is a kind of sporting event, with the staff racing against time and the demands of the waiters. From the first beat, when Daldry magnifies the rumble and groan of the ovens as they're ceremonially lit for the day, he misses no opportunity to be sensational. He uses the faces of his well-chosen actors like brushstrokes on a canvas of movement: Tony Rohr's lantern-jawed butcher, Max, a rolled cigarette dangling from his mouth; Annette Badland's beef-trust vegetable chef, Bertha, casting her hangdog looks at the world through wire-rimmed glasses; Lorraine Ashbourne's Monique, a waitress whose bravado and beehive hairdo have captured the heart of the German boiled-fish cook, the manic flaxen-haired Peter (the compelling Christopher Fulford), the play's main character. For this production, which Wesker himself directed at the University of Wisconsin in 1990, he has written snatches of dialogue for the waitresses which give them a wash of personality and problems. Daldry, who had his cast tutored in the culinary arts, has them all moving to their own specific agendas of needs and actions, which he orchestrates in masterly fashion amid the belching ovens and the caterwauling waitresses. The cacophony of hurled lines and clattering plates builds to a hellish and wonderful first-act finale, with the lights going red in the frenzy of activity. One white light remains on the sweet-faced young newcomer—Kevin, the fried-fish cook (Dermot Kerrigan). "Jesus, is this a bloody madhouse!" he shouts. "Have you all gone barking-raving-bloody-mad?"

In his diaries Wesker was in no doubt. "I do not care about people who need to eat a meal out—there must be other ways," he wrote in his 1956 diary. "No one should work like this to produce anything—anything! Nothing in the world is more important than a man's humanity, his dignity." Fortunately for Wesker, his metaphor gets the better of his gift of socialist gab, and the play speaks mostly through the poetic spectacle of the kitchen's hubbub. The acrobatic accomplishments of the actors invest the staff's labor with a sense of prowess, and not polemics. The play only once allows Wesker to indulge his penchant for rabbinical finger-wagging, and it takes an actor as expert as Teddy Kempner, who plays Paul, the pastry chef, to make it palatable. At speed, there is no time for thought, let alone dreaming. While the staff members are between shifts, in the interlude that begins Act II, they get to talking about dreams. "When a man dreams, he grows big, better," says Peter, the cutup and bully, trying to get the others to reveal themselves. Peter, the immigrant to whom the restaurant is home and who is desperately possessive of the married Monique, won't risk self-disclosure himself.

But the others are coaxed out of their solitude to confide a longing for something other than cash. Daldry and his actors successfully negotiate this sticky patch of the play by letting gestures speak louder than words: the brash red-headed egg cook, Michael (the excellent Thomas Craig), kicks a cardboard box around the stoves while imagining himself a goal-scoring winner against Arsenal; the sausage cook, Hans (Stefan Marling), plays his guitar and exits to his own imagined standing ovation; Monique casts a tender glance in Peter's direction after another of their squabbles over her leaving her husband. These miniature moments are crosscut in cinematic fashion with the detail of kitchen routine to build a sense of place and individual history.

The thought has occurred to Wesker that his quick-cut, pacy narrative juxtapositions have had their effect on more popular entertainment, and if that's true it may be because the play owes its style and its naïve documentary ambitiousness—which originally imagined thirty people on the stage—to Wesker's experience in film. It was written after Wesker's return to England from Paris and a stint as a would-be writer-director at the London School of Film Technique, in Brixton. But in the end it's the vision of steam, shouts, and sweating bodies which makes "The Kitchen" so meaningful and so memorable. As the second shift begins, Peter's life seems to be unravelling before us. "You serving yet, Peter? I want three turbot. Special for Marango," says the hoity-toity waitress Violet (superbly played by Sandra Voe), speaking of the Tivoli's pin-striped proprietor. What we know about Violet is only her comical grandiosity from her having worked "at the old Carlton Tower." That's enough of a plot point for Wesker to build on. As Peter starts to crack under the strain of his fraught love life and the pressure of work, Violet takes it upon herself to get her own orders. This small transgression is gigantic in the ceremony of kitchen work. "I'll serve you," Peter commands. "Me! Me! Is *my* kingdom here. This is the side where *I* live. This." Violet calls Peter a "bloody German bastard." Her insult is the last straw. Peter goes berserk and trashes the kitchen. It's a terrifying, demented moment. Plates are swept to the floor, a meat cleaver cuts through a gas fixture to stop the stoves, the staff dives for cover as Peter, chopper in hand, staggers into the dining room followed by the sound of crashing plates. When Peter returns, Daldry maximizes the standoff, with the cast cowering stage right and Peter, bleeding and exhausted, against the white-tiled walls. Peter doesn't explain himself, but the restaurant and its punishing pace are brought to a standstill. Marango (Ric Morgan) inspects the damage. "I give work, I pay well, yes," he says to those assembled. "They eat what they want, don't they? I don't know what more to give a man. He works, he eats, I give him money. This is life, isn't it?" He turns to Peter. "What is there more? What is there more? What is there more?" And on that bemused note, which raises issues that the play and the playwright can't begin to analyze, the staff members slowly, inevitably, wipe Peter's blood off the tiled walls and go back to the alienation that is their life.

In Wesker's original notes for the play, he wrote, "The times force people to take second best because it does not allow them to find the best. I come back to an old idea of mine: people are not responding, they are reacting." The sense of lost opportunity that fired the intellectual rebellions of the sixties is writ large in Britain in the nineties, only it translates as entropy. Daldry's revival is shrewdly chosen for the present hapless moment in British history, when the resignation at John Major's nineties has superseded the jubilation at the false boom of Thatcher's eighties. Britain is as sour as the Tivoli's soup. The hard rule of the kitchen seems to be the same as the implacable rule of the land: if it's on the table, eat it.

CLIFFORD ODETS

WAITING FOR ODETS

IN CHICAGO, A RAGGED MAN
stood on the corner of North Halstead and Willow, down the street
from the new, five-hundred-seat Steppenwolf Theatre, where Clifford
Odets's first full-length play, "Awake and Sing!" (1935), was being
revived. It was late. The street was empty. The man shuffled in laceless
sneakers to keep warm. He held out a paper cup and jiggled it. The next
day, Chicago's famous Schwinn Bicycle Company filed for bankruptcy.
Over the decade, Chicago's manufacturing job base has shrunk from
thirty percent to less than twenty percent, and despite the prosperous
shine of downtown's Miracle Mile things aren't good for the immigrants
who built the city: they can no longer count on factory work as their
gateway into society. It was Odets who said, "A job is a home to a
homeless man," and it is Odets who, fifty-eight years after he bushwhacked his way into the American consciousness with his agitprop one-
acter, "Waiting for Lefty," still speaks to that sense of stalled blessing
which haunts the land.

According to Odets, the fundamental activity of the characters in
"Awake and Sing!" is the "struggle for life amidst petty conditions"—
an activity that has again come to preoccupy a distressingly large number
of Americans. Except for David Mamet, Odets is the only American
writer to put low life as well as high life on the stage with a crackling
poetic authenticity that encompasses what he called "the American
gallery," which "remains uncelebrated and unexpressed." For decades,
critics have been trying to write off Odets as "dated"; this is a bias long
held by the *Times,* and it's why New Yorkers have been almost entirely
deprived of his voice since 1984. But to call Odets dated is to see only
the surface of his nineteen-thirties dramatic conventions, and not the

depth of his perceptions about character, language, and the punishing waste of spirit in democracy's obsession with success, which he once called "the peritonitis of the soul." All drama is by definition "dated," the product of a particular moment, and, as Odets's friend and original director, Harold Clurman, once remarked, "We do not dismiss Homer's epic because wars are no longer engaged in over a beautiful girl." History, however, has dealt society a wild card, and now, perhaps for the first time since the Depression, Odets's vision and his craft can be seen for what they are. Even in a production like Steppenwolf's, which gets as close to the rumble of panic under the play as Ponce de León did to the Fountain of Youth, Odets's big, brave voice has important things to tell us, about then and now.

"Here without a dollar you don't look the world in the eye. Talk from now to next year—this is life in America." So says Bessie Berger, the matriarch of Odets's Bronx family, who knows in her own way what Veblen meant about America when he said, "Esteem is awarded on evidence." In a capitalist society, that evidence is a show of wealth. Odets's accomplishment is to create a climate of humiliation which settles in around the Berger household like a thick fog. "I could die from shame," Bessie says of her son Ralph's girlfriend—to her, a "nobody." The judgmental eye of others—the scorn of the winners in a competitive society—is what terrifies Bessie and turns her into a termagant of manipulation. She forces her pregnant daughter, Hennie, into a loveless marriage with a newly arrived immigrant; she puts the kibosh on Ralph's friends ("I don't like my boy to be seen with those tramps") and his girlfriend; she even contrives to cheat Ralph out of some insurance money, only to explain when she's caught, "Ralphie, I worked too hard all my years to be treated like dirt." Bessie's house is spotless; what's soiling is the demands and disregard of the world. It's not just Bessie's soul that shrivels. The entire household is debased in various ways by economic necessity. Her husband, Myron ("He is heartbroken without being aware of it," the stage direction says), studied law but has spent his life in haberdashery. He retreats into nostalgia and badinage. "My scalp is impoverished," he says, referring to his bald pate, but his emptiness is more than skin deep. Bessie's father, Jacob, has retreated into utopian fantasies of a better world, and her moneyed brother, Morty, to whom life is "hot delicatessen," displays a smug indifference to others. His defense against humiliation is a success that humiliates them. In contrast to Morty's self-aggrandizement is the self-loathing of Hennie's sad-sack husband, Sam Feinschreiber. Failure, as Odets joked in another play, has gone to his head. He craves the invisibility of the shamed. According to the stage direction, Sam is "conditioned by the humiliation of not making his way alone." He spells it out, in a confession made all the more humiliating because nobody seems to care. "To my worst enemy I don't wish such a life," says Sam, who pleads to Hennie for her love and is rejected before our eyes. "Nobody likes me."

"When one lives in the jungle one must look out for the wildlife," Odets says, describing Bessie's vigilance. And, like any species that inhabits a hostile environment, Odets's characters develop a hard carapace, which serves both to protect and to attack. The wisecrack, as Odets reinvents it onstage, is the linguistic shell behind which his characters alternately hide and lash out. "Cut your throat, sweetheart. Save time," the gimpy small-time gangster Moe Axelrod, who boards with the Bergers, says to Hennie about her proposed marriage of convenience. Odets puts a fine spin on the sludge of street talk, and gives it a vibrant new currency and prominence. "I wouldn't trade you for two pitchers and an outfielder," Axelrod says to Ralph at the finale, in an exit line so strong that it lifts the bad odor of Axelrod and Hennie's running off together and abandoning her child. The act of speaking, as Odets dramatizes it, becomes a show of power in a powerless life. Laughter, according to Nietzsche, is an epitaph on an emotion; in Odets's hand, Jewish laughter is particularly ghostly, resounding with all the silent deaths of dreams deferred. His characters smile with cold teeth. Take this shrewd, oblique two-line exchange over dinner:

JACOB (*ironically*): If it rained pearls—who would work?
BESSIE: Another county heard from.

In the banter of these characters Odets shows language having a stage-managed revenge on life. Jacob's political bitterness momentarily vanishes when he lobs his sardonic grenade into the bourgeois patter of the dinner-table conversation, and Bessie's put-downs keep alive her illusion of potency in a life that is out of control. The terrific talk of Odets's characters mourns as it laughs.

Such is the power of Odets's dialogue that it works even in the Steppenwolf production, where the only poverty in evidence is a poverty of imagination. The mixed metaphor of Michael Merritt and Kurt Sharp's set, with expressionistic tenements looming above the naturalistic Berger house like anti-aircraft guns above a destroyer, announces the show's confusion of realms and its nervousness about creating a climate of claustrophobia on the stage. "I never in my life even had a birthday party," Ralph moans, but nothing on the set conveys the threadbare or the pinched. In fact, the house looks like a nicely converted Northside Victorian floor-through: shiny hardwood floor, candles in the candelabras, cut glass on the table and in the kitchen door. This is poverty seen through a suburban lens. And the racial memory of unmanning fiscal panic seems as far from this cast as a sustained Jewish accent. Without the Jewish rhythms and the mordant whine of the Jewish humor, which echoes the gloom of centuries, the production can't find a core of belief. Only Nathan Davis, who plays Jacob, and on whose lined face life has left its mark, comes anywhere near the vicinity of the play. Otherwise, the cast is almost uniformly too callow and too young. Francis Guinan's Myron, lumbered with a ludicrous wig, speaks a language of entropy but crosses the stage with a spring in his step. Jeff Perry's genial, corn-fed Moe Axelrod gets none of the chip that the war-wounded gangster carries. And Sheldon Patinkin's unfocussed direction lets Barbara Robertson turn Bessie's flop sweat into frenzy, on the theory, I guess, that when one is skating on thin ice, safety is in speed.

Steppenwolf has been bold enough to program Odets but not shrewd enough to find a voice for a play that is all about sounding off. Odets wrote "Awake and Sing!" when he was twenty-eight, and it became a kind of self-fulfilling prophecy, reversing a lifetime of botched missions. He had failed at school, failed as an actor, and failed even as a suicide. (He tried three times.) Song was Odets's metaphor of transformation. He built song not only into the title of his first major play but into the names of subsequent major characters, like Cleo Singer, in the 1938 play "Rocket to the Moon" ("Talent!—I'm talented. I don't know for what, but it makes me want to dance in my bones!''), and Leo Gordon, the philosophic voice in ''Paradise Lost'' (1935), who in early drafts of the play was called Kantor. Odets liked to compare himself to Walt Whitman (whose name Odets gave to his only son), and often invoked Emerson's dictum about the poet—''half song thrush, half alligator.''

Odets had been one of life's bottom feeders, living off dimes and dreams as an actor with the Group Theatre. ''I was sore at my whole life,'' he explained about the genesis of ''Awake and Sing!'' Before he discovered the insecurity of success, he'd lived the terror of poverty. The son of a first-generation Russian-Jewish émigré who had changed the family name from Gorodetsky, which means ''urban man,'' Odets became the chronicler of the pathos of Jewish assimilation into American city life. In ''Awake and Sing!'' he pitted American optimism, which was grounded in the myth of abundance, against the demoralized resignation that came with the fact of scarcity. Odets's spokesman is the stymied twenty-two-year-old, Ralph, who broadcasts lack of opportunity in the play's first words: ''Where's advancement down the place?'' In his next breath he bleats, ''All I want's a chance to get to first base!'' At the finale, with a windfall left him by his beloved grandfather Jacob, whose suicide is just one of many mutations in the play brought on by the shaming pressures of poverty and powerlessness, Ralph faces down his frustrations: ''My days won't be for nothing.'' Odets, too, held his face up to the world, and the world kissed it. Dubbed the new O'Neill, he became the spokesman of the thirties. He was on the cover of *Time*. Walter Winchell coined the word ''Bravodets.'' Cole Porter dropped his name in the song ''I'm Throwing a Ball Tonight,'' from ''Panama Hattie.'' (With prescience, Porter rhymed ''Odets'' with ''regrets,'' and ''Awake and Sing!'' made memorable that particularly punishing American sense of loss at the failure to become your best self—a failure that Odets's career came to exemplify.)

''Nobody knows how to act Odets anymore,'' the playwright William Gibson complained in 1988, in his introduction to Odets's forties diary, ''The Time Is Ripe.'' He invoked the names of the heavyweight Group Theatre ensemble that originally made Odets's work sensational —Lee J. Cobb, Luther Adler, Morris Carnovsky, John Garfield, to mention a few. But the generalization is not true. As a series of excellent London revivals over the last two decades has shown, Odets can be done, and done well. His plays, despite what Clurman called his "lyric afflatus" and their ideological full dress, are a quirky blend of deep Jewish pessimism and a very American desire to shine. Their world is gray, not black and white, and they reflect the split in Odets's own personality. The peculiar paradox of "Awake and Sing!" (and of Odets's work in general) is that it celebrates both the dream and the sure knowledge that a dream is something you wake up from. His ironic music is apt for the postimperial blues that America is starting to sing.

NEIL SIMON

SHTICK BALL

"Funny is money," says one of the joke writers who feed a TV monster called Max Prince in Neil Simon's "Laughter on the 23rd Floor," at the Richard Rodgers. On this principle the bulwark of American entertainment was built. No one has been more successful at mining the mother lode of the culture's avidity for distraction than Simon himself. "Laughter on the 23rd Floor," which was sold to the movies at its first staged reading, is Simon's twenty-seventh Broadway play. He has also written nineteen movies that he acknowledges. On any given day of the year, in both the western and the eastern hemispheres, an audience is gathered together to hear Neil Simon's version of funny. Sometimes, if he stops to think about it (which he rarely does), his gift puzzles him. "I said five funny things to my wife last night that made her nearly fall off the bed laughing," Simon told me, over lunch this summer in Los Angeles, where he lives. "I don't know how they come so quickly. We were playing poker last night. Somebody said, 'Pinky Lee died recently. How old was he?" And I said, '*Theventy Theven*.' They broke up laughing. I told that to my wife. She said, 'How'd you think of that so fast?' My line came directly on 'How old was he?' The message that is sent from your brain to your tongue is so swift it amazes me." This freakish talent, which turns envy, rapacity, aggression, egotism, and revenge into joy, is the subject of "Laughter on the 23rd Floor." The play puts the audience back in the closed world of the writers' room, where Simon, along with Larry Gelbart, Mel Brooks, and Mel Tolkin, collaborated with Sid Caesar in writing "Your Show of Shows." Here Simon is doing what he does best—telling jokes about the making of laughs.

The premise of "Laughter on the 23rd Floor" calls out of Simon an affection and a passion that put the play in the circle of his finest comic efforts, along with "The Odd Couple" and "The Sunshine Boys," which are also about combative and largely male domains. (Carol, the sole female jokesmith in the new play, admits, "I don't want to be considered a woman. I want to be considered a writer.") Simon brings us news both of the golden age of TV comedy and of the process of comedy-writing itself. The jokes are played out against a backdrop of public and private panic. Outside, in 1953, the McCarthy hearings are taking place; inside, the TV show is under siege from the network. Critics of the play, who claim that it doesn't illuminate the period, miss the point of Simon's bankable laughter: to turn denial into a form of delight. Divorce, illness, witch-hunts—in fact, all loss—are the stuff that these professional funnymen are trying to evade. In the writer's life, the room is the universe. "I remember walking down the street with Mel Brooks. We were walking toward the office," Simon told me. "And I said, 'Are we going to our life, or is our life when we go home?' "

The hubbub of outrageousness in the Writers' Room is a kind of comic vamping, a way of extending the ecstatic moment. "Those were the best days I ever had," Simon said. "Oh God, you laughed so hard at each other. We would get furious at Mel Brooks. We got in at ten in the morning. At a quarter to one, Mel still hadn't been in. We'd start a sketch. We'd say, 'Goddammit, that's it with Mel. We're just gonna have it out. Either he comes in on time or some punishment has to be meted out to this guy.' And then Mel would come in with a straw hat, throw it across the room, and say, 'Lindy's made it!' We'd just laugh our heads off and forgive him, because he was so hilarious." The noise, the competition, the ad-libs, the crazy oxygen that these wise guys generated in the room is as exhilarating to Simon as it is to the audience. "I had the idea a number of years ago," he told me. "I said to myself, 'How am I gonna write a play where *everybody* in the room is funny?' Here everybody is funny, but not in telling jokes. They're funny in other ways—in self-deprecating ways, in abusive ways, in ignorant and witty ways. I really had to go to some deep places and say to myself, 'Am I gonna deal with Sid Caesar's drinking and his taking tranquillizers?' I talked to Sid, and said, 'Sid, I'm writing a play about "Your Show of

Shows" and I'm gonna deal with that stuff.' He said, 'You do what you have to do.' I said, 'All right, but I'm gonna show you the play before I ever put it on.' He loved it. We all hated the movie 'My Favorite Year,' because it had nothing to do with the life of the writers. People always used to say, 'I wish I were in that room.' Moss Hart dropped in. Paddy Chayefsky dropped in just to watch how the show was written. We'd pair up, go away, and work on a sketch. Then everybody would congregate in the room and tear the work apart. There'd be fighting. Mel Brooks would say, 'Take this shit out of it. This is pure shit.' Then the castigations would come. I remember coming home one night to watch the show. My wife said, 'That's your line—I can tell.' And I said, 'I swear I have no idea if it was mine or not.' You yelled and you didn't remember what it was that you yelled. You just threw it in. Sid would sit at this table facing Michael Stewart, who acted as kind of a stenographer. We'd be around him in a semicircle—the Sun King and his courtiers.''

Significantly, "Laughter on the 23rd Floor" begins and ends with jokes about food. Even Tony Walton's set features food, with a coffee urn and an assortment of bagels, rolls, sliced pound cake, and Danish at the front of the stage. Nourishment is part of the metaphor of comedy. "When I walk in here, Max Prince laughs," Milt says, justifying his funny outfits to the rookie Lucas. "And if Max Prince laughs my kids eat this week." But joke writing is about psychic as well as physical survival. Simon's collection of lunatics and card-carrying narcissists use jokes as a way of feeding themselves—as a way of insuring a regular diet of pleasure, attention, and stimulation, which the funnymen can't trust the world to provide. In the opening minutes, the Russian-born Val (the superb Mark Linn-Baker), who is the paranoid Mel Tolkin character, holds up a bagel and proclaims, "Look at this. Already sliced. *This* is why my father brought us to America." Milt (the irrepressible Lewis J. Stadlen, looking and sounding like Groucho with a Durante spin) adds, "Mine came for chocolate pudding. In Poland they could make it but they couldn't get it in the cups." Max, even when he's drunk, finds it difficult to express love directly. "Whoo! Boy! Why is that so hard?" he says. "We never said it in my family. . . . We said *Eat!* . . . *Eat* was love. Potatoes was love. Brisket of beef was a *lot* of love.''

As Max, Nathan Lane prowls the stage in a whirlwind of isolated energy. His hair slicked back, his face a little fist of fury, he gives the character the dynamism and danger that the script calls for. "He exudes great strength," the stage directions read. "His strength comes more from his anger than from his physique." Simon superbly captures the loopy solitude of comic genius. "Sid's syntax was insane," Simon told me. "He would say all the wrong things. He'd speak in shorthand sometimes." The play has great fun dramatizing Caesar's articulate inarticulateness. "Mug," says Max, pacing and suffering one of his "Wolf Man" headaches. "Mug." He means coffee, no cream, four sugars. Max is never more funny than when he's earnestly trying to rally his troops to fight the network's cuts. He invokes "Spartacus in the war against the Byzantimums," and sounds the call to battle with "Remember what Churchill said? 'Never have so many given so much for so long for so little for so few for so seldom.' " The star comedian is a law, and a psychology, unto himself. He is noble and infantile at once. Max enters and immediately takes off his suit jacket and pants, so they can be cleaned and pressed. Later, he puts his fist through a wall, then orders a Tiffany frame and plaque to surround the hole. "Does Max have any enemies?" Lucas asks. Kenny (John Slattery), the WASP in Simon's collection of ethnic voices, chimes in, "Nobody hates Max the way Max hates Max." It's a throwaway comment, but a shrewd observation, borne out by Max's fulminating and erratic behavior. When one writer suggests that they reason with the NBC people, Max launches into a wacky monologue. "NBC is not a people," he says. "They're not like us. They wear black socks up to their necks. Crew neck socks . . . They come home from work and before dinner they dance with their wives. . . . They put up wallpaper in their garages. . . . You can't talk to them."

In this atmosphere of real and stage-managed combat, memorable comedy was born. The play serves as a kind of lexicon of comic maneuvers. When the tall-talking, Hollywood-bound Irish gag writer, Brian (well played by J. K. Simmons), comes on, his entrance is written with an old pro's sense of economy and character. "I'm sorry. I just stopped to—" Brian coughs, and starts again. "I stopped to—" He stops again, coughing uncontrollably. Finally, he gets his breath and says, "I stopped to get some cigarettes.'' Brian and the hypochondriacal Ira (played with terrific brio by Ron Orbach) are forever baiting each other. ''You goddamn leprechaun!'' Ira taunts him. *''Catholics* are not funny . . . Protestants are not funny. Methodists are not funny. Baptists are funny but only underwater.'' They have a funny-name contest, which ends with Ira heaving Brian's and his own shoes out the window. A similar kind of craziness fuels the creative competition over Max's parody sketch of Marlon Brando in the film ''Julius Caesar.'' As Max looks up at a ''clustah of stahs in da heavens,'' a character asks him what the cluster is called. ''It is called Stelluh,'' he says. ''Stelluh! . . . Stella for Stahlight!''

The sweet literacy of the parody soon became a thing of the past in commercial comedy. As the play demonstrates, ''Your Show of Shows'' fell victim to the homogenizing of public taste. ''America wanted comedy closer to their own lives,'' Lucas says toward the end. '' 'Julius Caesar' wasn't as familiar to them as kids named Beaver and fathers who knew best.'' Meanwhile, the stripling Lucas makes the writing team; Milt gets divorced; Carol gets pregnant; Val, with elocution lessons, gets to say ''Go fuck''—not ''fock''—''yourself''; and Brian gets to Hollywood. ''I'm telling you guys, Hollywood is great. You'll love it,'' he says at the finale. To which Val replies, ''Listen! If you're a Jew, you end up in the desert no matter what.'' Good joke. Good timing. Good meat-and-potatoes direction from Jerry Zaks, who keeps the fun machine ticking over and the actors crisply hitting their punch lines. ''Laughter on the 23rd Floor'' will start no aesthetic revolutions. But it's too easy to dismiss Simon. Like the ''low comics'' of an earlier generation, he is too popular to be considered ''art'' and more subtle, especially when writing about comedians and comedy, than the public fondly thinks. Time will sort out the critical assessment. But in this outing, anyway, Simon is certainly artful. And, within its limits, ''Laughter on the 23rd Floor'' is well written. ''Oh, I had a lot of fun writing it,'' Simon told me. ''I want to keep doing it. I've started to think about a sequel.''

BRIAN FRIEL

SIGHT UNSEEN

THE GLORIES OF DUBLIN'S
Abbey Theatre are not architectural. From the outside, it's a dumpy,
unpromising building a few blocks off O'Connell Street, the noisy main
drag, where the memories of great political protests hang as thick as
wishes in the air. Inside the theatre, lining the walls that lead, inevitably,
to the bar, are portraits of the artists who have contributed to its legend
—W. B. Yeats, Brendan Behan, Cyril Cusack, and the current jewel in
the theatre's literary crown, Brian Friel, whose newest play, "Wonderful Tennessee," opened on June 30, 1993. A Friel play is a national
event, and the first night of "Wonderful Tennessee" was reported on
the front page of the *Irish Times* and was attended by the President and
the Prime Minister of the Irish Republic and by a battery of Cabinet
panjandrums. On the second night, Friel himself was at the bar, looking
ruddier and more owlish than the cigar-smoking portrait of him, which
was just over his shoulder. He declined to discuss his new play, claiming
a hangover after the buoyant local reviews.

Friel is a master; and the new play, a follow-up to his international
hit "Dancing at Lughnasa" (1990) is a stylistic but not a thematic
departure, attempting in a new theatrical language to incarnate spiritual
grace. In the previous play, dancing became a bridge to some acknowledgment of the mystical—"as if this ritual, this wordless ceremony, was
now the way to speak, to whisper private and sacred things, to be in
touch with some otherness." In "Wonderful Tennessee," that otherness takes the form of an actual place—an island called Oileán
Draíochta, which one of the characters translates as "Island of Otherness, Island of Mystery." On a summer's night, three partying middle-
aged couples wait in vain, singing and telling stories, to be ferried there

from a remote pier in northwest Donegal. Their singing, like the danc-ing in "Lughnasa," is emblematic for Friel of the struggle to get beyond orthodoxy to faith—an exercise not just to "kill time" but to inform the heart.

Significantly, "Wonderful Tennessee" begins and ends in the silence of a windswept coast—"an environment," according to the stage direc-tions, "of deep tranquillity and peace." Friel establishes the moral debate of his play in the opening few seconds. The lights come up on Joe Vaněk's stunning set, a dilapidated two-tier concrete pier, which stretches nearly the width of the stage and is dominated at its center by a cruciform life-belt stand, with old ropes and a desiccated life belt hanging from it. The revellers who will inhabit this derelict arena are heard approaching long before they are seen. "Lost. Help! We're lost!" are the play's first words, which waft onto the vastness from offstage. Are they lost? The evening is dedicated to testing the certainty of this desolation.

The island has been bought "sight unseen" by the leader of the group, a bookie and concert promoter named Terry Martin (Donal McCann), who is the first onstage, and stares out at it on the horizon while holding his panama hat worshipfully over his heart. The others soon invade the stage in a frantic conga line, which brings them rumbus-tiously down from their tour bus and onto the pier—heads rolling and arms flying. "A hint of the maenadic," the stage directions say. Almost immediately, they're singing "I Want to Be Happy"; but the air is filled with the static of human complaint.

Terry's neurotic wife, Berna (Ingrid Craigie), a lawyer, has had a breakdown. She ends the first scene poignantly singing about the Im-maculate Heart and ends the second by jumping off the pier wall into the sea. Terry's sister, Trish (Marion O'Dwyer), nurses her husband, George (Robert Black), who is dying of throat cancer and provides joyous accordion music. Berna's sister, Angela (the sardonic and power-ful Catherine Byrne), a classicist by profession, is being hotly pursued by Terry and confides to him that "getting through the day is as much as I can handle." She is idealized by her frustrated husband, Frank (the droll John Kavanagh), who has been freed from his mundane day job by

Terry's financial support. Frank has pinned his hopes for a "break-through" on his improbably titled magnum opus, "The Measurement of Time and Its Effect on European Civilisation," and in the early hours he confesses to being one of "the goddamn failures . . . Husband—father—provider—worthless."

The play is a brilliantly notated fugue of laughter and lament, in which Friel's visions of Heaven and Hell vie to assert themselves. Here, for instance, in short strokes of asides and furtive glances, Terry inspects the abundance of a picnic hamper while, nearby, Berna confides the impoverishment of their marriage to her sister:

> TERRY: Marinated quail and quince jelly. God!
> TRISH: The delights of the world—you have them all there.
> ANGELA: There are times when all of us—
> BERNA: He has no happiness with me—Terry. Not even "about to be happiness."

The island, once the home of St. Conall and now a place of pilgrimage, offers a mythic counterpoint to the material anxieties of their lives. It's hard to see, and none of them can agree on its exact position or quite get it in focus. These unwitting pilgrims pick over the island's past and contemplate the ritual function of prayer and penance and the need, as Trish says, "to attest to the mystery." This brings a smile to Terry's face. "And why not!" he says. "I'm a bookie for God's sake." A gambler by instinct as well as by profession, Terry has wagered not just on the island but on faith, which is a defiant commitment to the unknown. "Believe me" is a frequent part of his litany. He has organized the outing and paid for it, and assures his friends that the ferryman will arrive. "He'll come. Believe me," he says. As they wait and talk, the island becomes an embodiment of hope, the wonderful Tennessee of the title, which is echoed in a song they sing:

> Come, my love, come, my boat lies low,
> She lies high and dry on the O-hi-o.

As in the song, this stranded collection of lost souls lives in hope of safe harbour. They try to manufacture contentment in their songs and stories. The ferry never shows up, the island is never reached. On the surface, anyway, their trip is, as one of them observes, a "useless, endless, unhappy outing." But as the group bears witness to mystery its collective sense of life is deepened. Berna tells a fantastical story about a flying house and defends it by recollecting a law professor dubbed Offense to Reason, who thought reason was the key to truth. "A flying house . . . marches up to reason and belts it across the gob and says to it, 'Fuck you, reason. I'm as good as you any day. You haven't all the fucking answers—not by any means,' " she says. "That's why I like it. . . . It's stupid, futile defiance."

"Wonderful Tennessee" is a similar act of defiance: a defense—some have said a misguided one—not so much of illusion as of the miraculous. Oileán Draíochta reawakens the characters' ancestral sense of the sacred—the longing to go beyond the vanity of despair and to acknowledge even in pain the wonder of life. The experience makes them believers. "Even if we don't get there," Trish says of the Island of Mystery, "well at least we know . . . it's there." Friel shows them unconsciously recapitulating the island's rituals. A game of stones that Trish plays in the second act gradually turns into a piling up of stones— "doing the *túras*," which, the program explains, was part of the ritual of pilgrimage to Inishkeel Island—and is accompanied by other vestigial ritual gestures, like the taking off of shoes and socks, doing the "rounds" by walking around the *túras* at least three times, and bottling water from the "holy well," which in this case is a puddle of rainwater. In the manner of pilgrims, the group hangs scarves, pieces of cloth, a bouquet of wildflowers on the life-belt stand. Each touches it before leaving the hallowed ground and travelling back to the unholy world. Friel sounds one final note of defiance. Angela, the agnostic, vows to return to the place every year: "Not out of need—out of desire! Not in expectation—but to attest, to affirm, to acknowledge—to shout Yes, yes, yes! Damn right we will, Terry! Yes—yes—yes!" She puts her sun hat at the top of the life-belt stand, giving the cross an intimation of human form. She exits with George, who is playing his accordion, and the two of them jauntily refuse death its dominion as they "loudly, joyously, happily" sing the play's title song.

Friel's allegory is unavoidably schematic. Despite the power of his poetry and his shrewd construction, the play's meaning seems more imposed by the author than earned by the characters, who are given problems but only a patina of personality. Friel's appeal to the heart is made largely through the head. (Even the respectful second-night Dublin audience gave the play only two curtain calls.) The director, Patrick Mason, makes an elegant asset of this limitation by mounting the play in a style as defiantly formalized as Friel's parable. His friezelike staging denies the expectation of depth and the comfort of naturalism. He places his actors on diagonals, which emphasize their silhouettes and exaggerate every turn of the head and body. "From my point of view, the intention is that the life of the interstices—the spaces between the characters, the connection of looks—is what's important," he told me. "Everyone has to be precisely placed. Every look, every gesture, every tableau has to be filled with narrative." Mason, who has had a long-standing superb collaboration with Friel, quoted the playwright: " 'We have a dialogue here on this island between ourselves. If we are overheard and understood, then that's icing on the cake.' " Mason added, " 'Wonderful Tennessee' is part of that dialogue. When the characters lift those stones, when they touch those cloths, there are generations stirring in the air of this theatre. I know it. I feel it every night. People know it in their bones."

Mason's production of "Dancing at Lughnasa" has gone around the world; and "Wonderful Tennessee" is scheduled to open on Broadway, at the Plymouth Theatre, in October. Its arrival on the island of Manhattan is as problematic as the arrival of Friel's pilgrims on the Island of Mystery. Broadway, which sanctifies profit, not prophecy, has lost a sense of what or how to celebrate. Whether the living heart of faith can be grafted onto the dead body of American show business is anybody's guess. "I'm not giving up," Terry says, ever hopeful of success in the journey. "Two–one against. Even money." I'd say the odds for "Wonderful Tennessee" 's surviving more than a heartbeat on Broadway are longer than that. But I hope it reaches its destination, and wins the hard and important battle to be heard.

❖

The epigraph to Brian Friel's new play, "Molly Sweeney," is from Emily Dickinson's poem about the proper way to stage a literary ambush. "Tell all the Truth, but tell it slant. . . . The Truth must dazzle gradually or every man be blind." "Molly Sweeney" is about the dilemma of a blind woman who briefly regains partial sight; it's yet another attempt by Friel, who studied for the priesthood between the ages of sixteen and eighteen, to find a new way of speaking about faith. In "Dancing at Lughnasa," the very act of dancing becomes a means of approaching the religious: as if, the narrator says, "this wordless ceremony was now the way to speak, to whisper private and sacred things, to be in touch with some otherness." In his most recent full-length play, the allegory "Wonderful Tennessee," Friel embodies that mystical otherness in real estate—the unreachable and alluring island that his erstwhile pilgrims call Oileán Draíochta (the Island of Mystery). But his most probing salute to the terror and intoxication of otherness is "Faith Healer" (1979), in which he explores the mind's flirtation with the miraculous through a character named Frank, a faith healer, who describes his freakish gift as "a craft without an apprenticeship, a ministry without responsibility, a vocation without a ministry." Frank, perched, like any artist, between the marketplace and the marvellous, acknowledges those moments of grace when his gift flows mysteriously from his soul directly into the hearts of a skeptical public: "I had become whole in myself, and perfect in myself and, in a manner of speaking, an aristocrat, if the term doesn't offend you." But the price Frank pays for his weird and unreliable talent is his relationship with other people. Frank displaces the pain and guilt of his self-absorbed life by turning the facts of it into fictions. Friel retells Frank's compelling version of his life from the differing, and ironic, viewpoints of his distraught, suicidal wife, Grace, and his Cockney manager, Teddy. "He kept remaking people according to some private standard of excellence of his own, and, as his standards changed, so did the person," Grace says when the time comes for her to recount her tragic story. Frank's obsession is part of her tragedy. "Many, many, many times I didn't exist for him. But before a performance this exclusion—no, it wasn't an exclusion, it was an erasion—this erasion was absolute: he obliterated me,'' she says.

"Faith Healer,'' which is the granddaddy of "Molly Sweeney'' in form and theme, also intersects with the new play on the issue of things seen and unseen. When Frank is practicing or summoning up his gift, he is blind to others ("He looked at me, no, not at me, past me, beyond me, out of those damned benign eyes of his''); and, as his creative eye turns inward, people like Grace feel themselves invisible. Molly, who could see for ten months as a baby and then went blind, inhabits an entirely invisible world—an otherness that has been imposed on her by fate but in which she is comfortable and surprisingly free. The thought that she is missing much of life doesn't dawn on her, so she tells us, until midlife, after her marriage and the first of two operations. Up to then, her vision had been wholly inward; and the sudden predicament of having to learn how to see at forty-one raises fascinating intellectual and spiritual problems. In the material, sighted world, seeing is believing. But in the realm of faith believing is *not* seeing; it is accepting the unknowable as fact. Molly trusts her unsighted world in the way that a writer of Friel's exhilarating capabilities trusts his unconscious—as a deliverance into the unknown, which brings one closer both to the essence of things and to the miraculous. Imagination and talent are gifts of God, which are served only by a rigorous attentiveness to their possibilities. Friel makes the point in Molly's wonderful soliloquy about the delights of swimming: "Just offering yourself to the experience— every pore open and eager for the world of pure sensation, of sensation alone—sensation that could not have been enhanced by sight—experience that existed only by touch and feel; and moving swiftly and rhythmically through that enfolding world; and the sense of such assurance, such liberation, such concordance with it.''

"Seeing isn't understanding,'' says Molly's eye doctor, Paddy Rice, when he recalls making his vainglorious, myopic decision to try to restore Molly's sight (an operation with a success rate, he admits, of "twenty in one thousand years''), and the remark turns out to be a self-fulfilling prophecy. "What has she to lose for Christ's sake?'' Mr. Rice says, echoing the words of Molly's husband, Frank. "Nothing! Nothing at all!'' What Molly loses for a time is the solace of her imagination. She has known the world in a different way—an emotional, playful, boundaryless way, which has given her another intuition about experience. Sight literalizes her experience, imposing boundaries on her imagination and inhibiting her rich intuitive life. "Seeing," Molly says, speaking of her inability to communicate the sensuous pleasure of swimming to her sighted friends, "in some way qualified the sensation; and that if they only knew how full, how total my pleasure was, I used to tell myself that they must, they really must envy me." It's her different knowledge—and the loss of it through partial sight—that Friel emphasizes by contrasting the serenity of Molly, who receives the sensory world so deeply, with the smug prowess of Mr. Rice and the autodidactic greed of her husband, who skitters as restless as a water bug on the sea of knowledge. Molly goes into a long and loving account of the shenanigans of her neighbors at a party at her house the night before the operation. Then she adds, "I was afraid that I would never know these people as I knew them now, with my own special knowledge of each of them, the distinctive sense each of them exuded for me; and knowing them differently, experiencing them differently, I wondered— I wondered would I ever be as close to them as I was now."

"Molly Sweeney" is a metaphysical case study posing as a medical one. By regaining partial sight, Molly is delivered into a condition of seeing but not knowing—a condition, Frank tells us, that Freud in this context dubbed "agnostic." "Yes. Agnostic. Strange," Frank says, putting his finger unwittingly on the spiritual malaise behind Molly's depression after her "miracle" operation. Literally and thematically, Molly, a woman of faith, is sandwiched between two agnostic forces. The play is a series of thirty-seven monologues, crosscut between Molly (Catherine Byrne), sitting downstage center, and her ophthalmologist, Mr. Rice (T. P. McKenna), and the funny, feckless Frank (Mark Lambert), who flank her. As in "Faith Healer," the characters speak to us but not to each other. Behind them is a cyclorama painted in a pinwheel of primary colors, which dissolve at the edges into darker hues, and a toppled sundial lies upstage among scattered leaves. The structure of the play and the disposition of the chairs on the simple set broadcast the nature of Friel's game: we must, as a character says in "Translations," "interpret between privacies."

What we hear from Paddy Rice is the depth of his ambition. He personifies overachievement and underinvolvement. A fallen "rogue star" from the galaxy of ophthalmic luminaries, he finds in Molly a chance to shine again, even from the remote backwater of Ballybeg. T. P. McKenna, an accomplished character actor, with a jowly, silver-haired, portly presence, plays Rice with a handkerchief foppishly drooping from his coat pocket. He has the right outline but the wrong pitch to catch the character's poignant dread. Friel's beautiful words don't rumble quite properly through the great tuba of his body. "What is the vulgar parlance?" Rice says, in the formal, pedantic speech that signals his detachment. "The chance of a lifetime, the one-in-a-thousand opportunity that can rescue a career—no, no, transform a career—dare I say, restore a reputation." Rice has been in a "terrible darkness" of his own making for seven years. His single-minded obsession with his career ("Insatiable years. Work. Airports. Dinners. Laughter. Operating theatres. Conferences. Gossip") led to the departure of his wife with a rival high-flying eye specialist, Roger Bloomstein. "I withdrew from medicine, from friendships, from all the consolations of work and the familiar," Rice says. But his retreat has not brought wisdom. He himself is an example of "blindsight," the diagnosis he makes of Molly's post-operative condition: a kind of vision that proves totally useless. Rice's expertise doesn't help him relate to others or to lead a moral life. He tells an anecdote about first hearing the word "blindsight," but doesn't catch the irony in it. "Beautiful lady. You *do* know that?" Bloomstein says to Rice about his wife. "I said of course I did," Rice tells us. " 'That's not how you behave,' he said. 'You behave like a man with blindsight.' " And Rice still does: he's separated from his children, from the community of others, and from himself. Even Molly's operation doesn't seem to have shifted his emptiness. He tells of discussing the operation and Molly's subsequent depression with a famous eye specialist at a memorial service for Bloomstein. The specialist tells him, " 'They don't survive. That's the pattern. But they'll insist on having the operation, won't they? And who's to dissuade them?' 'Let me get you a drink,' I said, and I walked away." The moment is shocking. Rice has kept this knowledge from Molly and blocked it from himself. He literally can't imagine Molly's suffering. The operation restored his faith in his technical prowess but has left him in bad faith. The irony is lost on him but not on us.

If Paddy Rice has a head but no heart, Frank has an untutored heart but no head. Mark Lambert invests Frank's perfervid curiosity—what the doctor calls the "indiscriminate enthusiasms of the self-taught"— with terrific energy and charm, which almost but not quite mask his restless emptiness. "Brilliant" is Frank's favorite adjective: Molly's psychotherapist is brilliant; an article on "engrams" is brilliant; even his friend Billy, with whom he has a hapless adventure trying to rescue two badgers, is brilliant. His eye can't resist (or dismiss) anything that distracts his attention from himself and the purposelessness of his life. Inevitably, his plans go awry. But he puts a funny face on his many botched schemes, the best of which is a nearly four-year stint on a windswept Irish island trying to raise Iranian goats, because they purportedly produce more milk. "All that time their metabolism, their internal clock, stayed Iranian," he explains. "They lived in a kind of perpetual jet lag." At first, Molly is just another of the reckless flutters of a man desperate for meanings, and she suspects as much. "He couldn't resist the different, the strange," she says, and quotes her best friend's observation about their prospective match: "All part of the same pattern, sweetie: bees—whales—Iranian goats—Molly Sweeney." Actually, Molly is a consuming mission, one that gives him both purpose and a narcissistic sense of goodness. He bones up on blindness at the library before their first date, and figures that dancing is the perfect activity. "I am your eyes, your ears, your location, your sense of space. Trust me." Only once, at the end of the badger escapade, does the despair underneath his manic avidity for action and ideas bubble up. "Why don't you stay where you are?" he says to himself. "What are you looking for?" Friel gives him one last expletive, spoken in disgust but echoing through the play with ironic resonance. "Oh, Jesus," he says.

Molly's loss is spiritual, but neither the doctor nor Frank has any sensitivity to that. (Frank looks up the term "gnosis," which the doctor uses for her impaired vision, and finds that it means "mystical knowledge." "Good Old Molly!" he says to himself. "Molly's full of mystical knowledge!") At the party before her operation, Molly already anticipates herself in "exile," estranged from her old world and unable to come to grips with her new, sighted one. "Homesickness" is the only word she can find for her desolation and her sense of separation. Catherine Byrne conveys Molly's sharp intelligence, if not the radiance of wisdom that the character has on the page. Molly takes us through the agitation of new sight ("all that movement—nothing ever still—everything in motion all the time") and the overload of color ("Just one more colour—light—movement—ghostly shape—and suddenly the head imploded and the hands shook and the heart melted with panic"); and her increasingly erratic behavior lands her eventually in the sanitarium where her mother once lived, and where she is visited occasionally by the ghosts of her parents. These fantasies and the facts about Frank's newest adventure, in Ethiopia, are woven seamlessly together in her translucent monologue. She has retreated within herself to a place somewhere between fact and fiction. "My borderline country is where I live now," she says. "I'm at home there. Well . . . at ease there." But from this borderland, somewhere between the sacred and the profane, the real and the imagined, she has found more knowledge of herself and of life than either her husband or her doctor has. In her stoicism there is dignity, and even a kind of freedom. Unlike the other characters, Molly, as she speaks her elegiac final soliloquy, explores the stage. Her physical liberation is the barometer of an internal one. "It certainly doesn't worry me anymore that what I think I see may be fantasy or indeed what I take to be imagined may very well be real— what's Frank's term?—external reality," she says, speaking for Friel's faith in the transforming power of the imagination. "Real—imagined— fact—fiction—fantasy—reality—there it seems to be. And it seems to be all right. And why should I question any of it anymore?"

"Molly Sweeney" is storytelling on a grand scale but theatre on a small one. Friel has an extraordinary word-hoard and a brave poetic gift, which can make words feel like actions. "Molly Sweeney" is a riveting chamber piece. But I look forward to the symphonies—of dialogue, song, and dramatic action—that Mr. Friel, one of the few modern masters of his craft, is capable of delivering.

TOM STOPPARD

BLOWING HOT AND COLD

IN TOM STOPPARD'S 1966
novel, "Lord Malquist and Mr. Moon," Malquist remarks, "Since we
cannot hope for order, let us withdraw with style from the chaos." This
notion has made Stoppard a very rich man. He says that his favorite line
in modern English drama is from Christopher Hampton's "The Philan-
thropist": "I'm a man of no convictions—at least, I *think* I am." Over
the years, in twenty-one plays, Stoppard has turned his spectacular
neutrality into a high-wire act of doubt. "I write plays because dialogue
is the most respectable way of contradicting myself," he once explained. The three-ring circus of Stoppard's mind pulls them in at the
box office, where news of the intellect, as opposed to the emotions, is a
rarity. Marvel at his marriage of Beckett and Shakespeare in the death-
defying clown act of "Rosencrantz and Guildenstern Are Dead"
(1967). Watch him play with logical positivism and the meaning of God
in "Jumpers" (1972). See him juggle Tristan Tzara, James Joyce, and
Lenin in "Travesties" (1974). Stoppard's mental acrobatics flatter an
audience's intelligence and camouflage the avowed limits of his plotting
and his heart.

In "Arcadia," at the Vivian Beaumont—to my mind, his best play so
far—Stoppard is serving up another intellectual stew (the recipe includes "a seasoning of chaos and a pinch of thermodynamics following a
dash of quantum mechanics," he says), but with a difference. Stoppard,
whose stock-in-trade is parody, which is skepticism in cap and bells, has
found a metaphor that takes him beyond parody to vision. Here, despite
some casting glitches, Trevor Nunn's elegant production pits the heart
against the head in a subtle theatrical equation, which factors out into a
moving ambiguity.

The play begins and ends with an image of Eden before the Fall. In this lush, tranquil landscape, painted onto a curtain, lit from behind, that wraps around the thrust stage like a kind of illuminated lampshade, no animals and no fear intrude on perfect pastoral harmony as Eve holds out to Adam the Apple of Knowledge. Only scudding gray clouds in the background suggest the confusion about to beset mankind once Adam takes a bite. The consequence of curiosity, once the curtain goes up, is a vaudeville of consciousness in a fallen world. "Septimus, what is carnal embrace?" the thirteen-year-old math brain truster Thomasina Coverly (the pert Jennifer Dundas) asks her handsome tutor, Septimus Hodge, in the play's first line. The question mirrors the image of Paradise about to be lost, and Stoppard's play goes on to answer her question. To embrace the flesh is also to embrace all the sins that the flesh is heir to— the sins to which Stoppard's labyrinthine plot, whose ingenious twists and turns involve greed, rapacity, vainglory, skulduggery, cruelty, delusion, confusion, and genius, bears ample witness.

The brilliance of "Arcadia" is not so much in the wordplay as it is in the construction. Stoppard has built his story along two time lines: life at Sidley Park, the Coverlys' country house in Derbyshire, in 1809, and life at present in the same house, where a couple of academics are picking over the bric-a-brac of Coverly family history. The action is set in a high-ceilinged room of grand Georgian design, which is dominated by a large oblong table cluttered with books, implements of learning, and a dozy pet turtle. A fissure in the cupola of Mark Thompson's shrewdly designed interior is the only physical hint of the skewing of world views that takes place around the table as the play shuttles back and forth in a nanosecond between centuries. (Actors in one time frame exit as actors from the other enter.) By crosscutting the Coverly family story and the story of the contemporaries trying to reconstruct it, Stoppard utilizes the ironies of history—the symmetries and accidents that lead, nonetheless, to a kind of order—as a way of demonstrating the outcome of chaos theory; that is, as the program note explains to us scientific simpletons, how reality "can be both deterministic and unpredictable." This is an enormous theatrical feat—a kind of intellectual mystery story—in which Stoppard provides the audience with the exhilarating illusion of omniscience. We become cosmic detectives, outside time, solving the riddle of history from the clues and connections that we see but the characters, who are caught in time, do not. For instance, the equation that Thomasina works out to explain the asymmetry of a leaf, her "New Geometry of Irregular Forms," later turns out, with the help of computers, to undo the assumptions of Newtonian physics. She is to classical mathematics what Picasso is to art history. The spirited youngster, who shouts "Phooey to Death!" in the first scene, works out a formula that, by the last scene, prophesies the ultimate doom of the universe, which is collapsing like a chocolate soufflé from the slow loss of heat. Even Thomasina's offhand doodle on the landscape architect's plans for a Gothic vista at Sidley Park—she sketches a hermit to inhabit the planned Romantic hermitage—turns out to have been a prophecy of Septimus Hodge's destiny. The caprices of history, like the accidents that become inevitabilities in a plot, are the charms of chance that Stoppard and the audience stand in awe of.

Life's terrifying randomness is a mystery that compels mankind to impose order. Chaos is psychologically intolerable; man's need for coherence is greater than his need for truth. Landscape, like ritual, is consoling because it holds the magical promise of permanence. "English landscape was invented by gardeners imitating foreign painters who were evoking classical authors," says Hannah Jarvis (Blair Brown), a modern who is writing a book about the Sidley Park hermitage and the garden. The imaginative ideal is made into a reality; and Stoppard contrives to dramatize a moment in the life of the estate when the old illusion of reality is being adapted to fit a new one. At Sidley Park, Nature was originally tamed according to a neoclassical symmetry. The projected Romantic version, for which Stoppard supplies fascinating visual aids, is a triumph of the picturesque over the well proportioned. The planned irregularity and "naturalness" of the reimagined landscape capture the nineteenth-century drift toward Romantic individualism: from formality to spontaneity, from aristocratic public space to middle-class privacy, from the balance that reflects the Enlightenment's God of Reason to the brooding Romantic freedom that makes a god of the self. "The decline from thinking to feeling, you see," Hannah says. No wonder Septimus (Billy Crudup, making a persuasive Broadway début) refers to the landscape architect who engineers the loss of this particular version of Paradise as the Devil. "In the scheme of the garden he is as the serpent," Septimus says. The wildness of the picturesque style is an attempt to contain chaos by building the unpredictable into the landscape, just as Thomasina, in her algebraic equation, is unwittingly introducing chaos into the physical laws of life.

Meanwhile, the lives and loves of these citizens take their apparently ordinary lustful course. The philandering Septimus cunningly evades a duel with the cuckolded poet Ezra Chater (Paul Giamatti), who enters in fury and exits in flattery, inscribing Hodge's copy of his poem "The Couch of Eros," after the tutor, lying, promises to review it favorably. "Did Mrs. Chater know of this before she—before you—" Chater sputters, seeing his wife's infidelity not as a leg over for her but as a leg up the literary ladder for him. Septimus encourages this delusion, and Chater is triumphant. "There is nothing that woman would not do for me," he crows, thereby illustrating Stoppard's larger theme—that people will rationalize anything to avoid chaos.

The compulsion for coherence has its comic apotheosis in the biographical sleuthing of Bernard Nightingale, a don from Sussex University who is a whirlwind of spurious intellectual connections. Nightingale (played with swaggering and hilarious arrogance by Victor Garber) has stumbled on the copy of Chater's "The Couch of Eros" that contains both the poet's inscription and an unnamed challenge to a duel, and he has traced the volume to Byron's library. A literary climber of the first order, Nightingale sniffs a mother lode of lit-crit kudos in making the connection between Byron and Chater. No one is better at this kind of academic flimflammery than Stoppard, and he has a good time teasing the literary second-guessing that too often passes for biography. Within minutes of insinuating himself into Sidley Park, and Hannah's orbit, Nightingale is spinning his academic wheels and turning what we know to be Septimus's face-saving deceit into a sensational case of adultery, literary infighting, and the death of Chater in a duel with Byron after the latter poet's devastating review of Chater's work appears in *Piccadilly Recreation*. "Without question, Ezra Chater issued a challenge to *somebody*," Nightingale says, reading from his completed paper in the tour-de-force opening of Act II. "Without question, Lord Byron, in the very season of his emergence as a literary figure, quit the country in a cloud of panic and mystery, and stayed abroad for two years at a time when Continental travel was unusual and dangerous. If we seek his reason—*do we need to look far?*'' Hellbent on literary glory, Nightingale rushes past the truth—''Is it likely that the man Chater calls his friend Septimus Hodge is the same man who screwed his wife and kicked the shit out of his last book?'' The paper is proof positive of the cynic's adage that ''history is something that never happened written by someone who was never there.''

''Arcadia'' uses intellectual argument as a kind of riptide to pull the audience under the playful surface of romance with which the characters in both time frames fill their days and nights. In ''Arcadia'' 's comic conceit, seismic intellectual shifts are treated as superficial, while superficial changes of the heart are treated as monumental. For the evening to work, the audience must feel the pull of sexuality as well as the play of knowledge. In London, with Felicity Kendal, Emma Fielding, and Harriet Walter in the major female roles, the erotic amperage was high; here, though, the American actresses can articulate the words but not the sexy twinkle beneath them. As Hannah, Blair Brown shows a sharp intelligence, but she can't give Stoppard's lines that nervy bluestocking spin which flirts with learning and turns the alarming into the charming. ''Oh, shut up,'' she tells Nightingale, when he is upbraiding her after discovering she has written a letter to the London *Times* giving the facts of Chater's death. (He was killed by a monkey bite in Martinique after discovering the dwarf dahlia.) ''It'll be very short, very dry, absolutely gloat-free,'' she says of her letter. ''Would you rather it were one of your friends?'' The strut of Stoppard's epigrams is also missed by Lisa Banes as Lady Croom, who delivers some of the most delightful *mots* without the louche aristocratic aura of entitlement that makes them properly pay off. ''Do not dabble in paradox,'' she says to Captain Brice (David Manis). ''It puts you in danger of fortuitous wit.'' Even the pint-size Jennifer Dundas, who has the smarts to make Thomasina a credible, if cloying, prodigy, hasn't the stature to make her a compelling object of desire. The cumulative effect is not to undermine the production but to dim it.

Still, the brilliance of Stoppard's metaphor shines through. In the final scene, Thomasina is horsing around with her brother when Septimus enters with her latest diagrams under his arm. "Order, order!" Septimus shouts to his rambunctious pupil, now nearly seventeen years old, who would rather waltz than work. By the end of the scene, when Septimus comprehends her latest equation, he sees that order—the Enlightenment notion of it—has entirely collapsed. Now the time frames merge, with the characters in the present overlapping with and commenting on the issues raised by characters in the past. "It's a diagram of heat exchange," says Valentine Coverly, a graduate student of mathematics (played expertly by Robert Sean Leonard), looking at the same diagrams that Septimus is studying. Septimus looks up. "So, we are all doomed," he says. "Yes," Thomasina answers cheerfully, not knowing that she is soon to become another integer in her equation of chaos. (She will perish the same night in a fire; and Septimus will become the hermit of Sidley Park, speaking to no one except his pet turtle.) But for the moment, with the geometry of the universe's doom in his hand, Septimus says, "When we have found all the mysteries and lost all the meaning, we will be alone, on an empty shore."

At the prospect of such an awesome, godless void, Thomasina suggests that they dance, and finally gets Septimus to his feet. The audience knows the outcome but the dancers don't: they live in the comedy of the moment, not in the tragedy of history. Hannah waltzes with Gus Coverly (John Griffin), a smitten teen-ager who has given her the final piece of the puzzle of Septimus's story. Together, the couples whirl around the old table covered with the inventory of centuries of learning. The ravishing image moves the play, in its last beats, from story to statement. The dance becomes the dance of time: one awkward, one graceful; one in celebration, one in resignation. The waltz, an act of grace in the face of gloom, is a perfect embodiment of Stoppard's spiritual standoff. Playwriting, like the dancing, is a way of giving off heat in a cooling universe: an assertion and an abdication at the same time. It's the dance of a stoic, and, from where I sit, it is brave and very beautiful.

PART 3
MUSICALS

GEORGE AND
IRA GERSHWIN

CITY SLICKERS

BROADWAY MARKS THE
spot where the new momentum of America's twentieth century found
its first wonderful playground. "Prosperity never before imagined,
power never reached by anything but a meteor had made the world
irritable, nervous, querulous, unreasonable and afraid" is how Henry
Adams characterized New York in 1905. To both comprehend and
assuage these powerful new industrial agitations, the new American
rhythm required new and powerful magic. On Broadway's Golden Mile,
prosperity and exhaustion, power and personality, dynamism and panic
coalesced in their most vigorous and unrepentant forms. In its songs,
Broadway provided a backbeat of promise; in its happy endings, an
escape from defeat; in the pratfalls of its clowns, the hope of resilient
survival. America has always been a percentage play, and Broadway
turned the gamble into fun. It was the stage on which the nation first
acted out the quintessential drama of the American sweepstakes. In its
pageant of big winners and big losers—a show that never closes—
Broadway bore gaudy witness not only to the abundance in the land but
also to the particularly vindictive nature of its idea of triumph, in which
it was possible to make both a name and "a killing." The commonest
citizen could rise by pluck, luck, and talent into the aristocracy of
success.

Broadway, like its stars, had to glow. And it did. Brilliance has always
been Broadway's defining element and its central metaphor. Lights
turned Broadway into "the Great White Way," "the Street of the
Midnight Sun," "the Midtown Coney Island." Broadway held back the

night just as it resuscitated high spirits. "It is a glowing summer afternoon all night," the French novelist Paul Morand wrote about Forty-
second Street. "One might almost wear white trousers and a straw hat.
Theatres, night clubs, movie palaces, restaurants are all lighted at every
porthole. Undiscovered prisms, rainbows squared." Miles of cable,
thousands of pulsing bulbs, millions of watts of energy blended people
with products in an extravaganza of self-promotion. Names sizzled in
the night sky, branding the heavens with their imperialism. Reflecting
on Broadway signs, the English critic G. K. Chesterton wrote, "What a
glorious garden of wonders this would be to anyone who was lucky
enough to be unable to read." But to the American, filled with the
century's sincere itch for progress and perfection, there was no more
sensational signpost of identity than to "see your name in lights."
Broadway stardom made a romance of individualism, and every theatre
marquee made spectacular the self's separation from others: the name
illuminated, the name rewarded, the name tyrannical. "When I do a
show, the whole show revolves around *me*," said Ethel Merman, one of
Broadway's greatest musical-comedy stars and *philosophes*, "and if I
don't show up, they can forget it!"

Broadway made a myth of show *business*, and the great stars of its
heyday—playful simulacra of the new corporate man whom Henry
Adams saw emerging "with ten times the endurance, energy, will, and
mind of the old type"—regarded themselves primarily as businessmen.
"I am a salesman of songs and jokes," Al Jolson said. "Just as any other
man sells merchandise, I have to sell my goods to the audience. I got
selling experience in small stores; these stores were called vaudeville."
In Broadway's hubbub of market forces, fame was box-office vigorish,
and was therefore dearly prized. The particular virulent American kind
of fame was cooked up on Broadway long before Hollywood mastered
the merchandising of celebrity. Fame (the word has its root in the Latin
word for "rumor") spawned that journalistic mutation—part reporter,
part fabulist—the Broadway gossip columnist. Leonard Lyons, Earl Wilson, Ed Sullivan, Louis Sobol, and especially, the Big Daddy of ballyhoo,
Walter Winchell, became the unofficial biographers of the rialto, turning Broadway into a whispering gallery of urban glory. Winchell coined
a telegraphic style to capture the breathless, reckless, impudent thrill of

Broadway, whipping up the sense of anticipation that made both the street and the society so distinctive. Eugene O'Neill called Broadway a "showshop," and he wasn't wrong. Seriousness, which has had many victories on Broadway—the plays of O'Neill, Tennessee Williams, Arthur Miller, Edward Albee, and Arthur Kopit—has never fared as happily in its raucous entrepreneurial environment as frivolity. But Broadway's frivolous entertainment, in its refusal to suffer, has itself become a metaphor, giving weight and dimension to that most mischievous and ambivalent of American guarantees—"the pursuit of happiness." The comedians who until the Second World War dominated the Broadway stage as its "low comics" became the models for the next generation's high art, inspiring such theatrical innovators as Antonin Artaud, Bertolt Brecht, V. Meyerhold, and, of course, Samuel Beckett, whose first American production reached Broadway in 1956.

Although this year, 1993, Broadway celebrates a century around Times Square, the Broadway of legend really began in the twenties. The Broadway that now seems old to us was substantially new to the generation of twenties artists who made it legend. They were not only making a new theatre but inhabiting a new landscape. The Music Box Theatre was new (1921), and so were the Martin Beck (1924), Madison Square Garden (1925), the Guild (1925), the Mansfield (1926), the Alvin (1927), the John Golden (1927), and the Majestic (1927). Neon and the Gershwins arrived on Broadway the same year, 1924; both made the city sensational in different ways. The lights turned Times Square into a sight; the songs turned Manhattan into a legend.

"Lady, Be Good!," whose seventieth anniversary is being celebrated by the Shaw Festival in the tranquil setting of Niagara-on-the-Lake, in Ontario, Canada, audaciously mixed highbrow and lowbrow, and introduced to Broadway the new musical team of George and Ira Gershwin. "Lady, Be Good!," which ran for three hundred and thirty performances, was also the occasion of the first starring roles on the American stage for Fred and Adele Astaire, who, like Gertrude Lawrence and Ethel Merman after them, rode the chromatic brilliance of a Gershwin score to glory. "He wrote for feet," Astaire said of Gershwin's music. In its syncopation and conversational sass, his score caught the boisterousness of the city and turned its momentum into an enduring urban romance. Gershwin shortened the musical line, added blue notes, and brought the musical up to speed with the metropolis. "We are living in an age of staccato, not legato," said Gershwin (who wrote "Rhapsody in Blue" in the same year as "Lady, Be Good!"). "This we must accept. But this does not mean that out of this very staccato utterance something beautiful may not be evolved." At twenty-six, Gershwin— self-confident, streamlined, prodigious—was a child of his century; and he expressed its twin deliriums of output and energy.

The twenties notion of Manhattan as a playground, "an isle of joy," starts, more or less, with the sibling fairy tale of Dick and Susie Trevor in "Lady, Be Good!" As the audience discovers at the overture, they not only are out of money but have been turned out, furniture and all, onto the street. "We were trying to do something that hadn't been done before," Astaire said; and among the show's many innovations—a thematic danced opening, songs that helped tell a story, two pianos in the orchestra—was the celebration of the city's blessings. No matter how far afield the locales of the American musical might be, its heart and soul were situated in New York City. Guy Bolton and Fred Thompson make the point in the first words of their script: "Sidewalk in front of the old Trevor homestead, Beacon Hill, R.I. This scene shows a sort of small 'square'—a cul de sac such as Sutton Place or MacDougal Alley." On their uppers but not down in the dumps, the Trevors make ingenious use of the city. When a strolling policeman refuses to take out a street light so that the Trevors can plug their electric stove into the lamppost, Susie says brazenly, "Very well, then I can! Now we'll have current, and no current expense." In the twenties musical, the Big City always provides. Even a passing hobo, Jack Robinson by name, catches Susie's eye; he turns out—as hoboes do in musicals—to be a millionaire. Abundance is the message both of the musical and of its version of urban life. The wondrous sense of bounty corresponded to the Gershwins' experience of what Ira called their "peregrinatory Manhattan boyhood," whose "Epicurean Delights of Childhood on the East Side" he listed in his diary: "1) Chinese Nuts 2) Polly Seeds 3) Hot Arbis 4) Sweet Potatoes 5) Lolly Pops 6) Candy Floss 7) Half Sour Pickles." The clamor of the city, the "metropolitan madness" that

George Gershwin spoke of, was another form of abundance and a signal of "our incomparable national pep." In "Lady, Be Good!," the city's feverish pace is first dramatized as a thrilling but punishing alienation in the showstopping "Fascinating Rhythm":

> What a mess you're making!
> The neighbors want to know
> Why I'm always shaking
> Just like a flivver.

By the finale, when the song is reprised, the incessant rhythm has become a kind of redemption, holding out the promise of delight, not disintegration:

> Fascinating wedding
> Say, that appeals to me.
> Fascinating wedding,
> I hear you calling.

If George Gershwin absorbed the music of the city, his twenty-eight-year-old brother cocked a sharp ear for the poetry of street talk. "Listening to the argot in everyday conversation results in pay dirt for lyric writers," Ira said. At the Shaw Festival, "I've Got a Crush on You," from "Treasure Girl" (1928), is grafted onto the production, and we get to hear Ira's colloquial cunning at its most charming: the beloved addressed as "Sweetie Pie" and the besotted admitting that his words of love are "mush."

Ira, who characterized himself as a "floating soul," was a dreamer whose words helped define that particularly American sense of expectation (another presenting symptom of America's abundance) which is summoned up by "The Man I Love," a superb song that was dropped from the original show but has been reinstated in the current production:

> Maybe I shall meet him Sunday,
> Maybe Monday—Maybe not;

Still I'm sure to meet him one day—
Maybe Tuesday
Will be my good news day.

Although the proscenium arch of the Royal George Theatre is decorated with painted American five-dollar bills and coins of the realm,
Glynis Leyshon's skeleton production of "Lady, Be Good!" cuts back
drastically on the show's orchestra, its chorus, and its celebration of
prowess. Musicals shouldn't, and perhaps can't, be done on a beer
budget. Watching a vintage piece like "Lady, Be Good!" performed
by the festival's competent ensemble of actors, you can't help notic-
ing the loss of technique that has accompanied the attrition of the
musical. In their heyday, musicals like this one were star vehicles, and
it's not hard to see why. You have to care about the characters, but as
they're written they are doodles lumbered with flat dialogue. Stars
brought to the party the appeal of extraordinary personality. The As-
taires were inimitable; and, while nobody would expect the actors
playing Dick and Susie Trevor to equal them, they should at least have
some charm. Paul Gatchell's Dick Trevor manages merely a sort of
strained niceness, and Patty Jamieson's Susie calls attention to herself
with a terminally cute Baby Snooks voice. It's left to the gangling Todd
Waite, as the eccentric Bertie Bassett, and Richard Binsley, as Watty
Watkins, in goggle-eyed imitation of the comedian Walter Catlett, who
originated the role, to add energy to the evening and vigor to the
comedy. Binsley enters with a ukulele and plays it for "Fascinating
Rhythm." The expertise is welcome. The small stage is otherwise
underpopulated and usually underwhelming. The cast, which has a few
big voices, contains only one person who can actually tap-dance, although the chorus gets away with some simple, well-drilled steps.
William Orlowski, who has also done the show's tap choreography,
serves as a kind of one-man tap chorus. It's he who launches into a Bill
(Bojangles) Robinson routine, tapping up and down steps that light up
like pinball bumpers when touched. Orlowski has the moves but never
quite the illusion of ease. The others in the time-stepping chorus revolve around him like so many trainers with a performing workhorse.
It's a funny sight, but its threadbareness is topped at the finale, when

Dick and Susie, thanks to the prospect of marriage, are back in the money. In musical terms, this is cause for rejoicing; but here, against a background of painted balloons, a paltry dozen real balloons are dropped from the flies—a grace note that has as much clout as a popgun.

RODGERS AND HAMMERSTEIN

CAROUSEL

O N THE ENGLISH STAGE,
Americans are forever depicted as the clowns of capitalism—predatory,
credulous, barbarous, and loud. If there has been a positive portrait of
an American by a major English playwright in the last twenty-five years,
I'm not aware of it. But when it comes to American musicals, the
English can't get enough. Currently, there are five American musicals
on London's West End; two more are scheduled for the spring. What's
endearing about this fascination is how ineptly most of the musicals are
performed. The fundamental problem is spiritual. The British don't
believe that everything's coming up roses, and that something's coming
—something good—if you can wait. American optimism, which is
built on abundance, is not fathomable by the British imagination, because England is a culture of scarcity, and its favored idiom is irony,
which insists on limits to expectation. As a result, American musicals in
England frequently lose a part of their energy and their resonance in
translation. They also lose a lot of their production values, because the
English will not—and usually cannot—spend enough to get the shows
to work properly. So it's a strange and wonderful twist of theatrical fate
that the Royal National Theatre's daring, elegant production of Rodgers
and Hammerstein's "Carousel" should blast away the aspic in which
the show has been preserved and reinvent this classic "musical play"
along darker, more ironic lines, making it compelling for the American
nineties.

The nine musicals of Richard Rodgers and Oscar Hammerstein II
engineered a revolution in American entertainment. Hammerstein was

forty-seven when he joined forces with the forty-year-old Rodgers, in 1942. He'd been a co-author of some of the biggest hits of the twenties ("Rose-Marie," "The Desert Song," "Show Boat"), but his fascination with operetta ran aground in the theatrically conservative, and he had a decade of failures. On the other hand, since 1935 Rodgers, partnered with Lorenz Hart, had produced a string of eight sassy hits, including "Pal Joey" and "By Jupiter." The new Rodgers and Hammerstein partnership smashed the old Broadway formula of "no girls, no gags, no chance." Before Rodgers and Hammerstein, there was "musical comedy," in which smart songs and capering star turns elevated frivolity into an art form. After "Oklahoma!" (1943) and "Carousel" (1945), America had musical theatre. Rodgers and Hammerstein's discovery did for the precision of musical production what the interchangeable part did for mass production—insured quality control. The musical became "actor proof," a fun machine in which the makers, not the stars, controlled the product, and in which song, star, and choreography served a finely tuned story. "Song is the servant of the play," Hammerstein said. "It is wrong to write first what you think and then try to wedge it into a story. . . . A rhyme should be unassertive, never standing out too noticeably. . . . If a listener is made rhyme-conscious, his interest may be distracted from the story."

And in "Carousel" it's the story, Hammerstein's faithful, cunningly filigreed adaptation of Ferenc Molnár's "Liliom" (1909), that elevates the show's main characters—the wife-beating carnival barker, Billy Bigelow, and his masochistic jailbait, Julie Jordan—into dramatic literature. Currently, our musicals are full of moralizing but are unconnected to the moral universe of narrative. Character, context, and plot have been replaced too often by idiosyncrasy and abstraction. What memorable characters have emerged from our recent musical theatre? Tevye in "Fiddler on the Roof." Mrs. Dolly Levi in "Hello, Dolly!" Sweeney Todd in Stephen Sondheim's masterpiece of the same name. That takes musical theatre to 1979. Since then, owing largely to the experiments of Sondheim, who was Hammerstein's protégé, the musical has gone down a postmodernist road, which only Sondheim can travel with any sense of occasion. "The form Rodgers and Hammerstein developed tells a story through character and song," Sondheim said in 1978, after he'd begun "to explore the reduction of human character in a situation of its most succinct form." And he added, "It expands the characters, and the characters therefore cause things to happen in the story, and it goes song-scene, song-scene, song-scene." While acknowledging Hammerstein's importance to his own work ("Oscar taught me how to construct a song like a one-act play"), Sondheim deconstructed the Rodgers and Hammerstein musical and gloated over its demise. "Their work appeals mostly to those over fifty, which doesn't bode well for posterity," he said.

But the concept musical that has evolved from the musical play is too often merely a song cycle. Audiences seem to get smaller as the songs get smarter. A smart lyric in the mouth of a stick figure is a theatrical nothing. This mutation has robbed the musical of an essential playfulness and penetration. Atrophy has been declared art, and instead of being a game of show-and-tell the musical has become a song-heavy game of tell-and-tell. Recently, the arrival of George C. Wolfe's "Jelly's Last Jam" opened the musical up to new mythologies and new aesthetics, showing Broadway how to be at once pertinent and populist. And now the success of the reinterpreted "Carousel," which may arrive on Broadway as early as next fall, has thrown down another challenge to the aridity of current musical storytelling techniques. "I don't think anybody in the nineties could recapture the optimism of the forties," says the director, Nicholas Hytner, whose previous musical megahit was "Miss Saigon." "But I would hope that this production might give those people writing musicals faith to approach material again in the way Rodgers and Hammerstein did."

Hytner, who has a fine partnership with the designer Bob Crowley, had three years to prepare for the show. Every inch of the National's Lyttleton Theatre is filled with the painstaking boldness of their imaginative collaboration, and it gives the play a hard scenic and intellectual edge. " 'Carousel' is one of those shows that have outgrown the theatrical conventions of their first performance," Hytner told me just before the show went into rehearsals, last October. "I think it's the best of the great romantic musicals. I was surprised at how tough and real it was when I read it: Julie Jordan *picks up* Billy Bigelow—you could never do that on the stage in 1945. There's a very interesting tension between the sweetness of the music and the powerful sexual undercurrents of the play. In this 'Carousel,' the dark, subterranean sexuality, which has traditionally been kept in the background of productions, explodes into the foreground.''

The sense of heat is evoked first by the set: a vast Shaker-blue box fronted by a scrim displaying an abstract blue circle with a wispy corona of red, like an eclipsed sun. It's a powerful, authoritative mark, which foreshadows the sense of smoldering passion Hytner manufactures in the first beat of the musical. Instead of opening the show with the famous dance prelude at the fairground, Hytner brings the curtain up on the claustrophobic, shadowy New England textile mill where Julie and her friend Carrie Pipperidge work. The sumptuous sweetness of Rodgers' "Carousel Waltz" plays underneath that image and underscores the frustrated liberty of these wage slaves. The circular emblem on the scrim transmogrifies into the luminous face of a clock: the natural order of the heavens giving way to the unnatural order of the workplace. So when the clock strikes six and the girls are released into the twilight of the New England spring, the thrill of the fairground hubbub and the exhilaration of their momentary freedom gorgeously coalesce with Richard Rodgers' sweeping melody. It's an extraordinary theatrical moment. Suddenly, the empty blue box—a blue that demarcates the sea and sky of this nineteenth-century coastal community—is swarming with carnival life. Bearded, tattooed ladies; Uncle Sam on stilts; a house of horrors spin in and out of sight as the carousel is put together before our eyes. And when Billy Bigelow brazenly scoops Julie up and onto an orange wooden horse, with the merry-go-round's neon canopy fanning out above them like the petals of a flower, the stage is brilliantly set for passion.

Traditionally, Billy Bigelow is cast as a macho beefcake baritone who carries his balls in a wheelbarrow (John Raitt, Howard Keel, Gordon MacRae). But Bigelow, like Liliom, is a lethal combination of pugnacity and panic—he's wild rather than bad. His easy sexual charm and braggadocio hide an anger that he can't explain but that he exhibits in sudden, unaccountable abusive outbursts. ''I was looking for James Dean with a voice,'' Hytner says about discovering Michael Hayden, who was just out of Juilliard when he was given the role. ''After we'd had two years of auditioning the 'Soliloquy,' maybe two hundred times, Hayden was the only one who made us listen. Until him, only Chippendales with voices were coming in."

From the moment Hayden throws his leg over the rearing head of the carousel horse to face Julie Jordan on her ride, his sexual brazenness is never in doubt. He is a strong, if not a seasoned, performer: a fascinating amalgam of the vulnerable and the volatile. He has the pint-size muscularity of Gene Kelly, for whom the part was conceived, and is a restless, lupine presence. This quality is magnified in the ingenious staging of the terrific duet "If I Loved You." Here Billy and Julie are positioned on a rolling hill bounded by a picket fence that climbs sharply upward to a colonial church in the background. Billy can't sit still. The set, like the delicate music underneath the lovers' stage-managed skepticism, pitches them toward each other despite their efforts to stay apart. Hayden doesn't have a pure, crisp, effortless singing voice, like that of Joanna Riding, who plays Julie, and this takes some of the shine off his dazzling attack. In the seven-minute "Soliloquy," at the end of Act I, in which Billy first imagines himself as a father and concludes prophetically by imagining stealing to provide, Hayden acts the song well, but he is sometimes flat in the upper registers, and this keeps "Soliloquy" from clinching its overwhelming emotional moment. "The more he plays the part, the more his voice will open out," Hytner says. Even now, though, the success of "Carousel" is rooted in Hayden's clever connection of violence to self-hatred, which makes Bigelow compelling and redeemable.

By another stroke of good casting karma, Hytner chose Clive Rowe as Mr. Snow, the subject of Carrie Pipperidge's delightful "When I Marry Mr. Snow." Snow, who rises from fisherman to fishing-fleet owner, is everything Billy is not: dutiful, homeloving, hardworking, bursting with bourgeois dreams of glory. In her song Carrie (Janie Dee) confides everything about him to Julie—or *almost* everything. In this production, Mr. Snow is black. When he pops up in the middle of Carrie's reprise about their imminent wedding, singing, "Then I'll kiss her so she'll know," the pause that ensues announces the surprise of both the characters and the audience. On the first day of rehearsal, according to Hytner, Rowe introduced himself to the cast saying, "I'm

Clive Rowe. I play Mr. Snow, and that's the first and last time you'll laugh at that gag.'' Fortunately, the audience laughs with delighted surprise every night, and this bold piece of non-traditional casting adds a considerable dimension of poignance and charm to the show's embodiment of American pluck and luck. "There aren't many black people in Maine now, and there probably weren't then,'' says Hytner, who chose Rowe for his ringing tenor voice, with a heroic top A, and his warm, roly-poly stage presence. "But they didn't dance classical ballet as a regular form of discourse, either.'' The casting is shrewdly in keeping with the provocative racial overtones of "Liliom,'' where the subplot love interest was a Jew who becomes a successful restaurateur. And the importance of community, which was one of Hammerstein's abiding liberal themes, has its apotheosis in the image of Mr. Snow and his nine variously hued children melding happily into this closely knit New England town at the high-school-graduation finale. "I don't see how you could end a show with 'You'll Never Walk Alone' and be staring at thirty-nine white faces,'' Hytner says.

Among the many astonishments of this "Carousel'' is seeing the National Theatre, which is notorious for overdesigning contemporary plays whose action cannot otherwise fill the enormous stage, function at its full technical and scenic capacity in a show that actually demands large, eloquent space. Hytner and Crowley use the stage revolve poetically, fading in and out of scenes with wonderful images, among them sand dunes, sun-blanched clapboard docks, a party of rowboats, and a spectacular streamlined Heaven, complete with a phantasmagoric tapered Shaker box that holds the stars and rises high into the ozone. The spectacle doesn't push the customers back in their seats—it draws them forward in participation. They have to work to make all the show's articulate emotional connections.

Sir Kenneth MacMillan's restaging of Agnes de Mille's pioneering choreography also makes scintillating links with the story. "I actually saw the original London production in 1950, and it's a very serious thing I've been asked to do—to try to equal what Agnes de Mille achieved,'' Sir Kenneth said to me last fall, before rehearsals. "Nowadays, dance has disappeared from the musical. Jazz dancing features a lot in musicals like 'Cats.' You can get away with an awful lot, but there's been nothing to really challenge dancers in a way that would stretch their technique. Perhaps this show will restore the balance.'' Sir Kenneth, who died a few weeks later, in the middle of rehearsals, certainly created exciting challenges for the accomplished dancers in the prelude and in Louise's ballet (beautifully danced by Bonnie Moore and Stanislav Tchassov). But the choreography of ''June Is Bustin' Out All Over'' and ''Blow High, Blow Low'' is more athletic than inspired, and it leaves at least one old pro, Patricia Routledge, who plays Nettie Fowler, seeming not too pleased to have her heft shifted about so vigorously onstage.

Rodgers thought that ''Carousel'' was his finest score, and when the patina of forties bonhomie is scraped away from the stage pictures, Hammerstein's adaptation and lyrics also look to be among his best. The scenes, which follow Molnár's traffic plan and use great chunks of his dialogue, are complex and well constructed. And the issues of abuse bring the show right up to the minute. Molnár, who in Budapest café society was rumored to be a wife beater, tried to face the combination of omnipotence, emptiness, and denial in Liliom, who will admit to neither love nor shame. ''Who's ashamed?'' he says of his abused wife's weeping to the Heavenly Magistrate (Hammerstein changed this to the more benign Heavenly Friend), whom he meets in the next world, after his suicide, and he goes on:

> But I couldn't bear to see her—and that's why I was bad to her. . . . We argued with each other—she said this and I said that—and because she was right I couldn't answer her—and I got mad—and the anger rose up in me—until it reached *[points to his throat]* and then I beat her.

In Hammerstein's version, Billy Bigelow admits perhaps more shame and forgiveness but no more clarity about the perverse hungers of the human heart. Billy is as fierce in his mistreatment of Julie as she is accepting of his abuse. She embodies the romantic ideal of suffering with reward. As she sings in ''What's the Use of Wond'rin' '':

> So, when he wants your kisses
> You will give them to the lad,

And anywhere he leads you you will walk.
And any time he needs you,
You'll go runnin' there like mad.
You're his girl and he's your feller—
And all the rest is talk.

The show, like the song, allows good and bad, joy and pain, to co-exist onstage, as they do in life. "It's possible, dear, fer someone to hit you—hit you hard—and not hurt at all," Julie says to her teen-age daughter, Louise, who is slapped by Billy when he comes down from Heaven a generation later to set things to rights. Both Molnár and Hammerstein wimp out on the slap, which is to Louise's hand when it should be to her face. ("We may gain courage with that later on," Hytner says.) Hytner prefers to think that Julie's controversial line about hurt, like all the stories about Billy that Julie tells Louise, is false. But this doesn't answer the questions of balance and of healing, which Hammerstein's finale tries to stage. "I see plays and read books that emphasize the seamy side of life, and the frenetic side, and the tragic side," Hammerstein said. "I don't deny the existence of the tragic and the frenetic. But I say that somebody has to keep saying that isn't all there is to life. . . . We're very likely to get thrown off our balance if we have such a preponderance of artists expressing the 'wasteland' philosophy."

From the distance of half a century, the finale seems a far more mature and resonant ending than the saccharine pieties of the film, which is what the general public remembers of "Carousel." Hytner reduces the religiosity by cutting "The Highest Judge of All" and by paying scrupulous attention to psychological detail. With Billy whispering to Julie, as her face lightens, "I love you, Julie. Know that I loved you!" and the Doctor telling Louise and the rest of her graduating class, "Don't be held back by [your parents'] failures. Makes no difference what they did or didn't do," the finale reads as metaphor both for the acceptance of loss and for the need to achieve gratitude for what remains of life after the losses. The moment speaks as powerfully now, in the midst of a pulverizing recession, as it did in 1945, after a world war. As the song says, "Walk on, walk on, with hope in your heart . . ."

The reinterpretation of "Carousel" is a vivid antidote to the boulevard nihilism that has so soured the American musical, which once made legends of hope and now makes legends of despair. What's important about Hytner's revival is that it doesn't deny the darkness but shows how to fit that darkness into some larger picture, which includes sun, stars, and earth. "I believe in wind and willow trees," Hammerstein once told Sondheim, who didn't. And perhaps, before the musical can evolve beyond Sondheim's blasted joys and lucid doubts, which are now the state of the attenuated art, musical theatre has to return somehow to its big-hearted origins. This is why Hytner's approach to "Carousel" is important to ponder. In it, the murderous and the miraculous share the stage. Ambiguity replaces both optimism and anxiety as the prevailing credo, and in the show's updated modernity both nostalgia and deconstruction are kissed goodbye. "Carousel" is not "through-sung." It submits the audience to the differing pleasures of song and prose. Song is an enchantment (in fact, the word "enchantment" has its root in the Latin for "to sing") that is palpable and long-standing. A song makes an audience feel, but prose makes it discriminate. Those are fighting words to the Young Turks in musical theatre, but "Carousel" belies the so-called advances of the new musicals. Its well-balanced narrative approaches some deeper sense of life, which is theatrically more satisfying for embracing both misery and mystery. As St. Teresa said, "All the way to heaven is heaven."

JULE STYNE

MR. BROADWAY

Jule Styne, who died last week, at eighty-eight, was a small man with a big gift for melody. He belonged to Broadway's heyday, when being brilliant and corrupting an audience with pleasure were part of the job description. He was the last of his talented, bowwow breed. Once, in his early years, when he had a band and was tinkering with one of his compositions at the piano after a gig, a dapper man tapped his shoulder and said, "Keep it simple but harmonically attractive." The man, Styne found out later, was Vincent Youmans, the composer of "No, No, Nanette" and other Broadway hits. And Styne did just that. He wrote memorable musicals—"Two on the Aisle," "Bells Are Ringing," "Gypsy," "Funny Girl"—when the musical was still selling confidence instead of impotence. "Everything's Coming Up Roses," "Don't Rain on My Parade," and "Diamonds Are a Girl's Best Friend" are brilliant examples of the sense of fun and wonder that Styne found in the material world, enabling him to give people anthems of expectation.

Billeted until recent years on the second floor of the Mark Hellinger Building, on West Fifty-first Street, Styne worked not at the piano but at his desk while chain-smoking cigars. An obsessive gambler (he visited OTB every day of his adult life) as well as a fertile composer, he wrote with the radio tuned to the racing results. When he had fleshed out an idea, he'd pick up the paper and say, "Let's hear how it sounds." "God forbid you should say, 'I loved it, Jule, but the bridge . . .'" says Susan Birkenhead, who wrote the lyrics to "Jelly's Last Jam," and who had been lifted from obscurity by Styne to collaborate on "Treasure Island" in the early eighties. "Rather than *potchky* with the lyric, he'd rip it up and start again. He had this bottomless well of music in him."

Styne, a cocky, well-dressed man, never hid his light under a bushel. "I'm pulling my score!" he'd threaten when he was throwing a tantrum. Betty Comden tells of Styne's dropping a song through the transom of a Hollywood producer's office with the declaration "May I say, another hit!" At parties, Styne would make a beeline for the piano and play what he called "a medley of my Academy Award losers," which included "I'll Walk Alone," "It's a Great Feeling," and "Change of Heart." Then, peering over thick, tinted glasses—a sartorial trademark—he'd say, "And what song of mine do you think finally won?" Then he'd play "Three Coins in the Fountain."

When Styne was nervous about a show tune, he would growl to his lyricist, "We gotta have a home run here." He always knew how to swing for the fences, and usually delivered that rare stroke, almost impossible to encounter these days: a blast of joy. Styne had, by his count, fifteen No. 1 Tin Pan Alley hits, yet he was also a musical dramatist who knew how to write for stars. "They're stars for a reason, and don't you forget it," he lectured his lyricists, and his music turned talents into legends. He gave Carol Channing "Diamonds Are a Girl's Best Friend" and "I'm Just a Little Girl from Little Rock"; he gave Barbra Streisand "People," and, most memorably, he gave Ethel Merman "Everything's Coming Up Roses" and "Rose's Turn." When he was writing "Bells Are Ringing," Judy Holliday told him she would sing anything but a ballad. "Jule knew that Judy loved to sing harmony," says Betty Comden, who co-wrote the show's lyrics with Adolph Green. "He took Judy into another room and said, 'This is the harmony part in this number.' She learned it and sang it perfectly. He said, 'Well, that's the song.' It was 'The Party's Over.' "

GEORGE C. WOLFE

JELLY'S LAST JAM

WHEN YOU'RE TALKING
about the American musical, you're talking Broadway religion: the
salvation of applause, the beatification of the bottom line, the gospel of
good times. This faith has been sorely tested over the last generation,
and the musical has gone into the wilderness. What America is the new
musical singing about? Vietnam put paid to legends of abundance and
righteousness which were formerly the musical's manifest destiny. The
musical lost confidence in its content, its form, its audience, and its
country. German fairy tales, French *pointillisme*, Victorian England,
thirties Berlin—many of the most celebrated recent musicals seem
prepared to sing about anything but America. Musicals gave the society
myths of triumph; now, in the society's retreat from power, the musical
is making myths of anxiety. The musical was fun before it was art; but
give or take a few blips of buoyancy ("Hair," "A Chorus Line,"
"Chicago"), anxiety has become the new abundance. The musical, like
the winded culture it reflects, seems at a loss to know what or how to
celebrate. Pluck 'n' loathing has replaced pluck 'n' luck as the prevailing
credo, the delirium of hope giving way to the delirium of despair. "The
more he bleeds, the more he lives/He never forgets and he never
forgives," chants the chorus about the demon barber of Fleet Street in
Stephen Sondheim's masterpiece "Sweeney Todd." The lines could be
the epitaph of the sour dreams and articulate entropy that the paying
customers have been asked to applaud in these wilderness years where
joy has been banished from the contemporary musical's definition of
maturity.

But joy and irony—the adult acknowledgment of liberation *and* limitation, blessing *and* barbarity—can exist on stage as they do in life, and

"Jelly's Last Jam" has arrived to show Broadway that it's possible to be kinetic and not camp. The show is a watershed, engineered by its playwright/director George C. Wolfe and an extraordinary array of theatrical talent. The fact that this is Mr. Wolfe's first Broadway play, his first Broadway libretto, and his first shot at directing a Broadway musical is a kind of showbiz miracle in itself. But the real significance of the occasion is the redemption that "Jelly's Last Jam" holds out for the future of the American musical. The show opens the musical up to new mythologies, new aesthetics, and a new historical sophistication. The message behind the musical, as well as Jelly Roll Morton's songs, is spelled out for the audience by a character called Jack the Bear. Says the Bear: "High life or no life, ya still gotta live yo' life." That's news to Broadway, whose celebration of the good life has rarely included ordinary life.

"What I've been trying to evolve is a visual and emotional vocabulary which is as evocative and as subliminally powerful as black music," says Wolfe, who writes the blues with words, images, and music. The blues are irony in action; in them, the contradictions of hurt and happiness coalesce. "Jelly's Last Jam" walks it like it talks it. "To relive your past without pain is a lie," says the Chimney Man, the *deus ex machina* in this all-singing, all-dancing Last Judgment, as he indicts Jelly Roll Morton for a moral amnesia that mirrors the commercial musical's practice of removing pain for gain. "Jelly's Last Jam" shows what it means to properly stimulate an audience instead of tickling it to death. "The conventional Broadway wisdom is 'When in doubt give 'em spectacle,' " says Wolfe. "But a human being going through emotions is the best sort of event you can witness."

The first of many accomplishments of "Jelly's Last Jam" is to raise the amperage of passion and to sanctify the moment. In "Jelly's Last Jam," the audience cheers a New Orleans belter called Miss Mamie whose "story lasted 'bout as long as my song," when she concludes "Michigan Water," singing "So all you gumbo-eatin' bitches, can kiss my ass goodbye!" The song is an exhibition of being: slangy, sensuous, and sensational. The defiance in Miss Mamie's voice echoes the defiance in "Jelly's Last Jam," which wants a mass communication but, unlike the influential musicals of Sondheim and his imitators, doesn't disdain the mass.

"Jelly's Last Jam" returns character to the concept musical where all too often a few strokes of personal idiosyncrasy pass for characterization. "Jelly's Last Jam" redresses some of this narrative imbalance. The shrewd lyrics of Susan Birkenhead make an event of plot and personality, and not her brilliance. Luther Henderson's low-down, sumptuous jazz score, inspired by Jelly Roll's music, punches out the subtext of Birkenhead's tasty words with bold stokes whose dissonances invoke the black American jook and not the European avant-garde. The show brings rambunctiousness and noise and a sense of lived-life back to Broadway. If the standing ovations "Jelly's Last Jam" received when I saw it in New York and in Los Angeles (where, at the time, it was the highest grossing show in the Mark Taper Forum's twenty-five-year history) are accurate barometers, "Jelly's Last Jam" has finally found a sophisticated hush of museum theatre and is returning it to the rousing hubbub of the mass from which the form's power springs.

Wolfe is a folklorist, and his vivacious characters exude the high definition and the high style of self-contained, unoppressed denizens of a black world. The paradoxical Jelly Roll Morton, the self-proclaimed Creole "inventor of jazz" and a traitor to his race, is the central raffish figure whose racism the musical controversially debates, but there are others: Jack the Bear, Foot-in-Your-Ass Sam, Too-Tight Nora, Three-Finger Jake, Sweet Anita, The Hunnies who capture a variety of moments, moods, and styles of black life as the story of jazz works its way with Jelly Roll from New Orleans to Chicago and to New York. These characters revel in their power and in their prowess. "I try to write characters with an outrageous sense of self because, in their presence, they're the opposite of oppressed," says Wolfe. "I love people who carry their power with them. It's one of my theories that black folks carry all of their stuff with them all the time because they didn't have time to pack the first time around. They don't keep their arrogance, their humility, their anger, their passion locked in little boxes. So that the next time, if somebody tries to take it away, they'll have it *all* with them."

The first black Broadway musical, Noble Sissle and Eubie Blake's

"Shuffle Along" (1920), made it to Broadway by pandering, as its title suggests, to downtown racial stereotypes. Nothing too much had changed over the years until "Jelly's Last Jam."

A number of black shows from "Ain't Misbehavin' " to "Bubbling Brown Sugar" to "Five Guys Named Moe" have brought black music and black talent to Broadway but refused to put the ravishing energy in a proper historical context. The shows are another form of shucking, what Wolfe calls "cultural strip mining," that robs black expression both of context and of ideas. Wolfe's chilling Act One finale, "Dr. Jazz," makes a spectacle of this denial. In blackface and bellhop caps, the chorus struts the fun-loving racist stereotype behind Jelly as he sings about the delightful spell of his music, whose syncopation is meant to make the public forgive and forget the sin that made it and his own transparent shortcomings.

> Listen people, here comes Doctor Jazz
> He's got glory all around him, yes he has
> When the world goes wrong
> n' you got the blues
> He's the man what makes you get out
> Both your dancin' shoes. . . .

In "Jelly's Last Jam," Wolfe is not reflecting a white world but debating a black one. He celebrates Afro-American culture not as a sociological problem, but as a way of being.

"Every phase of Negro life is highly dramatized," wrote Zora Neale Hurston, whom Wolfe successfully adapted for the stage in "Spunk" and whose famous essay "Characteristics of Negro Expression" is gospel to Wolfe. "There is an impromptu ceremony always ready for every hour of life. No little moment passes unadorned. Whatever the Negro does of his own volition, he embellishes." The Afro-American will-to-adorn glories in survival and the ability of the race to reinterpret white civilization for its own use. The stylishness of "Jelly's Last Jam" is witness to the originality and the ever-changing energy of the black aesthetic. Morton's jazz motifs decorate the melodic line of his songs, tap dancing decorates motion, and the trio of Hunnies with legs up to their armpits decorate just about everything else. From the sinking of a pool ball to the slamming of a door to the re-creation of the L.A. landscape (a couple of upstage zigzag lines of neon), Wolfe's visual language misses no opportunity for startling invention. The asymmetry and angularity of Wolfe's stage pictures, which make the musical dynamic and fresh, are also part of the black aesthetic. "There's a tribe in Africa that ploughs its fields in perfect squares but leaves one square that isn't perfect," explains Wolfe. "It's embracing the imperfection as opposed to being haunted by it."

"Jelly's Last Jam" also reclaims the gorgeous power of tap dancing as part of musical storytelling. Jelly Roll Morton was a piano player, not a tap dancer; but in Wolfe's script, tap becomes a percussive beat which is at the root of the rhythm and the anger. In fact, the tap dancing begins when young Jelly learns syncopation from the cries of New Orleans street vendors as the Root Man shouts "roots, roots, roots," and soon launches into a show-stopping tap competition with Jelly. "Simply because a silhouette is deemed offensive," says Wolfe of the reactionary overtones of tap, "you don't throw away the silhouette or the content, you reclaim it." And so he has: tap becomes a metaphor of Jelly Rolls' frustration as well as creation. It's awesome to watch.

Wolfe's story turns the tables on the imperialism of self which Broadway musicals and its stars have traditionally made glorious. In this time of riot and recession, "Jelly's Last Jam" sounds a new note on the Broadway musical stage. The show dramatizes "destiny of me" being transformed into the destiny of we. This is also news. "When you're dependent on those around you in order to survive, you negotiate a sense of the collective, you evolve this sense of 'we,'" says Wolfe. Jelly Roll learns finally that he's the messenger, not the message. Sings the ensemble at the finale:

> All the lovin'
> The leavin'
> The losin'
> Who we are
> And what we used to be

It's in the music
Play the music for me. . . .

Jelly Roll's music expresses the stories of people we'll never know; but "Jelly's Last Jam" dramatizes the sin of separation that we know all too well. Jelly abandons the mythology of individualism to embrace the new mythology of community, which puts the show at the spiritual center of the American moment. "Go forth, Armstrong! Go forth, Ellington! Go forth, Bassie, Bolden, 'n' Bechet," says the Chimney Man. "Go forth, Morton!" A door festooned with African hieroglyphs opens, and Jelly Roll passes through it into history. But history is fable agreed up. And "Jelly's Last Jam" astutely renegotiates the audience's idea of black culture and the nature of the musical itself. It's a tremendous imaginative feat, and a tremendous show, and a tremendous step in the right direction for an art form which, like the society itself, has lost touch with the best part of itself.

SAVION GLOVER

TAP MESSENGER

O<small>N A BALMY SEPTEMBER</small> night in 1994, at the end of a thrilling gig, the tap dancer Savion Glover, then twenty years old, and wearing an old T-shirt and a new growth of beard, leapt into the moat that was part of the set for the Shakespeare Festival's production of "Two Gentlemen of Verona" at the Delacorte Theatre, in Central Park. Glover's impetuous cannonball instantly earned him a place in the annals of theatrical joy. He was soon joined by the street drummers known as Drummin 2 Deep, who had accompanied him on plastic pails during the show and by a group of young tap dancers he's been training for the last few years, under the name of Real Tap Skills. The finale, which brought the audience to its feet, was, like everything Glover did that night, an encounter with the extraordinary. Glover was splashing down to earth after two hours in musical orbit.

Tap dancing is an explosion of spirit. Although it can be recorded, filmed, and even written about, the real glory of the art is the exhibition of mastery in the living moment. Those who bore witness to Glover that night—many of the younger people literally danced out of the Park, and some were spotted still dancing down in the subway—saw an old art form taking a new direction. Glover hardly looked at the paying customers or faced them as he tapped. There was no toothy smile, no waving of arms, no tuxedo (although he owns one). Glover, in fact, made no concessions to conventional entertainment. He was a picture of disheveled command—not out to please but to find himself inside the beat. "These are our expressions," he says, referring to his punkish style of tap. "People have to come into our circle. Of course we're entertaining, but on *our* terms." Lurching forward in his baggy shorts, as if following the lead of his size-12EE feet in a fugue of taps, Glover was in his own ecstatic zone—"reachin' for the rhythm," as he puts it. "I'm not thinking about where I am on the stage, about what my arms are doing. I'm just listenin' to the music." He calls it "goin' for self" when he finds a groove. "I'm hearin' big bands and stuff. I'm hearing orchestrations: drums, horns, bass. I'm not thinking about the audience. I'm not even thinking that I have tap shoes on. My toes are my sounds. I treat them like instruments. All types of music going." But it's the hip-hop rhythms that Glover's virtuosity is most notably taking off the street and onto the American stage. His kinetic language has all the vibrancy of street talk, which is what he compares it to. "See, it's like we have English, right? English, French, Spanish—and then we got slang. The steps that we usin' now is like slang. There ain't even no name. We can't say 'shuffle step' or 'flap' or 'cramp roll' or something like that. It's just live *vrap-um-ba-boom*."

Tap has always been a ceremony of survival, and Glover's dance is a brilliant assertion of the anger, energy, intensity, and arrogance of African-American youth. One of the people who saw Glover that September night—and whose arts foundation had picked up the tab for the evening—was Herb Alpert, a musician and the co-founder of A & M records, the largest independent label in the world, which he'd sold in 1992 for around four hundred and fifty million dollars. Alpert, who is no slouch at talent spotting, had first encountered Glover in George C. Wolfe's "Jelly's Last Jam," in 1992, when he raised the roof tapping with his mentor and friend Gregory Hines. "He has the whole tool kit, the whole shot from bebop to hip-hop," Alpert says of the jagged edge of Glover's complex sound. "Man, he's like his own rhythm section." As Glover and his crew clambered out of the makeshift canal, gleefully shaking the water off themselves like puppies, Albert turned to Margo Lion, who had commissioned and co-produced "Jelly's Last Jam" and was sitting beside him. "Savion is to tap what Charlie Parker is to jazz," he said.

Once upon a time, when the Broadway musical was young, it took its defining, irresistible energy from the streets of the city. At a stroke, Glover's Park performance brought musical theatre up to date; his upbeat energy showed a glimpse of how the musical might find its way out of decadence back to dynamism. "My style is just raw," Glover says. "My style is young. Funk." When pressed for a definition of funk, the chin of Glover's boyish face drops down toward his chest, and his head slowly eases its way back and forth on his neck. "Funk is real *under*," he says, snapping his fingers. "Against the beat. Just *ridin'*. It's the bass line. Funk is anything that get your head on bop. It's like a pulse. It's dead, but it's right there." Recently, when George C. Wolfe was trying to conceive a project for Glover at the Public Theatre, and asked him what he wanted to do, Glover replied, "Bring in the noise, bring in the funk!" That was it: he gave Wolfe the title and the trajectory of the show they're doing together. Words are not Glover's main medium, but in that simple sentence he sounded the call of his dance revolution: to put tap back into a contemporary black context. In the subtitle for the show, Wolfe spelled out the mission behind Glover's dancing and expressed his own anthropological fascination with rhythm, calling it, in full, "Bring in Da Noise, Bring in Da Funk: a tap/rap discourse on the staying power of the beat." To Wolfe, tap is a metaphor for all that's buried inside rhythm. The show, in a series of musical tableaux, decodes black rhythms as they move from Africa to slavery in the South, to urban communities, and finally to the present moment. "My theory is that what's buried inside rhythm is whatever the historical, cultural, political, and spiritual truths of the day are," Wolfe says. "So, if you really dissect, say, ragtime, there's a complexity, but there's an innocence and joy, too, because a country had just asserted itself as a world power." He adds, "Inside of Savion are the rhythms of all this."

As Glover waited for rehearsal to begin on a recent weekend, swigging from a pint of Nestea, he hardly looked like an encyclopedia of the beat. When he is not on the floor working on his steps, he exudes a calm, gentle naturalness. In his blue Shaq 32 shirt, with a black balaclava that he's contrived to wear on the top of his head so that his hair pokes through the opening where the face should be, he appears just like any other unprepossessing homeboy. In fact, he's a prodigy. "Savion is possibly the best tap dancer that ever lived," Gregory Hines says. And Glover's wiry body has become the repository of an extraordinary tap legacy. "I call him the Sponge. He learns very quickly," says the tap choreographer Henry Le Tang, who taught the Hines brothers in the fifties and taught Glover briefly before putting him into "Black and Blue," a tap revue he mounted in Paris in 1987. Glover has not merely studied and appropriated the moves of the great old tappers; he has been tutored by them. Along with Le Tang and Hines, Jimmy Slyde, Chuck Green, Lon Chaney, Honi Coles, Sammy Davis, Jr., Buster Brown, Sandman Simms, and Arthur Duncan have been Glover's teachers, passing their steps along to him since he first went public with his big talent at the age of ten, on Broadway, in "The Tap Dance Kid." By the time he was fifteen, Glover played opposite Hines and Sammy Davis in the film "Tap," where he was cast in the role of tap dancing's heir apparent. By November, when he will be twenty-two, myth will have become reality: Glover, the future of tap, has arrived.

"God's hand was on him," said Yvette Glover, Savion's mother, when I asked her about her son's gift recently. But the family gene pool also had something to do with it. Glover has a raffish athletic and musical pedigree. His great-grandfather on his mother's side, Dick (King Richard) Lundy, was a shortstop in the Negro Leagues and went on to manage eleven Negro League baseball teams, including the Newark Eagles. Glover's grandfather, Bill Lewis, was a big band piano player and vocalist, and his grandmother Anna Lundy Lewis, now in her eighties, was for many years the minister of music at Newpoint Baptist Church in Newark; she played for Whitney Houston when Houston was singing gospel. It was Anna Lewis who first noticed Glover's musicality when, as a fretful baby, she tried to calm him by picking him up and humming to him. "Savion looked up at her and started smiling and humming," Yvette Glover recalls. "She and I looked at each other. She said to me, 'This baby's anointed. There is no doubt. He's anointed.'" By the age of two, Savion was leaving a trail of fingerprints around the house as he beat out rhythms on everything he touched. "Walls, pots, closet doors," says Glover, of playing with his brothers. "We'd get different sounds out of everything." When Yvette Glover would come home from work, Savion would say, "Mommy, sit down and collapse yourself," and then he and his brothers, who had been organized by their grandmother, would give a musical performance. To his mother, Savion had "scary rhythm," by which she means, "unusual, impeccable rhythm.'' When Savion was about four and a half, she put him in a Suzuki drumming class, only to be greeted one day soon after his enrollment by Glover's teacher, who told her, ''Savion's got to go.'' As Yvette Glover recalls, ''I said, 'Excuse me?' She said, 'He's got to go.' I said, 'Oh my God, what did he do?' She said, 'No, he doesn't belong. He is too far advanced for this class.' '' The teacher had arranged an audition at the Newark Performing School of the Arts, and Savion became the youngest recipient of a scholarship in the school's history. When Glover found tap, he found his bliss. ''Even if I wasn't doing shows,'' he says. ''I'd still be tap dancing.'' ''There's no place I haven't seen Savion tap,'' Yvette Glover says. ''Once he hit the floor to get up in the morning, what you'd hear is tapping. He would tap in the bathroom. When he used to walk to school, he tapped.''

When Glover was seven, he began to learn show tap at the Broadway Dance Center, in New York; at the age of eight, he saw Chuck Green and Lon Chaney's exhibition of rhythm tap—a form of tap in which the whole foot, not just the heel and toe, are used to make sound. ''Savion loved the fact that it was the foot, the whole foot, that could be used to make those African drummed rhythms, those in-depth sounds,'' says Yvette Glover. She carted him into the city from Newark, New Jersey, every weekend to music and dance classes, along with his two older brothers, Carlton and Abrom. She remembers Savion (his name was her abridged version of ''saviour'') turning to her after Green and Chaney's performance and saying, ''Mommy, this is what I want to do.''

Since he turned his tapping into a profession, twelve years ago, Glover has earned over a million dollars, doing shows, films, concerts, and special appearances including a five-year stint on Sesame Street. When he was eighteen, he bought a four-bedroom house for his mother in Upper Montclair, New Jersey, and he occupies the large wood-panelled basement apartment, with his own sound studio and portable dance floor. (Glover enjoys mixing and making his own music tracks.) Since ''Jelly's Last Jam,'' he has been dating the singer Tiffany Caldwell. His other major social activity is basketball, about which his agent, Carol Davis, says ''he's a freak.'' ''I always wanted to dunk,'' says Glover, whose first choreographed dance was with a basketball. ''Basketball is like my exercise. I can't get away from basketball. My brother

Abrom was like mad into basketball. Abrom could just—one bounce off the verti—just woof it. I'm woofin' with my feet.''

Not long ago, Glover wrote a rap about tap dancing, invoking Chaney, who died last year (and taught him, among many steps, the paddle-and-roll) and Jimmy Slyde, whom he considers ''the godfather'' of tap:

> I do a wing on the left
> Paddle my roll real loud—
> Then get funky like that bass line
> From ''Move That Crowd.''
> When I slide like Jimmy
> You can't stop my taps
> Cause they comin' from tha feet
> Of tha Dancin' Maniac

Tap is a folk art, and, in the exhilaration of the moment, Glover's joyful improvisations carry a sense of the past. ''A lot of times he'll do somebody's step,'' Hines says. ''I know whose step it is. He'll do it, and he'll work it into his thing. It's like an homage—a real playful, respectful thing.'' Glover feels this historical imperative strongly. (A few years ago, at the memorial service for Honi Coles, Glover did an a capella tap, ending with a flash move that Coles loved but Glover rarely does: a back flip into a split from a standing position, and getting up without using his hands.) ''I feel like it's one of my responsibilities to keep the dance alive, to keep it out there, to keep the style,'' he says. This is why Glover, who has been teaching since he was fourteen, set up Real Tap Skills, why he taught classes in all the sixty-five cities he visited last year on the road tour of ''Jelly's Last Jam,'' and why he's planning to start a school to encourage young tappers. His mission is to reclaim the beat that he feels got lost when tap dancing was recycled—first on Broadway, where it was brought downtown from Harlem, with Sissle and Blake's 1921 musical ''Shuffle Along,'' and then in the Hollywood fun machine. ''The dance just got lost,'' he says. ''It started to be this entertainment-type thing. Instead of keeping it real, keeping the rhythms there, people started mixing tap with jazz dance. They would shy away from the rhythms: all the turns and trenches, big swings of your body.'' He adds, ''Tap dancing really has nothing to do with arms or big smiles or anything like that.'' Glover's dance brings tap back to where it originally lived: below the waist. ''He wants the blackness, the roughness, the rhythm of the black tappers to be heard,'' says Yvette Glover, who was an administrative secretary before becoming a professional singer and actress. ''He wants it to be a credit to all of those who died penniless, who never had a chance to expand their gifts. He wants the recognition of where tap dancing came from; he wants to honor that authentic African-rooted sound.''

In most states in the pre–Civil War South, the slaves were forbidden to have drums, because of their owners' fear of revolt. Inevitably, percussion was displaced to the feet, and part of tap's mystery and power—what Zora Neale Hurston called the ''dynamic suggestion'' in black dance—is the connection of the tap beat to that subversive liberation. Many hoofers have played the drums—Harold Nicholas, Gregory Hines, Bill (Bojangles) Robinson, even Fred Astaire—and it's no surprise that Glover, too, went from the drums to tap. (At the age of seven, he played in a group called Three Plus One; he insisted on standing up and dancing while he drummed.) ''Tap is like a drum solo,'' Glover agrees. ''I believe you can get so many tones out of using your foot. Your heel is like a bass drum. The ball of your foot is the snare. The side is like a rimshot. A regular tap dancer knows ball and heel; he don't know about the side of your arch, the side of your foot. We get sounds from the pinkie toe to all sides of the foot, back to the heel. I try to get these stupid wings—'' He stops, stands up, and demonstrates a wing, sliding his feet rapidly apart and making a graceful, swishing sound. ''It's like brushes,'' he explains, adding, ''Drummers carry around their sticks, we carry around our tap shoes.''

Glover has what is called in the trade ''a heavy foot.'' He says, ''I dance heavy. Loud and hard. And I just wanna be heard, all over the place.'' Frequently, in discussions with Wolfe about hiring extra dancers to fill out the different tap styles to be represented in the show, Glover is heard to say, ''He can't hit.'' ''Hitting'' is tap talk for expressiveness—what in the old days was called ''laying down some iron.'' If a dancer can hit, in Glover's terms, he's ''somebody who can complete a phrase, complete a tap sentence . . . *say* something." If a dancer can't hit, in Glover's opinion, he's somebody like Tommy Tune. "He is like sensationalism. He don't express himself," Glover says. "He hasn't reached that point. Tune and all those guys are still doing classroom stuff. That's why tap dancing don't go nowhere. It'll probably go somewhere now we got young hands in here. All these years they been teachin' the same thing—shuffle, cramp-roll, flap. They give you like a vocabulary—maxi pull-back, buck-and-wing, maxi ford. But they don't tell you *shaff-da-boom.* . . . My teachers are still like Jimmy Slyde. He told me, 'Yo, hit.' " Glover sometimes waxes philosophical on the subject of hitting. "If you can't hit, you can't express yourself," he says, his feet rippling the floor with taps as he speaks. "Execute a rhythm to the fullest. If you gonna come up here and do somethin' that you learned in class, that's cool and everything, but I wanna see what *you* got. I wanna see *you* hit. The complete expression of you in the moment. No restrictions. How you feel. How you hear the rhythms."

Just how hard Glover hits and how much rhythm he hears has been captured on a new record, "Battle of the Bands: San Antonio vs. New Orleans" (Riverwalk Live, Vol. 4). The producers staged a kind of imaginary challenge between a tapper and a hoofer: Bill (Bojangles) Robinson singing and tapping to "Doin' the New Low Down," against Glover tapping to the same song. The contest, which lasts almost two minutes, is a walkover. Robinson—who was known as the "Mayor of Harlem" and was probably the most popular tapper of his day (when he died, he had a hundred-car funeral cortège that attracted a crowd of more than a million people)—produces his crisp, syncopated sound with his heel and toe. But Glover is a dynamo, tripling the number of taps in each musical phrase as his feet dissect the song into a barrage of intricate rhythms.

The challenge of improvisation is the centerpiece of tap. "The toughest thing for any tap dancer is to get out there and improvise," Hines says. "Not only do you have to make it up, but you've got to do something that tops the previous dancer. The challenge is a rite of passage. It's also one of the ways we kept the art form moving." When the challenges are real, as they were between Hines and Glover in "Jelly's Last Jam," theatre is pushed to the limits of astonishment. "It's terrifying to have to be in a dance challenge with Savion," Hines says. "Winning was never in question. For me, the only thing was whether I could get one in on him. Savion liked to play basketball between shows. Meanwhile, I'm getting massages, taking naps." Hines, who liked to knock on Glover's dressing room door and ask, "Are you tired?" recalls a Saturday matinee, after Glover had been out all night partying, when he saw his advantage and thought, Oooh, by the evening show, he'll be exhausted, and I'll really nail him. He continues, "When he came back for the evening show, he was exhausted. So we go out onstage, and we're doing it, but I can see he's not a hundred percent. I do my first step, the step I usually do. Then he does a step. I pull something out, and I riff on it, so that even the people onstage are 'oohing.' So now he blinks a couple of times like a rhino that hadn't seen me coming, but now he's spotted me. Now he reaches for something very interesting. But it's still not, you know, there. I finish off. I spin. I go up on both my toes, and I just stay there, and I come down with a flourish. And now I can see his nostrils flaring and his eyebrows wrinkle. His lips come pouting out like they do, and he does an amazing step—he spins around, goes up on *one* toe, and then he hops on the toe to some kind of percussive thing that pissed me off. And when he did that, a roar went up like it was a bullfight. The people onstage started laughing, because they knew I thought I had him."

As Glover takes his dancers through the steps in rehearsals for "Bring on Da Noise," he improvises on his feet, and he frequently stops and corrects them saying, "Hear the beat?" Glover has a unique sense of music, and he hears a lot more of what's going on in the music than they do. He can translate the rhythms directly to his feet (and if he forgets a step, he has only to play back a tape of the rhythms to recall it). "I just hear songs. Just like solos," he says during the break. "Like that just now—" He stops and listens. Behind us there is the clatter of tapping, but Glover's ears have picked up the lighter sound of someone tapping a cup. He goes on, "I hear music in the street. When the cars are screechin'. Trains, subways, people talkin', basketballs, motorcycles—all types of sounds." Glover's obsessive search for rhythms gives his dancing its distinctive intensity. "People think I dance angry," he says.

"But I'm reachin' for a different tone." As Wolfe describes it, "It's like all of a sudden someone figured out how to make the clarinet have twenty more notes. You go, 'Where did that come from?' "

Glover doesn't know, and he doesn't worry about it. "When I choreograph, I like to make it up right there on the spot," he says. (In 1992, he received an National Endowment grant in choreography, making him the youngest recipient in N.E.A. history.) "He's completely available to the moment," Wolfe says. "Therefore, in the rehearsal room, anything can happen, as opposed to actors trying to cover themselves or to protect what they don't know." Today Glover has started slowly. He's struggling with Wolfe's concept of layering Reg E. Gaines's rap and Ann Duquesnay's bluesy voice over his taps to convey the controlled violence of a summer day in the late sixties. "Hot fun in the summertime," Ann Duquesnay wails, and underneath this Gaines is saying, "Cats hangin on corner/Sippin grapeless wine/Late wit' my pay, and my rent due (too)/Hydrant streamin'/Black top steamin'. . . ." Wolfe keeps an eye on Glover, who works the other dancers around the floor, trying to find the movements to narrate the sudden flare-up of a street fight. "Now he's starting to get it," Wolfe whispers. "I direct the same way. I know it inside, and I just have to clear myself out of the way, and then it comes out. He's got all these rhythms that are just in him. It's genius is what it is. You have to tap into it, and it comes out. He's as much a composer as he is a choreographer."

Glover paces and taps in front of the mirror, hearing phrases, repeating them, building up a tapestry of intricate sound, which sometimes frustrates Real Tap Skills, who struggle to keep up with him. "Let's go again," he says, and they stolidly assume their positions and start over. Watching them work makes you think of a brass rubbing: each new pass brings the outline into slightly higher definition. Musical ideas flow as easily as moods through Glover's body. As he lurches and slides— sometimes on point, sometimes spinning on his heels—he sends out volleys of clattering rhythm, and seems to be playing the floor.

"I follow the sound," Glover says of his rehearsal method. "I'm feelin' the stage for sounds. You might find a spot on it that gives you that bass; you might find a spot on the floor that gives you that dead-type tom-tom sound." On this particular day, he finds a spot and hits it with the side of his ankle. He likes the sound and the look of it. Over the next three hours, he works this sound up into an elaborate rhythmic geometry. In fact, watching Glover build and orchestrate the complex weave of rhythms is like watching a mathematical equation being set up and factored out. At the beginning of the morning, there was no scene; by the three o'clock lunch break, Glover and his group have got four sensational minutes. Wolfe laughs, his body rocking to the beat, as the dancers go through their noisy, brilliant paces for him. "It's all right," Wolfe says afterward, his eyes shining. Later, out of Glover's earshot, Wolfe adds, "I think what makes Savion an incredible artist is his extraordinary joy in what he does. He is able to live inside that state of joy and not compromise his emotional complexity like the earlier tap dancers had to."

Not long ago, watching her son preview some of the new routines for "Bring in Da Noise, Bring in Da Funk," Yvette Glover had a strange experience. "I sat there and I actually saw my son—I'm not crazy— emerge from his body," she says. "Like I said, 'There goes my baby.' When he hit that floor, I just saw the old Savion stay there and then a new transformation take place. I could not believe what I was seeing."

In the tap world, Glover's emergence as a role model is there for all to see. "When I was fifteen, I looked up to Honi Coles, Sammy Davis, and Sandman Simms," Hines says. "A fifteen-year-old kid now is trying to do Savion. So five years from now, what we'll be getting is a whole new wave of tap dancers who are in their early twenties, led by Savion, who at that point will be in his mid-to-late twenties. It will be a pool to draw from for serious tap choreographers like we've never seen."

Glover seems unfazed by his responsibility or his new adulthood, assuming both with a cool, disarming command. Last year, when he set off on the national tour of "Jelly's Last Jam," he stood with his mother in the kitchen of their New Jersey house. "I actually said good-bye," Yvette Glover says. "He will always be my baby, but I realize that he's a young man. It was hard to see him go. I said, 'Lord, what am I gonna do? There goes my last child.' "

"Mommy," Glover said. "You raised me right. Now trust me."

LERNER AND LOEWE

SHAW BUSINESS

IN 1913, THE YEAR BEFORE
Mrs. Patrick Campbell, at the age of forty-nine, played the eighteen-
year-old Cockney ragamuffin Eliza Doolittle, in "Pygmalion," she
broke off her affair with the play's author, George Bernard Shaw, who
wrote to her in a huff worthy of its curmudgeonly central character,
Professor Henry Higgins. "I have treated you far too well, idolized,
thrown my heart and mind to you (as I throw them to all the world)
. . . and what you make of them is to run away," he said. "Go then:
the Shavian oxygen burns up your little lungs: seek some stuffiness that
suits you. . . . You have wounded my vanity: an inconceivable audacity, an unpardonable crime. Farewell, wretch that I loved." Out of this
hurt Shaw made what he called a "shameless potboiler"; and Alan Jay
Lerner and Frederick Loewe, in their great adaptation of that potboiler,
made one of the finest musical romances ever staged on Broadway—
"My Fair Lady," which opened in 1956 and closed six years later, after
two thousand seven hundred and seventeen performances.

"It is impossible for an Englishman to open his mouth without
making some other Englishman despise him," said Shaw, who rightly
believed that with the proper accent in England you could get away with
almost anything. Lerner and Loewe rephrased the point, putting more
pep in Shaw's polemic:

An Englishman's way of speaking absolutely classifies him
The moment he talks he makes some other Englishman despise him.

Phonetics—and speech as a source of class division—was the bee in
Shaw's bonnet, but Howard Davies' new production, at the Virginia

Theatre, settles for just bonnets: a whole scrim full of them painted on a light-blue backdrop in a Magritte-inspired addition to Ralph Koltai's original set. The image, at once startling and wrong, typifies the production's panic about a point of view. Of all the modern musicals, few are so staunchly rooted in the reality of a place and a problem as "My Fair Lady," where the English class system is writ large in the transformation of Eliza from street urchin to society belle. "My Fair Lady" has two distinct locales: the raffish Cockney working class of Covent Garden and the imperial Edwardian upper class of Wimpole Street. The musical, like the play, is a satire about the landscape of English manners, not about an inner landscape. "Pygmalion" and "My Fair Lady," each in its own way, are models of engagement, whereas Magritte's images are models of estrangement. Instead of liberating the play's meanings, the design has the curious effect of obfuscating them. The visual jokes substitute conundrums for content. In Higgins's study, for instance, Davies replaces the professor's bust of Plato with a behemoth phrenological head that occasionally lights up, turning the room into a kind of de Chirico dreamscape. In place of the "recording machine" with which Higgins sifts through the strange mutations of English speech, Davies opts for a gargantuan upstage Rube Goldberg contraption, as if Higgins were developing an H-bomb instead of a theory of speech. And in the famous "Ascot Gavotte," where society toffs in blasé song report on the horse race—"What a gripping, absolutely ripping/Moment at the Ascot op'ning day"—other singing swells and belles now drop from the flies in imitation of Magritte's "Golconde." The image calls attention to the director but not to the dialectic of the play.

Musicals may be the staple of Broadway's commercial theatre, but there aren't many American directors capable of expertly handling such mass maneuvers, which are the theatrical equivalent of war. Davies is the latest recruit from the first rank of English directors—Trevor Nunn, Nicholas Hytner, Terry Hands, Mike Okrent—to be trained for this most lucrative art form. "My Fair Lady" is Davies' maiden voyage with an American musical (he's done many memorable straight plays in Britain, including "Les Liaisons Dangereuses" and Tennessee Williams's "Cat on a Hot Tin Roof"), and, with some uncredited help from Tommy Tune and Jeff Calhoun, who punched up the choreography of the show's big-boffo comedy numbers, "With a Little Bit of Luck" and "Get Me to the Church on Time," he has done well enough to insure himself another outing. This is lucky for him, and maybe even lucky for us. Still, although this musical can't fail to give pleasure, it seems odd that an Englishman could not get the Americans in his cast to sound remotely English. (The inclusion of the Pearly King and Queen in this production is even more incongruous, as if to establish visually a Cockney presence that can't be clinched vocally.) Odder still is that when we first encounter Eliza, selling flowers in Covent Garden, she is a kind of suburban Cinderella: although the script describes her as dirty, she is very well turned out, with hardly a smudge on her. This tatterde-malion tidiness undermines the drama of Eliza's transformation, which Melissa Errico, despite a fine voice and an attractive presence, also helps to diminish, by lampooning the Cockney sound that at first circum-scribes Eliza's life. The parody serves mostly to curry favor with the audience, but then currying favor is what this genial production is all about.

Its congenital affability is typified by Davies' casting of Richard Chamberlain as the smug, blustering, bullying Higgins, whom the stage directions describe as "rather like a very impetuous baby." Chamber-lain, all charm and suave good looks, smooths the edges of Higgins's prickly personality, so that the character's overbearing arrogance, his fits of rage, his blinkered misogyny are there in the wit of the lyrics but not in the chemistry of the actor. In "Why Can't a Woman Be More Like a Man," for instance, Higgins's special pleading of maturity belies his infuriating narcissism:

> Would I start weeping like a bathtub overflowing?
> And carry on as if my home were in a tree?
> Would I run off and never tell me where I'm going?
> Why can't a woman be like me?

But there is nothing intemperate or foolish or dangerous about Chamberlain. He can't work himself up into a fine delusional lather that will winkle from the songs their nuances of humor and character. Still, Chamberlain handles the complicated songs well enough. In fact, he gives a thoroughly pleasing performance, as neat and as well made as the tweedy Patricia Zipprodt outfits he wears. Paxton Whitehead's pukka Colonel Pickering not only provides Chamberlain with excellent support but comes closer to filling in the emotional outline of the script with the proper period attitude. When, together, the two linguists teach the caterwauling Cockney the Received Pronunciation in "The Rain in Spain," the moment still lives up to Wolcott Gibbs's judgment of it, in these pages, as "just about the most brilliantly successful scene I remember seeing in a musical comedy."

The success of the songs in "My Fair Lady" owes as much to their dramatic placement as to their construction. What we are watching in "The Rain in Spain" is the creation of a social face. In "The Ascot Gavotte," the sensational sangfroid of the upper class is topped at the conclusion of the scene, with Eliza shouting at the horse, "Come on, Dover!!! Move your bloomin' arse!!!" Her face has not yet been perfectly "composed," but in the next test of her new persona, when Higgins introduces her at a ball, she comes up against the ruthless scrutiny of Higgins's arrogant Hungarian pupil, Zoltan Karpathy—a drama of exposure that usually brings down the first-act curtain but here opens the second act. Then, in "You Did It," Lerner and Loewe exhibit their dramatic and lyric brilliance in a song that is at once a celebration of Higgins's success and an announcement to us of Eliza's curious defeat. The moment is musically and dramatically golden, and is as carefully managed as the lyrics. Higgins and Pickering revel in vindictive triumph over Karpathy—a victory, as they see it, of the professor's, and not Eliza's.

Eliza is reconstituted as a lady, at once a stranger to her class and to herself. Both the play and the musical make the point that once the experiment is a success and Higgins has won his bet there is no independent future for her. As a working-class girl, Eliza sold flowers, but as a lady she can sell only herself, in marriage. In "Pygmalion," she goes off with a Hooray Henry named Freddy Eynesford-Hill, but Alan Jay Lerner respectfully disagreed with Shaw's ending. In the musical, Eliza is pursued in vain by Freddy (Robert Sella), who is camped out on her doorstep in what seems permanent, open-throated adoration. In "Show Me," Eliza superbly exhibits her agitation in 3/4 time, evidently discovering that Easy Street is a blind alley. She is drawn to the tyrannical Higgins as her Prince Uncharming.

The working out of this scenario is more delightful than its final resolution, but in the current production two incidental pleasures should be saluted. Dolores Sutton, as Higgins's high-society mother, who gives her son and his bad temper a wide berth on social occasions, has no song but is memorable nonetheless for the droll, slow pitch of her delivery. "Charles," she says to her chauffeur upon learning that her eccentric son has brought a flower girl to Ascot, "you better stay by the car. I may be leaving abruptly." The central comic turn, though, is Eliza's father, the blackmailing dustman Alfred P. Doolittle, who, like his daughter, finds himself a victim of middle-class morality. The great music-hall star Stanley Holloway made a legend of his two showstopping numbers—"With a Little Bit of Luck" and "Get Me to the Church on Time"—which are rollicking hymns to hedonism. The part has now been passed down to his son, Julian Holloway. Following in one's father's footsteps may not be good for the soul, but it's good for the show. Holloway *fils* has a raucous spirit and a rumpled face, and he has a grand time delivering Lerner and Loewe's wonderful songs and his father's comic business. He lifts the show so successfully that nepotism may join capitalism as the musical's prevailing credo.

BEAUTY AND THE BEAST

THE SHOCK OF THE NEUTRAL

FOR MONTHS NOW, BROAD-
way's high-stakes gamblers have been worrying about the Walt Disney
Company's joining their game, and speculating about just how the
newcomer will play its high card, the stage version of "Beauty and the
Beast," which in its prior incarnation, as an animated movie, grossed
something in the region of three hundred and fifty million dollars. Even
in Broadway's present climate of retreat, the pot is still very rich; and
some Broadway panjandrums are squawking that Disney is playing with a
stacked deck. Thanks to a sweetheart deal from the city and the state,
Disney has acquired the derelict New Amsterdam Theatre, on Forty-
second Street, used by Florenz Ziegfeld as a temple for his extravagan-
zas, and plans to restore and then occupy it, presenting Disney and
perhaps other productions. Disney has produced "Beauty and the
Beast," now at the Palace, on its own, taking no outside investors and
anteing up a reported twelve million dollars. Even if the show were to
flop (something Disney wouldn't allow), "Beauty and the Beast" would
lose less than the cost of any of Disney's movies. Some Broadway people
argue that Disney has raised the producing stakes so high that it will
force out competitors, while, at the same time, it is sure to lower the
standards of the Broadway game. Disney certainly has more chips than
anyone else to back its taste, and that makes it the envy of every hard-
scrabbling producer. Disney has already ponied up an extra eight hundred thousand dollars for the cast album, and the company's deep
pockets give it the advantage, in the light of the mixed reviews the show
has been receiving, of being able to pay the *Times*'s advertising rates,
which bring so many struggling shows to grief. But in all the backbiting
chat about Disney's arrival, and about the art of the musical versus

commerce, there is a certain amount of Broadway pretension, which, as Disney's *Übermensch,* Michael Eisner, decodes it, means that "they are it, and everybody else is plebeian, animals, no-talent swine." The Broadway musical, which glorified its risk capital as "angels" and its entrepreneurial talent as "stars," is what made a legend of show business. "If it wasn't business," Eisner says, quoting Woody Allen, "it would be called show show."

I met up with Eisner in the commissary of Disney Studios in mid-March, on the day that Euro-Disney was saved from collapse, so humble pie was still on the menu. "Theatre to me is a little bit like religion," said Eisner, who grew up on New York's Upper East Side and wrote a couple of plays at Denison University ("so I could date a girl in the Theatre Department," he said). "I saw every show from 'Oklahoma!' to 'Foxy.' When we were growing up, birthday parties, anniversaries, weddings—what you did was go to a show. Whereas now, with my kids, you go to a movie. The theatre is not part of the celebration experience, whether you live in California or anywhere else."

Theatre culture is dying because large segments of the society have been excluded from it not just by price but by content. Disney's emergence on Broadway at such a demoralized moment is a fascinating turn of events, and results partly from Eisner's instinct about the increasing need for community. "I'm a complete contrary on the information highway," he says. "Assuming we get gun-control legislation to make it safe to go out, our position on the information highway is outside the house. Our theme parks. Our movies. Our sports teams. Legitimate theatre. You're with your family, doing something you can do together. You can talk about it on the way there. You can talk about it on the way home. The point is—and our rides are built this way—you all go on together." Eisner's social formula seems shrewd; his formula for Broadway profit-taking seems surefire; but the formula for "Beauty and the Beast"—rewriting a wonderful fable into a tale of loss without pain, and pleasure without joy—is more problematic. He and his company will certainly get their Broadway money-spinner, but it's like stripmining the subconscious of its most valuable material while claiming you're a friend of the environment.

"Beauty and the Beast" calls itself a musical, but it is really an

American cousin of another English genre—the pantomime, which began in the eighteenth century and gave the kiss of life to the refinements
of the harlequinade, and which traditionally retells fairy tales with jokes,
slapstick, song, and double-entendre. In "Beauty and the Beast," for
instance, when Belle needs to borrow a dress to dine with the Beast, the
Wardrobe (Eleanor Glockner) strikes the perfect saucy pantomime
note. "Let's see what I've got in my drawers," she says. Pantomime's
authenticity is not in the story but in the irresistible holiday impudence
of its working-class idiom. "Beauty and the Beast" belongs to this long
tradition of bantering folderol. "Ah, chérie," says Lumière, the Mau-
rice Chevalier of candelabras, to the flustered French duster, Babette,
"you cut me to the wick." Even the stolid clock, Cogsworth (the
impish Heath Lamberts), gets into the spirit. "If it's not baroque," he
says, taking Belle on an architectural tour of the castle, "don't fix it."

At its best, Disney's "Beauty and the Beast" has a few moments of
solid-gold theatrical amazement. The movie version featured music by
Alan Menken and lyrics by Howard Ashman; the musical has been
beefed up with additional lyrics by Tim Rice. The boffo "Be Our
Guest" turns into a kind of showstopping culinary cabaret, in which the
gilt cutlery, kitchen utensils, and plates of the enchanted castle parade
around Belle as she's introduced to the Beast's enchanted world by
Lumière (played with endearing gusto by Gary Beach). This high-camp
extravaganza is better onstage than on film, because its design and its
energy parody the theatrical inventions of Erté, Ziegfeld, and Busby
Berkeley, which are funnier and more sensational in the flesh. It's a field
day for the costume designer, Ann Hould-Ward. Here showgirls in
bodices descend a stairway of plates, bearing Cubist cups and saucers
over their breasts and wearing headdresses piled high with tilting cups.
Other chorines, dressed as flatware, sashay across the stage and weave
among still more showgirls, with spinning plates attached to their backs.
Ziegfeld eroticized objects; Disney makes a joke of them. A bevy of
utensils and napkins also soft-shoe and hitch-kick their enchanted hearts
out. For breathtaking dopiness, the spectacle beats even the concentration-camp ballet in "Exodus." It's a vision of sublime, almost poetic
frivolity in which, for once, Ashman's lyrics deliver what they promise:

> Singing pork, dancing veal
> What an entertaining meal
> How could anyone be gloomy or depressed?
> We'll make you shout encore
> And send us out for more
> So be our guest
> Be our guest
> Be our guest.

Into this routine the director, Robert Jess Roth, interpolates a little burlesque hilarity: a giant vaudeville hook in the shape of a candlewick is manipulated by the grumpy Cogsworth as he tries vainly to yank Lumière off the stage. At the end of the song, Roth tops this delicious hokum by tilting behemoth champagne bottles in from the wings and, as the corks pop, showering the stage with sparks that whip the audience into a cheering frenzy. Roth, who only rarely rises above the pedestrian, also stuns the audience at the finale. Belle sobs her love over the Beast's dying body, and the spell is broken: the Beast not only feels love but wins it. Here, with a trick of the lights and God knows what technology (provided by Jim Steinmeyer and John Gaughan, who are in charge of illusions), the Beast's body levitates and then, apparently weightless, spins in space. When the body is deposited back on the ground, the Beast's terrifying horned and hairy visage has vanished, and the re-deemed Prince stands magnificently before us. It's a theatrical moment to remember.

Disney's "Beauty and the Beast" works hard at neutralizing the dark and disturbing emotional issues that the fable raises. In the authoritative, long-winded version, by Gabrielle Susanne de Villeneuve (1740), the spell was cast on the Prince by a vindictive nurse/fairy. "She wanted me to love her not as a mother, but as a mistress," the Prince explains. In "The Uses of Enchantment" Bruno Bettelheim points out that many subsequent versions of the tale adopt the motifs of another fable, that of Cupid and Psyche, where beastly form is punishment "for having se-duced an orphan." Sexuality is at the center of the fierce and fearful story: the man learning to tame his bestial rapacity, and the young girl learning to accept new and dangerous feelings as she transfers her allegiance from her beloved parent to someone who at first appears a monstrous animal, and who could, at any moment, devour her. The fable shows that it's the acceptance of the monstrous both in the other and in oneself which brings happiness. But Disney's version, which preaches "Don't be deceived by appearances," is all surface. In Disney's retelling, the Prince, who is "spoiled, selfish, and unkind," is turned into a monster for the uncharitable act of refusing a beggarwoman shelter. In the opening dumb show, the Prince, displaying no more disdain than a maître d', stands in the doorway of his castle while the witch zaps him with what, from the explosion, seems like an Exocet missile. The emotional picture is immediately muddied, and the fable never quite adds up. In Villeneuve's story, the father, trying to honor his daughter's wish, gets into trouble by stealing a rose from the Beast's garden as a coming-home present. The rose, Bettelheim writes, "symbolizes both his love for her and also an anticipation of her losing her maidenhood, as the broken flower—particularly the broken rose—is a symbol for the loss of virginity." The rose as a symbol of virginity doesn't come into Disney's story, and neither, really, does sex. In the Disney version, Belle is all mind (she loves books), and the Beast is all anger. His incivility is in contrast to the solicitous Beasts of earlier versions, who are distinguished by their generosity and continually betray their own sexual longing by asking Beauty, in vain, to marry them. Disney's Beast (the excellent Terrence Mann) hides himself and his sexuality away. He deals only in power and tirade.

The fable was originally intended to teach domesticity and self-sacrifice, but the Disney version has no truck with either submissiveness or the painful struggle of child separating from parent. (Almost as an afterthought, in the play's last beat Belle's father, played by Tom Bosley, gives her hand in marriage to the Prince.) Disney's Belle has spunk; and Susan Egan, who has a fine voice and a sweet, strong nature, is a perfect embodiment of the American ideal of decent self-sufficiency. The adolescent ambivalence of leave-taking is pinned on the provincialism of place, not the possessiveness of parent. "Every morning just the same / Since the morning that we came / To this poor provincial town," the restless Belle sings. Later, she offers herself as hostage for her father in the Beast's castle and expresses very uncharacteristic sentiments about the trade. "For Papa I will stay," she sings, "but I don't deserve to lose my freedom in this way." In the Disney version, the father is no longer a rich merchant come upon hard times but a dithering inventor who loves his daughter the way she is. "No Matter What" is a paean to their unconditional love—a relationship that the story detours around in order to make room for the cute brute Gaston, who sees in Belle's beauty the only match for his own. With a quiff of hair like Elvis's and a chin like Victor Mature's, Burke Moses has great fun as the posturing hunk. In "Me" he wows the audience and would stop the show if Tim Rice's sendup of narcissism were sharper and Moses himself didn't seem to be in on the joke.

"As a company, we always try to *exceed* the expectations of the audience or the guest," Eisner told me. "If you exceed the expectation, then you'll do well. Most people just try to get away with it. That's why I want a fourth showstopper." Even if Eisner didn't get a first-rate score, he almost gets his quota of showstoppers. "Human Again" is as much fun as the Academy Award–winning song "Beauty and the Beast" is moving, especially when the latter is sung by the poignant voice of Beth Fowler, who plays Mrs. Potts, the teapot, and has the added chore of pushing her son Chip (Brian Press), the teacup, around on a portable table that has the unnerving effect of making the kid look like a severed head. For the rest, the Disney team does adequate work. Stan Meyer's sets have all the gimcrack realism of a Disney ride. Matt West's choreography doesn't exactly light up the stage; it's energetic, but over at "My Fair Lady," at the Virginia Theatre, the Cockney cutups singing "With a Little Bit of Luck" are clanking tankards almost the way they do here in "Gaston." Eisner gets a slick pantomime libretto from Linda Woolverton, who serves up the jokes and the pathos as required with some nifty rhythmic twists. One plot point, however, beggars the imagination: the Beast, who lives alone in his castle, has a library as big as the reading room of the British Museum—but he can't read. A Prince not read? Ignorance is traditionally part of the curse, not part of the cure. Here Belle reaches the Beast through reading. As it turns out, love of learning, not lust, is what brings Belle and the Beast together. *That,* in these illiterate times, really does exceed the expectations of the audience.

STEPHEN SONDHEIM

LOVE IN GLOOM

There are animals in the jungle that survive by playing dead, and Fosca, the heroine of Stephen Sondheim's "Passion," is one of them. Ugly, hysterical, unrelenting, joyless, she's an amalgam of alienations, and personifies both romantic agony and the dead end to which Sondheim, in his perverse brilliance, has brought the American musical. In "Passion," the charm of angst replaces the charm of action, and the American musical, once a noisy, vulgar, bumptious exhibition of our appetite for life, is deconstructed into an elegant flirtation with death. Sondheim's "revolution" is not really one of form (most of his shows are lyric-heavy and not well integrated) but one of intellectual ambition: his shows substitute the prestige of pain for the prestige of enjoyment. Here, for instance, the audience is encouraged not to applaud but to listen. The songs are treated as narrative, and are not even listed in the program. Sondheim, whose musical ideas are rarely as bold as his lyric ones, is in rebellion against "tunes" (which is why he doesn't provide many) and the notion of himself as a "tunesmith." We are coaxed to see Sondheim as a thinker and the musical as a statement. But the formal qualities of verse —rhyme's combination of rigor and delight—make it a blunt analytic instrument, "unsuitable for controversy," as W. H. Auden pointed out. Nevertheless, the public, ever mindful of Sondheim's greatness ("Is Stephen Sondheim God?" a *New York* headline asked recently), sits reverently, without intermission, to receive the pieties and the pontificating of "Passion," which, typically, has no passion, only ratiocination. What we get in this listless epistolary musical, where the main characters spend much of their time singing love letters to and from each other, is the result of Sondheim's recent experiments with the play's director and librettist, James Lapine: not the big heart but the dead heart; not the joy of the pleasure dome but the hush of the lecture hall; not dancing but reading.

Sondheim's eye for excellent material far exceeds his ability to plumb it. "Assassins" (1991), for instance, offered him the extraordinary panorama of American psychopathy and infamy, but from it he drew merely a dark cartoon. "Passion," which is set in Italy in the eighteen-sixties and was adapted from the Ettore Scola film "Passione d'Amore," poses a mesmerizing psychological conundrum in the story of Fosca's erratic behavior and her eventual seduction of the handsome, promising captain, Giorgio (superbly sung by Jere Shea), but Sondheim can't musically come to grips with its issues of love and emotional tyranny. The production prefers to stay on the surface of the romantic formula of suffering without reward. The startling first image—the naked body of Giorgio's lover, Clara (the voluptuous and fine-voiced Marin Mazzie), astride her hairy-chested package of military testoster-one—has the look of passion but not the hunger. They are talking their pleasure, not taking it, and this mutual meditation on ecstasy is cut short at the end of the first song by Giorgio's announcement that he's being posted to a backwater. The lovers' words speak of perfection with a lyric conviction that the music can't match:

> Some say happiness
> Comes and goes.
> Then this happiness
> Is a kind of happiness
> No one really knows.

Giorgio's happiness and his heroic reputation (he has rescued a wounded soldier in a skirmish with the Russian infantry) are tested by Fosca, an orphan, whose only kin is a cousin, the colonel of the regiment to which Giorgio is posted. She interrupts the banality of military dinner-table badinage with an offstage scream. It's the first we hear of her, and the noise is sensationally appropriate. Fosca (in a stunning performance by Donna Murphy) is intrusive. She knows no boundaries, and the scream broadcasts her inability to contain herself. "She is a kind

of medical phenomenon,'' a doctor tells Giorgio. ''A collection of many
ills.'' As staged, she is also a collection of iconic trappings from gothic
romance: the shadowy figure descending the long, gloomy staircase; the
black-shrouded silhouette; the doomed, spectral presence. Fosca but-
tonholes Giorgio with her sharp intelligence while Clara, in a gorgeous
pink gown, simultaneously materializes before us to sing her letter to
him. Clara conjures a world of joy: the ''sultry afternoon'' and their
sumptuous sex. Fosca, on the other hand, is a gourmand of griefs. She
clutches a book; and when Giorgio, out of politeness, offers to lend her
material from his library, his decency gives Fosca an opening and an
audience. She has taken death as her dominion, and she loses no time in
selling herself as an aristocrat of anguish. ''Sickness is normal to me, as
health is to you,'' she tells Giorgio, startling his soldier's imagination.
Sondheim's characterization of military life is wholly unconvincing—
drumrolls, marching soldiers, and some trite lyrics:

> Group: This military madness
>   This military
> All: Uniforms, uniforms
> Giorgio: Military madness.

But when Fosca sings to Giorgio about why she reads, at once
disguising and admitting her defensiveness, Sondheim is in his element,
and he delivers an astute soliloquy about resignation. ''I do not dwell on
dreams,'' she sings to Giorgio in the show's finest song. ''I know how
soon a dream becomes an expectation.'' She goes on, exalted:

> I do not hope for what I cannot have!
> I do not cling to things I cannot keep!
> The more you cling to things,
> The more you love them,
> The more the pain you suffer
> When they're taken from you . . .
> Ah, but if you have no expectations, Captain,
> You can never have a disappointment.

Fosca haunts the outpost with both her grief and her envy. She is inconsolable. She will not eat. She will not laugh. She humiliates herself. She can take pleasure only in things that reflect her sense of collapse, like the ruined castle to which she offers to take Giorgio. "I find it lovely," she says. "Probably because it's ruined, I suppose." She uses her sense of blighted life to extract pity from Giorgio, whose mind is full of Clara, and whose mouth is full of romantic, symbiotic mush about "love that fuses two into one." Giorgio is a victim of his own decency. He struggles to fend off Fosca's panic-stricken emotional demands. "This woman has no friends. No one to talk to. I know the power I have over her," he explains to Clara, who has cautioned him to keep his distance. "I didn't ask for this power—she bestowed it upon me, but somehow it carries responsibilities that I can't seem to shed." Fosca plays on Giorgio's youthful omnipotence. "Understand me, be my friend," she sings to Giorgio—a plea whose pathos and empowerment he finds impossible to refuse. "They hear drums / We hear music. / Be my friend."

No barrier that Giorgio can put between them keeps Fosca away. She will not be denied. She is beyond hope or shame. This is not passion but obsession—a distinction that Sondheim's show doesn't make clear. Fosca follows Giorgio up a mountain, onto a train. She is even prepared to kill herself to get his attention, taking to her bed after she receives his Dear Fosca letter. "You rejected her love—which doesn't surprise me," the doctor tells Giorgio. "This woman is letting herself die because of you." The doctor prevails on Giorgio's chivalrous nature to help save a life, but in agreeing to be a savior Giorgio loses control of his own life. Fosca is so emotionally impoverished that she doesn't trust the world to give her pleasure, and the musical's best scene is a chilly display of her overweening narcissism. Giorgio, thinking Fosca is dying, allows her to dictate words of love, and he dutifully writes them down and signs them as his own. The letter will later be misconstrued by Fosca's cousin and lead to a near-fatal duel, but the writing itself is a death-dealing moment. The eerie act of ventriloquism, an un-love song, demonstrates the insidiousness of Fosca's control and shows Sondheim at his dramatically most astute. It's a powerful moment of psychological wretchedness, couched in the language of the romantic sublime:

For now I'm seeing love
Like none I've ever known,
A love as pure as breath,
As permanent as death,
Implacable as stone.

Sondheim and Lapine fudge the issue of Fosca's infantile behavior by giving her a history (doting parents; a feckless first husband, who absconded with her money) that in no way adequately explains the trauma of abandonment that her hysteria acts out. They opt for glib sociological shorthand: shame at her husband's rejection, and humiliation, as an unmarried woman in a patriarchal society, at forever being a "daughter." Similarly, Giorgio's emotional volte-face after Clara refuses to run away with him (she's married, and would lose custody of her child) is dramatically confusing. On the rebound from Clara, he sees Fosca with new eyes, and transfers his romantic hyperbole to her almost instantaneously—as if losing the ideal of love were worse than losing the object of it. The moment is meant, I hope, to be ironic, but it is not played or received that way. Giorgio is betrayed by his romantic imagination. Fosca's possessiveness is refashioned by him into a delirium of unrequited love:

Love without reason, love without mercy
Love without pride or shame.
Love unconcerned
With being returned . . .

"Unconcerned with being returned"? Fosca's tyrannical behavior has been entirely devoted to forcing a response from Giorgio. He doesn't hear his own befuddlement; and although the lyrics address the confusion, the words have no proper purchase on the audience's imagination, since we don't hear lyrics in the same way we hear prose. Fosca and Giorgio's embrace is the creepiest I've ever seen onstage—a kind of vampire clinch, in which Giorgio's health is exchanged for Fosca's sickness. The production cops out on this ambiguity, which the stage directions emphasize in the penultimate scene, when Giorgio thinks he has killed Fosca's cousin and lets out a high-pitched scream—"a cry that could only be reminiscent of Fosca's." But "Passion" won't explore, or even acknowledge, this irony. It is just as commercially compromised as the musicals it pretends to be in rebellion against—it's forced, presumably for box-office reasons, to claim a triumph for love at the finale ("Your love will live in me!" Fosca and Giorgio sing to each other), while never dramatically proving it. In fact, everything we've been shown in the musical belies the purity of the finale's romantic ardor. The author can't quite admit his ambivalence toward the predatory Fosca, but it makes itself felt anyway, in the curious absence of pulse in his workmanlike score.

Sondheim's music has a surface sophistication, a fussy accompaniment that allows no strong melodic arc but serves the conversational tone of the lyrics. Lapine's book also promises more than it delivers. Only Giorgio and Fosca are vividly drawn; the others are given a wash of personality, and an occasional line that gets a titter. The military scenes —and there are a lot of them—are uniformly lackluster, and some are actually repetitious, reminding the audience of what it already knows: Fosca's unhappy, Giorgio's got a future, and soldiers are boorish. La- pine's organization of plot points is clunky; and the dialogue is too often of "The pheasants will be ready shortly" variety. His staging is more elegant. A former set designer as well as a filmmaker, Lapine conjures up strong, if sedate, stage pictures, using bold vertical lines made by panels that slide in from the wings and also work, in a cinematic way, to create dissolves. But, in a play where so much is verbalized and so little said, the grandness of the design trivializes rather than enhances the play's statement. In between the romantic wafflings, you find yourself studying Adrianne Lobel's beautifully painted backdrops, which suggest the hazy Italian countryside, or admiring the well-lit stippling on the movable panels.

On the night I saw "Passion," the audience was both unmoved and unconvinced. They were right to be. "Passion" feels like a rushed and unfinished portrait, in which the head and the hands are complete but the rest remains an unexplored outline. Yet again, Sondheim and Lapine have loaded a musical with fascinating intellectual freight—a burden that, finally, it can't carry.

THE WHO'S "TOMMY"

FULL TILT

WHEN PETE TOWNSHEND hit upon a pinball wizard as the central figure of his rock opera, "Tommy," he found a solid-gold metaphor for the psychic numbness and the weird optimism of England at the tail end of the nineteen-sixties. It was a brief, bumptious moment of possibility, for which "Tommy" is one of the most splendid epitaphs. Trauma and triumph seemed then to be the integers of pop life, and nobody lived or sang about both parts of that equation more sensationally than Townshend and his group, The Who. Tommy, the aforementioned wizard, is struck deaf, dumb, and blind at the age of four, when his father returns from the war and the child sees him kill the man he finds in his wife's arms. Tommy's famous silence keeps both his family and his splintered self together. To compound his distress, his uncle Ernie abuses him. Salvation comes in the shape of a pinball table. Tommy's playing of this electric fun machine becomes the gimmick—like Townshend's guitar-wrecking, windmill style of playing—through which he makes himself felt by the world and is lured out of his brooding, impossible solitude. In the end, Tommy gains not only fame but wisdom. No wonder the story has been retold so often: in billions of inches of newsprint about The Who; on The Who's own tours; in the Ken Russell movie; and now in the Broadway show "The Who's 'Tommy,' " at the St. James Theatre. It's the marriage of capitalism and mysticism, in which the hipoisie finds its heart.

In the original recording, Townshend insisted, correctly, that The Who, and not an orchestra, perform the music. A rock opera had to have rock musicians; and The Who—singer Roger Daltrey, drummer Keith Moon, bass guitarist John Entwistle, and, of course, Townshend himself—were virtuoso performers, whose personalities gave added drama and dynamism to a story in which they not only took parts but had participated as writers. The tale itself was about London, narcissism, celebrity, fans, and the sheer, giddy luck of talent. In other words, it was about them. But the impulse behind a "rock opera" was business, and this is where the current Broadway show and the original hybrid coalesce. Before "Tommy," Townshend had experimented with two "mini-operas," "A Quick One" and "Rael," but the managers of the band, Kit Lambert and Chris Stamp, hadn't been sure about pursuing the form. "We were worried about the airy-fairy connotations of calling it an opera," says Stamp, who now lives in New York. "After all, The Who were a rough, streetwise bunch of London kids." But he goes on to say, "Rock touring was really shitty. We thought, Why should rock audiences have to listen to music in fuckin' aircraft hangars? What attracted us to the rock-opera idea was that opera houses were run by committee, and not by greedy carnival people, who were always looking to rip us off at the gate. We hit up the opera managers with 'This is opera and opera's for the people.' We thought we'd be able to browbeat them into giving us their opera houses, and we did. We got them dirt cheap."

At the St. James, instead of banks of amplifiers, there's scaffolding studded with TV monitors to broadcast Tommy's electronic celebrity; instead of the band onstage, there is an orchestra under it; instead of a song cycle with great musicians breaking new ground and making new music, there are adequate actors and dancers illustrating the words in prosaic Broadway-musical choreography; instead of a youth culture celebrating its newfound strength, there is a middle-aged audience applauding the memory of youth. "Don't Miss a Word!" says a sign above the stall offering headphones in the lobby, as if clarity were what The Who, one of the loudest rock bands ever, were about. The Who were a fierce experience, not a suburban shuck. "The Who's 'Tommy,' " which is going to make everybody a lot of money, is the polyester version—shiny, easy to handle, and thin.

Still, from the first brazen chords of the overture, Townshend's music —however muted for Broadway—has an indubitable thrill. It's strong stuff—full of vigor, melody, shrewd insight, and the almost messianic conviction of one of rock and roll's finest messengers. Just to hear the licks again is enough to rouse an audience that has become inured to both the vacuous blowhard bravado and the intemperate whining of the composers who usually work Broadway. Townshend's questing, prickly intelligence comes through loud and clear. If a generation's longing for attention and transcendence needed an anthem, he provided it in Tommy's plaintive reprise, "See me, feel me, touch me, heal me." When the opera is sung by The Who in concert, Tommy's predicament is fleshed out in the imagination of the auditor. But when the songs— however superb—are enacted by others, they run into theatrical trouble.

Des McAnuff's production (he also collaborated, with Townshend, on the book, and is the artistic director of the La Jolla Playhouse, in San Diego, where the show was developed) is caught on the horns of a theatrical dilemma, which no amount of slick, if exhausting, spectacle can resolve. The hero of this famous score is spectacularly passive. The fact that Tommy is, for most of the show, "deaf, dumb, and blind" means that the songs can comment on him, but he can't reveal himself to us through action. The central character is unreachable, unknowable, and therefore essentially undramatic. McAnuff's production huffs and puffs to make the scenic surface of the show compelling when the characters can't be. Caught somewhere between light show and light opera, McAnuff misses no opportunity to fill the shallows with dazzle. He does the Second World War in the first five minutes, complete with spinning airplane propellers, Churchill voice-over, machine-gun fire, parachuting soldiers, and a bit of upstage concentration-camp barbed wire. He conjures the teen-age Tommy, like a jack-in-the-box, out of a mirrored closet at which his two younger personas gaze. These maneuvers are adroit without being inspired. With John Arnone's sets and Wendall K. Harrington's projections, McAnuff is especially effective in the pinball-arcade scene, as Tommy discovers his métier, and, later, in his breakthrough into greatness, when the pinball machine sparks, smokes, and rises toward the heavens, like some German Expressionist whirlwind. It's an all-blinking, all-flashing, all-caroming bit of showmanship, which nicely matches the energy of the song:

> He's got crazy flipper fingers
> Never seen him fall . . .
> That deaf, dumb, and blind kid
> Sure plays a mean pinball.

"Tommy" is most arresting when it tries to fathom both the liberation and the trap of fame. "Sensation" captures better than any other rock song I know the imperialism of fame's enchantment, that "new vibration" the song celebrates:

> I'm a sensation.
> I leave a trail of rooted people
> Mesmerized by just the sight
> All these lovers feel me coming
> Love as one—in love tonight.

Being spellbound, either by oneself or by others, is one of the fascinating issues the music addresses. The mirror into which Tommy looks, and which holds the memory of the lonely child, is the show's recurring image and its primary clue. Tommy learns to turn his gaze from his own reflection and out to others. In so doing, he moves from the infantile to the adult, from selfishness to community. He also learns disenchantment. As in all fairy tales, it's not the enchanted but the disenchanted who are free. To the fury of his fans, Tommy starts to think against his celebrity:

> I'm free—I'm free
> And freedom lies here in normality.

But normality on Broadway is about as welcome as modesty in a whore. The audience is paying for the extraordinary. And here, at the finale, Townshend brings the audience to its feet with a thematic fillip that is more cunning than all McAnuff's directorial pyrotechnics. Tommy, who has spent a good part of two and a half hours looking at his own reflection, now stares out at the audience and sings:

Right behind you I see the millions
On you I see the glory.
From you I get opinions
From you I get the story.

Having begun as a hymn to the self, the song turns into a hymn to the customers, reminding them that it is *they* who are the magic and the miracle. At a stroke, pandering to the masses is elevated to the level of metaphysics. The audience, quite naturally, goes crazy. It's a point of view that Broadway musicals, which make a myth of individualism, rarely sing about. But, even if it's suspect in the context of a multimillion-dollar production, the sentiment is welcome on the American scene, and so is Townshend. With the touring-company dates selling briskly (the show's going on the road for two years), with a book about the making of the musical in progress, and with what feels like a long stay at the St. James virtually assured, "The Who's 'Tommy' " will not be as modest as the pinball wizard about owning its success. But then it's best not to take a star's public protestations of humility too much to heart. Instead of watching Townshend's words, watch his billing. Meanwhile, even those who don't like the show can sit back in their yellow-and-black "Tommy" T-shirts and enjoy the marketing experience.

ISAAC BASHEVIS SINGER

BRING BACK THE CLOWNS

A LINE IS AN UNUSUAL
sight at any theatre these days; so it seemed especially promising on a
sunny afternoon on Memorial Day weekend to see a double-domed
Harvard audience queuing at the Loeb Drama Center, in Cambridge,
for tickets to the American Repertory Theatre's world première of
"Shlemiel the First," a musical about the imaginary town of Chelm, a
village of fools invented by Isaac Bashevis Singer for his children's
stories. Conceived, and splendidly adapted for the stage, by the
A.R.T.'s artistic director, Robert Brustein, the musical is built around
the clamor of a klezmer band performing traditional Jewish music.
"Storytelling has become a forgotten art and has been replaced by
amateurish sociology and hackneyed psychology," Singer wrote in a
postscript to a collection of his children's fiction. The same is true of
the contemporary musical. Playfulness has been replaced by pontificating, comedy by commentary. "Events never get stale," Singer said.
"Commentaries often are stale from the very beginning." And commentaries are what has been sinking the plots of the lyric-heavy, sol-
emn-swaggering contemporary musicals. For instance, "Tommy," a
"rock opera," acts out the Second World War in its first five minutes;
"Kiss of the Spider Woman" waves photographs of "the disappeared";
"Miss Saigon" serves up a helicopter, Vietnam, and snapshots of *bui-
doi,* the abandoned children of Asians and United States military person-
nel; "Cats" ends with an image of feline resurrection; "Passion" pur-
veys Stephen Sondheim's cant about love ("as permanent as death") as
if it were philosophy. When the musical was "musical comedy" (a term
in rapid decline by the mid-forties, with the prestige of Rodgers and
Hammerstein's "musical play"), the clowns brought vulgarity and hu-

manity to the proceedings. But nowadays, in the musical, pretension has superseded celebration. Brustein has often inveighed against this mutation from his catbird seat at *The New Republic,* where he has been drama critic for most of the last thirty-five years. According to him, "Shlemiel the First" is meant to be an antidote to the genre's atrophy of heart, whose aim is "to get back to a musical form that has joy in it."

And "Shlemiel the First" is busting its buttons with joy. From the opening beats of David Gordon's fresh and elegant production, "Shlemiel the First" announces its liberation from banality. Chelm is no slice-of-life shtetl but a surreal landscape that is impossible to second-guess. The play's world is a clown's world—a world turned upside down in Robert Israel's witty, lopsided design, which filters a traditional tale through an avant-garde aesthetic. The set broadcasts a fable's innocent logic: the raked stage floor has crimps in it; the threshold and the tables are vividly abstracted and angled; the stacked dresser drawers have no bureau; and two backdrops—one of gray clouds branded with Miró curlicues, the other a centerpiece of pink—capture in their contrasting intensities the bittersweet undercurrents of both the story and the music. (The klezmer sound, like the blues, has irony built into its clamor: sorrow in joy and joy in sorrow.) When the curtain comes up, Shlemiel (Larry Block) and his disgruntled wife, Tryna Rytza (Rosalie Gerut), are asleep, but their bed is vertical. From the start, our perspective is playfully jolted out of the habitual. The production demands that we enter its topsy-turvy world, and the authority of the direction compels belief in its wacky logic.

When Tryna Rytza gets out of "bed" and begins to dress, she spells out her resignation to their arranged marriage:

> What's the difference what I feel?
> Someone somewhere made a deal.
> There's the rub, here lies my zhlub.
> I married a shlemiel.

Shlemiel is a beadle by profession—a synagogue sexton, or gofer. To his wife, he is a "crazy fool," who uses a dreidel to make decisions, and whose low estate her song deftly defines:

Can you believe that this is all I got?
Not a learner, not a scholar,
Doesn't earn a single dollar.
I could spend all day telling what he's not.

Shlemiel is a recognizable throwback to the musical's earlier tradition. He is a species of low-comic innocent: a link between Yiddish theatre and the capering buffoons of Broadway musicals in the twenties and thirties and the musicals of our own sour, pseudo-sophisticated moment, in which goodness as well as high jinks has been banished. In the old days, Shlemiel's role could have been taken by any number of funnymen—Bobby Clark, Ed Wynn, Jimmy Durante, or Jack Gilford, to name only a few. Here the agreeable Larry Block exudes a puckish sweetness but brings none of a real clown's sad-sack presence or antic instincts to the part.

In Singer's story, Shlemiel is called upon to spread the wisdom of Gronam Ox around the world. Ox is the wisest member of the village's council of six sages, having earned the laurel by solving a sour-cream shortage in the shrewdest of ways: by merely changing the term "sour cream" to "water." This solution has serious emotional repercussions. His wife, the aptly named Yenta Pesha, no longer pleases him with her blintzes, which are now thin and runny—something that Yenta (the clever and caterwauling Marilyn Sokol) makes clear while occasionally pausing to slug him with one of the pickles she carries, like six-shooters, tucked into her capacious apron. The effect is charming, and Sokol doesn't miss a laugh as she bitches about the decline of her love and her blintzes:

My man of wisdom! My man of wisdom!
The man I cooked my heart out making blintzes for.
He isn't very bright.
He don't know I'm always right!
And he doesn't like my blintzes any more.
Gevalt!

Sokol doubles as the sixth wise man, and Gordon frequently has her change into her Yenta schmatte onstage to debate the sorry crew. While a dummy takes Sokol's place at the wise men's table, she whips off her beard and assumes the blowsy, heavy-hipped outline of a Jewish mama. Sokol literally steps into the zaftig stereotype, at which the production winks while milking it for all it's worth. Later, a few of the men don the women's Old World armor to fill out a chorus of kvetchers.

This is broad but funny stuff, and a great deal of its tastiness belongs to the affectionate precision of the lyricist, Arnold Weinstein, who has cooked up one of the finest sets of lyrics I've heard in recent years. Weinstein, whose works include "Dynamite Tonite!" (1963) and "Casino Paradise" (1990), is completely at home with the material, and his smart words sit gracefully on the notes of the gorgeous score that Hankus Netsky has composed and adapted (with additional music by Zalmen Mlotek), never pressing for insight but delivering it nonetheless. In Weinstein's showstopping "Geography," a rewrite of the Yiddish comic standard "Rumania, Rumania" (which Brustein had him do as an audition piece to test the depth of his Yiddishkeit), the meticulous rhymes sparkle with delight as they contemplate Gronam Ox's fame and keep up with the song's manic rhythm. Weinstein can make one well-chosen word lift a song into a special zone of pleasure. His sprightly lines manage to get laughs even amid the hilarious sight of dancing dunces led by Gronam Ox (Charles Levin, having a field day) himself. Between the "zets, zets, zets" and the "hay diga diga"s, Gronam's vaunting vainglory comes over loud and clear:

> Everywhere, religious leaders
> Will become my biggest readers.
> Shiva, Buddha and Mohammed
> Make way for the real Melamed!

Gordon, who both directed and choreographed the piece, has a particularly good time in "Geography." The wise men dance their chairs downstage and proceed to stomp on them, do-si-do around them, slap syncopated rhythm on their backs, and then, when they finally sit down, carry out a variety of finger-popping, leg-crossing, shoe-tapping maneuvers in unison. It's a wonderful sight, whose minimalism also slyly teases the vulgar lavishness of contemporary musicals. Gordon misses no opportunity to make ingenious stage pictures. When Shlemiel goes on his hapless missionary journey, a narrative Waterloo for any story, Gordon uses the splendid Klezmer Conservatory Band not only as travelling music but as a scenic element. As Shlemiel moves through the shifting landscape, full of leafless trees and red papier-mâché boulders, Gordon manufactures the sense of a long, eventful journey by having the band move with him onstage. Its members, led by the trombonist and followed by the banjo player, the violinist, and the clarinettist, are lugged, one by one, from the wings and pulled around the stage on blankets. When Shlemiel stops to relieve himself, the band stops, too. By the time Shlemiel meets up with the Rascal (Remo Airaldi), who steals his food and points him in the wrong direction, the band is nearly offstage and back in the pit. Shlemiel may be lost, but Gordon and his collaborators definitely know where they're going.

To Singer, children's fables were "the last vestige of storytelling, logic, faith in the family, in God, and in real humanism." Inevitably, in its playfulness, "Shlemiel the First" touches something humane and consequential. In Act II, Shlemiel finds himself back home. But he comes to the witless conclusion that this is a second Chelm, and that the people who claim to be his wife and children are not related to him at all. His confusion is oxygen to the story. Husband/parent turned to stranger is a profound fear, which the musical's farce finds a way of probing. In her frustration, Tryna Rytza appeals to the wise men for a ruling. True to form, the wise men, taking Noah's ark as a precedent, reason themselves into folly and agree with Shlemiel. "If God made everything in twos, why not Jews?" Gronam Ox sings, convincing all the villagers that there are indeed two Chelms and that they are looking at Shlemiel the Second. Now confirmed as a stranger, Shlemiel is experienced as one by Tryna Rytza, who immediately falls in love with him. Mr. and Mrs. Shlemiel talk to each other like adulterers and go through all the envious badinage of infidelity. "You have a younger touch," Shlemiel tells Tryna Rytza when she inquires about his wife. "Your eyes are brighter, your voice is sweeter, your skin is smoother." And, of course, it's true: a change of heart has been engineered by the power of the imagination to see the other from a new perspective. Old angers are directed at their "absent" partners. Shlemiel worries that Tryna Rytza's husband will "tear her to pieces" when he finds out; and she counters, "Who knows what he's doing with that bitch of yours in Chelm Number One?" A sense of sin, so absent from contemporary life and the musicals about it, fuels the erotic thrill of their romance. In "Can This Be Hell?" they sing:

> Can we be bad?
> This feels too good for that.
> The taste,
> The smell . . .
> What on earth can heaven be
> If this is hell?

In the end, the sages and the confused lovers are brought to their senses by Yenta Pesha. The world is put to rights, the way only musical comedy can do it. Gronam Ox learns humility, which has its reward not in heavenly bliss but in Yenta's heavenly blintzes. ("Now his brain has immigrated to his heart," she sings. "So tonight extra zaftig blintzes à la carte.") Tryna Rytza has also had a change of heart, and now looks on Shlemiel with tolerant affection. "Husband One or Husband Two," she sings. "Each will do if either's you." This harmony accords with Singer's sense of the miraculous, and with his almost mystical detachment and refusal to suffer. Life's truths and its mistakes, the show implies, are all delusions. That is a radical point of view, which disabuses the musical and the audience of the smug comforts of boulevard nihilism. In 1974, when "Shlemiel the First" had its début as a straight play, at Yale, where Brustein was then the theatre wallah, Singer told him, "My work should be done fast, like Shakespeare—not slow, like Chekhov." "Shlemiel the First" meets Singer's requirements of pace and adds an element of wonder. In fact, it dares the musical to go back to its beginnings and start again.

KERN AND HAMMERSTEIN

MISSISSIPPI MUD

"SHOW BOAT" WAS BORN "big and meant to stay that way," said Oscar Hammerstein II, who was present at the conception. It was billed as "An All American Musical Comedy," and so it was. This watershed musical, about a group of touring riverboat players who worked the towns along the Mississippi, spanned forty years of American history, ranged across a panorama of classes, colors, and careers, and told its sprawling story using the wide variety of popular musical styles that had captivated the American public for the past sixty years. "Show Boat," which opened on December 27, 1927, was a radical departure in musical storytelling, marrying spectacle with seriousness. It was conceived as a discourse on American musical and social history, and nothing like it had ever been seen on the American stage. The size of its ambition and its cast were symptomatic of the buoyancy of Broadway, which was at its peak in the 1927–28 season, when two hundred and sixty-four shows were produced in seventy theatres. "Show Boat" arrived under the auspices of Florenz Ziegfeld, Jr., the entrepreneur of Broadway musical extravaganza, and under the authorship of Hammerstein and Jerome Kern, the architects of Broadway musical change. Ziegfeld, whose contract with the authors originally called for the delivery of a script within three weeks of signing, was paying for fun, not ferment. He feared adding gravity to the musical's habitual good times. "In its present shape," Ziegfeld told Kern, complaining about the complicated plot of family unhappiness, tragedy, and miscegenation, "it hasn't got a chance except with the critics, and I'm not producing for critics and empty houses." But Hammerstein and Kern were adamant that a musical should mean something; and "Show Boat," in its broadest sense, was meant to mean

America. The show was inclusive, not exclusive. Its capaciousness, like that of the land itself, pronounced its abundance—of talent, of heart, and, in its acknowledgment of race, of the society's sins as well as its dreams. Here was a musical that, at a stroke, did away with the traditional Broadway folderol and brazenly offered up a picture of the democracy. "Show Boat" was democratic in the focus of its story, in its themes, in its music, in its interracial cast. And, as its many revivals and three films attest, "Show Boat," like all democratic experiments, was constantly revising itself.

The latest superb revision, Harold Prince's hard-nosed and scintillating six-and-a-half-million-dollar production, which last weekend opened Toronto's luxurious new North York Performing Arts Centre, has, in keeping with the controversial ambitions, if not the democratic spirit, of the musical, caused a rhubarb. Since April, the Coalition to Stop "Show Boat," a collection mostly of leaders of Toronto's black community, has been trying to run "Show Boat" aground. The coalition has been hard at it, lobbying Ontario's Human Rights Commission and, even before previews began, mounting weekly demonstrations of as many as a hundred people outside the theatre. At the preview I saw, there was a whiff of autumn and of Weimar in the air. About forty armed police, some helmeted and mounted, stood behind police barricades outside the building while inside plainclothesmen, stationed at every exit of the massive eighteen-hundred-and-fifty-seat Main Stage Theatre, watched the audience. In 1927, Hammerstein and Kern wanted to open a theatrical discussion about race relations in America; in 1993, the Coalition to Stop "Show Boat," branding the show "racist, anti-African propaganda" and a "discriminatory and harmful cultural experience," was noisily trying to close it down. The brouhaha that has been percolating over the last several months began as the bleatings of the uninformed on behalf of the underrepresented and ended in anti-Semitic catcalling. "Most of the plays that portray blacks or any other ethnic groups in a negative way is always done by a white man, and always usually a Jewish person is doing plays which denigrate us," Stephnie Payne, a black member of the North York board of education, said in a television interview, referring to the producer of the show, Garth Drabinsky, and his director as well as to Ziegfeld, Hammerstein, and Kern. Ms. Payne later apologized for her remarks, but the racial slurs of the self-styled anti-racists have clung to the production. One protester's sign read, "Show Boat Is Not Kosher (Unclean)." But is it?

Certainly there's little to defend in Edna Ferber's gushing bestseller on which the musical is based. Ferber writes like a teen-ager on diet pills: "The Mississippi itself was a tawny tiger, roused, furious, blood-thirsty, lashing out with its great tail, tearing with its cruel claws, and burying its fangs deep in the shore to swallow at a gulp land, houses, trees, cattle, humans, even; and roaring, snarling, howling hideously as it did so." Her novel is a kind of hilarious anthology of bad writing, and it does include some unconscionable racial caricatures. "Almost invari-ably," she writes of the blacks rushing to see the riverboat, the *Cotton Blossom,* as it pulls along shore with its calliope blasting, "some magic-footed Negro, overcome by the music, could be seen on the wharf executing the complicated and rhythmic steps of a double shuffle, his rags flapping grotesquely about him, his mouth a gash of white." But the book is not the play—a distinction that the coalition can't quite fathom. "Since the play is based on the book," one of its members said, "the play has to be racist." Well, no, it doesn't. Hammerstein and Kern imbued Ferber's characters with their own concerns, putting a new chassis on the story and souping up the old engine to make a theatrical vehicle for themselves. In "Ol' Man River," which Hammer-stein characterized as "a song of resignation with a protest implied," the Mississippi is transformed from Ferber's symbol of romantic chaos into one of Christian redemption. Through Joe, sung here by Michel Bell with an almost freaky cavernous basso that seems to echo down the ages, Hammerstein makes injustice sensational in the song's very first words:

> Dere's an ol' man called de Mississippi;
> Dat's de ol' man dat I'd like to be!
> What does he care if de world's got troubles?
> What does he care if de land ain't free?

The song is a hymn of anguish and endurance in the static post-Reconstruction South. Although the published lyric now substitutes "colored folks" for "niggers" (Hammerstein made the change for the 1946 revival), the original shocking, bitter refrain was truer to the outraged spirit of the slaves and to the metre of the song, whose fury, even in its bowdlerized form, is clear for those who have ears to hear:

> Colored folks work on de Mississippi
> Colored folks work while de white folks play.

Hal Prince's version of "Show Boat" displays—as much as a Broadway musical can—a sense of black humiliation amid jubilation. After all, this is a show in which two troupe members, Steve and Julie, take themselves away when Julie's "mixed blood" is discovered. But describing racism doesn't make "Show Boat" racist. The production is meticulous in honoring the influence of black culture not just in the making of the nation's wealth but, through music, in the making of its modern spirit. The point is made adroitly in the orchestrations of Robert Russell Bennett and William David Brohn, in the montage that takes over the story from the turn of the century to the twenties and moves, sharpish, from ragtime to jazz to Charleston—all jaunty expressions of black liberation. "Show Boat" 's curtain call makes a spectacle of integration, while the musical's story pointedly does not. It begins in the eighteen-eighties with two water barrels at the side of the stage, one marked "Colored Only," the other "White Only"; and it closes in the nineteen-twenties with Kim, the celebrated granddaughter of the show boat's captain, at the end of "Kim's Charleston," perched on top of a ticket box that reads "Balcony: Colored Only." The lives of the white folks have taken wild turns of fortune, but the black stories remain fundamentally static. (In the original finale, part of which has fortunately been cut by Prince, both Kim and the child of the play's comic performing couple, Frank and Ellie, are redeemed by theatrical stardom, whereas Joe and the black community make do with the salvation of the gospel.) This was the shaming state of civil rights in 1927, about which the musical comments:

> Let me go 'way from de Mississippi
> Let me go 'way from de white man boss.

Far from depicting blacks as "subhuman savages, dim-witted, child-like, lazy, drunk, irresponsible, and devoid of any human characteristics," as one of the coalition members put it, Prince's "Show Boat" clearly dramatizes the reverse. The sources of wisdom (Joe), of courage (Julie, who leaves the *Cotton Blossom* only to later sacrifice her Chicago singing job—and probably her life—so that her abandoned white friend, Magnolia, can work and feed her young child), of comfort (Queenie's kitchen), and of musical delight (the gospel, blues, ragtime, and jazz numbers, and the accompanying cakewalk, shimmy, strut tap, and Charleston) are black. The black experience, in both its triumph and its tragedy, is at the heart of the show's perception of America.

The linchpin of "Show Boat" is Cap'n Andy Hawks, the dithering and adorable owner of the *Cotton Blossom*. He manages to hire the gambling bounder Gaylord Ravenal for his acting company, to coach his sheltered and beloved daughter, Magnolia, to play opposite the new man, and, finally, to get the two star-crossed lovers married. Cap'n Andy is, as Ethan Mordden has pointed out in these pages, Hammerstein's "cockeyed optimist," whose dreamy eccentricity helps him survive the cussedness of his wife, and who, at the finale, even manages to engineer a last-minute reconciliation of the long-parted lovers. Robert Morse makes a wonderful Cap'n Andy, and it's a thrill to watch him work. Morse is a genuine star turn. He owns the stage with his relaxed, puckish whimsicality. As Cap'n Andy, Morse is all fluster and bluster. His hands, like Andy's shambolic personality, seem to be all over the place—flapping at the heavens, poking into his pockets, resting on his now protruding belly. Morse, who is good on his feet and has a great comic silhouette when he's wedged into a chorus line, gets every bit of humor and poignance out of the role. His style of delivery can best be described as racing to meet a red light. Morse takes a run at a sentence, only to break off in the middle and lay his smoky voice down on just the right word. It's a piquant mannerism. When his wife, Parthy Ann, collapses at the news of her daughter's imminent marriage, someone exclaims, "She's fainted!" Morse takes a beat and says with a twinkle, "Are you sure?" Elaine Stritch is Parthy Ann and makes as much of this thankless role as anyone can. She towers above Morse, and serves as a droll comic foil for his capering benevolence. Stritch's chin juts out at the world like a fist. Ramrod straight, her consonants as hard as her attitude, Stritch is very sour and very funny. She rattles around in her craggy voice, which is capable of stopping the show, but in this outing, where she sings "Why Do I Love You?" to Magnolia's new baby at the redesigned opening of Act II, she's allowed to be merely endearing.

Even in musical plays of "Show Boat"'s calibre, characterizations are usually not so well drawn that they don't benefit from the extra dimension of personality called "star quality." It's hard to define, but when you see it onstage it's hard to miss or forget. Almost all the couples in "Show Boat" bring something extraordinary to their roles. In a fine scene that, incidentally, dramatizes the blues corrupting the white world with pleasure, Lonette McKee, who plays Julie, gives "Can't Help Lovin' Dat Man" a terrific, swinging interpretation. Her forlorn rendition of "Bill" is equally well judged and moving. Rebecca Luker, as Magnolia, is full of beans and acting talent. With the help of the handsome and very charming Mark Jacoby as the feckless Gaylord Ravenal, she makes the "love at first sight" hokum of "Make-Believe" and the passion of "You Are Love" credible and exciting. As Queenie, Gretha Boston gets her gorgeous voice behind "Mis'ry's Comin' Aroun'," the stunning dirge that foreshadows Julie's exposure as a mulatto. Boston exudes a warmth and humor that make it transparent why Magnolia would want to take refuge from her flinty mother in Queenie's kitchen.

In emphasizing the social content of the show, Prince and his designer, Eugene Lee, haven't forgotten the fun of its spectacle. They give us a stern-wheeler that docks before our eyes, a footlit theatre, cotton bales stacked on a Natchez levee, even an electric train that steams across the stage in the distance. Susan Stroman's choreography calls attention not to itself but to the new momentum of the democracy, to which black culture gave voice and, in its vivid dances, also body. In bringing together good and bad, optimism and outrage, celebration and resignation, "Show Boat" demanded a new maturity from musical theatre and from its audience. "Show Boat" insists—and Prince's expert production makes the point irresistible—that the past must be remembered for its sins as well as for its triumphs. History is ambiguous, and so is the idealism of love and hate. "Show Boat" puts that paradox center stage. The show chronicles slavery not to condone it but to deplore it. Anyone with a demitasse for a hat can see the intention. Not, however, the coalition, a politically correct sign of our winded times, which wants freedom for everything but thought. Adamance without information only trivializes protest. That's why the coalition's cries of racism have had all the impact of a popgun; and why, after seven decades, "Show Boat" still speaks to the informed heart of the democracy.

PART 4

PRODUCTIONS

INGMAR BERGMAN

GRAVITY AND GRACE

On November 25, 1970,
the novelist Yukio Mishima orchestrated his famous suicide, committing
hara-kiri and then having his head cut off. At a stroke, the mind-body
split he wrote about was finally resolved. Mishima's death, at forty-five,
was, like his life, an act of fanatical will and aesthetic principle. He had
written forty novels, twenty volumes of short stories, and eighteen
plays, among the last of which was "Madame de Sade" (1965), a
meditation on the metaphysics of desire. De Sade, who, like Mishima,
was a voluptuary of the perverse, never appears in the play, but the
memory and the import of his libertinism dominate six women who
wait and worry about him through his long incarceration. Mishima
projected onto de Sade his own quest, in which perversion became an
act not of debasement but of discovery. In a late poem, "Icarus,"
Mishima wrote:

> Why, still, should the lust for ascension
> Seem, in itself, so close to madness?
> Nothing is that can satisfy me;
> Earthly novelty is too soon dulled.
> I am drawn higher and higher, more unstable.

Both Mishima and de Sade were romantic individualists who embraced pain as a way of defeating boredom and extending the limits of
consciousness. In this romance of the self, both were quintessentially
modern: destroying themselves for meaning. De Sade had a prodigious
genius for perversion, and Mishima seems to have instinctively understood the sense of blessing implicit in the monstrous. His play makes a

case for the necessity of evil. Recounting de Sade's being beaten with a broom eight hundred and fifty-nine times, Comtesse de Saint-Fond, the play's female libertine and de Sade's disciple, says, "If you increase numbers until they are no longer believable, evil itself becomes a miracle." She argues that de Sade, whose miracles "have nothing in common with the miracles lazy people merely wait for," works for his spiritual enlightenment.

So does the director Ingmar Bergman, who understands the deeply religious nature of Mishima's inquiring into the profane. Bergman's formidable gifts of penetration and design turn "Madame de Sade," which on the page is apparently all talk, into a magnificent exhibition both of Mishima's subtle moral debate and of his own incomparable stagecraft. It is one of the most noble evenings I've ever spent in the theatre. The show is part of a Bergman doubleheader (along with "Peer Gynt") and will play for three days at the Brooklyn Academy of Music. For four years, it has been in repertory intermittently at Stockholm's state-subsidized and exquisite art deco Kungliga Dramatiska Teatern (where I saw it three weeks ago). In it Bergman sets himself the challenge of containing the play's turbulent passions within the formal spirit in Japanese drama. He does away with all period décor. He streamlines Mishima's baroque text (herein quoted from Donald Keene's translation). He allows his actors no excessive gestures. The play speaks through the dramatic interplay of groupings, costume, color, words, and subtext. Every acting moment is filled, every inch of stage space is dynamic. It's a thrilling and educational encounter, which makes American theatre and most European theatre, by comparison, look like minorleague stuff.

"What I like about Ingmar is that he very rarely speaks about what he means," says Donya Feuer, the American-born choreographer who worked with Bergman on his film of "The Magic Flute" and his opera version of "The Bacchae" and has perfectly realized the "choreographic spirit" behind Bergman's reading of "Madame de Sade." "By what he does, you understand what he means. Everything Ingmar does is emotion. To give a place for this emotional response, he has to get the actors in the same place he is—to touch them in the most secret part of their imagination. In 'Madame de Sade' we didn't want to do anything that was Japanese in itself. But the exactness of Mishima's language demanded an exactness in the actors' movements and in their attack. The way they looked and didn't look. The way they listened onstage, and waited, and exited. Since it's an open space and very exposed, all the tension and the boundaries had to be created by the women themselves in relationship to each other. We began to work with that. There isn't a moment in this performance which doesn't fit Ingmar's plan. In every scene Ingmar searches for a space—a kind of rectangle, which varies several inches one way or another—that he calls 'the acoustic and optical center' of the stage. From this glowing place everything comes. Every single moment has a form.''

From the play's first beat, when the housekeeper, Charlotte (Helena Brodin), scurries onstage in Japanese fashion but dressed as a period French servant, Bergman announces the game of contrasts he is about to play. Charlotte, previously the housekeeper of Comtesse de Saint-Fond, is a bridge between the worlds of liberty and respectability. Bergman uses her like a kind of silent chorus, alternately astonished and appalled as she eavesdrops from behind the background arches. The boundaries of the debate are established at once when the "saint," Baronesse de Simiane (Margaretha Byström), whose piety will put her in a nunnery by the finale, comes face-to-face with the "sinner," Comtesse de Saint-Fond. Bergman uses Charles Koroly's magnificent costumes to make palpable the implications of this battle between denial and freedom. Simiane, soon to be joined by her counterpart in containment—the hostess, Madame de Montreuil—is decked out in the periwigged and corsetted formality of eighteenth-century high fashion. A wall of fabric and wire barricades both women off from the world. By contrast, Comtesse de Saint-Fond (the brilliant and brazen Agneta Ekmanner) enters in streamlined riding gear, her breasts clearly visible through a pale-marigold tunic. The effect is as teasing and shocking as her personality. She is neither powdered nor periwigged. The red of her lipstick and the small ruby pendant she wears hint at blood.

"It's a very dangerous part," Ekmanner told me. "I feel very exposed onstage. But it's no time to lie. You can't offend the public in doing this extremely difficult part—full of sorrow and longing—without doing it as honestly as possible." Ekmanner lays herself recklessly open to the audience, just as Saint-Fond does to the women on whom she has come to call, and who dismiss her as decadent. Montreuil wants Saint-Fond to trade sexual favors with the High Court officials in exchange for their lifting de Sade's death sentence. Saint-Fond recounts the offenses that have brought de Sade to this pretty pass: a menu of infamy that includes orgies with whores, the use of Spanish fly, sodomy, and flagellation. This news sends a *frisson* of fear through Baronesse de Simiane, who in the script protects herself from contamination by making continual signs of the cross, and in Bergman's version does so by hiding half her face behind her fan.

When Madame de Montreuil enters, the minuet of vanity and outrage steps up a pace. Montreuil (played with regal detachment by Anita Björk) is as chilly as her pale-blue dress, and as imposing. She is baffled by de Sade's capers but admits that "the one thing I *could* understand was honor." She wants de Sade's freedom for the sake of her distraught daughter, Renée, who is de Sade's long-suffering wife and whom she dubs "the bride of the King of Hell," and for the honor of the family name. Saint-Fond reads Montreuil's snobbery correctly, and continues to tweak the vanity of Montreuil's righteousness with her unrepentant knowledge of the flesh. "The most striking characteristic of the marquis' illness is how pleasant it is," she tells her. "Immorality has always been for me a perfectly appointed, completely self-sufficient preserve. It has its shepherds' cottages and its windmills, its brooks and lakes."

In Stina Ekblad's delicate and sharply defined interpretation, Renée puts her intelligence and her longing for meaning into the myth of her fanatic devotion, and allows de Sade to carry both the darkness and the passion that she won't own in herself. "Bergman gave me inspiring word pictures for the role," Ekblad told me. "For instance, of Anne, my sister in the play, he said, 'She's building a cathedral around her in which she is worshipping herself.' Of my character, Renée, he said, 'She's a hymn echoing in this cathedral.' Renée is more of a tune—changing, echoing. She's like a bell." In Act I, Renée gives lip service to conventional behavior. She presents herself in the role of dutiful and heroic victim. Saint-Fond brings this hypocrisy into focus with a mischievous question. "How does he treat you?" she asks Renée. The impropriety sends Montreuil and Simiane plunging behind their upturned fans. Decadence and duty square off. "If you were to see our marital bed," Renée says, saving face for the moment, "there would be nothing I should ask you to keep a secret."

Renée is wedded as much to the idea of marriage as she is to de Sade. In her transparent goodness, she lives up to her mother's idea of repute. Madame de Montreuil exhausts herself restoring the family name, and Renée is no less tireless both in living a blameless life and in whiting out the dark parts of her life. She rationalizes de Sade's yearning for blood —she says it's related to "the glory of his distant ancestors who served in the crusades"—and she refuses to listen to her mother's pleas to leave him. But what on the surface seems devotion is also a rigid defensiveness. In this, she is definitely her mother's child. But she is also a weird, refracted image of her husband. Both de Sade and Renée are in the avant-garde of suffering. Both are strangely inconsolable. De Sade acts out his anger on others; Renée murders parts of herself. He fiercely admits himself; and she, just as fiercely, hides herself away. The play skillfully brings this ambiguity to a head at the end of the first act, when Madame de Montreuil's other daughter, Anne, returns from Italy. The stunning and capricious Anne, superbly played by Marie Richardson as a languorous Fragonard seductress whose eyes sparkle with self-regard, announces that her companion in Italy was none other than de Sade, escaped from prison and in hiding. Montreuil begs her not to tell Renée. "She knows we went to Italy," Anne tells her flabbergasted mother, who has only just finished hearing Renée's entreaties to save her husband from prison. "And where Alphonse is hiding." Both Renée's devotion to de Sade and Montreuil's devotion to getting him released are at a stroke called into question. The carapace of convention —what Mishima calls "the unoriginal concepts of duty"—has cracked from the dangerous pressures it's meant to contain: the temptation of the imagination.

Life seems to have changed for the de Sade household at the beginning of Act II, as the curtain comes up on Renée reading Anne the court order announcing de Sade's pardon and his release from prison. In the intervening six years, which take us to the fall of 1778, de Sade has been internalized differently by each character. His genius for suffering has somehow deepened them and—on the surface, at least—made them mellower. To capture the change in the quality of their suffering and their passion, Bergman first changes his palette. At the opening of the act, a flamelike tree is projected against a red cyclorama, foreshadowing the fierce passion to follow. Time has left its mark on the sisters; and Koroly's dresses, in resonating shades of dark red and terra-cotta, convey an earthier, weathered sense of life. Renée's denial now takes the form of claiming kinship with de Sade. "My unhappiness has at last reached the level of Alphonse's sins," she says. A tone of resignation and skepticism has come into her voice. She understands that claims of happiness are a tapestry of denial, in which the woman "painstakingly weaves in, eye by eye, solitude, boredom, anxiety, loneliness, terrible nights, frightening sunrises." And when Anne bitchily suggests that de Sade never loved anyone, including Renée, she can hear the idea, while deflecting its hurt. "Everyone is free to have fantasies," she says. "Alphonse taught me the power of fantasy." The intoxication with suffering is most clearly dramatized by Saint-Fond, who, announcing her boredom with licentiousness, describes being stripped naked and used as the altar for a black mass. In this speech, full of grief and strange glory, Saint-Fond recounts the rebirth of feeling at an orgy where the blood of a sacrificial lamb coursed over her naked body and candles dripped hot wax on her outspread palms. She holds up her arms and points to scars like stigmata. She has been crucified and redeemed in the flesh, not in the afterlife. "Alphonse was myself," she says. They are bound together by a sense of absence which perversion turns into a kind of heroism.

Bergman savors every twist of plot and passion, then makes it pay. Saint-Fond tips the decorum of Madame de Montreuil's house toward delirium when she informs Renée that the pardon was merely a trap set by her mother to rearrest de Sade, and that he is now in jail again. The stage is then left to the play's most extraordinary passage—a furious, stylized battle between Montreuil and Renée. Mother and daughter at first circle one another, with Renée begging her mother to free de Sade, and Montreuil asking what happiness his freedom would bring her. "The happiness of poverty. The happiness of shame," Renée says, in a hymn to her masochistic devotion. "That is the happiness with which I shall be rewarded for setting Alphonse free." The words outrage Montreuil, and in a sudden and stunning outburst she throws her fan across the floor: "You're lying, lying." She paints a lacerating word picture of an orgy at which her informant witnessed the conduct of Renée and de Sade, during another of his brief escapes from prison. Montreuil stands above her daughter, with her arms crossed in imitation of Renée's bound hands as her whipped nude body hung from a chandelier. "You dangled half unconscious in pain," she says. "With his tongue, he cleansed your body. It wasn't only blood he cleansed." She tears at the bodice of Renée's dress to expose her scars. Bergman sends mother and daughter reeling in fury to opposite ends of the proscenium, and then launches them toward each other in a flurry of accusations. As they descend on one another, their bodies lower to the ground like snarling animals in a standoff. "You never attempted, even in your wildest dreams, to imagine what it would be like to unlock the strange door that opens on a sky full of stars," Renée taunts, defending de Sade for opening her up to extremes of experience where "holiness and shame imperceptibly switch appearances." Hunkered down in front of her daughter, Montreuil counters, "That's right. We never tried to open the gates of Hell." De Sade has called out of Renée a demonic force. In this coruscating stage picture, Bergman demonstrates that Renée has been infected not only by de Sade's ideas but by his manic metabolism. On the last beat of the act, Renée, too, is saying "Alphonse is myself."

Projected clouds and the rumble of wind forecast the threatening wild card that history deals the de Sade ménage at the opening of Act III. Twelve more years have passed, and we are at the beginning of the French Revolution. The change in public mood is prefigured by Charlotte, the housekeeper, who now wears her hair loose on her shoulders. In her transparent insolence and her assertive walk, she registers the bumptious new democratic spirit. The violent search for new answers and new freedoms has made the dead Comtesse de Saint-Fond an icon of liberation, and even de Sade will become one of the Revolution's spokesmen. He is soon to be released from prison, and Madame de Montreuil, always with an eye to survival, now looks forward to his return. "Alphonse's vices may serve as a bill of acquittal not only for himself but for our whole family," she says, rationalizing de Sade's evil as a source of potential good. Renée's actual goodness has not been rewarded; in fact, she has been debased by de Sade in his novel "Justine," which cannibalizes her years of devotion to make a myth of vice. "Justine is myself," she says. Unexplained scars on Renée's wrists recall Saint-Fond's "stigmata" but not her redemption. Renée's public humiliation persuades her to take holy orders. And there is a still greater paradox about de Sade to be faced. "His fascination with destruction ended in creation," Renée says. In pursuing the light, she has learned through de Sade that it can come from improbable dark sources. The play neatly brings the audience to the spiritual impasse of modern life: one person dedicating the self to God and the other making a god of the self.

At the finale, de Sade arrives at the house and knocks on the door. "Tell me how the marquis looks," Renée says twice, a heartbreaking repetition. Charlotte describes an old, fat man with sallow skin and nervous eyes. "Please ask him to leave," Renée says. "And tell him this: 'The marquise will never see him again.' " With that, Renée exits, leaving Charlotte to pick up the discarded volume of "Justine." She starts to step on it, then reconsiders, and instead of destroying it she takes the book and walks off with it under her arm. Renée's history with de Sade may be over, but de Sade's life with the public imagination and the complex notion of individual freedom is about to begin. On that grace note, Bergman ends this flawless production, in which his genius is entirely in the service of the play's meaning. Next year, Bergman will be doing two plays at the Kungliga Dramatiska Teatern. Believe me, I will be there.

ARIANE MNOUCHKINE

CAPRICE OF THE GODS

THE NEW YORK THEATRE
season began in big bowwow fashion on the first weekend of October.
By 2:30 P.M., an hour before show time, on a cloudless Saturday, a line
the length of a city block had formed outside the 14th Regiment Armory, in Brooklyn, where Ariane Mnouchkine's Théâtre du Soleil and
its two-day, ten-hour cycle of Greek tragedy, "Les Atrides"—combining Aeschylus' "The Oresteia" with Euripides' "Iphigenia in Aulis"—
was being produced by the Brooklyn Academy of Music. Beleaguered by
the collapse of the economy, the collapse of their city, the collapse of
Woody and Mia's romance, New Yorkers seemed happy to turn their
attention to the collapse of the House of Atreus. The city's highfliers, to
most of whom "Attic" probably means "storage space," rubbed shoulders with the hoi polloi. Occasionally, a hopeful theatregoer panhandled
the line, plaintively asking, "Tickets? Tickets?" An official, wearying of
the trek around the block, said, "We'll be opening the doors soon. Pass
it back." The words echoed down the line like the news of Agamemnon's return to Argos.

Once inside, the ticket holders were herded past the sixty-foot playing area—a kind of squared bullring, with scuffed blond walls bearing
rust-colored smears that discreetly hinted at dried blood. Only as they
jostled to park their backsides on folding chairs that had been crammed
onto behemoth gymnasium risers towering above the stage did the
paying customers twig to the fact that Mnouchkine's bold attempt to
reimagine the marathon experience of Greek tragedy included the ass-
aching discomfort of sitting through it.

For over a quarter of a century, working out of an old ammuni-
tion factory on the outskirts of Paris, Mnouchkine and her company

have been fashioning their own brand of explosives—a series of elegant and exciting theatrical events, including "1789," "Mephisto," and a samurai-inspired "Richard II." Mnouchkine is a mistress of ceremonies who is interested in the civic dimensions of drama. A conservative avant-gardist, she is one of that rare breed which wants mass communication and actually loves the mass. And in her hands "The Oresteia," which is a hymn to democracy, becomes a democratic spectacle. You can't pay to get the best seat. There are no reserved seats, there are no intermissions, and no one can be seated after the play starts. The audience has to want to be there. In order for performance to factor into pleasure, both parts of the theatrical equation—audience and actors—have to be prepared. Here the actors are housed behind the grandstand, in a warren of cubicles under a makeshift pine pagoda lit by flickering kerosene lamps. Their wigs and belts are draped over the rafters, their makeup is meticulously laid out, their ravishing headdresses perch on forms beside the dressing tables. Flowers are placed strategically around the dressing area, whose cushions, carpets, and incense give it the feel of a Turkish bazaar. The actors white their faces, comb the long strands of their wigs, cinch themselves into corsets and long skirts. No telegrams on mirrors, no champagne in the fridge, no clutter of cards or clothes: the atmosphere of "Les Atrides" is one of scrupulous attention to detail. Performer and public are moving inexorably from the ordinary into the extraordinary. This concentrated focus creates an enormous sense of occasion for the actors and the audience alike. So when Jean-Jacques Lemêtre's kettledrums rumble, they announce both onstage and in the grandstand a gorgeous exhibition of energy.

Mnouchkine rightly claims intellectual kinship with, among others, the great Russian avant-garde director V. S. Meyerhold, who, in his attack on naturalism and the teachings of Stanislavski, felt that "words in the theatre are only embellishments on the design of movement." Meyerhold took as his theatrical model the fairground cabotin, the seventeenth-century strolling player who combined the clown's poetic agility with an appetite for surprise. While nothing in the punishing violence of the Atreus saga is jokey, the spectacle is imbued with the clown's rebellion against the habitual. Lemêtre's orchestra of four, which takes up a quarter of the stage, employs an exotic array of string and percussive instruments whose weird sonorities call up a world preyed upon by gods, ghosts, and murderous vendetta law.

And when the chorus of "Iphigenia in Aulis" makes its first entrance, pushing through the upstage double doors and dancing toward us in the stutter steps of Indian kathakali, Mnouchkine immediately puts the audience in another spiritual realm, where the rhetoric of movement matches the strangeness of the choric odes. At a stroke, Greek tragedy is stripped of its familiar associations, and we are lured into that otherness which is the terrain of myth. Hints of Greek folk dance, Balinese dance, Kabuki aragato ("rough stuff and bombast") are also layered into the wild geometry of the plays, which by their very nature are encounters with the marvellous. The production speaks its passions not just to our heads but to our senses. It opens the audience up not only to the poetry of language but to the silent metaphysics of color, gesture, fabrics, and space. The cumulative effect is hypnotic, as if we were walking in our dreams. Mnouchkine's attack mirrors the structural arc of "The Oresteia," which is established in the first image of the first play, when the Watchman in "Agamemnon" waits for a sign of light, and culminates with "The Eumenides," when the Furies are called out of the dark and into the democratic gaze of the citizens.

Where most modern drama is too small for the heroic spaces of large institutional theatres, "The Oresteia" bursts their bounds. The plays address the issue of how to heal wounds we carry for sins we didn't commit, how to evolve justice, how to turn the dark, destructive forces in both the self and the state into creative ones. And in "The Eumenides," when Athene, a goddess born from a man's head, casts the deciding vote that allows Orestes to walk free and elude destruction by the Furies for killing his mother ("I favor the male side. . . . I wouldn't give preference to a woman"), we bear witness to the incarnation of patriarchy. By beginning the cycle with "Iphigenia in Aulis," the only extant Greek tragedy that dramatizes Agamemnon's sacrifice of his daughter to gain victory over Troy, Mnouchkine wants to spell out the family story and sympathetically reinterpret Clytemnestra, turning her from a virago into a rebel whose actions reject women's second-class citizenship in fifth-century Athens. Clytemnestra's murder of Aga-

memnon is both an act of revenge and a liberation—a point that Aeschylus implies and that Mnouchkine underlines by tacking Euripides' irony
onto the majesty of Aeschylus' democratic optimism. It's like having a
first act of "Carousel" written by Stephen Sondheim.

But although "Iphigenia in Aulis" gets "Les Atrides" off to a rousing
start, it has the curious effect of helping to sink "Agamemnon," which
follows from it and recapitulates the saga of the sacrifice. The audience
palpably sags under the weight of now unnecessary exposition. You
come away thinking that the play is undramatic, when in fact it is
Mnouchkine who has excised the central dramatic image—the crimson
carpet—around which the battle between Agamemnon and Clytemnestra is fought and their natures are revealed.

Clytemnestra gives "red-carpet treatment" a whole new meaning.
Her revenge is not just to murder her vainglorious husband but to
demonstrate her superiority over him. "Don't turn me into a woman
with your softness," he says. But that's what she does. The crimson
carpet, which begins as a sign of flattery and then becomes a taunt to the
gods, ends as an emblem of the Greeks' fear of female engulfment:
Clytemnestra uses it as a net to trap Agamemnon while she stabs him. In
this production, though, the carpet is discussed but never shown; and so
the subtlety of their battle is not dramatized. It is a major omission, and
a missed scenic opportunity, by a director who usually loses no opportunity to make thrilling stage pictures. The loss is symptomatic of
Mnouchkine's unnecessary special pleading in her attempt to humanize
Clytemnestra. To this end, she has cast the powerful and appealing
Juliana Carneiro da Cunha, whose doleful eyes and elegant dignity play
down the text's repeated allusions to Clytemnestra's mannish nature.
And, where Aeschylus introduced a Nurse to undermine Clytemnestra's
claims for herself as a mother in the scene before she pleads with her
son for her life, Mnouchkine diffuses the power of the Nurse's indictment by staging her as the Hellenic equivalent of a pantomime dame.
Elsewhere, Mnouchkine, who claims that "our duty as directors is to be
good readers," misreads and simplifies the story with politically correct
bowdlerizations. At the conclusion of her version of "The Eumenides,"
for instance, Athene promises the Furies a place of honor in the city:

"In future times Women will be more revered." The lines do not exist in the Greek text. They are Mnouchkine's sop to sisterhood.

Mnouchkine's great achievement here is to crack the theatrical bugbear of the chorus. She largely succeeds in restoring to Greek tragedy a sense of the expressive possibilities of the savage, demonized world of the plays. There is a kind of intoxication in the swirling hubbub of the chorus as it vaults the walls, skirts flying, at the finale of "The Libation Bearers," or circles around the prostrate Clytemnestra in the awful delirium of war at the finale of "Iphigenia in Aulis." The tumult of Mnouchkine's chorus is just the kind of poetic revelation Artaud had in mind when he wrote about theatre that "plunges us into that state of uncertainty and ineffable anguish which is characteristic of poetry." The chorus, however agitated, is always poised in some strategic, kinetic balance that adheres to classic symmetry and to the aesthetics of harmony so central to ancient Greek culture. Nowhere is Mnouchkine's interpretative and scenic genius more powerful than in her evocation of the Furies. Terrible cries of birds and growls of dogs well up from below the grandstand and echo in the vast building. And when the Furies arrive they bolt onto the stage on all fours from subterranean lairs behind the bullring walls—a pack of snarling, red-eyed, baboon-faced dogs rooting for Orestes' blood with their pointed snouts. The dogs' high, swept-back quiffs of black hair throw long, eerie shadows on the armory's brick wall. The image is electrifying and exact. Somehow, Mnouchkine occasionally contrives to have the dogs, who remain on all fours throughout the evening, leap high into the air, as if levitating with voracity. The execution is flawless, and the masks, by Erhard Stiefel, are inspired. The dogs are a yapping, frenzied, predatory correlative for all those unseen destructive forces which hunt man down and push him to the point of madness.

Once, when Charlie Chaplin was asked to describe his art, he quipped, "Entrances and exits." The same could be said of Mnouchkine. She provides a raked trolley to whip her characters—in telling friezelike postures—on and off center stage from an entrance built into the middle of the grandstand. It's an effective, if overused, device, which adds both momentum and a mythic dimension to the storytelling. The Prophetess (well performed by Nirupama Nityanandan, who also plays Electra and Iphigenia) is dramatically lifted from the back of the grandstand and deposited center stage by shrouded guards to begin "The Eumenides." And "The Libation Bearers" ends memorably, with Electra unable to push offstage the pallet on which Clytemnestra and Aegisthus lie murdered. The gravity of the murder is made manifest. Only at the play's last moment does the pallet, with the help of the chorus, disappear—sensationally—from sight. Mnouchkine attends to every nanosecond of stage time. Although her scenic powers may outweigh her analytic ones, she puts the production in the service of the text. This inevitably means longueurs for a contemporary audience. But these lapses are more than compensated for by the imagery. When Orestes (the athletic Simon Abkarian, whose heroic features also serve well for the vain Agamemnon and for Achilles) dances exultantly over his dead mother's body, heaving and twisting as if in some spiritual convulsion, the image chills the blood and sears the brain.

In Aristophanes' "The Frogs," Dionysus, at whose festival the tragedies were performed, goes down to Hades to find a poet to save Athens in its moment of danger. Euripides and Aeschylus debate, and in the end, choosing wisdom over cleverness, Dionysus picks Aeschylus. "Off you go," says Pluto, the god of Hades, as Aeschylus heads back to earth. "Go with your sound advice and save the City for us. Educate the fools —you'll find a good many." Theatre was how that education took place. In the arena, ideas were tested, language was minted, and the citizens were called into a community to share and be shaped by the events. No wonder, then, that the word "civilization" has its root in "city," with the cross-fertilization such collectiveness implies. The movement from barbarity to community, from exclusion to acceptance, is caught in one stunning final image by Mnouchkine: the Furies abandon their predatory posture to walk upright off the stage. They have been joined to the civic domain.

RALPH FIENNES

MATINÉE IDOLATRY

"Hamlet" is a play that tests the best actors of each generation, and also each generation's sense of itself. Over the last thirty years, in England, no fewer than three "Hamlet"'s have served as such cultural bellwethers. In 1965, during the Vietnam War, David Warner gave us an untidy undergraduate Hamlet who was frustrated by Denmark's military-industrial complex. In 1980, as Britain's economy went into a weird free fall, Jonathan Pryce's Hamlet was possessed by the ghost of his father, who spoke through him in a frightening supernatural flirtation with madness. And now, in the neutral, post-Thatcher nineties, Ralph Fiennes has pitched his drop-dead matinée-idol profile and the modesty of his sensitive soul into a postmodern "Hamlet" whose refusal to risk interpretation reflects Britain's current bland and winded times.

Fiennes, an intelligent, reticent player, seems almost as unwilling to enter the vortex of Hamlet's torment as Hamlet himself is to take action. Fiennes radiates an elegance of spirit that rivets the audience with its sense of unspoken mystery. His performance is a stylish event, much more the "mould of form" than the "glass of fashion." He has a mellow, reedy voice that filters Shakespeare's gorgeous complexity and gives the language an accessible colloquial ring. Fiennes is not one for grand histrionic gestures. His personality doesn't take up a lot of space. He compels attention by his decency, not by his declaiming. Fiennes, who has limpid green eyes and tousled chestnut hair, and who is a laid-back, brooding, romantic star, is catnip to the public and oxygen at the box office. (The Almeida Theatre Company's production, which began its much ballyhooed life at the Hackney Empire, the wonderful old music-hall venue in London's East End, has arrived at the Belasco for a fourteen-week Broadway engagement.) This "Hamlet" has been designed to be a people's "Hamlet," which is to say a "Hamlet" in which the plot, not the psychology, is complicated, and in which the cast works the room instead of working for meaning. Inevitably, therefore, Fiennes's Hamlet is not a navel-gazing scholar or an alienated adolescent or a demented psychological case study. His Hamlet turns out to be the guy Horatio always said he was: a "sweet prince," a sort of rogue and *pleasant* slave.

The director, Jonathan Kent, who last year transferred the Almeida's "Medea," with Diana Rigg, to Broadway with great success, has set the play in Edwardian England and has lopped an hour off the playing time. The speed favors breadth over depth; the streamlining suits the cut of Fiennes's jib, and he wears James Acheson's period clothes well. What we have here is a ripping Shakespearean yarn that shows off the thrills and chills of the story's melodramatic elements: the ghost of a murdered king, a mother's hasty marriage to her husband's murderer, a prince driven to near-madness and revenge, a lovelorn suicide, a lot of ghoulish high jinks around graves, a terrific sword fight, and a quadruple poisoning. The result is lucid without being moving: a kind of aerobic "Hamlet," which works hard to keep up the pace while going nowhere.

The lights come up on a bare, raked stage, and the sound of crashing waves fills the auditorium. In the background, the environs of Elsinore are suggested by faint, blurred beams of light projected through a murky scrim on which the outlines of rocks are just visible. A sentinel climbs up through a trapdoor—more for effect than for sense, it seems, like many things in this production. "Who's there?" he calls. That's the play, the whole existential ball of wax. Hamlet's entire dramatic journey is foreshadowed in these first words. He, too, must penetrate the surrounding darkness and tease out the reality of his parents, of the corrupt court, and of himself. By finally taking action—which means accepting loss, including the loss of his own life—Hamlet sees clearly into the heart of things and achieves his adulthood. In this sense, "Hamlet" is both a detective story and a metaphysical investigation. The practical and the philosophical aspects of the tale need time to build properly; as the saying goes, "No delay, no play." But here, with the proceedings speeded up, the text is not so much examined as *done*. It's significant that Fiennes attacks the "To be, or not to be" soliloquy, which sets out Hamlet's spiritual quandary, by coming toward us in manic stutter steps and turning the famous meditation into yapping thought. He skirts the issue of interpretation by turning talk into behavior. The image is novel; but little nuance comes across the footlights. In this ranting mode, dissembling a madness that is really giddy grief, the barefoot Fiennes grabs Ophelia's crotch and insolently shoves Claudius's shoulder. But Fiennes can't really get up a convincingly antic head of steam. He is slow to kindle and never really burns. He's not so much tormented as pissed off.

Fiennes has his best moment with the Gravedigger (the excellent, grizzled Terence Rigby, who also plays Hamlet's father's ghost and the Player King). Listening to the Gravedigger expound matter-of-factly on how a body decomposes, and learning that a skull he has unearthed belonged to Yorick, the former King's jester, Hamlet gently takes this relic of his old acquaintance from the Gravedigger. "This?" Fiennes says, uttering the word with a huge sense of recognition, wonder, and sadness. His sensitivity and the mournfulness of the moment coalesce. "Where be your gibes now? your gambols? your songs? your flashes of merriment, that were wont to set the table on a roar?" Fiennes says, with a delicacy that delivers Shakespeare's observations about mortality like a punch to the heart.

The production's obsession with surface has its most effective expression in Peter J. Davison's sets. He creates a dark, lugubrious officialdom of behemoth ceilings, heavy brown-stained doors, and large shuttered windows that turn the actors into scuttling Lilliputians. Hamlet is first seen framed by one of these gigantic windows, standing upstage with his back turned away from the bustle of power, whose aggrandizement is reflected in the monumentality that surrounds it. Still, Davison, too, succumbs to the production's impulse to startle rather than compel. The ghost is conjured up on a high platform behind the scrim. There, lit from above by the white glare of a halogen lamp and announced by a jolt of electronic sound, Hamlet's dead father appears twice, in his carapace of armor: a "Star Wars" effect that is a projection of commercial instincts more than of Hamlet's unconscious. Similarly, Jonathan Kent's eye for business is sometimes shrewder than his eye for detail. When Laertes and Hamlet take turns leaping into Ophelia's grave and embracing her body, each trying to outdo the remorse of the other, the poor dead girl bobs up and down like a hand puppet. And at the finale, when Fortinbras (Rupert Penry-Jones, who is also Fiennes's understudy) arrives to take over the kingdom that Hamlet has died to save, his Aryan good looks and the gray capes of his lieutenants make it seem as if the Luftwaffe had invaded Denmark.

In American theatrical circles, the definition of a genius is anybody from England. But the prestige of this production can't hide the unevenness of its seasoned supporting cast, who prove the adage that British actors are either tours de force or forced to tour. Besides Terence Rigby, only the lanky, bearded Peter Eyre, as Polonius, breathes distinctive life into his role. Eyre plays the meddling bureaucrat as a long drink of cold water: cleaning his pince-nez as he counsels his hotheaded son to "neither a borrower, nor a lender be," and withholding his hand from Laertes when he goes, Eyre misses no opportunity to have fun with the old blowhard's pedantry. Polonius rushes to the Queen with a letter that Hamlet has sent his daughter, and reads it to her as a presenting symptom of Hamlet's lunacy. Reciting " 'To the celestial and my soul's idol, the most beautified Ophelia,' " Eyre's Polonius bristles with dopey patrician disdain. "That's an ill phrase, a vile phrase, 'beautified' is a vile phrase," he says, and gets one of the evening's best laughs.

Others are not so much at home in Shakespeare's climate of delirium. Tara FitzGerald, a talented young actress with a bright future, flounders as Ophelia. There is nothing fractured or vulnerable about her, and when Ophelia goes mad FitzGerald won't let her rip. FitzGerald's behavior—the compulsive walking back and forth, the sexual taunts directed at Claudius—feels tame and glib: a trick of the mind, not a journey of the heart. Often, when English actors are nowhere near the center of their parts they rely on the power of their articulate voices; James Laurenson's Claudius falls into the trap of such posturing. Claudius is John Gotti with a pedigree—carnal, vicious, power-hungry, ruthless—but Laurenson gives us chicanery on the half shell. He does a lot of Urgent Shakespeare Acting. A few wheeling turns upstage, some nips at the top of his hand, a little booming oratory, and—presto!—you have a villain. This stock rep stuff is also dished up by the beautiful Francesca Annis, as a Gertrude who can't manage much grief at the sight of Ophelia's dementia but does manage a long, lingering kiss with Hamlet. It's a bit of business that has become the theatrical baggage of the role in this century, but the incestuous overtone seems inappropriate, especially in such an unanalytic production.

A word about Hamlet's duel. Jonathan Kent and the fight director, William Hobbs, have built up this face-off between idealism and treachery into a scintillating contest that takes excellent advantage of the story's melodrama. A cream-colored tarp is rolled downstage for the match, and the court sits watching upstage right, in gray upholstered chairs. Hamlet fights with graceful, playful enthusiasm, unaware that he's up against the double whammy of Laertes' poisoned sword and Claudius's poisoned chalice. Hamlet gets the first couple of touches; then Laertes' temper flares, and he cuts Hamlet. They scuffle, and in the hurly-burly their swords get mixed up. Hamlet chases Laertes around the room, sending chairs flying and courtiers scurrying for safety. It's exciting and well-staged hokum, in which Laertes ends up hoist with his own petard. At that point, the Queen, who has drunk from the chalice, collapses; then the Grand Guignol of Shakespeare's ending quickly plays itself out. At the finale, Fortinbras's men lift Hamlet's corpse on their shoulders and, swaying, carry him slowly upstage and toward the light beyond. Fiennes's head falls back, giving the audience one last glimpse of the star. Even backward, upside down, and dead, Fiennes exits looking good.

INGMAR BERGMAN

THE BATTLE OF THE VANITIES

Alceste, the central figure of Molière's comedy "The Misanthrope" (1666), is probably the greatest refusenik in dramatic literature. He makes the dour Ancient Mariner look like a party animal. He is in the grip of a terrible fury at the sinfulness of the world, a man drawn both to the life of the court and to the flesh but unable to abide the fallibility of either. He will accept life only on his own terms of impossible purity. "I wish no place in a dishonest heart," he proclaims. Among literature's heroes of absurd negativity—Kafka's Hunger Artist, Melville's Bartleby the scrivener—Alceste, with his clownish outbursts, is surely the funniest. He's adolescent hell on a short fuse; he rails against the vanity of the corrupt and acts out the vanity of the righteous. But how honest is Alceste? This is the question that Ingmar Bergman explores in his third attempt at the play (he directed earlier productions in 1957 and 1973), on the main stage of the Royal Dramatic Theatre of Sweden, in Stockholm. In Bergman's reinterpretation, Alceste's idealism is a mask for his sexual jealousy, and Alceste himself is as much a victim of appearances as the world he hectors. What Bergman engineers in masterly style is both a wonderful comedy of manners and a subtle dissection of the nature of manners themselves.

The curtain comes up on a painted scrim of Watteau's "La Partie Quarrée": three seated figures and a standing Pierrot figure, whose back is to us, are shown conversing against a background of Arcadian tranquillity. But comedy, in general, and "The Misanthrope," in particular, are anything but tranquil. The scrim makes a spectacle of pastoral containment—an approach that Bergman immediately begins to test in the realm of manners. Another Pierrot figure, this one in the flesh and facing us, watches from the side of the stage as the scrim starts to play tricks on our comforting sense of coherence. A peephole opens in the gold skirt of one of the Watteau maidens, and an actor peers through it, then waves. Behind the curtain, there are sounds of laughing and then screaming, then a sudden silence, then the clatter of pails, and then the scrim itself starts to wobble, as if shaken by a poltergeist. The contradiction between the serene surface and the rowdiness behind it becomes, as we soon discover, the theme of the play.

When the scrim rises, we see the entire cast, in all its fustian regalia, about to begin a game of blindman's bluff. Alceste's beloved Célimène (the gorgeous Lena Endre) has been blindfolded and is being spun around in the middle of a circle by Pierrot, who is the spirit of comedy and Bergman's alter ego. The dance—the ritualized dance of manners, which Veblen called "a symbolic pantomime of mastery on the one hand and of subservience on the other"—begins around her. Célimène's groping is a metaphor of the play's inquiry. At issue here is not just whom Célimène will favor as her lover but how to find and hold on to status, how to search out who and what are real. Alceste (the handsome Thorsten Flinck, wearing an austere black frock coat) breaks out of the dancing circle in disgust, stopping the game just as Célimène finds herself on her knees, fondling the crotch of one of her foppish suitors, Oronte (played with superb swagger by Jarl Kulle). As the moment has been choreographed, by Donya Feuer, it captures in one unforgettable image the polarities of libertine court life: a hypocritical world of social constraint and sexual concupiscence, veering, as it were, between snow jobs and blow jobs.

The game of blindman's bluff leads swiftly into a procession, with the actors walking upstage through large green doors, beyond which an array of delicacies, on a sumptuous candlelit banquet table, is briefly glimpsed. No sooner have the doors closed behind the court revellers than they open again and Alceste is flung out. He sprawls downstage in front of us, his knees bleeding and his dander up. The scrim, the dance, the banquet, and the expulsion are all part of Bergman's brilliant preamble to Molière. The play proper begins with Philinte (Thomas Hanzon) asking his friend Alceste, "Now, what's got into you?" (The play is performed in Swedish; I'm using Richard Wilbur's English trans-

lation.) The answer, it turns out, is nothing. Alceste can't partake of
life's banquet. He is a kind of moral anorexic, who won't take in the
world except in his own irrational and controlling way. Alceste spoils
things for the world while claiming that the artificiality of court life is
spoiling him. He lectures Philinte:

> Ah, no! we should condemn with all our force
> Such false and artificial intercourse.
> Let men behave like men; let them display
> Their inmost hearts in everything they say;
> Let the heart speak, and let our sentiments
> Not mask themselves in silly compliments.

In the abstract, Alceste's indictment rings true, but in reality what
Alceste is proposing is a form of social suicide. Philinte politely suggests
to him:

> Wouldn't the social fabric come undone
> If we were wholly frank with everyone?

Alceste won't gild any lily. What he misses—and what Molière and
Bergman understand—is the essential theatricality at the core of personality, "personality" being a word whose Latin root means "mask."
Manners are the ritual care that human beings—little deities of a self-
created universe—require as worship: the ceremony that insures for the
participants a sense of public congruence with their idealized selves. To
maintain "social face," some form of dissimulation is necessary: seeming prevails over being. "The Misanthrope" is all about the protecting,
the hiding, and the refusing of "face." In this production, Alceste
frequently stands turned away from others. He wants to remove his face
from public view, to avoid the inevitable collusion that manners require:

> Sometimes, I swear, I'm moved to flee and find,
> Some desert land unfouled by human kind.

When, in Act I, Oronte flounces in, his speech piled as high with rhetorical flourishes as his periwig is with blond curls, Alceste won't make a symbolic show of friendship. It's a hilarious battle of the vanities. Oronte fishes for compliments from Alceste for the banal sonnet he has penned. But Alceste refuses to reflect even a smidgen of Oronte's grandiosity back to him.

ORONTE: Others have praised my sonnet to the skies.
ALCESTE: I lack their art of telling pleasant lies.

Oronte, with his good manners, tries to disarm Alceste, but his subsequent humiliation leads him first to pull his sword on Alceste and then to pull a fast one by supporting another man's suit against Alceste for slander. "Social face," the sociologist Erving Goffman wrote, "is only on loan . . . from society; it will be withdrawn unless [the individual] conducts himself in a way that is worthy of it." Manners, inevitably, put mankind under wraps.

The twin predicaments of manners—self-inflation and self-imprisonment—are translated with spectacular success in the exaggerated silhouettes of Charles Koroly's magnificent costumes; they go beyond the baroque to the rococo. "It's screwed-up rococo," Koroly told me. "This rococo does not exist, it's so completely artificial. It's as if we had created a world of beautiful and poisonous insects." Koroly, who spent ten months designing the costumes, most of which weigh about twenty pounds apiece, added, "Rococo is not coming close to other people or being close to your own feelings. It's being encapsulated in a mannerism and a form of manners." In a sense, Koroly's costumes are the real set of the play; Bergman has kept his stage almost bare, so the actors can give full meaning to the bulky carapaces of fabric which house them. From the second week of Bergman's eight-week rehearsal schedule, the cast was wearing the show's coats, shoes, crinolines, and corsets, not just to eliminate obstacles in wearing them but to let the costumes inform the artificiality of the characters. In such outfits, you can't sit, stand, walk, or breathe in a natural way, and the architecture of unnaturalness brings its own inevitable mutation of character.

Alceste is besotted by Célimène, who is his exact emotional opposite: warm, witty, politic, mature, calm. The alluring Célimène is given the most seemingly natural of silhouettes. Bergman stages Célimène's second appearance boldly: she is lolling over breakfast with Alceste in her pale-green canopied bed. As Célimène, Lena Endre is potent stuff: a radiant intelligence. Her loose-fitting white linen negligee and her mane of auburn hair signal spontaneity and naturalness. The illusion engendered by someone as physically exquisite and fresh as Célimène is that she must also be morally exquisite. "All your speeches are enraged and rude," she tells Alceste, dabbing jam on his impertinent nose. "I've never been so furiously wooed." Endre could send the salmon upstream in the flintiest of male hearts; and the appearance of two courtly dandies at her levee—the smug Acaste (clever Mats Bergman), who lubriciously dangles a cameo from its fob into the open mouth of a kneeling servant girl, and the epicene Clitandre (the leggy and ludicrous Claes Månsson), who flashes a long red nail on his little finger—fuels Alceste's jealousy. To Célimène, Alceste's passion only confirms the power of her sexual appeal and its novelty value in the ritualized tedium of court philandering.

Alceste, who is an expert at lying to himself, claims to be incapable of dissimulation; but the flirtatious Célimène is a master of it. She faces down the puritanical Mme. Arsinoé (the superb Agneta Ekmanner), who fancies Alceste herself, and who scuttles around the stage, in a layered purple-black dress, like an Egyptian scarab; clutching a prayer book, she delivers salvos of spite in a pinched voice full of piety. "One must avoid the outward show of vice," Arsinoé warns Célimène, who for most of this sensational war of words has her back turned to Arsinoé or glides around her, so that her face never loses its marvellous composure under the older woman's onslaught of malice. Ekmanner, who radiates a regal inner fire, has a field day in the role. Her austere elegance and the frozen angularity of her neck and hands reinforce her starchy propriety as Célimène herself goes on the attack. Célimène says, "When all one's charms are gone, it is, I'm sure / Good strategy to be devout and pure." Arsinoé takes revenge on her by showing Alceste a compromising letter from Célimène to Oronte. (She later provides him with letters from *all* of Célimène's suitors.) When Alceste confronts

Célimène with the letter, she is calmly arranging roses in a vase whose dragon design is the only predatory clue; she brushes her face occasionally with a bloom as she gives him a disarming answer. "Pretend, pretend, that you are just and true," Alceste begs, dropping to his knees and holding her hand to his cheek. "And I shall make myself believe in you." Significantly, at this moment of crisis Alceste has more faith in his powers of denial than in the power of love. Célimène touches his face, and in that gesture—electric with feeling and with irony—she brazens it out: "Just why should I *pretend?*"

By Act V, Alceste, scandalized by the victory against him in the courts for slander, is almost levitating with rage. He fumes to Philinte:

> This age is vile, and I've made up my mind
> To have no further commerce with mankind.

Here the intemperate Alceste suddenly walks through an upstage wall. The spectacle is hilarious, and Alceste's notorious virtue takes another pratfall when Oronte forces Célimène to choose between him and Alceste. This turns into a kind of jamboree of humiliation, during which all Célimène's lovers and the hated Arsinoé (now dressed in a harsh black-and-red gown and emitting little squeals of vindictive triumph from behind her fan) congregate across the width of the proscenium to witness Célimène being confronted with her own bitchy private thoughts about her lovers as Acaste reads them aloud. Célimène is turned toward the audience with chagrin on her face and nowhere to hide. Faced with true feeling, society collapses around her. One by one, the betrayed men exit, pouring scorn on Célimène's beautiful, turned head, which she struggles to hold high. Acaste is the last to leave. He approaches Célimène in her humiliation and holds out a fan—the instrument for saving face and "composing herself"—and then, in a huge theatrical moment, drops the fan at her feet as he exits. It's a chilling revenge.

Alceste offers to marry the ostracized Célimène, but on the condition that they go "To that wild, trackless, solitary place/In which I shall forget the human race." Célimène protests that she is only twenty and would be bored. She starts to make another proposal, but Alceste cuts her off in a rage. She will accept life on his terms or not at all. He rejects her out of hand. Alceste cannot take anything in but himself; he is incapable, finally, of any mutuality. Quite naturally, in this production, Célimène runs screaming from him. Alceste then makes a breathtaking volte-face and, in the next beat, is talking about proposing marriage to Célimène's cousin, the idealistic Eliante (Nadja Weiss). When she confesses her love for Philinte, Alceste bids them, and us, a self-pitying farewell:

> Meanwhile, betrayed and wronged in everything
> I'll flee this bitter world where vice is king,
> And seek some spot unpeopled and apart
> Where I'll be free to have an honest heart.

Alceste's flight from court life is also a flight from his own problematic inner life. His legendary negativity is shown in Bergman's majestic production to be a defense against any emotional surrender.

On opening night, the burghers of Stockholm began clapping politely at the end of the play, as if surprised that Molière's comedy should come to such an abrupt and unsettling conclusion. But by the third curtain call, quite unexpectedly, the applause turned to stomping. After a while, the audience seemed to rise en masse from the plush blue seats and kept up the huzzahs for about ten minutes, until both they and the actors were exhausted. The Swedes know greatness when they see it.

STEPHEN DALDRY

THE VIRGIN AND THE DYNAMO

THE ROYAL NATIONAL Theatre's production of Sophie Treadwell's 1928 Broadway succès d'estime, "Machinal" (which was also revived at the Public Theatre in 1990), brings together two awesome theatrical phenomena: the hydraulic system of London's Lyttelton Theatre and Fiona Shaw. "I'm not controlling the evening. It's a new thing for me," Shaw said in the actors' bar after the show. Even so, Shaw, one of the genuinely great actresses in the British Isles, battles Ian MacNeil's extraordinary set to a draw. In the set's corner, weighing eight tons and costing twenty-six thousand pounds, is a behemoth cast-iron ceiling. It hovers, drops, tilts, opens, clangs—and does virtually everything but take a bow. Against the oppressive gravity of this enormous grille, often draped with workers who shower the stage with welding sparks, Shaw pits her pale, nervy sensibility, which has its own acute inner fire. This is the battleground on which Treadwell's character, an Everywoman called Miss A., fights for her life in nine scenes without intermission. "The woman is essentially soft, tender, and the life around her is essentially hard, mechanized," Treadwell wrote in her stage directions. "Business, home, marriage, having a child, seeking pleasure—all are difficult for her—mechanical, nerve nagging."

The production is directed by Stephen Daldry, whose staging of J. B. Priestley's "An Inspector Calls" comes to Broadway in April, and it begins with the echo of hammer blows and immediately immerses the audience in industrial sound—the wheezing, whistling, hissing, grinding noise of twentieth-century American power asserting its freedom. Amid the din, the safety curtain opens to reveal Shaw standing upstage, almost at the back wall of the mammoth theatre. Her first expression is a hyperventilating gasp: she stands paralyzed in the hubbub, trying to suck in life from the fetid air. Her panic and her isolation are as glaring as the bank of lights that is being winched up the back wall. No other contemporary actress can take an audience so articulately to the dark outer reaches of emotional experience. "I'm often bored by the theatre," Shaw told me. "As actors, it's our duty to push the envelope, to go farther faster. It's a bit like the Olympics. You've got to decrease your lap time with each performance or stagecraft will get stuck. If you're complacent or too comfortable, I don't think much gets communicated." Shaw's daring is mesmerizing. Even before we know Miss A.'s problems, we witness a character at the crossroads of her life. "The day a play starts, something cataclysmic has already occurred," Shaw explains. "Miss A. is going to work in dread. She can barely walk, because there's a man who's going to ask to marry her." Shaw is expert at engaging her character's frustration and magnifying it to the point where, as she says, "domestic frustration and the universal intersect and where suicide dwells in cottages and council houses." Miss A. is a female victim of the new century's alternately punishing and exhilarating industrial momentum. "Prosperity never before imagined, power never yet wielded by man, speed never reached by anything but a meteor, had made the world irritable, nervous, querulous, unreasonable and afraid" is how Henry Adams memorably characterized this mutation of consciousness in "The Education of Henry Adams." "All New York was demanding new men, and all the new forces, condensed into corporations, were demanding a new type of man—a man with ten times the endurance, energy, will and mind of the old type—for whom they were ready to pay millions at sight."

Treadwell, who graduated from Berkeley in 1906, came of age with the century's industrial boom. An actress, journalist, and feminist, and the author of four novels and more than thirty plays, six of which were mounted on Broadway, she seems to have reflected, as well as chronicled, the era's restless obsession with productivity. In "Machinal," the heroine is not a corporate highflier but a young, poorly educated stenographer who is swept up in the slipstream of the century's velocity, where she cannot find "any place, any peace." (Neither, really, could men, although, as the Adams quotation indicates, men built this world, which then trapped them in a different kind of alienation.) In "Machinal," which is French for "mechanical," the city is the antagonist, and its inhabitants are merely cogs in the inexorable drama of production. From the play's first beat, Daldry brilliantly submerges Miss A. in the stench and shadows of the metropolis. Never before has the oppression of industrial capitalism looked so beautifully brutal. Prior to Treadwell's Expressionist solution, the numbing mechanization of modern life had been addressed in the theatre for more than a decade, both in the dreamwalkers of its scripted comedies ("Merton of the Movies," "Beggar on Horseback," "The Show-Off") and in the high jinks of its low comedians. Treadwell's play calls for "the variety and quick changingness of its scenes" to conjure a sense of the new momentum, which found its truest and most sensational theatrical metaphor in the pratfall. In this one resilient, low-comic image, panic and promise coalesced in a way that matched a new rhythm with a new kind of laughter. The clowns were parodies of the new corporate man and the new energy. "I was alien to this slick tempo," Charlie Chaplin wrote, in "My Autobiography," of his first visit to New York, in 1910, and he immediately worked the city's speed and violence into his American brand of comedy. "Even the owner of the smallest enterprise acts with alacrity. The shoeshine boy flips his polishing rag with alacrity, the bartender serves a beer with alacrity. . . . The soda clerk, when serving an egg malted milk, performs like a hopped up juggler." At a certain speed, all things disintegrate, and the low comedians made a spectacle of this collapse, turning the citizen's dazed survival into a form of delight.

Treadwell's goal, although bold, is theatrically more sombre and highfalutin than the funnymen's. In Daldry's production, it's the set, not the society, that does most of the collapsing. Miss A., as her name implies, is a generality, an idea in search of an interpretation. And Treadwell imposes one. Miss A. is a model of alienated labor, a victim of economic necessity, whose life factors out neatly in a Marxist equation, which explains the long and successful run of "Machinal" in the U.S.S.R. The murderous energies of capitalism, in which all life is dedicated to "making a killing," are transmuted into a numbed female heart. "The plot is the story of a woman who murders her husband,"

Treadwell wrote in her first stage direction, "an ordinary young woman, any woman."

Miss A., like Hedda Gabler, whom Shaw recently played in a production that was generally agreed to be the best in living British memory, finds herself with—and pregnant by—the wrong man. "Hedda knows she's a coward and can't do anything about it—that's the tragedy of her life," Shaw says. "Miss A., on the other hand, has no ability to connect with her inner life. She's entirely emotional. That's why I was interested in playing her. In my private life, I'm on a high frequency. My mind goes too fast. I sometimes get swamped by problems. That's why I find Miss A. hard to play."

With the expert help of Quinny Sacks, who orchestrated the movement, Daldry builds the oppressive rhythms of office life and the badinage of office talk into a symphony of generalities, which becomes the music of the group's homogenized, unreflective shared experience. Language as well as life undergoes a mutation. Not emotion but productivity is what is stressed in talk. "American language heads for the nouns," Shaw observed. "The fact. The concrete things. Not the verbs and adverbs that discriminate." The office badinage is of a very special, ritualized kind, demanding a response but no connection:

> Telephone Girl: Hello—hello—George H. Jones Company—
> hello—hello—
> Stenographer: I'm efficient. She's inefficient.
> Filing Clerk: She's inefficient.
> Telephone Girl: She's got J. going.
> Stenographer: Going?
> Telephone Girl: Going and coming.
> Filing Clerk: Hot dog.

Treadwell has been praised by some American critics as a precursor of the vernacular discoveries of Odets and Mamet. This is stretching it. She catches in city speech what she describes as "its brassy sound, its trick of repetition." She does not, however, hear the poetry in its sludge, or plumb the drama in its defensive swagger. Miss A., like the other office workers, can't think. When she finally speaks, in the first scene, struggling to cope with the advances of her boss, Mr. Jones, what we hear is the atomized speech of a mind fragmented beyond reason by the new industrial rhythm.

> Young Woman (Miss A.): George H. Jones—straight—thin—bald—don't touch me—please—no—can't—must—somebody—something—no rest—must rest—no rest—must rest—no rest—late today—yesterday—before—late—subway—air—pressing—bodies pressing—bodies—trembling—air—stop—air—late—job—no job—fired—late—alarm clock—alarm clock—alarm clock—hurry—job—ma—nag—nag—nag—ma—hurry—job—no job—no money—installments due—no money—money—George H. Jones—money—Mrs. George H. Jones—money—no work—no worry—free!—rest— . . .

Miss A. marries Mr. Jones—played by the svelte and boutonnièred John Woodvine, who manages somehow to convey bewildered humanity behind an oafish chauvinism. On their honeymoon, she cowers in the bathroom, flummoxed by disgust and terror, which she vainly tries to disguise as shyness. Outside, the husband counts down the seconds. "I want somebody," she sobs when she finally comes out. Mr. Jones says, "You've got me, haven't you?" Miss A. can't find any authentic emotional connection. "Somebody! Somebod—" are the last words on her lips as she is electrocuted for his murder. Miss A. has been steered by Treadwell through the frustration of parental misunderstanding, the ambivalence of childbirth, the loneliness of co-habitation, the thrill of a brief affair, and the final liberation of murder. "Is nothing mine?" she says, protesting as prison barbers shave her head for the execution. "The very hair on my head—" The feminist point is starkly made: nothing *is* hers. Treadwell at this point imposes her own idiom on the character. "I will not be submitted!—this indignity!" Miss A. says, trying to employ a vocabulary of outrage quite beyond the parameters of her personality. She has been reduced to an object in the marketplace and treated like a possession in the home. Her only gesture of autonomy in a lifetime of submission to other people's authority is the act of murder. "Why?" the judge asks, after the bullying prosecutor (excellently played by Colin Stinton) gets her to confess to the deed under cross-examination. "To be free," she answers. "But if you wanted freedom, you could have divorced him," the judge says. "Oh, I couldn't do that!!" Miss A. says, in a stunning line that exposes her primitive, unexamined inner life. "I couldn't hurt him like that!"

In the end, the voltage that runs the industrial dynamo runs directly through Miss A. She ends as she began—gasping for air. As she recedes from view, convulsing before our eyes in the electric chair, the audience is left with the sound of sizzling and the sight of smoke. It's an apt image both of Miss A.'s waste and of Treadwell's fury. In dramatizing an anonymous woman, Treadwell brazenly took her argument beyond psychology to ideology. She was ahead of her time, and certainly ahead of the debate that most theatre then was having about family, male authority, and women's rights. (The show ran for ninety-one performances on Broadway.) But Daldry, who has pulled out all the scenic stops and has used the Lyttelton stage as it has never been used before, gives the production a significance that the text, finally, can't bear. This won't please some of the admirers of "Machinal," like the literary scholar Judith E. Barlow, who bemoans its having been "erased" from the cultural history of its time. "The obscurity into which she and her play fell obviously has much to do with her gender," she writes in the program note. I don't think so. There are good plays that are not important, and important plays that are not good. "Machinal" falls into the latter category. Even this outstanding revival will not put "Machinal" in the canon of American dramatic literature. The failure is due not to sexual politics but to writing. "Machinal" provides no substantial character development for its heroine and only one dimension for the subsidiary characters, who remain stick figures. Even Fiona Shaw, who invests Miss A. with a magnificent vulnerability, admitted that "the play is legless," and said, "It's like fighting with one hand behind your back." Daldry's pyrotechnics pump up "Machinal" with scenic steroids to make it look like a heavyweight contender, but the enormous effort betrays a suspicion that the text is lightweight.

PETER BROOK

LOSING THE PLOT

What we call "I"—
the self that we spend a lifetime making and remembering—is really a
story that we tell ourselves and that is reflected back to us by the world.
When both versions of this narrative are more or less in synch, you have
sanity; when they aren't, you have madness. And when, for neurological
reasons, the mind can't even assemble the plot of its story, you have the
discombobulated world that Oliver Sacks famously describes in his collection of essays "The Man Who Mistook His Wife for a Hat." "To be
ourselves we must *have* ourselves—possess, if need be repossess, our
life-stories," Sacks writes of the blighted lives his book deals with. "We
must 'recollect' ourselves, recollect the inner drama, the narrative of
ourselves. A man *needs* such a narrative, a continuous inner narrative, to
maintain his identity, his self."

The tragic spectacle of what happens when this kind of discourse goes
awry has inspired the visionary director Peter Brook to reinvent Sacks's
book for his own theatrical purposes. "The Man Who," an apt, verbless
title for stories of lives that have lost a through line, is part of Brook's
lifelong exploration into the mystery of communication, which he's
carried out in Paris since the early seventies, at his International Centre
of Theatre Research. Here, in a terse, anecdotal, unpolemical play,
Brook and five of his performers submerge the audience in the caprices
of nature and in the delicate, miraculous balance on which consciousness
rests. Even though "The Man Who" apparently dramatizes grievous
mental losses, its scrupulous attentiveness to the humanity of each
struggling patient makes us feel an appropriate awe at the incomprehen-
sibility of the workings of fate in human life. This awe is part of Brook's
antidote to what he sees as the spiritual impasse of modern theatre. In

seeking to address this impasse, he has mounted more than fifty productions in his long and distinguished career; many of them—like "Marat/Sade," "A Midsummer Night's Dream," "Conference of the Birds," and the nine-hour exploration of the Hindu epic, "The Mahabharata" —have been seminal storytelling experiments. "The Man Who" has been on a five-city standing-room-only tour of England and Scotland, concluding at the Royal National Theatre's Cottesloe stage, in London, where I caught up with it. The production marks Brook's first major return to England since 1976 and the tour of "The Ik," his adaptation of Colin Turnbull's "The Mountain People," which was a devastating anthropological study of a starving Ugandan mountain tribe and the breakdown of community. In a sense, "The Man Who" is an extension of "The Ik" 's inquiry into the "broken current" of communal connection. Here, however, it's the circuitry of the brain, and not the catastrophe of economic circumstance, that cuts off illumination. The new play, which lasts just an hour and forty minutes, and which Brook calls "a commando work," is the product of the company's own neurological research as well as of Sacks's. The characters are "unmemoried men," unable to decipher, variously, their bodies, their external world, their inner life, sometimes even their language—all the elements that reflect the self back to itself—and they are therefore beyond the comforts or the creation of ritual. In fact, they are trapped in the very opposite of ritual—the constantly changing, meaningless moment.

When the lights come up on "The Man Who," the audience is staring at technological equivalents of the brain's function: two large upstage TV monitors, a video camera, and a VCR, which are used to provide biofeedback for the patients. These devices dominate what is otherwise an unremarkable space; a white chair is positioned at center stage, and three others, along with three tables, have been pushed to the periphery. The play begins with a patient taking the center-stage seat while the doctor, a part played at various times by all the actors and sometimes by two or three at once, slowly applies an electrode to different parts of his brain. The patient moves an arm, blinks, twitches, speaks a memory, which may be a confabulation. "It's strange," the patient finally says to the doctor. "I was there and here at the same time.'' And so are we, as the performers shuttle us between known and unknown realms.

Brook turns the audience, like the neurologists, into instruments of attentiveness. "There is a terrible shock when you first encounter the painfulness of their condition, which is something you could never have believed," Brook told me recently. "But it is *rapidly* replaced with a strong feeling of identification and closeness." Sacks calls his subjects "travellers to unimaginable lands," and positions them and their often extravagant behavior "at the intersection between fact and fable." Brook deftly manages to walk a comparable dramatic tightrope, and refuses to sensationalize or fictionalize the material. "Some people have been very surprised that we haven't made this literally, in the way that Sacks has done, in the sense that Sacks gives what belongs to a writer— the background, the past, the future," Brook said. "In fact, I felt all through the work that in the theatre this would be clouding. You don't need to know the biography of someone. They're carrying their biography in their bodies and in their spirit." He went on to connect "The Man Who" to his acting experiments with "The Ik," saying, "Direct behavior enables an audience to see through that behavior to a real predicament without using storytelling, without using fiction." And he later added that when the dramatist and screenwriter Jean-Claude Carrière (his collaborator on "The Mahabharata") tried to adapt the company's neurological research for the stage he couldn't write twenty lines without getting into fiction. "That's why we had to avoid any thought of a story line," Brook said.

The danger of putting these freakish mutations of consciousness before an audience is that in less adroit hands they could become a kind of "Dr. Sacks's Believe It or Not." But Brook's trust in his actors' mimetic gifts is borne out by "The Man Who." We see this when, early in the show, a patient (the gangling, sweet-faced Sotigui Kouyate) talks to a doctor about his unhinged condition. "I'm who I am. I don't know. Whoopee. My head's like a plate of porridge," he says. The doctor tests his disorientation, standing behind him and asking the patient to locate him. The patient doggedly turns his chair a hundred and eighty degrees, until he finds a figure to go with the voice. "All is crystal clear," the patient jokes. "Whoopee." Kouyate's good spirits find dignity beneath deracination.

"I've lost all the senses of my body," says another patient, skillfully inhabited by David Bennent. "My head moves, but from my neck to my feet I can't feel my body anymore. If I don't look at it, I don't know it's there, it's as though it doesn't exist." Bennent wrestles with his ungainly and recalcitrant limbs as he mobilizes himself, then staggers around the stage like the Tin Man without oil for his joints. His lubrication is self-consciousness. "I've found out that if I look at my arm I can guide it with my eyes," he says, and he adds later, "Every day is a mental marathon."

In this world, where the patients are strangers to themselves, comedy and terror coexist, and "The Man Who" confidently steers its way between hurt and hilarity. At times, the scenes play like wonderful vaudeville slapstick, only with no rebounding from the pratfalls. For instance, a doctor holds up a red glove:

> DOCTOR: What's this object? No, don't touch.
> PATIENT 1: It's a grey rectangle prolonged by five descending cylinders one of which is shorter than the others and slightly on a diagonal. . . .
> PATIENT 2: A sort of receptacle.
> DOCTOR: What does the receptacle contain?
> PATIENT 2: It contains its contents.

These two men suffer from visual agnosia, a condition in which nothing seems familiar, and the individual, like the eponymous man who mistook his wife for a hat, is lost in a world of lifeless abstractions. Their distortions are internal and sometimes disguisable; but the whole haywire neurological nightmare is externalized in the extravagant brainstorm of Tourette's syndrome, whose clownish tics, sudden scatological explosions, and hyper-self-consciousness make Robin Williams's schizoid frenzy look lethargic. In Tourette's syndrome, the mind is a kind of whirlwind of conflicting compulsions. "I see myself as though I'm cut in two," says the Ticker, played superbly and with edgy vividness by Bruce Myers. "One Me ticks all the time, while the other Me says to him:

'Stop.' No, no, steady, you're out of your mind, it's ridiculous, idiotic, I said 'Halt! Verboten!' '' Myers's voice shifts to a lower register like a racing car dropping down a gear. ''The blind force of the subcortex always wins in the end,'' he says. There's a comedian's heroism in his clowning, which defies fate even as he acknowledges it. The Ticker can't stop himself from mugging at the video camera, or resist teasing Sacks about having a tic himself. ''No one wants to know us but we are in fashion,'' he says. ''Yes, everyone wants Tourette's. You want Tourette's, take mine. You want it, you can have it, you want it, you can have it.'' He exits shouting a defiant ''Fuck you!''

''The Man Who'' bears ample witness to the vast, ghostly domain of the mind. A patient (Yoshi Oida) is asked to shave, and does only one side of his face. ''Have you forgotten anything?'' the doctor asks. ''No,'' the patient says, and then checks himself on the video screen. He feels his cheek, shaves the clean side again, then looks once more at the screen. Grief falls slowly across his face. ''Please stop,'' Oida says, crying. ''Stop now.'' The awareness that without memory man cannot ''compose himself'' is as unbearable for an audience as it is for the afflicted. We cling to the sentimentality that there is salvation in forgetting, but onstage, as in life, the shock of tragedy comes with the sudden echo of self-awareness. The point is made best in a brilliant piece of found poetry where the patient (Bruce Myers, in another cameo tour de force) chats happily with a doctor, who records his words—words that, although delivered with great verve and sincerity, are nonsense. ''I'm not completely nor,'' he begins, in answer to a question about how he is. ''I haven't narrd nothing new extraordinary I can remain nothing in a clear precise way-too long perhaps-it's the thought that something comes . . .'' Myers turns this nonsense into gorgeous Beckettian music, whose intensity communicates both the anguish and the vigor of the patient's personality. The scene builds dramatically from fellowship to fun to fury when the patient's reading from Gray's ''Elegy'' (''Groy's Olegy in a contry cheched'') is played back to him. The patient, full of life but with no words for it, is locked inside his unfathomable, torturing head, and there is no key to release him or his word horde. The replayed tape forces this desolating awareness. Despite the doctor's pleas, the patient wants to end the session and, maybe, his life:

PATIENT: But you've no necessity to make beauty-you've no necessity to do-it's goodnot-it's dead-black-it's finished-it's not more truth-can't go on-what you were recruiting-what you can finish something that will be good to do-to black-it's finished-it's well done and yet God knows I would like a thingamer-revolver-a crime-a bat-a bite-to end that-that's all-no-no more life.

DOCTOR: Please.

PATIENT: You-you have very well you very good-and the other people-yes-but-because I was I-I can't do it-I am too young too ancient age-since my age finish very old-yes-72, 88 years that I am old now badmade-by law-I am scraped-botch. I am dead-do you see, beauty-you can't do it-no-with all of beauty's kindness to all things-no! no! life no more truth-absolutely not.

"The Man Who" ends with images of the brain, in radiant primary colors, spinning before our eyes on the TV screens like some distant galaxy. The images, like the ravishing nonsense sounds that precede them, are scrambled and beautiful and mysterious. "The Man Who" brings news of the weird outskirts of consciousness and of the humanity of those who have taken up residence there. Brook and his company hear music in the weirdness, and, through their discipline, they lead the audience to hear it, too.

ANNA DEAVERE SMITH

UNDER THE SKIN

ANNA DEAVERE SMITH IS
a lithe, clear-eyed, forty-two-year-old actress and Stanford theatre professor who has done a great thing. She has gone into this noisy republic
and, combining the editorial skill of the biographer and the precision of
the mimic, has brought onto the American stage the voices of the
unheard. She is offering, in what she calls "a parade of color," a new
framework from which to assess race and class in American culture. She
is not writing polemical theatre but, better, doing theatre politically.
"It's crucial that whites in the audience find points of identification,"
she wrote in a memo to one of the dramaturges of her most recent
piece, "Twilight: Los Angeles, 1992," which currently is at L.A.'s
Mark Taper Forum. "Points of empathy *with themselves,*" she added. "To
create a situation where they merely empathize with those less fortunate
than themselves is another kind of theatre. . . . My political problem
is this: Privilege is often masked, hidden, guarded. This guarded, for-
tressed privilege is exactly what has led us to the catastrophe of non-
dialogue in which we find ourselves. I'm not talking about economic
privilege. I'm talking about the basic *privilege* of white skin which is the
foundation of our rare vocabulary."

Smith wants to breach this fortress by including both people of color
and their unofficial language in the public debate. She speaks heart to
heart with her subjects, who, in turn, speak memorably to us. There is
no buttonholing, no buzz of sound bites, nothing from the bargain
basement of sociology. Instead, like the Billie Holiday song, she asks
heartache to come in and sit down. That she succeeds completely is a
testament to the integrity both of her performance and of the complex,
often poetic feelings she coaxes out of her subjects. "Twilight," which

distills more than a hundred and seventy interviews into an hour and three-quarters, attempts, through twenty-seven narratives, to take the pulse of Los Angeles between the Rodney King incident, of March 3, 1991, and the federal trial that ended this April with the conviction of two L.A. policemen for violating King's civil rights. The play—the fourteenth installment of a series she calls "On the Road: A Search for American Character," which came to national attention in 1991 with her award-winning "Fires in the Mirror," about Brooklyn's Crown Heights riots that year—is a bold, prodigious, democratic gesture that calls to mind Walt Whitman's dictum: "The United States themselves are essentially the greatest poem." Whitman's great poem, of course, invoked the voices of America but celebrated only himself. Smith, who speaks verbatim the words of the voiceless, is really writing a poem with them in public. In this heroic undertaking, she is conducting one of the most sophisticated dialogues about race in contemporary America.

When the lights come up on Smith, the eyes struggle to find her amid the clutter of chairs and tables strewn in some Surrealist pattern around the thrust stage. ("Anna's always saying 'It's not domestic. It's not domestic,' " says the director, Emily Mann, who puts Smith neatly through her paces.) The epic nature of the piece is reinforced by the large, undecorated gray back wall, at the center of which is a recess that becomes, variously, a TV split screen, a hodgepodge of graffiti, an office window. Onstage, barefoot and with her hair pulled back, to make the changes of costume and sex easier, Smith somehow neutralizes herself in the task of giving shape to the multifarious voices of others. (In rehearsal, with earphones on, she literally lets the characters take her over, playing back their unedited talk and speaking their words until images and gestures emerge from the rhythms.) "As a student learning Shakespeare, I became fascinated with how the spoken word works in relationship to a person's psychology," she says. "It's the *manipulation* of the words that creates character, not just the words, not just the emotion. My earliest exercise was to take Queen Margaret's speech from 'Richard III'—a vicious speech—and say it over and over again. I did it for three hours. I felt that I'd entered this awful world and this strange woman. I was completely taken over. That became my point of reference for acting. I kept wondering why that wasn't happening in more realistic plays. Why the words didn't really hold. In Shakespeare, the words held not just the psyche of the person but also the psyche of the time.''

By demonstrating that to be "literature" a narrative doesn't have to be "educated," "Twilight" goes right to the heart of the issues of race and class. "The process of creating literature is natural. It isn't dependent on a pen and paper. It's a person using their voice and the making of words to come to consciousness of what they know," she says, pointing to the print on my newspaper. "This little thing on a page is just a capsule. The real magic happens when the word hits your breath.''

Certainly in her case it does. I saw "Twilight" twice, and it was thrilling to watch different parts of the Los Angeles community face their reflection. At the first performance—a truncated one, which was part of the Taper's Young Audience Program—things didn't look good for Anna Deavere Smith. A rambunctious audience of more than seven hundred students from eleven L.A. high schools began laughing at the TV images of looting which open the section she was about to perform. But Smith soon tamed them. As Julio Menjivar—one of the innocent Latinos with no criminal record who were nonetheless rounded up by the police during the riot—she was describing in Spanish the police abuse, then suddenly stopped and said to the audience, "I don't think I should say what the police said. Your teachers will mind.'' The kids shouted back, "No they won't!'' So Smith said, "Get up, motherfucker! Get up!'' What had started in laughter ended in a standing ovation. The next day, a predominantly white and paying adult audience also rose to its feet at the finale. "She's the closest thing to a professional athlete I know,'' the Taper's producing director, Robert Egan, told me. "There's a willingness to go out into the field of play and just do it. She's got a uniquely instinctive instrument. She also learns as much dialogue as anybody I've ever seen.''

"Twilight" is both a metaphor for a scarred city and the tag of one of Smith's characters, Twilight Bey, who helped to organize the L.A. gang truce, and whose poetic interpretation of his name gave Smith the idea for her title. "I can't forever dwell in darkness,'' he said to her of the limbo his name signifies to him. In Smith's script, for reasons of rhythm and memorization, the words are printed like poetry, falling unpunctuated down the page. Here, for example, is Bey, a kind of night watchman of his grim neighborhood, discoursing about his name:

> So twilight
> is
> that time
> between day and night
> limbo
> I call it limbo
> so a lot of times when I've brought up ideas to my homeboys
> they say
> Twilight
> that's before your time
> that's something you can't do now
> when I talked about the truce back in 1988
> that was something they considered before its time
> yet
> in 1992
> we made it
> realistic
> so to me it's like I'm stuck in limbo
> like the sun between night and day

But in its ruthless probing of both the language and the life of its subjects Smith's piece embodies another aspect of twilight. "The twilight hours are a time when it's harder to see, but they become a more creative time, because you have to participate more," Smith told me. "We might see more because we have to look harder." Her show looks for no scapegoats and offers no solutions. "It'd be horrible to give an answer," she says, "because there hasn't been an examination."

"Twilight" is the beginning of the inquiry. It bears theatrical witness to the barbarity not just of violence but of envy, which in Los Angeles drives both rich and poor crazy. Smith shows people struggling to make coherent their sense of rage and pain. Over the phone, a former Black Panther activist socks it to a militant about armed struggle: "If you just

want to die, and become a poster, go ahead and do that." A Korean
wife tells of hospital visits to her husband, who has been partially
lobotomized by a rioter's bullet fired at point-blank range. "At night,
and all the day long, and I spend all my time and in my heart for him,"
she says, in halting English. Almost all of Smith's subjects struggle to get
to the point. Smith tracks her subjects through their quirky syntax and
their repetitions. "The process of getting to the point is where I think
character lives," she says. "Shoshana Felman, in 'The Literary Speech
Act,' says that people talk and talk in order to have an experience of
themselves. The sludge is the journey to understanding. The sludge is
the self." In "Twilight," out of the groping for words Smith creates a
sense of spiritual static. For example, here (with punctuation added) a
Hollywood talent agent, trying alternately to deny and to admit that
winning in the American sweepstakes means somebody else's losing, ties
himself up in the kind of semantic knots that David Mamet would envy:

> But maybe—not maybe but, uh—the system plays unequally.
> And the people who were the "they" who were burning down the
> Beverly Center had been victims of the system. Whether well-
> intentioned or not, somebody got short shrift, and they did. And I
> started to absorb a little guilt and say, uh, I deserve . . . I
> deserve it. I don't mean to get my house burned down. The "us"
> did not in—not (I like to think)—not intentionally . . . But
> maybe so. There's just . . . It's so awful out there.

The agent never finishes his thought. To Smith, who is fond of
quoting to her students Allen Ginsberg's "The breath is the inspiration," the agent's stammering is a metaphor of his moral stalemate.
"I'm not interested in who's responsible," she says. "I'm interested in
catching this particular agent, who wears Armani suits and is a neat guy.
Where is he? That inability to express is itself a reality."

Listening is one of "Twilight" 's major unspoken dramas. In making
the audience hear the characters, Smith is also showing it how to listen
to the strangers in its midst. She creates a climate of intimacy by
acknowledging the equality of the other. She waits out the anger. She
accepts the contradictoriness. She cleverly notes the body language. And

sometimes even her right to listen is tested. Angela King, the aunt of Rodney King, says at the end of her interview, "You understand what I'm sayin' now. You do? Alright." "That 'alright' is her allowing me to listen. I'm passing the test," Smith explains. "There is also the issue of 'Am I worthy to hear them?' I like it that in some cases the dance that you have to do to get to the position of being allowed to listen is difficult. That's why I'm interested in a character like Big Al, who says to me, 'You got to live here to express this point, you got to live here to see what's goin' on.'"

The information for which Smith listens is not facts but the inner conflicts of the soul and how they express themselves in everyday speech. There's no mistaking the former L.A. Police Chief Daryl Gates's slip of the tongue when he refers to Rodney King as "Rodney Thing." "You can't appreciate the blossom without the sludge," she says, and her extraordinary interview with Reginald Denny proves her point. Denny, who was pulled from the cab of his truck and nearly beaten to death, became the media's totem of ghetto barbarity: his beating but not his rescue by four blacks got the TV coverage. Smith follows Denny's meandering vacuity—"I didn't usually pay too much attention of what was going on in California, or in America, or anything"—which leads to a moment of eloquence: "How does one say that someone saved my life? How does a person . . . How do I express enough thanks for someone risking their neck? And then I was kind of—I don't know if afraid is the word—I was just a little awkward meeting people who saved me. Meeting them was not like meeting a stranger but it was like meeting a buddy. There was a weird common thread in our lives." Smith says that Denny's phrase brought something into focus for her and her desire to dramatize difference in the community. "What I'm offering—and I never started thinking about it until Reginald Denny's piece—is a kind of an aggressive response to the damage the search for sameness has done for us. We're never going to be the same. It wouldn't be the worst thing in the world for whites to acknowledge it. Then we really could say, 'We have this weird common thread,' which is racism."

The discrepancy between surface and seriousness is pointed up by Jon Stolzberg's "videowall," with its elegant use of iconic L.A.-riot reportage ("image looters" is what the South Central locals dubbed the media), which never approaches the depth of discourse of Smith's speakers. We hear from Theresa Allison, whose nephew was murdered and whose son is in jail, how the L.A.P.D. fakes drive-by killings and sometimes eliminates a project youth by merely picking him up and dropping him into enemy-gang territory. Angela King remembers the young Rodney King standing up to his ankles in a stream, so alert and agile that he could catch trout with his hands: "I said, Boy, you sure you ain't got some African in you? Ooh, yeah, I'm talkin' 'bout them wild Africans, not one them well-raised ones. Like with a fish hook?" A juror in the first trial, which cleared the L.A.P.D. of any wrongdoing in Rodney King's beating, cries in Smith's presence, recounting public reaction to the decision: "One of the most disturbing things—and a lot of the jurors said that— The thing that bothered them that they received in the mail—more than anything else, more than the threats—was a letter from the K.K.K. saying we support you and if you need our help, if you want to join our organization we'd welcome you into our field. And we all just were—*No!*" A juror from the federal trial agreed to talk to Smith after her lawyer saw a preview of "Twilight." Her interview, restricted by contract from quotation or publication, is one of the most fascinating of the evening—a hilarious and touching account of the back-room frustration in which the deadlocked jurors (one Hispanic, two blacks, and nine whites) had to face their own racial guilt before they could finally find two of the policemen guilty of violating King's civil rights.

Twice in the play, characters refer to waking up. Elvira Evers, a cashier whose life was saved by the elbow of her unborn baby when she was hit by a stray bullet, concludes, "So it's like—open your eyes. Watch what is goin' on." And Reginald Denny is aroused almost to a fury at the thought of racism as he says, "I just want people to wake up." "Twilight" aspires to disenchant a community whose major industry is the business of enchantment. "How do we encourage people to grow up?" Smith wondered out loud to me. "Will there ever be a sobering moment?" She then confided a dream she had had the night before.

In her dream, Smith went into a hospital room, where she was alone

with a Japanese man whose head was shaved and who had a perpendicu-
lar incision on the front of his forehead. She realized that the man didn't
know what had happened to him and was terrified. "This is the place
where I relate to Reginald Denny," she said of the dream. "It's a very
terrifying place, to tell you the truth. It's a place that has to do—it's
very, very deep—with coming into consciousness. Of the *terror* of
coming into consciousness, whatever that consciousness is. So, for me,
my point of connection with Denny is when he's in the hospital, not
knowing who's there and having to put together why he's there."
Smith's eyes shone suddenly with tears. Her voice cracked. "I guess
that's what makes me so sad about America. I know we haven't yet
come to consciousness. To me, there is something *very, very* dark and
very, very disturbing about the inevitability of having to wake up after this
horrible, horrible accident, which is racism. The only way to master this
fear of coming into consciousness is by coming into the consciousness of
others, mimicking how other people did it, because it's terrifying to
come into my own."

In its judicious daring, "Twilight" announces that a multicultural
America is here and functioning and is capable of noisy but brilliant
collaboration. Smith herself was struck by the reality of this diversity as
she watched on the TV monitors of the Taper lobby her many-hued
dramaturges discussing the play with a preview audience. The next day,
she sent them a note, which read, in part:

> In my life, in this moment
> you are proof
> that
> "a change's gotta come"
> has come.

Her victory is hard won, and theatre throughout America is better
for it. "Twilight" goes some way toward reclaiming for the stage its
crucial role as a leader in defining and acting out that ongoing experiment called the United States.

INGMAR BERGMAN

WINTER SONGS

I_N INGMAR BERGMAN'S majestic production of Shakespeare's "The Winter's Tale" at the Royal Dramatic Theatre in Stockholm, the play begins with the program. In it Bergman pretends to be the translator of a letter (actually, it's by Bergman himself) written in 1925 by a German professor who was returning a nineteenth-century theatre poster to the Royal Library of Stockholm. The poster is reproduced on the opposite page. It announces "The Winter's Tale" as part of Miss Ulrika Sofias's nineteenth-birthday celebration, over Christmas, in the Grand Hall of Hugo Löwenstierna's hunting castle. The professor has underlined one of the cast, the writer Jonas Love Almqvist, who has a bit part, and, in passing, mentions that another professor considered him "as good as Strindberg." On that throwaway, faux-naïf sentence the full weight of Bergman's knowing, gorgeous production rests; his "Winter's Tale" is presented as part of Löwenstierna's Christmas festivities. (The production comes to the Brooklyn Academy of Music next May, along with Bergman's "Madame de Sade" and, possibly, "The Misanthrope.")

Almqvist (1793–1866) is one of Sweden's great literary figures; his poetry, novels, songs, and progressive educational ideas made him one of the most controversial figures of his day. Almqvist was an early champion of Shakespeare in Sweden, so his presence at this Christmas production has some historical rationale. Bergman uses Almqvist's music, which delicately mixes Romantic melancholy with Christian idealism, to frame in a kind of lyric embrace Shakespeare's perplexing tale of murderous jealousy and improbable redemption. Almqvist songs begin and end each of the play's two acts, and intensify the realms of regret and spiritual longing that Bergman meticulously explores. And

Almqvist's own story hovers around this haunted play like yet another ghost. Almqvist, like Leontes, seems to have perpetrated an act of absurd violence: he was accused of killing a moneylender in 1851 and fled to America, where he lived until 1865. He died an outcast, protesting his innocence, in Bremen, Germany, in 1866, and his body was not returned to Sweden until 1901. The conceit of a Christmas celebration gives Bergman a brilliant scenic framework with which to keep the play's polarities of tragedy and joy, loss and rebirth always dynamically visible, and the stunning complexity of his structure perfectly suits the arabesque quality of Shakespeare's writing in the late plays.

When the audience takes its seats, the pre-play festivities are already in progress, and the Grand Hall of the hunting castle turns out to be a subtle replica of the Marble Hall of the Royal Dramatic Theatre. The theatre's Art Nouveau windows, its gold Egyptian light fittings, its gilt columns, and even part of Carl Larsson's ceiling fresco, "The Birth of Drama," are reproduced in Lennart Mörk's elegant set. The world of the play and the world of the theatre are one. In a swirl of song, dance, and party hubbub the guests foreshadow aspects of their Shakespearean personae. The shambolic man struggling with his lines will become Autolycus (Reine Brynolfsson). The no-nonsense lady calling for the songs to begin and leading a young boy across the stage will be the tenacious Paulina (Bibi Andersson), who faces up to Leontes. A youngster, who will play Mamillius, looks over his shoulder for his parents in the same way that Mamillius will watch the disintegration of his parents' relationship in the play. The pure, compelling voice of Irene Lindh serenades the assembled with Almqvist's "The Heart's Flower," a song that sets the play's ambiguous spiritual stakes of suffering and mercy with the lines "The heart asks God why did you give this rose to me/ God's heavenly answer, the blood from your heart has given the color to the rose." And then, in one of the many magnificent transitions that Bergman engineers, the bittersweet mood is reversed when the children at the party start ringing bells and calling for the play to start.

As the Shakespearean exposition begins in the foreground, the children, now wearing white-faced masks of comedy and tragedy, pull a platform bearing the host and hostess and a friend of theirs down toward the action. When the platform reaches the front of the stage, these three have become the blue-robed Leontes (the superb Börje Ahlstedt), the green-robed Polixenes (Krister Henriksson), and the charming Hermione (Pernilla August, who played the lame servant girl in Bergman's "Fanny and Alexander" and Bergman's mother in "The Best Intentions," and who here, draped in a vibrant-red Empire gown, radiates serenity and an irresistible generosity of spirit).

Why does Leontes, who begins the play by asking Hermione to use her charms to make his beloved brother stay at court, suddenly go berserk when she succeeds? As a tragic character, Leontes poses a theatrical problem for any director. Unlike Othello or Lear, he doesn't smolder with inner turmoil. He simply crashes and burns in a blaze of jealousy. He acts out passion's awful agitation, which Shakespeare himself records in Sonnet No. 147: "Past cure I am, now reason is past care, / And frantic mad with evermore unrest." (The sonnets were published in 1609; and "The Winter's Tale," the thirty-fifth of Shakespeare's thirty-six plays, was first produced in 1610–11.) Bergman's Leontes suffers from the dementia of the perception of a love triangle similar to the one in which Shakespeare was caught—between the third Earl of Southampton (Henry Wriothesley), who was his patron, and the Dark Lady. Here the sexual charge of Hermione is unmistakable. Pernilla August gives Hermione a sense of ripeness and openness. She continually touches her husband's body, and he playfully drapes her red shawl around his neck; but when she turns to Polixenes the intimacy between them is also palpable. She's so comfortable with both men that if you can't understand Swedish it's not clear at first just who is husband and who is brother-in-law. The power of her connection with Polixenes hits Leontes like a brainstorm, and he suddenly begins to demonize his wife. His braying hatred is the flip side of idealized passion—the vindictive volte-face that Shakespeare makes in Sonnet No. 147:

> For I have sworn thee fair, and thought thee bright,
> Who art as black as hell, as dark as night.

As Leontes begins his litany of accusation, the red shawl of passion, which once connected them, now lies between them like a river of blood. Leontes plots to murder his brother and settles on exiling him from his kingdom; nearly stomps his newborn daughter, Perdita, to death in her cot before sending her into uncertain exile; generates the grief that his son, Mamillius, dies from; and imprisons Hermione and then calls her before his kangaroo court, which, so it seems, kills her. Bergman handles the melodrama of this fury in brilliant collaboration with the choreographer Donya Feuer. When Leontes glimpses Hermione and Polixenes circled in a dance—a stunning image of exclusion, which evokes the furious isolation in Edvard Munch's "The Dance of Life"—a rush of stabbing anguish overcomes him; he's grabbed the live wire of possessiveness and can't let go. Leontes breaks into the circle, casting Polixenes out and embracing Hermione. He holds her at arm's length while she nestles his hand gently against her cheek. Suddenly, Leontes whispers something obscene to her, and Hermione breaks away. Leontes grabs a nearby female member of the court and begins to rape her. It's a beautifully staged and awful moment. What compounds Leontes's passion and his violence, Bergman seems to be saying, is the middle-aged king's unconscious terror of impotence. In its opening moments, the play hints at the brothers' sexual prowess when Polixenes talks to Hermione about the vigor and innocence of their idyllic youth. "You have tripp'd since," Hermione coyly jokes, and Polixenes adds, "Temptations have since then been born to 's." But Bergman makes Hermione much younger than her husband, and eliminates from the first scene any visible sign that she is nine months pregnant. Later in Act I, when Leontes overrules the Delphic oracle, which has proclaimed Hermione innocent, he flails the behemoth Sword of Justice—a gesture that broadcasts both tyranny and sexuality. Leontes's hectoring and violence are self-hypnotic gestures, magically reinforcing his sense of potency.

In his productions, Bergman always maps out a thirteen-by-twenty-foot playing area that he calls "the optical and acoustic center." Here, having cut the text to the logistical minimum and concentrated the drama on the business of living and dying, he has turned over to Feuer twice the space—twenty-six feet by forty—in which to choreograph the subtext. It's a bold collaboration, which physicalizes the multiplicity of messages and mysteries in Shakespeare's new minting of the English language. "There is movement in his text—real physical movement,

which you experience in speaking it, hearing it, even working with it,"
Feuer says. "His language was a carrier all the time of other meanings
and other messages. This is part of Shakespeare's choreographic spirit."
Together, Feuer and Bergman deliver unforgettable stage pictures.
When Leontes decides to put Hermione on trial, the *figuranter* (chorus
members) reappear out of a bleak snowy landscape as passersby off the
street: an organ grinder, a thief, a cripple, a chimney sweep—ghostly
figures whose ragged gray presence mirrors Leontes's fragmented, unreceptive self-involvement. His baby daughter's tempest-tossed journey
into exile is dramatized by a billowing gray cloth hurtling around the
stage, with a clipper ship held aloft on sticks, while veiled women in
ribbed gray skirts writhe like waves to the sound of a wind machine as
it's cranked before our eyes. In the final act, Hermione is traditionally
revealed to Leontes as a statue—an unreachable, idealized object, who
turns into flesh and blood when she's perceived as a person, and literally
comes off her pedestal. Here Hermione is carried in from the wings on
a catafalque by four *figuranter,* who march at a funereal gait. The moment, like so many of Bergman's solutions, is simple and daring.

"It is a bawdy planet," Leontes says in Act I, and Bergman never lets
the audience forget that in the midst of death there is life. He breaks off
the gloom and apprehension of Act I with a call to dinner. The bear that
has chased Antigonus as per Shakespeare's famous stage direction "Exit
pursued by a bear" reappears happily for supper carrying his costume
head in his hand and a little girl on his shoulder. This is, after all, a feast;
and even in the last part of the play, which begins sixteen years later in a
monastery, with Leontes abasing himself in front of a living statue of the
Virgin Mary, a laurel wreath from the Midsummer Festival is hung
unobtrusively on the corner of a screen. The Madonna to whom Leontes prostrates himself is the Bleeding Maria, with a sword plunged in
her heart, and her body held up in a posture of crucifixion. Bergman
subtly carries the symbols of Christian rebirth through the production:
the evergreen Christmas tree in the Grand Hall of Act I; the Midsummer Festival tree—a cross decorated with ivy and a Swedish flag—in
Act II; and, in the finale, the Crucifixion itself. In the intervening years,
Leontes has tortured himself with remorse. When he rises to meet the
banished Perdita, now to be married to his brother's son, Florizel, his

flagellated back and stomach have bled through his shirt. Hermione, who, unbeknownst to him, has been in purdah awaiting the oracle's promise of her daughter's return, comes to life before his eyes. Leontes and Perdita fall to their knees in shock, and Leontes is held up by his brother. "Present your hand," says Paulina, who orchestrates this stage-managed resurrection. The moment is also theatrical revelation. Leontes is beyond forgiveness, and he knows it. He has accepted grief as his destiny and his due. He sits down beside Hermione and slowly, tentatively, stretches his hand over hers. Perdita does the same. "O, she's warm," Leontes says. Perdita lays her head in her mother's lap. Hermione's head brushes against Leontes's shoulder. It's an immense gesture, a miracle of the heart, which Bergman stages like a Pietà. Hermione speaks almost inaudibly to her daughter: "Where hast thou been preserv'd? where liv'd? how found/Thy father's court?" Perdita and Leontes raise Hermione up, and Perdita places her parents' hands together. They exit hand in hand to continue the conversation offstage. At that moment of salvation, snacks are announced. Life's banquet goes on.

"A sad tale's best for winter," Shakespeare says in the play. The mayhem of "The Winter's Tale," like a horror movie's submersion in death, is meant to renew the living's sense of life. Here, in the liquid Northern moonlight, Bergman calls up the spirits of Almqvist and Shakespeare and himself in one final song, the prayer "The Listening Mother of God":

> O my God, how beautiful it is,
> To hear the sound of a holy angel's voice,
> O God, how wonderful it is,
> To die to music and to song. . . .
> Quietly sink, O my holy spirit, in
> The arms of God, the Living, the Good.

On that note of grace, Time (Kristina Adolphson) rises from the front row of the orchestra section and, having opened Act II, now ends the play. She is a regal, white-haired lady in a formal black dress with a red train. She holds a cheap brass alarm clock and now sets it on the lip of the stage. As she moves upstage to leave, she looks back over her shoulder at us, and a smile plays briefly across her face. The clock's hands are at five minutes to twelve. For Shakespeare in "The Winter's Tale," for the seventy-six-year-old Bergman, and for us in the theatre, Time is almost up. In this eloquent production, imbued with the calm authority of genius, Bergman leaves us with the ticking of the clock and the urgency of forgiveness and blessing.

INDEX

ABOUT THE AUTHOR

John Lahr is the theater critic of *The New Yorker* and the author of fifteen books. Among them are his bestselling biographies of his father, the comedian Bert Lahr, *Notes on a Cowardly Lion,* and Joe Orton, *Prick Up Your Ears,* which was made into a feature film. His most recent book, *Dame Edna Everage and the Rise of Western Civilization: Backstage with Barry Humphries,* was awarded the 1992 Roger Machell Prize for the best book on the performing arts in England. Mr. Lahr has been the literary manager of the Tyrone Guthrie Theater in Minneapolis and the Vivian Beaumont Theater at Lincoln Center in New York. His stage adaptations have been performed at the Royal National Theatre in London, the West End, the Royal Exchange in Manchester, and the Mark Taper Forum in Los Angeles. Mr. Lahr has twice won the George Jean Nathan Award for Dramatic Criticism, first in 1969 when he was the critic of *The Village Voice* and *Evergreen Review,* and most recently in 1995 for his work at *The New Yorker.* He lives in London.